INTERNATIONAL ECONOMIC ASSOCIATION

General Editors: Sir Austin Robinson (1950–80), Sir Douglas Hague (1980–6), Michael Kaser (1986–)

Kenneth J. Arrow and Michael J. Boskin (*editors*)
THE ECONOMICS OF PUBLIC DEBT

Béla Balassa and Herbert Giersch (*editors*)
ECONOMIC INCENTIVES

William J. Baumol (*editor*)
PUBLIC AND PRIVATE ENTERPRISE IN A MIXED ECONOMY

Ansley J. Coale (*editor*)
ECONOMIC FACTORS IN POPULATION GROWTH

Béla Csikós-Nagy and Douglas Hague (*editors*)
THE ECONOMICS OF RELATIVE PRICES

Béla Csikós-Nagy and David G. Young (*editors*)
EAST-WEST ECONOMIC RELATIONS IN THE CHANGING GLOBAL ENVIRONMENT

Marcello de Cecco and Jean-Paul Fitoussi (*editors*)
MONETARY THEORY AND ECONOMIC INSTITUTIONS

Léon H. Dupriez and Douglas Hague (*editors*)
ECONOMIC PROGRESS (Second Edition by Austin Robinson)

Martin S. Feldstein and Robert P. Inman (*editors*)
THE ECONOMICS OF PUBLIC SERVICES

Armin Gutowski, A. A. Arnaúdo and Hans-Eckard Scharrer
FINANCING PROBLEMS OF DEVELOPING COUNTRIES

Karl Jungenfelt and Douglas Hague (*editors*)
STRUCTURAL ADJUSTMENT IN DEVELOPED OPEN ECONOMIES

T. S. Khachaturov and P. B. Goodwin (*editors*)
THE ECONOMICS OF LONG-DISTANCE TRANSPORTATION

Pierre Maillet, Douglas Hague and Chris Rowland (*editors*)
THE ECONOMICS OF CHOICE BETWEEN ENERGY SOURCES

Edmond Malinvaud and Jean-Paul Fitoussi (*editors*)
UNEMPLOYMENT IN WESTERN COUNTRIES

R. C. O. Matthews and G. B. Stafford (*editors*)
THE GRANTS ECONOMY AND COLLECTIVE CONSUMPTION

Franco Modigliani and Richard Hemming (*editors*)
THE DETERMINANTS OF NATIONAL SAVING AND WEALTH

Jósef Pajestka and C. H. Feinstein (*editors*)
THE RELEVANCE OF ECONOMIC THEORIES

Mark Perlman (*editor*)
THE ECONOMICS OF HEALTH AND MEDICAL CARE
THE ORGANIZATION AND RETRIEVAL OF ECONOMIC KNOWLEDGE

Austin Robinson, P. R. Brahmananda and L. K. Deshpande (*editors*)
EMPLOYMENT POLICY IN A DEVELOPING COUNTRY (2 volumes)

Paul A. Samuelson (*editor*)
INTERNATIONAL ECONOMIC RELATIONS

Christian Schmidt (*editor*)
THE ECONOMICS OF MILITARY EXPENDITURES

Christian Schmidt and Frank Blackaby (*editors*)
PEACE, DEFENCE AND ECONOMIC ANALYSIS

Joseph E. Stiglitz and G. Frank Mathewson (*editors*)
NEW DEVELOPMENTS IN THE ANALYSIS OF MARKET STRUCTURE

Richard Stone and William Peterson (*editors*)
ECONOMETRIC CONTRIBUTIONS TO PUBLIC POLICY

Nina G. M. Watts (*editor*)
ECONOMIC RELATIONS BETWEEN EAST AND WEST

ECONOMIC GROWTH AND RESOURCES

Edmond Malinvaud (*editor*)
1   THE MAJOR ISSUES

R. C. O. Matthews (*editor*)
2   TRENDS AND FACTORS

Christopher Bliss and M. Boserup (*editors*)
3   NATURAL RESOURCES

Irma Adelman (*editor*)
4   INTERNATIONAL POLICIES

Shigeto Tsuru (*editor*)
5   PROBLEMS RELATED TO JAPAN

HUMAN RESOURCES, EMPLOYMENT AND DEVELOPMENT

Shigeto Tsuru (*editor*)
1   THE ISSUES

Paul Streeten and Harry Maier (*editors*)
2   CONCEPTS, MEASUREMENT AND LONG-RUN PERSPECTIVE

Burton Weisbrod and Helen Hughes (*editors*)
3   THE PROBLEM OF DEVELOPED COUNTRIES AND THE INTERNATIONAL ECONOMY

Victor L. Urquidi and Saúl Trejo Reyes (*editors*)
4   LATIN AMERICA

Samir Amin (*editor*)
5   DEVELOPING COUNTRIES

STRUCTURAL CHANGE, ECONOMIC INTERDEPENDENCE AND WORLD DEVELOPMENT

Victor L. Urquidi (*editor*)
1   BASIC ISSUES

Silvio Borner and Alwyn Taylor (*editors*)
2   NATURAL AND FINANCIAL RESOURCES FOR DEVELOPMENT

Luigi Pasinetti and Peter Lloyd (*editors*)
3   STRUCTURAL CHANGE AND ADJUSTMENT IN THE WORLD ECONOMY ECONOMY

John H. Dunning and Mikoto Usui (*editors*)
4   ECONOMIC INTERDEPENDENCE

The first fifty IEA conference volumes published by Macmillan are available as a set.

Please see the copyright page for information on Series Standing Orders.

The Economics of Public Debt

Proceedings of a Conference held by the
International Economic Association at Stanford, California

Edited by
Kenneth J. Arrow
and
Michael J. Boskin

in association with the
INTERNATIONAL ECONOMIC
ASSOCIATION

© International Economic Association 1988

All rights reserved. No reproduction, copy or transmission
of this publication may be made without written permission.

No paragraph of this publication may be reproduced, copied
or transmitted save with written permission or in accordance
with the provisions of the Copyright Act 1956 (as amended).
or under the terms of any licence permitting limited copying
issued by the Copyright Licensing Agency, 33–4 Alfred Place,
London WC1E 7DP.

Any person who does any unauthorised act in relation to
this publication may be liable to criminal prosecution and
civil claims for damages.

First published 1988

Published by
THE MACMILLAN PRESS LTD
Houndmills, Basingstoke, Hampshire RG21 2XS
and London
Companies and representatives
throughout the world

Printed in Hong Kong

British Library Cataloguing in Publication Data
The economics of public debt: proceedings
of a conference held by the International
Economic Association at Stanford,
California.—(Macmillan/IEA; No. 85).
1. Debts, public 2. Economic
development
I. Arrow, Kenneth J. II. Boskin, Michael J.
III. International Economic Association
336.3'4   HJ8030
ISBN 0-333-46815-5

Series Standing Order

If you would like to receive future titles in this series as they are published, you can make
use of our standing order facility. To place a standing order please contact your bookseller
or, in case of difficulty, write to us at the address below with your name and address and
the name of the series. Please state with which title you wish to begin your standing order.
(If you live outside the UK we may not have the rights for your area, in which case we will
forward your order to the publisher concerned.)

Standing Order Service, Macmillan Distribution Ltd, Houndmills, Basingstoke, Hampshire,
RG21 2XS, England.

Contents

Acknowledgements	vii
The International Economic Association	viii
List of Participants	x
Abbreviations and Acronyms	xii
Introduction *Kenneth J. Arrow and Michael J. Boskin*	xiii

PART I PUBLIC DEBT AND MACROECONOMICS

1 Deficits, Monetary Policy and Real Economic Activity
 Robert Eisner and Paul J. Pieper   3

 Discussion   39

2 On the Relevance or Irrelevance of Public Financial Policy *Joseph E. Stiglitz*   41

 Discussion   75

3 Concepts and Measures of Federal Deficits and Debt and their Impact on Economic Activity *Michael J. Boskin*   77

 Discussion   112

4 Optimum Fiscal Policy when Monetary Policy is Bound by a Rule: Ramsey Redux *Edmund S. Phelps and Kumaraswamy Velupillai*   116

PART II PUBLIC DEBT AND EQUITY

5 Public Debt and Intergeneration Equity *Richard A. Musgrave*   133

Discussion	146
6 Debt Burden and Intergeneration Equity *Toshihiro Ihori*	149
Discussion	191

PART III   ASPECTS OF PUBLIC DEBT THEORY AND PRACTICE

7 Debt and Taxes in War and Peace: The Closed Economy Case *J. S. Flemming*	201
Discussion	224
8 Public Debt and Fiscal Policy in Developing Countries *Vito Tanzi and Mario I. Blejer*	230
9 Benefits and Burdens of Indexed Debt: Some Lessons from Israel's Experience *Ephraim Kleiman*	264
Discussion	287
10 Debt, Wealth and the Rate of Growth: An Exercise in Equilibrium Dynamics *Stefano Gorini*	292
Discussion	309
Index	311

Acknowledgements

The International Economic Association Conference on the Economics of Public Debt was made possible through the generous support and guidance of the Center for Economic Policy Research, the Koret Foundation, and the Rockefeller Foundation. Their assistance was an invaluable resource to the Programme Committee. We also wish to thank Stanford University for its hospitality and cordiality in serving as the site of the conference.

The International Economic Association expresses its thanks to the International Social Science Council under whose auspices the publications programme is carried out and to UNESCO for its financial support.*

PROGRAMME COMMITTEE

Professor Kenneth J. Arrow
Professor Michael J. Boskin
Professor Jean-Paul Fitoussi

The International Economic Association

A non-profit organisation with purely scientific aims, the International Economic Association (IEA) was founded in 1950. It is in effect a federation of national economic associations, at present fifty-eight in all parts of the world. Its basic purpose is the development of economics as an intellectual discipline with an international approach which recognises a diversity of problems, systems and values in the world economy.

The IEA has, since its creation, tried to fulfil that purpose by promoting the mutual understanding of economists from the West and the East as well as from the North and the South through the organisation of scientific meetings and common research programmes and by means of publications of an international character on problems of current importance. During its thirty-seven years of existence, it has thus organised seventy-nine specialists' round-table conferences on topics ranging from fundamental theories to methods and tools of analysis and significant problems of the present-day world. Eight triennal World Congresses have also been held, which have regularly attracted the participation of a great many economists from all over the world. The proceedings of all these meetings are published by Macmillan.

The Association is governed by a Council, composed of representatives of all member associations, and by a fifteen-member Executive Committee which is elected by the Council. The present Executive Committee (1986–9) is composed as follows:

President: Professor Amartya Sen, India
Vice-President: Professor Béla Csikós-Nagy, Hungary
Secretary General: Professor Jean-Paul Fitoussi, France
Treasurer: Professor Luis Angel Rojo, Spain

Other members:	Professor Kenneth J. Arrow, USA (President, 1983–1986)
Professor Edmar Lisboa Bacha, Brazil
Professor Ragnar Bentzel, Sweden
Professor Oleg T. Bogomolov, USSR
Professor Silvio Borner, Switzerland

The International Economic Association

                Professor P. R. Brahmananda, India
                Professor Phyllis Deane, United Kingdom
                Professor Luo Yuanzheng, China
                Professor Edmond Malinvaud, France
                Professor Luigi Pasinetti, Italy
                Professor Don Patinkin, Israel
                Professor Takashi Shiraishi, Japan

Adviser: Professor Tigran S. Khachaturov, USSR

General editor: Mr Michael Kaser, United Kingdom

Adviser to General Editor: Professor Sir Austin Robinson, United Kingdom

Conference Editor: Dr Patricia M. Hillebrandt, United Kingdom

The Association has also been fortunate in having secured the following outstanding economists to serve as President: Gottfried Haberler (1950–3), Howard S. Ellis (1953–6), Erik Lindahl (1956–9), E. A. G. Robinson (1959–62), G. Ugo Papi (1962–5), Paul A. Samuelson (1965–8), Erik Lundberg (1968–71), Fritz Machlup (1971–4), Edmond Malinvaud (1974–7), Shigeto Tsuru (1977–80), Victor L. Urquidi (1980–3), Kenneth J. Arrow (1983–6).

The activities of the Association are funded mainly from the subscriptions of members and grants from a number of organisations, including continuing support from UNESCO.

List of Participants

Professor **Kenneth J. Arrow**, Stanford University, USA
Professor **Ragnar Bentzel**, Uppsala University, Sweden
Professor **Douglas Bernheim**, Stanford University, USA
Dr **Mario I. Blejer**, International Monetary Fund
Professor **Silvio Borner**, Basel University, Switzerland
Professor **Michael J. Boskin**, Stanford University, USA
Professor **Béla Csikós-Nagy**, Hungarian Economic Association
Dr **Christophe Chamley**, World Bank
Professor **Phyllis Deane**, Cambridge University, England
Professor **Robert Eisner**, Northwestern University, USA
Professor **Jean-Paul Fitoussi**, International Economic Association
Mr **John S. Flemming**, Bank of England
Professor **Victor Fuchs**, Stanford University, USA
Professor **Stefano Gorini**, Sassari University, Italy
Professor **G. Bert Hickman**, Stanford University, USA
Professor **Toshio Ihori**, Osaka University, Japan
Professor **Ephraim Kleiman**, Hebrew University of Jerusalem, Israel
Professor **Mordecai Kurz**, Stanford University, USA
Professor **Gerald Meier**, Stanford University, USA
Dr **Bryan Motley**, Federal Reserve Bank of San Francisco, USA
Professor **Richard A. Musgrave**, University of California, USA
Professor **H. M. A. Onitiri**, United Nations Development Program
Professor **Edmund S. Phelps**, Columbia University, USA
Professor **Paul J. Pieper**, University of Illinois, USA
Professor **Sir Austin Robinson**, Cambridge University, England
Professor **Marc Robinson**, University of California, USA
Professor **Luis Angel Rojo**, Bank of Spain
Professor **Myron Scholes**, Stanford University, USA
Professor **Jaime Serra-Puche**, El Colegio de Mexico
Professor **Takashi Shiraishi**, Keio University, Japan
Professor **John Shoven**, Stanford University, USA
Professor **Joseph E. Stiglitz**, Princeton University, USA
Professor **Guido Tabellini**, University of California, Los Angeles, USA
Dr **Vito Tanzi**, International Monetary Fund
Professor **John Taylor**, Stanford University, USA
Dr **Adrian Throop**, Federal Reserve Bank of San Francisco, USA
Professor **Kumaraswamy Velupillai**, Aalborg University Center, Denmark

List of Participants

RAPPORTEURS

Professor William Gale, University of California, Los Angeles, USA
Dr John Roberts, Federal Reserve Bank, Washington, USA

Abbreviations and Acronyms

AEI	American Enterprise Institute
BEA	Bureau of Economic Analysis (of US Department of Commerce)
CBO	Congressional Budget Office
CD	certificate of deposit
CPI	consumer price index
DRI	Data Resources Incorporated (External Debt File)
FED	Federal Reserve System (of the USA) or Federal Reserve Bank
FDIC	Federal Deposit Insurance Corporation (USA)
IGE	intergenerational equity
GDP	gross domestic product
GNP	gross national produce
LIBOR	London interbank overnight rate
NBER	National Bureau of Economic Research Inc.
NIPA	National Income and Product Accounts
NNP	net national product
OASDI	Old Age Services and Disability Insurance
OLS	ordinary least squares
OPEC	Organisation of Petroleum Exporting Countries
PATAM	dollar denominated time and demand deposits (Israel)
PATAP	restitution deposits (Israel)
PCE	personal consumption expenditure
PDV	present discounted value

Introduction

Kenneth J. Arrow
and
Michael J. Boskin

Rising government deficits and public debt in both advanced and developing economies are one of the dramatic structural changes in the world economy in the 1980s. The economic causes and consequences of this explosion of public debt are the themes of this volume and were the reasons that the International Economic Association convened a conference on the Economics of Public Debt at Stanford University in the summer of 1986. The papers in this volume were presented, critiqued, and discussed at that conference.

The papers represent a wide range of issues concerning the economics of public debt. They include theoretical analyses of the conditions under which debt finance 'matters' for the real economy and/or the price level; the importance of domestic versus external debt; issues in the measurement of deficits and debt; and empirical analyses of determinants of the effects of deficits and public debt on real economic activity and its composition.

A theme running through many of the papers is the unsustainability of large deficits. The public debt to GNP ratio will inexorably grow as a proportion of the tax base (and income) if government expenditure exceeds tax revenues and if the interest rate exceeds the growth rate (all taken to exclude interest). Even if the growth rate exceeds the rate of interest, persistent deficits may result in a more or less rapid rise in the debt to GNP ratio toward levels which the private economy – including the rest of the world – may be unwilling to hold. Another important theme of the essays is the interaction of the measurement of deficits and debt with the rate of inflation. It is well known that unanticipated increases in inflation redistribute wealth from creditors to debtors. Several papers in this volume analyse the impact of such changes when the debtor is an economy's public sector.

Still another theme running through several papers in the volume reflects other potential interactions of fiscal and monetary policy. If monetary policy is bound by a fixed rule, what does this do to optimal fiscal policy? What is the interaction of indexation of government bonds with monetary policy? What are the limits to revenue generation via money creation in a developing economy with substantial public debt?

This volume is intended to emphasise these and related themes by presentation of theoretical and empirical studies of both advanced and developing economies, together with a synopsis of the conference discussion of them.

Robert Eisner and Paul Pieper discuss the potential measurement problems in using nominal budget deficits in an inflationary economy. In previous work, they concluded that conventional measures of fiscal policy in the late 1970s in the United States greatly overstated the extent of fiscal expansion; indeed, they argue that fiscal policy was essentially contractionary. Their earlier work did not examine the potential impact of monetary variables on real economic activity (and its composition). In the work presented here, Eisner and Pieper generalise their previous results by the introduction of monetary variables and ask whether these monetary variables abrogate the explanatory power of the fiscal variables. In their analyses, they conclude that the adjusted deficit measures are positively related to consumption and investment (implying crowding in of investment) and negatively related to net exports.

Joseph Stiglitz asks when will a tax for debt swap affect the real economy, affect the price level but not the real economy (the so-called classical dichotomy) or simply be irrelevant and affect nothing. Stiglitz stresses the need to account for the effects of all the financial policies of the governments simultaneously and that this is possible only within an intertemporal model with explicit assumptions with respect to the formation of expectations and the impact of financial policies on the intergenerational distribution of income. Stiglitz develops various relevance and irrelevance theorems. He particularly asks whan can the government provide that the private market cannot and concludes that most important are intergenerational redistribution and risk-sharing opportunities. Stiglitz strongly concludes that the basic reasons for the apparent failure of so-called Ricardian equivalence in the real world has to do with both fiscal illusion (economic agents do not fully capitalise all future tax liabilities in their current decisions) and credit market imperfections.

Michael Boskin presents alternative measures of government assets and liabilities along the way to alternative measure of deficits and debt. He discusses issues of aggregating various components of income when there may be systematic covariance among them. Boskin's annual time-series regressions for the United States conclude that alternative measures of deficits imply that a tax-for-debt swap increases real consumption about 25 cents per dollar. Changes in budget deficits also affect the composition of GNP, given its level. In these specifications, each dollar of deficit crowds out 25 or 30 cents of private investment and a like amount of net exports and induces about a 30 cent increase in private saving. Also important are various generalisations of a measure of government assets and tests for whether they have the same effect as private wealth on private consumption expenditures. Evidence is presented that public tangible capital may be a substitute for private savings.

Edmund Phelps and Kumaraswamy Velupillai discuss the appropriate fiscal policy when monetary policy is bound by a rule, for example a constant money growth rate rule. In the development of fiscal norms, early Keynesians stressed functional finance, the notion the government ought to run deficits to stimulate the economy when the economy slowed down and conversely when it was overheated. Neo-Keynesians such as Samuelson subsequently argued for neoclassical determination of optimal government spending and taxes, leaving stabilisation of output to monetary policy. Phelps and Velupillai examine the construction of a model in which one can ask the question of the appropriate stabilisation approach to fiscal policy and output in the economy in which monetary policy is tied by various rules. They conclude that there appears to be a case for scaling public expenditure up or down with a view toward its output and employment effects without violating basic Ramsey rules for optimal taxation and saving.

Richard Musgrave discusses the appropriate role of debt finance under alternative circumstances. In his view debt finance is part of the allocation function of the government in its attempt intertemporarily to synchronise the benefits of public expenditures with bearing of the costs of financing them. Musgrave distinguishes various cases in which intergenerational equity, by his definition, is automatically satisfied or tends to be violated.

Toshihiro Ihori begins by asking does financing government expenditure by borrowing rather that by taxation impose a greater burden on future generations and if so, how. His empirical work for Japan suggests that some burden is passed to the future. The theoretical model discussed demonstrates how the actual behaviour of government (with respect to the policy instruments chosen) is crucial in how debt burdens relate to intertemporal or intergenerational equity.

John Flemming discusses the role of budget of deficits and surpluses as smoothing tax rates in a stochastic environment. He builds on earlier work in which factor prices were determined by international trade or capital mobility. In the closed economy model considered, factor prices are endogenous. The model is stochastic in that a Markovian process generates two states of the world: strong or weak demand for government spending (hence the analogy to War and Peace). Flemming's major result is that the expected value of tax changes should be zero. In other words, one should not go on a public spending binge on a purely pay as you go basis (e.g. the finance of war). Flemming's paper also raises various issues concerning the nature of the instruments the government uses as debt finance.

Vito Tanzi and Mario Blejer discuss the recent tendencies in developing countries concerning the growth of public debt. Tanzi and Blejer stress important differences between advanced and developing countries in the constraints on the level of taxation relative to national income. Substantial inflexibility in the tax–GNP ratio limits it to one half or less in developing countries of what it is in advanced economies. In no case is there documented experience where the tax ratio has increased 10 to 20 percentage point of GDP in one or two decades or even by several percentage points in a few years. These economies also have substantial limits on domestic debt since internal capital markets are small and a limited role is played by financial intermediatries, combined with a high default and political risk. This implies that foreign source financing is extremely important to these economies.

Tanzi and Blejer analyse empirically external public debt growth and also determine a substantial negative correlation between the rate of growth of the economy and the foreign debt-GNP ratio. The pattern seems to be for a sharp increase in foreign borrowing obviously leading to a steep accumulation of foreign debt followed thereafter by a steep decrease in net foreign borrowing as credit becomes expensive. This implies a reversal of the net flow of funds to LDCs which then must run trade surpluses, and change their economic policies in the course of economic adjustment.

Ephraim Kleiman considers the burdens and benefits of indexed debt via a discussion of the Israeli experience. He notes that indexation leads to a decrease in wealth redistribution due to inflation, decreased real effects of inflation, and a large decrease in real money balances as indexed bonds substitute for cash. Various potential benefits of indexation are discussed in some detail by Kleiman.

Stefano Gorini works out the relationship between budget balance, wealth and growth in Domar-type models. Public debt is seen as an increase in private wealth. The model develops a unique equilibrium with budget balance or surpluses, but with budget deficits, two, one, or no equilibrium may exist. Gorini then turns to discuss the deficit policy necessary to support a potential growth rate.

The editors of, and contributors to, this volume hope that these essays and their discussion will add to our knowledge of the causes and consequences of public debt policies in advanced and developing countries and that knowledge can be a useful input to improving those policies and resolving the economic distortions and imbalances they create.

Part I
Public Debt and Macroeconomics

1 Deficits, Monetary Policy, and Real Economic Activity

Robert Eisner
NORTHWESTERN UNIVERSITY

and Paul J. Pieper
UNIVERSITY OF ILLINOIS

1 INTRODUCTION

The coincidence in the 1970s of apparently large, structural federal deficits, substantial and growing unemployment and inflation rising to double-digit levels brought widespread questioning of the hitherto dominant Keynesian paradigm. Indeed, Robert Lucas (Lucas and Sargent, 1978; Lucas, 1981) indicated this coincidence as a motivation for his own rejection of that paradigm and search for new macroeconomic theory. In short, he explained, the Keynesian model suggested that expansive fiscal and monetary policies might cause some inflation but would reduce unemployment. But to the contrary, he indicated, these policies begot accelerating inflation *and high unemployment*.

In earlier work (Eisner and Pieper, 1984), we have argued that conventional measures of federal deficits – both actual and structural or high employment – along with associated views of fiscal policy, were fundamentally flawed. We showed that they were particularly biased measures of fiscal thrust in periods of significant inflation. Conventional measures ignored changes in the market value of outstanding government debt due to changing interest rates and further changes in their real value due to changes in the general level of prices or inflation. Making appropriate adjustments for changes in the real value of debt forces revision of conventional measures of fiscal policy. Particularly from 1977 to 1981, what appeared to be substantial deficits, both actual and due to high employment, became substantial surpluses.

We reported further that high employment deficits adjusted to correspond to changes in the real value of net debt were positively associated with subsequent increases in real GNP and reductions in unemployment. In other work (Eisner and Pieper, 1985) we noted that the United States high employment budget deficits adjusted for inflation were positively associated with subsequent real growth in Canada, France, West Germany, Italy, Japan and the United Kingdom.

The relations we estimated were all single equation, reduced forms and doubts may reasonably be expressed as to whether our results will prove robust against underlying structural changes. Dealing only with the reduced forms, however, the question immediately arises as to whether deficits may have been associated with changes in the money supply, which had been omitted in the relations we estimated. Perhaps it was excluded monetary variables that accounted for the relations we observed.

In this chapter we will seek to answer that question. We will further estimate separately the role of the interest effect on the market value of the debt and deficit. In addition, we will extend our previous analysis with annual data to estimation of distributed lag relations involving quarterly time series. Finally, we will go beyond effects on the aggregate of gross national product to examine movements of the various components of GNP. This will enable us to cast some light on the extent to which deficits 'crowd out' or 'crowd in' investment. We will also find, in the impact of deficits on net exports, an explanation of the previously observed relation between United States deficits and GDP growth among our major trading partners.

2 THE ROLE OF MONEY AND DEFICITS: ANNUAL DATA

We have introduced two different measures of monetary policy into our relations, the monetary base and non-borrowed reserves, both expressed as the change in end-of-period real stocks as a percentage of GNP.[1] We use the high employment deficit, calculated for an unemployment level of 5.1 per cent, as a first order measure of the thrust of fiscal policy on aggregate demand. However, our preferred fiscal measure differs in two important respects from other studies. First, since it is clearly real wealth which is relevant to real economic activity, we have adjusted the high employment deficit for changes in the real market value of government debt due to both inflation and changes in interest rates. The latter affect the market value of federal debt while inflation further affects its real value.

Secondly, we relate changes in real economic activity to the level of the high employment deficit, expressed as a percentage of GNP, rather than its rate of change. Consumption is a function of wealth, and not just current income, in both the life-cycle and permanent income theories. A federal budget deficit increases desired consumption by raising current wealth in the form of the federal debt to the private sector.[2] To the extent that it is expected to continue it also raises expected future income. Thus the change in consumption should be a function of the change in government net debt, or the level of the deficit. The higher the deficit, the greater the increase in wealth and the greater the increase in consumption.

A greater federal debt may also stimulate investment, both directly and indirectly. A direct effect may stem from portfolio considerations. Firms finding themselves with greater wealth in the form of government securities may strive to restore balance by acquiring real assets. A perhaps more powerful indirect effect may stem from perceptions of increased current and planned future consumption which would generate demand for more capital to supply an increased output of consumer goods.

In our earlier work, since time series for high employment budgets have been constructed back to 1955, we were able to regress changes in gross national product and unemployment on lagged high employment budget surpluses for observations beginning with 1956. A consistent series for the monetary base is available from the Federal Reserve only for years beginning with 1959. Our regressions were therefore able to use observations from 1960 through 1984. We had previously estimated separate sets of constants and regression coefficients for observations in the less inflationary, pre-1967 period and for the ones beginning with 1967. With so few pre-1967 observations now available, we have specified separate parameters only for the constant terms but calculated common regression slopes.

In Table 1.1[3] we present regressions of changes in GNP on the lagged high employment surplus and the lagged real change in either the monetary base or non-borrowed reserves, all expressed as percentages of GNP. The results for the high employment surplus variables are consistent with our previous work with a somewhat different set of observations. First, a balanced official high employment budget would appear to produce a very substantial growth in GNP in the earlier less inflationary period but virtually no growth in the later more inflationary period. The difference is much less, as shown by the constant terms, in the price adjusted surplus regression. Secondly, the high employment surplus is significantly negatively related to subsequent growth in GNP

Table 1.1 High-employment budget, monetary aggregates and GNP

$$\Delta \text{GNP}_t = b_{01}X_1 + b_{02}X_2 + b_1 \text{HES}_{t-1} + b_2 \Delta M_{t-1}$$

$X_1 = 1, X_2 = 0: t = 1961\text{--}6$
$X_1 = 0, X_2 = 1: t = 1967\text{--}84$

Regression coefficients[a]

(1)	(2)	(3)	(4)	(5)	(6)	(7)	(8)	(9)
	Constants		High employment surplus		Change in monetary base	Change in non-borrowed reserves		
Equation	1961–6	1967–84	Official	Price-adjusted				
	(b_{01})	(b_{02})	(b_1)	(b_1)	(b_2)	(b_2)	$\bar{R}^2$	$D\text{--}W$
(1.1)	7.450 (0.879)	0.772 (0.602)	−2.577 (0.530)				0.547	1.68
(1.2)	8.662 (0.856)	4.328 (0.422)		−2.306 (0.370)			0.662	1.88
(1.3)	3.228 (0.722)	2.023 (0.409)			12.888 (2.282)		0.618	1.99
(1.4)	4.525 (1.034)	3.099 (0.588)				10.574 (7.311)	0.125	1.59
(1.5)	5.159 (0.977)	1.123 (0.499)	−1.426 (0.546)		8.790 (2.556)		0.701	1.58

(1.6)	6.417 (1.257)	3.353 (0.576)		−1.461 (0.501)	6.628 (2.907)		0.719	1.70
(1.7)	7.041 (0.882)	0.999 (0.594)	−2.501 (0.512)			8.331 (5.082)	0.581	1.86
(1.8)	8.423 (0.941)	4.343 (0.429)		−2.237 (0.390)		3.162 (4.781)	0.653	1.88

Notes:
[a] Ordinary least squares; standard errors are shown in parentheses.
ΔGNP = per cent change in GNP
HES = high employment surplus as per cent of GNP
ΔM   = real change in monetary base as per cent of GNP, or real change in non-borrowed reserves as per cent of GNP.

and again the relation is sharper, in terms of standard errors and coefficients of determination, for the price adjusted surplus.

As hypothesised, however, the real change in monetary base also proves a good predictor of subsequent increases in GNP. In the 1967–84 period, a constant real monetary base was associated on average with a 2.0 per cent increase in real GNP (and 3.2 per cent growth in the years 1961–7). Each tenth of a percentage point increase in the ratio of the real change in monetary base to gross national product (corresponding on average to a 2.13 per cent increase in the rate of growth of the monetary base) was then associated with a 1.3 percentage point greater growth in GNP. The coefficient of determination in the monetary base relation was 0.618, higher than the 0.547 value of $\dot{R}^2$ for the official high employment surplus equation, but less than the 0.662 for the price adjusted surplus equation. The real change in non-borrowed reserves performs poorly, with little explanatory power and a coefficient not significantly different from zero.

Regressing the real change in GNP on both the high employment surplus and change in monetary base reveals that both were significant. The absolute values of both sets of coefficients, however, were less than when they were the sole regressors. In the best fitting equation, involving the price adjusted high employment surplus and the change in monetary base, the role of the monetary base variable is minimised, with a coefficient of 6.628, as compared with 12.888 when it is the sole regressor and 8.790 when it is coupled with the official high employment surplus. The coefficient of the price adjusted high employment surplus variable is a robust -1.461, almost three times its standard error of 0.501. The coefficient of the price adjusted high employment surplus increases to -2.237 when the monetary base is replaced by non-borrowed reserves, while the coefficient of non-borrowed reserves continues to be not significant.

We have noted in earlier work that the price and interest adjusted high employment surplus required two years of lags to show most of its effect on GNP. We attributed this to the possibility that agents would view short-term changes in the market value of securities as in considerable part transistory. We have thus regressed real changes in GNP on lagged values of the high employment surplus and two year lagged values of the interest effect. Results are shown in Table 1.2.

As hypothesised, the lagged interest effects are significantly negatively related to changes on GNP. The high employment surplus, both unadjusted and price adjusted, is highly significant in all four regressions. Introduction of separate interest effects generally reduces the significance

Table 1.2 High employment budget, delayed interest effect, monetary aggregates and GNP

$$\Delta GNP_t = b_{01}X_1 - b_{02}X_2 + b_1 HES_{t-1} + b_2 IE_{t-2} + b_3 \Delta MB_{t-1} + b_4 \Delta NR_{t-1}$$

$X_1 = 1, X_2 = 0$ for $t = 1961\text{-}6$
$X_1 = 0, X_2 = 1$ for $t = 1967\text{-}84$

(1)	(2)	(3)	(4)	(5)	(6)	(7)	(8)	(9)	(10)
Equation	Measure of HES	Constants		Regression coefficients[a]					
		1961-6 (b_{01})	1967-84 (b_{02})	HES_{t-1} (b_1)	IE_{t-2} (b_2)	ΔMB_{t-1} (b_3)	ΔNR_{t-1} (b_4)	$\bar{R}^2$	D-W
(2.1)	OF	5.226 (0.872)	1.323 (0.453)	-1.330 (0.488)	-0.901 (0.364)	6.875 (2.408)		0.762	1.67
(2.2)	PA	6.300 (1.136)	3.357 (0.520)	-1.323 (0.456)	-0.846 (0.359)	5.166 (2.697)		0.771	1.70
(2.3)	OF	6.550 (0.763)	1.310 (0.513)	-2.065 (0.457)	-1.167 (0.389)		6.930 (4.319)	0.701	1.86
(2.4)	PA	7.722 (0.867)	4.093 (0.388)	-1.860 (0.370)	-0.997 (0.377)		2.880 (4.196)	0.733	1.80

Notes:
[a] Ordinary least squares; standard errors in parentheses.
GNP = per cent change in GNP
HES = high employment surplus as per cent of GNP
OF = official
PA = price adjusted
IE = interest effect as per cent of GNP
MB = real change in monetary base as per cent of GNP
NR = real change in non-borrowed reserves as per cent of GNP

of the monetary variables. The coefficient of the lagged monetary base is no longer significant in the equation with the price adjusted surplus (although it is significant, at the 0.05 probability level, in Cochrane–Orcutt autoregressive relations, now shown here), while non-borrowed reserves are not significant in both equations. The price adjusted high employment surplus variable performs slightly better than the official high employment surplus, in terms of goodness of fit, with either monetary variable (but not consistently so in the Cochrane–Orcutt estimates).

Further confirmation of the robustness of the fiscal variables may be seen in Table 1.3, which shows the results of annual regressions with the change in unemployment as the dependent variable. Holding the monetary base constant, an increase in the official high employment deficit of one per cent of GNP is associated with a reduction of 0.69 percentage points in the unemployment rate, while a similar increase in the price adjusted deficit is associated with a 0.63 percentage points decline in unemployment. As in the GNP regressions, the coefficients of both surplus variables and the lagged interest effects are highly significant, with t-statistics in most instances greater than three. The monetary base is significant only in the official surplus equation, while the coefficient of non-borrowed reserves is positive. Again, a balanced official budget (and constant real monetary base) appears expansionary in the earlier period, but contractionary, bringing significantly greater unemployment, in the more inflationary later years.[4]

3 RESULTS WITH QUARTERLY TIME SERIES

In analyses of quarterly time series we first worked with four quarter lags of official and price adjusted high employment budget surpluses and four quarter lags, as well, of three sets of monetary variables. Regressing the change in GNP on the budget variables alone produced a sum of the coefficients of the price adjusted surplus with a lower standard error while the difference in constant terms as between earlier and later periods was greater in the official surplus equations. These results again suggest an inflation error in the official surplus variables, partly corrected by separate constant terms for more inflationary and less inflationary periods. Two sets of monetary variables – the monetary base and total reserves – also showed sums of regression coefficients which were significant at least the 0.05 probability level, with the

Table 1.3 High-employment budget, delayed interest effect, monetary aggregates and unemployment

$$\Delta UN = b_{01}X_1 + b_{02}X_2 + b_1 HES_{t-1} + b_2 IE_{t-2} + b_3 \Delta MB_{t-1} + b_4 \Delta NR_{t-1}$$

$X_1 = 1, X_2 = 0$ for $t = 1961$–6
$X_1 = 0, X_2 = 1$ for $t = 1967$–84

(1)	(2)	(3)	(4)	(5)	(6)	(7)	(8)	(9)	(10)
		\multicolumn{2}{c}{Constants}			Regression coefficients[a]			
Equation	Measure of HES	1961–6 (b_{01})	1967–84 (b_{02})		HES_{t-1} (b_1)	IE_{t-2} (b_2)	ΔMB_{t-1} (b_3)	ΔNR_{t-1} (b_4)	$\bar{R}^2$ D–W
(3.1)	OF	−0.611 (0.337)	0.936 (0.201)		0.692 (0.217)	0.506 (0.161)	−2.208 (1.068)		0.746 1.93
(3.2)	PA	−1.052 (0.523)	−0.073 (0.239)		0.634 (0.210)	0.482 (0.165)	−1.539 (1.242)		0.736 1.72
(3.3)	OF	−1.171 (0.332)	1.010 (0.223)		0.944 (0.199)	0.621 (0.169)		0.788 (1.881)	0.691 1.83
(3.4)	PA	−1.738 (0.363)	−0.273 (0.162)		0.868 (0.155)	0.536 (0.158)		2.690 (1.757)	0.746 1.57

Notes:
[a] Ordinary least squares; standard errors are shown in parentheses.
UN = percentage point change in unemployment rate
HES = high employment surplus as per cent of GNP
OF = official
PA = price adjusted
IE = interest effect as per cent of GNP
MB = real change in monetary base as per cent of GNP
NR = real change in non-borrowed reserves as per cent of GNP

monetary base variables most clearly significant. The differences were not great but the coefficient of determination was higher in the budget equations and highest when the price adjusted surplus was used as the regressor.

When fiscal and monetary variables are both used as regressors, t-statistics are generally reduced. However, the price adjusted surplus variables remain significant in all regressions, while the official surplus variables are no longer significant at the 0.05 level in the monetary base equation and the only significant set of coefficients for the monetary variables is found in the equation including the official surplus and non-borrowed reserves.

The four-quarter lag regressions reported in Table 1.4 include price adjusted budget variables but exclude interest effects, that is, the par-to-market adjustment which captures capital gains and losses in the market value of outstanding federal debt. To estimate their role we again turn to longer lags and introduce, in this case as separate variables, interest effects lagged five to eight quarters. The sums of coefficients of the interest effect variables, as shown in Table 1.5, prove highly significant in all equations and are close in magnitude to the sums for the budget surplus variables. (Interest effects are defined as positive to the extent that they reduce the market value of net debt and thus contribute to a surplus. We should hence expect similar signs of coefficients of the budget surplus and the separate interest effects.) The monetary variables remain significant only in the regression including the official surplus and non-borrowed reserves. To the extent monetary variables do affect the rate of growth of output their role would appear to be largely captured in their wealth effect on the market value of government debt.

The results of quarterly regressions involving the change in unemployment are shown in Table 1.6. The sums of coefficients of the fiscal variables are consistently significant with a value in the neighbourhood of unity, or somewhat greater than the estimates from annual time series. None of the sets of monetary variables is significant in any of the six regressions.

Table 1.7 presents regressions, for both GNP and unemployment, involving eight quarterly lags of the price and interest adjusted high employment surplus and the change in monetary base. Once more, the adjusted budget variable fares considerably better when each is a sole regressor. When both sets of variables are introduced into the regressions, estimated parameters of the high employment surplus variables prove robust and highly significant. The monetary base variables lose all significance and actually reverse sign.

Table 1.4 High-employment budget, monetary aggregates and GNP, quarterly data, four-quarter lags

$$\Delta GNP_t = b_{01}X_1 + b_{02}X_2 + \sum_{i=1}^{4} b_{1i} HES_{t-1} + \sum_{i=1}^{4} b_{2i} \Delta M_{t-i}$$

(1) Equation	(2) Measure of HES and money	(3) Constants $1960.2-1966.4$ (b_{01})	(4) Constants $1967.1-1984.4$ (b_{02})	(5) HES (Σb_{1i})	(6) ΔM (Σb_{2i})	(7) $\hat{R}^2$	(8) $\hat{\rho}$
(4.1)	OF	6.459 (1.122)	1.411 (0.826)	−2.101 (0.695)		0.260	0.272
(4.2)	PA	8.153 (1.197)	4.235 (0.614)	−2.199 (0.528)		0.279	0.223
(4.3)	MB	3.047 (1.003)	1.940 (0.594)		13.788 (3.622)	0.248	0.211
(4.4)	NR	4.617 (1.109)	3.156 (0.665)		11.857 (6.769)	0.207	0.344
(4.5)	TR	4.654 (1.029)	3.267 (0.626)		21.950 (9.979)	0.212	0.292
(4.6)	OF, MB	4.798 (1.424)	1.113 (0.768)	−1.399 (0.813)	8.486 (4.472)	0.283	0.208
(4.7)	PA, MB	6.646 (2.036)	3.538 (0.974)	−1.630 (0.810)	4.998 (5.532)	0.272	0.200
(4.8)	OF, NR	6.267 (1.068)	1.306 (0.786)	−2.190 (0.669)	13.309 (6.326)	0.303	0.238
(4.9)	PA, NR	7.811 (1.218)	4.331 (0.606)	−2.107 (0.533)	8.286 (6.318)	0.316	0.224
(4.10)	OF, TR	6.222 (1.134)	1.458 (0.869)	−1.925 (0.712)	12.780 (9.789)	0.282	0.242
(4.11)	PA, TR	7.936 (1.400)	4.211 (0.617)	−2.055 (0.634)	5.485 (10.714)	0.279	0.225

Notes:
[a] Least squares with Cochrane–Orcutt first order autoregressive corrections; standard errors are shown in parentheses.
$X_1 = 1$, $X_2 = 0$, for $t = 1960.2$ to 1966.4; $X_1 = 0$, $X_2 = 1$, for $t = 1967.1$ to 1984.4
HES = high employment surplus as per cent of GNP
OF = official, PA = price adjusted
ΔM = real change in monetary aggregates as per cent of GNP
MB = monetary base; NR = non-borrowed reserves; TR = total reserves.

Table 1.5 High employment budget, monetary aggregates, interest effects and GNP, quarterly data

$$\Delta \text{GNP}_t = b_{01}X_1 + b_{02}X_2 + \sum_{i=1}^{4} b_{1i}\text{HES}_{t-i} + \sum_{i=1}^{4} b_{2i}\Delta M_{t-i} + \sum_{i=5}^{8} b_{3i}\text{IE}_{t-i},$$

(1) Equation	(2) Measure of HES and M	(3)	(4)	(5)	(6)	(7)	(8)	(9)
		Constants		Regression coefficients[a]				
		1960.2–1966.4 (b_{01})	1967.1–1984.4 (b_{02})	HES (Σb_{1i})	ΔM (Σb_{2i})	IE (Σb_{3i})	$\hat{R}^2$	$\hat{\rho}$
(5.1)	OF, MB	5.169 (1.301)	1.343 (0.708)	−1.462 (0.749)	5.155 (4.260)	−1.443 (0.565)	0.340	0.152
(5.2)	PA, MB	6.791 (1.876)	3.751 (0.898)	−1.574 (0.751)	2.169 (5.223)	−1.411 (0.571)	0.324	0.149
(5.3)	OF, NR	5.904 (0.959)	1.615 (0.714)	−1.848 (0.624)	11.873 (5.906)	−1.520 (0.535)	0.361	0.164
(5.4)	PA, NR	7.157 (1.151)	4.139 (0.558)	−1.750 (0.520)	7.000 (6.036)	−1.376 (0.547)	0.365	0.170
(5.5)	OF, TR	6.115 (1.016)	1.458 (0.786)	−1.834 (0.657)	4.584 (9.248)	−1.705 (0.574)	0.346	0.177
(5.6)	PA, TR	7.622 (1.301)	4.049 (0.569)	−1.891 (0.602)	−1.793 (10.232)	−1.581 (0.582)	0.335	0.177

Notes:
[a] Least squares with Cochrane–Orcutt first order autoregressive corrections; standard errors are shown in parentheses.
$X_1 = 1$, $X_2 = 0$, for $t = 1960.2$ to 1966.4; $X_1 = 0$, $X_2 = 1$, for $t = 1967.1$ to 1984.4.
HES = high employment surplus as per cent of GNP
OF = official, PA = price adjusted
ΔM = real change in monetary aggregates as per cent of GNP
MB = monetary base; NR = non-borrowed reserves; TR = total reserves.

Table 1.6 High-employment budget, monetary aggregates, interest effects and unemployment, quarterly data

$$\Delta UN_t = b_{01}X_1 + b_{02}X_2 + \sum_{i=1}^{4} b_{1i}HES_{t-i} + \sum_{i=1}^{4} b_{2i}\Delta M_{t-i} + \sum_{i=5}^{8} b_{3i}IE_{t-i}$$

(1) Equation	(2) Measure of HES and M	(3)	(4)	(5)	(6)	(7)	(8)	(9)
		\multicolumn{2}{c}{Constants}	\multicolumn{3}{c}{Regression coefficients[a]}		
		1960.2 1966.4 (b_{01})	1967.1 1984.4 (b_{02})	HES (Σb_{1i})	ΔM (Σb_{2i})	IE (Σb_{3i})	$\bar{R}^2$	$\hat{\rho}$
(6.1)	OF, MB	−0.494 (0.613)	1.214 (0.347)	0.931 (0.330)	−3.115 (1.909)		0.501	0.499
(6.2)	PA, MB	−1.575 (0.869)	−0.308 (0.434)	1.012 (0.339)	−1.144 (2.335)		0.500	0.509
(6.3)	PA, MB	−1.520 (0.799)	−0.341 (0.394)	0.961 (0.315)	−0.523 (2.177)	0.526 (0.218)	0.532	0.456
(6.4)	OF, NR	−0.911 (0.530)	1.107 (0.378)	1.131 (0.296)	−1.370 (2.335)		0.508	0.555
(6.5)	PA, NR	−1.814 (0.579)	−0.442 (0.305)	1.106 (0.241)	0.622 (2.327)		0.526	0.536
(6.6)	PA, NR	−1.524 (0.517)	−0.378 (0.263)	0.961 (0.224)	0.253 (2.199)	0.557 (0.212)	0.560	0.469

Notes:
[a] Least squares with Cochrane–Orcutt first order autoregressive corrections; standard errors are shown in parenthesis.

$X_1 = 1$, $X_2 = 0$, for $t = 1960.2$ to 1966.4; $X_1 = 0$, $X_2 = 1$, for $t = 1967.1$ to 1984.4.
HES = high employment surplus as per cent of GNP
OF = official, PA = price adjusted
ΔM = real change in monetary aggregates as per cent of GNP
MB = monetary base; NR = non-borrowed reserves; TR = total reserves
UN = percentage point change in unemployment

Table 1.7 High employment budget, monetary base, GNP and unemployment, quarterly data, eight-quarter lags

$$\Delta Z_t = b_{01}X_1 + b_{02}X_1 + \sum_{i=1}^{8} b_{1i}\text{HES}_{t-i} + \sum_{i=1}^{8} b_{2i}\Delta \text{MB}_{t-i}$$

(1) Equation	(2) Dependent variable (ΔZ_t)	(3)	(4)	(5)	(6)	(7)	(8)
		Constants		HES	ΔMB	$\bar{R}^2$	$\hat{\rho}$
		1961.2–1966.4 (b_{01})	1967.1–1984.4 (b_{02})	(Σb_{1i})	(Σb_{2i})		
(7.1)	ΔGNP	9.113 (1.231)	4.674 (0.630)	−2.544 (0.546)		0.316	0.217
(7.2)	ΔGNP	3.295 (1.189)	2.034 (0.631)		12.377 (4.759)	0.223	0.200
(7.3)	ΔGNP	9.498 (2.472)	4.758 (1.155)	−2.601 (0.909)	−1.207 (6.939)	0.291	0.216
(7.4)	ΔUN	−2.335 (0.577)	−0.601 (0.303)	1.146 (0.243)		0.531	0.515
(7.5)	ΔUN	0.381 (0.621)	0.657 (0.331)		−6.411 (2.330)	0.442	0.525
(7.6)	ΔUN	−2.491 (1.104)	−0.633 (0.534)	1.186 (0.391)	0.177 (3.146)	0.494	0.521

a Regression coefficients

Notes:
[a] Least squares with Cochrane–Orcutt first order autoregressive correction: standard errors are shown in parentheses.
$X_1 = 1, X_2 = 0$ for $t = 1961.2 - 1966.4$
$X_1 = 0, X_2 = 1$ for $t = 1967.1 - 1984.4$
HES = price and interest adjusted high employment surplus as per cent of GNP
MB = real change in monetary base as per cent of GNP
GNP = per cent change in GNP, at annual rates
UN = percentage point change in unemployment

We conclude, on the basis of these single equation estimates, that monetary policy, as evidenced by changes in either the monetary base or in total or non-borrowed reserves, does not explain – or explain away – the association of budget deficits with increases in gross national product and decreases in unemployment. Quite to the contrary, the high employment budget deficit, adjusted for changes in the real value of the debt due to inflation and changing interest rates, accounts for a substantial portion – in the eight-quarter regressions virtually all – of the effects otherwise attributable to the role of money. The monetary variables do not prove robust.[5] The adjusted surplus variables do.

4 COMPONENTS OF GNP

Government deficits may be viewed as constituting public dissaving, absorbing private saving and hence, if private saving is given, reducing private investment. Of course, if output is not fixed it is unreasonable to assume that private saving is given. As the issue was posed half a century ago, a stimulus to non-investment spending may bring about more or less private investment, depending on the relative reactions of the demand for money and of investment to interest rates and output (Lange, 1938). These in turn will relate to how close the economy is to full employment and hence how much output can in fact increase. Indeed, even at full employment it would appear that a deficit induced increase in aggregate demand need not reduce investment if the money supply is increased in proportion to the increase in interest bearing government debt. The only result then would be a higher price level, with no change in the real debt, real quantity of money, interest rates or investment (see Eisner, 1986, pp. 182–4).

In an open economy, government deficits may also affect the balance of payments via interest and output effects. To the extent they increase output they will increase imports. To the extent they raise interest rates they will attract foreign capital, raise exchange rates and add to the impetus to an 'unfavourable' balance of trade and a reduction in net exports. The inflow of foreign capital and goods would, however, both help accommodate an increase in investment.

The evidence that adjusted structural deficits have been positively related to the growth of GNP makes clear that it cannot be assumed that a deficit-induced stimulus to consumption must result in less private investment. The issue is an empirical one, and we are able to offer some striking results of further examination of our annual time series.

The effects on GNP of the budget deficit, and other variables such as changes in the monetary base, are the sum of their effects, direct or indirect, on the various components of GNP. We have hence regressed changes in these components, each expressed as percentages of GNP so that estimated parameters are comparable, on the price adjusted high employment surplus and changes in the monetary base. As shown in Table 1.8, equation (8.1), the surplus is, as expected, negatively related to consumption. Each percentage point of price adjusted high employment deficit as a ratio of GNP was associated over the years 1961 to 1984 with an increase in personal consumption expenditures equal to 0.646 per cent of GNP. But as also shown in Table 1.8, each percentage point of deficit was also associated with an even larger increase in gross private domestic investment, amounting to 1.371 per cent of GNP (8.2). While of course neither of these point estimates should be taken too seriously, it is worth noting that the signs of the coefficients are clearly statistically significant. Results shown in Table 1.9 indicate further that the deficit was similarly positively associated with the durable and the non-durable and services components components of consumption, and with the fixed and inventory components of investment. The adjusted high employment deficits were thus correlated positively with increases in *both* consumption and investment. Deficits were 'crowding in' investment, not crowding it out.

As predicted, however, deficits did have a distinct negative effect on net exports. Each percentage point of adjusted high employment deficit as a ratio of GNP was associated with a reduction of net exports of 0.392 per cent of GNP, as shown in Table 1.8, equation (8.4). And this was more than fully accounted for by an increase of imports equalling 0.436 per cent of GNP, as shown in Table 1.9, equation (9.8).

There are important consequences, domestic and foreign, of this negative effect of our budget deficits on net exports. On the domestic side, we have a 'leakage' of income and demand outside of our economy. We see in equation (8.6) in Table 1.8 that each percentage point of price adjusted high employment deficit is associated with an increase in 'domestic demand' equal to 2.125 per cent of GNP. With a reduction in net exports equal to 0.392 per cent of output, however, the estimated impact of one percentage point of deficit on GNP is only 1.571 per cent.[6] We find then that the deficit leads Americans to spend more and that stimulates more production, but some of it involves Japanese Toyotas and Sonys, French wine and English sweaters. The increase in imports thus permits a greater increase in domestic consumption and investment than the increase in domestic output.

Table 1.8 High-employment budget, changes in monetary base and changes in components of GNP

$$\Delta COM_t = b_{01}X_1 + b_{02}X_2 + b_1 PAHES_{t-1} + b_2 \Delta MB_{t-1}$$

$X_1 = 1, X_2 = 0$ for $t = 1961-6$
$X_1 = 0, X_2 = 1$ for $t = 1967-84$

(1) Equation	(2) Component (COM)	(3) Constants 1961–6 (b_{01})	(4) Constants 1967–84 (b_{02})	(5) Surplus $PAHES_{t-1}$ (b_1)	(6) Monetary base ΔMB_{t-1} (b_2)	(7) $\hat{R}^2$	(8) $\hat{\rho}$
(8.1)	Consumption	3.400 (0.676)	2.344 (0.305)	−0.646 (0.266)	2.427 (1.582)	0.580	0.095
(8.2)	Investment	2.569 (1.189)	1.133 (0.551)	−1.371 (0.422)	3.727 (2.425)	0.562	0.283
(8.3)	Government	1.178 (0.560)	0.478 (0.272)	−0.106 (0.174)	−0.629 (0.978)	0.352	0.476
(8.4)	Net exports	−1.682 (1.450)	−0.829 (1.202)	0.392 (0.137)	1.600 (0.813)	0.503	0.850
(8.5)	GNP	6.195 (1.301)	3.381 (0.591)	−1.571 (0.485)	7.266 (2.827)	0.733	0.173
(8.6)	Domestic demand	7.338 (1.527)	3.929 (0.689)	−2.125 (0.570)	5.380 (3.314)	0.700	0.161

Regression coefficients[a]

Notes:
[a] Least squares with Cochrane–Orcutt, first order autoregressive corrections; standard errors are shown in parentheses.

ΔCOM = change in component as per cent of GNP
PAHES = price adjusted high employment surplus as per cent of GNP
ΔMB = change in monetary base as per cent of GNP

Table 1.9 High employment budget, monetary base, and fine components of GNP

$$\Delta COM_t = b_{01}X_1 + b_{02}X_2 + b_1 PAHES_{t-1} + b_2 \Delta MB_{t-1}$$

$X_1 = 1, X_2 = 0$ for $t = 1961\text{-}6$
$X_1 = 0, X_2 = 1$ for $t = 1967\text{-}84$

Regression coefficients[a]

(1) Equation	(2) Component	(3) Constants $1961\text{-}6$ (b_{01})	(4) Constants $1967\text{-}84$ (b_{02})	(5) Surplus $PAHES_{t-1}$ (b_1)	(6) Monetary base ΔMB_{t-1} (b_2)	(7) $\hat{R}^2$	(8) $\hat{\rho}$
(9.1)	Consumer durables	1.034 (0.364)	0.603 (0.165)	−0.382 (0.140)	1.082 (0.802)	0.548	0.197
(9.2)	Nondurables and services	2.349 (0.400)	1.732 (0.180)	−0.258 (0.154)	1.438 (0.936)	0.510	0.085
(9.3)	Fixed investment	1.597 (0.696)	0.827 (0.333)	−0.800 (0.214)	2.780 (1.261)	0.664	0.448
(9.4)	Change in inventories	0.777 (0.593)	0.229 (0.265)	−0.444 (0.240)	0.848 (1.411)	0.340	−0.128
(9.5)	Federal	0.591 (0.530)	0.173 (0.256)	−0.091 (0.167)	−0.863 (0.936)	0.281	0.466
(9.6)	State and local	0.540 (0.252)	0.307 (0.128)	−0.011 (0.062)	0.187 (0.361)	0.515	0.611

(9.7)	Exports	0.004 (0.513)	0.277 (0.240)	0.007 (0.186)	1.742 (0.972)	0.204	0.400
(9.8)	Imports	0.942 (0.381)	0.734 (0.176)	−0.436 (0.149)	0.280 (0.856)	0.428	0.081

Notes:
[a] Least squares with Cochrane–Orcutt first order autoregressive corrections; standard errors are shown in parentheses.
ΔCOM = change in component as per cent of GNP
PAHES = price adjusted high employment surplus as per cent of GNP
ΔMB = change in monetary base as per cent of GNP

But if this 'leakage' reduces the favourable impact of budget deficits on our own output, it correspondingly contributes to the demand for foreign product. With US gross national product in the neighbourhood of $4,000 billion, each percentage point of deficit contributes a net increase in demand for foreign goods and services of $17.5 billion (0.436 per cent of $4,000 billion). We should then anticipate a role for the US budget deficit in the economies of other nations. The lesser increase in domestic output will have a counterpart in greater growth of output elsewhere.

This is of course precisely what we discovered in relating price adjusted high employment deficits in the United States to changes in gross domestic product in six major OECD countries. The US budget deficit contributed significantly to those nations' economic growth. The effects of deficits on the net exports component of US GNP point out the multiplicand in a substantial foreign trade multiplier.

We have again been able to improve the fit of our relations by introducing the interest effect lagged two years. Table 1.10 shows significant negative coefficients for the contribution of the interest effect to an adjusted high employment surplus in the equations for consumption (10.1) and investment (10.2) as well as for GNP (10.5) and domestic demand (10.6). The price adjusted high employment surplus remains highly significant in all of these equations as well as in the equation for net exports. The total effect of the adjusted high employment surplus, including the two-year lagged interest effect is uniformly increased.

Our regressions of components of GNP offer a few other interesting results. For those concerned that budget deficits fuel increases in government expenditures the message is apparently, 'Not to worry!' Each percentage point of adjusted high employment deficit, again as a ratio of GNP, was associated, as shown in (8.3) of Table 1.8, with increases in government expenditures of only 0.106 per cent of GNP, with the increase in federal expenditures alone accounting for 0.091 per cent of output, as shown in equation (9.5) of Table 1.9. And finally, the monetary base variable, while significant in the total GNP regressions (8.5 and 10.5) and uniformly showing the 'right' (generally positive) sign for the GNP components, was significantly different from zero at the 0.05 probability level only in the case of fixed investment (9.3), and even then only when the interest effect variable was excluded – which is also what a good Keynesian might have predicted[7].

Table 1.10 High employment budget, changes in monetary base and changes in components of GNP

$$\Delta COM_t = b_{01}X_1 + b_{02}X_2 + b_1 PAHES_{t-1} + b_2 IE_{t-2} + b_3 \Delta MB_{t-1}$$

$X_1 = 1, X_2 = 0$ for $t = 1961–6$
$X_1 = 0, X_2 = 1$ for $t = 1967–84$

(1) Equation	(2) Component	(3) (4) Constants		(5) Surplus $PAHES_{t-1}$	(6) Interest effect IE_{t-2}	(7) Monetary base ΔMB_{t-1}	(8) $\hat{R}^2$	(9) $\hat{\rho}$
	(COM)	1961–6 (b_{01})	1968–84 (b_{02})	(b_1)	(b_2)	(b_3)		
(10.1)	Consumption	3.280 (0.630)	2.326 (0.285)	−0.575 (0.243)	−0.383 (0.184)	1.898 (1.477)	0.642	0.153
(10.2)	Investment	2.250 (1.075)	1.037 (0.495)	−1.132 (0.436)	−0.671 (0.351)	2.698 (2.448)	0.617	0.096
(10.3)	Government	1.032 (0.586)	0.466 (0.296)	−0.069 (0.162)	−0.167 (0.118)	−0.885 (0.945)	0.381	0.558
(10.4)	Net exports	−1.472 (1.136)	−0.694 (0.864)	0.379 (0.128)	0.193 (0.100)	1.929 (0.758)	0.574	0.834
(10.5)	GNP	6.033 (1.152)	3.390 (0.522)	−1.467 (0.432)	−0.836 (0.336)	5.852 (2.551)	0.792	0.178
(10.6)	Domestic demand	7.145 (1.255)	3.945 (0.568)	−1.973 (0.479)	−1.151 (0.392)	3.349 (2.844)	0.793	0.127

Notes:

[a] Least squares with Cochrane–Orcutt, first order autoregressive corrections; standard errors are shown in parentheses. ΔCOM = change in component as per cent of GNP. PAHES = price adjusted high employment surplus as per cent of GNP. ΔMB = change in monetary base as per cent of GNP

5 CONCLUSIONS

1. Money does not explain away a strong relation between the inflation adjusted high employment surplus and changes in gross national product and unemployment. In regressions involving both fiscal and monetary variables, the fiscal variables prove generally robust. The relations are stronger and the monetary variables, while usually maintaining some role, generally lose significant when the high employment surplus is adjusted for price and interest effects. Thus failure to measure deficits correctly has not only contributed to a false view of fiscal impotence, but has possibly lead to an overestimate of the importance of money.

2. The adjusted high employment budget deficit is positively related to increases in both consumption and investment. Far from crowding out investment, deficits apparently crowd it in.

3. A damping effect of deficits is to be noted, however, in the negative relation between the adjusted high employment surplus and net exports. Aggregate demand of Americans is stimulated considerably more than the aggregate demand for American output. Thus, US budget deficits add a foreign trade multiplier stimulus to the growth in output in US major trading partners.

4. In the light of all the above, overly enthusiastic monetarists, those who would infer policy ineffectiveness from rational expectations, and those who would reject the Keynesian revolution of a half century ago – or its 'neoclassical synthesis' – might all take pause.

APPENDIX 1

Table 1.A1 Lag structure: official and price-adjusted high-employment surplus, real change in non-borrowed reserves and interest effect, and per cent change in GNP

(1) Lag	(2)	(3) Equation (5.3) Official surplus	(4)	(5)	(6) Equation (5.4) Price-adjusted surplus	(7)
	HES	ΔNR	IE	HES	ΔNR	IE
1	−0.799 (0.599)	0.863 (2.023)	—	−0.862 (0.488)	−0.883 (2.099)	—
2	0.450 (0.680)	5.855 (2.098)	—	0.371 (0.497)	5.407 (2.136)	—
3	−1.880 (0.644)	4.384 (2.227)	—	−1.333 (0.486)	2.711 (2.326)	—
4	0.381 (0.582)	0.772 (2.147)	—	0.075 (0.456)	−0.235 (2.140)	—
5	—	—	−0.504 (0.183)	—	—	−0.495 (0.185)
6	—	—	−0.574 (0.204)	—	—	−0.530 (0.207)
7	—	—	−0.199 (0.207)	—	—	−0.147 (0.210)
8	—	—	−0.242 (0.181)	—	—	−0.204 (0.183)
Sum	−1.848 (0.624)	11.873 (5.906)	−1.520 (0.535)	−1.745 (0.520)	7.000 (6.036)	−1.376 (0.547)

Notes:
HES = high employment surplus as per cent of GNP
ΔNR = real change in non-borrowed revenues as per cent of GNP
IE   = interest effect on federal debt as per cent of GNP

Table 1.A2 Eight-quarter lag structure: price and interest adjusted high employment surplus and real change in monetary base, GNP and unemployment equations

(1) Lag	(2)	(3) ΔGNP Equations		(5)	(6)	(7) ΔUN Equations	(8)	(9)
	(7.1) PIAHES	(7.2) ΔMB	(7.3) PIAHES	ΔMB	(7.4) PIAHES	(7.5) ΔMB	(7.6) PIAHES	ΔMB
1	−0.366 (0.165)	6.324 (2.099)	−0.306 (0.183)	3.290 (2.304)	0.084 (0.052)	−1.406 (0.666)	0.073 (0.058)	−0.503 (0.733)
2	−0.394 (0.176)	3.699 (2.130)	−0.330 (0.215)	−0.577 (2.624)	0.191 (0.063)	−1.645 (0.766)	0.182 (0.078)	0.129 (0.962)
3	−0.565 (0.173)	2.000 (2.186)	−0.563 (0.223)	−2.195 (2.571)	0.141 (0.061)	−1.004 (0.759)	0.155 (0.084)	0.744 (0.949)
4	−0.177 (0.173)	0.046 (2.282)	−0.273 (0.220)	−3.086 (2.651)	0.175 (0.060)	−1.333 (0.784)	0.202 (0.084)	0.427 (0.962)
5	−0.349 (0.173)	2.028 (2.269)	−0.456 (0.219)	0.354 (2.537)	0.223 (0.060)	−0.851 (0.776)	0.252 (0.083)	0.128 (0.894)
6	−0.415 (0.174)	1.516 (2.215)	−0.423 (0.219)	1.916 (2.263)	0.124 (0.061)	−0.324 (0.738)	0.129 (0.082)	−0.439 (0.962)
7	−0.068 (0.174)	−1.759 (2.053)	−0.028 (0.214)	0.283 (2.160)	0.139 (0.061)	−0.078 (0.737)	0.127 (0.078)	−0.353 (0.766)
8	−0.210 (0.166)	−1.476 (2.017)	−0.223 (0.189)	−1.193 (2.029)	0.069 (0.052)	0.231 (0.643)	0.065 (0.060)	0.044 (0.642)

Sum	−2.544	12.377	−2.601	−1.207	1.146	−6.411	1.186	0.177
	(0.546)	(4.759)	(0.909)	(6.939)	(0.243)	(2.330)	(0.391)	(3.146)
$\bar{R}^2$	0.316		0.223	0.291	0.531	0.442	0.494	

Notes:
PIAHES = price and interest adjusted high employment surplus as per cent of GNP
ΔMB = real change in monetary base as per cent of GNP
ΔGNP = per cent change in real GNP
ΔUN = percentage point change in unemployment rate

Table 1.A3 High employment surplus, changes in real monetary base and real non-borrowed reserves, as percentage of GNP, 1960–84

Year	High-employment surplus			Change in real monetary base	Change in real non-borrowed reserves
	Official	Adjusted for price effects	Adjusted for price and interest effects		
1960	2.39	2.83	0.89	−0.09	0.18
1961	1.35	1.99	2.45	0.08	0.03
1962	0.53	1.28	0.87	0.08	−0.02
1963	1.24	1.79	2.25	0.27	0.00
1964	0.17	0.78	0.72	0.25	0.05
1965	0.13	0.98	1.43	0.22	0.00
1966	−0.74	0.33	0.11	0.02	−0.09
1967	−1.89	−0.89	−0.34	0.20	0.15
1968	−1.26	0.06	0.18	0.15	−0.05
1969	0.52	1.94	2.74	−0.04	−0.11
1970	−0.46	0.77	−0.64	0.08	0.08
1971	−1.05	0.11	−0.25	0.13	0.05
1972	−1.02	0.02	0.39	0.44	0.06
1973	−0.72	0.89	1.14	−0.08	−0.10
1974	−0.02	2.15	2.01	−0.13	−0.04
1975	−1.88	−0.38	−0.54	−0.02	−0.06
1976	−1.01	0.22	−0.52	0.15	−0.04
1977	−1.06	0.46	1.30	0.13	−0.06
1978	−0.73	1.26	2.15	0.01	−0.06
1979	−0.08	1.72	1.91	0.00	−0.07
1980	−0.65	1.45	1.97	−0.10	−0.04
1981	−0.11	1.57	1.45	−0.15	−0.01
1982	−1.06	0.02	−2.01	0.16	0.03
1983	−1.66	−0.60	0.68	0.28	0.01
1984	−2.51	−1.36	−1.92	0.42	0.02

APPENDIX 2: SOURCES AND METHODS

1 Net Debt

Net debt is defined as total financial assets less financial liabilities. Federal government net debt includes totals for the government of the

United States, federally sponsored credit agencies, and the monetary authority. Current assets in federal employee and retirement funds are treated as offset by current liabilities. No consideration was made for future retirement obligations or associated future receipts.

The Flow of Funds section of the Federal Reserve Board is the data source for the par value of the net debt. US government securities, agency issues and savings bonds are converted to market values by indices taken directly or derived from Cox (1985). A market-to-par index for mortgage holdings was developed by discounting mortgage flows by the end of period yield on new home mortgages. A precise description of the procedure can be found in Eisner (1986).

2. Price Effects – Nominal-to-Real Conversion

Price effects are calculated as the change in the real market value of existing net debt, excluding gold, measured in average prices of the period. They may be described as:

$$PE_t = [(A-1)DM_{t-1} + (B-1)(DM_t - DM_{t-1})]1/B$$

where

PE = price effects,
P = GNP implicit price deflator in period t,
P^e = end of period price deflator,
DM = end of period market value of net debt excluding gold
$A = p_t^e/P_t$, and
$B = P_t^e/P_{t-1}^e$.

The end of year price deflator is calculated as the arithmetic average of the deflators in the fourth and first quarters. The deflator for personal consumption expenditures, which is available monthly, is used to calculate the end of quarter GNP price deflator. The formulation used is:

$$P_t^e = P_t(P_t^{c,e}/P_t^c)[(P_{t+1}P_t^c)/(P_t P_{t+1}^c)]^{.5}$$

where

P = GNP implicit price deflator
P^c = implicit price deflator for personal consumption expenditures

$P^{c,e}$ = end of quarter implicit price deflator for personal consumption expenditures. This is calculated as the average of the deflators for the last month of the quarter and the first month of the next quarter.

The last term, the ratio of growth in the GNP deflator to the PCE deflator, is intended to control for differences between the two indexes in trend rates of growth.

3 Interest Effects

Interest effects equal the total change in par-to-market revaluations:

$$IE_t = \sum_{i=1}^{5} [(1 - \text{MP}_{i,t})K_{i,t} - (1 - MP_{i,t-1})K_{i,t-1}],$$

where

$K_{i,t}$ = par value of the i-th financial instrument at the end of year t, expressed as a positive quantity if it is a liability and a negative quantity if it is an asset

$MP_{i,t}$ = market-to-par index for the i-th financial instrument at the end of the year t.

The five financial instruments are savings bonds, mortgages, agency issues, Treasury issues held by the Federal Reserve and US government and Treasury issues held by the public. Market-to-par indexes for all instruments except mortgages are taken or derived from Cox (1985). A market-to-par index for mortgages was developed by discounting mortgage flows by the end of period yield on new home mortgages. A precise description of the methodology used can be found in Eisner (1986). Quarterly interest effects are calculated in the same manner except that end of quarter per values and market-to-par indexes are used, and the total change in par-to-market revaluations is multiplied by four to convert from quarterly to annual rates of change.

4 High-Employment Budgets

The high employment surplus is defined for a 4.0 per cent level of unemployment in 1955, gradually increasing to 5.1 per cent in 1975 and remaining constant thereafter, as indicated below.

Year	High employment unemployment rate
1955–8	4.0
1959	4.1
1960–2	4.2
1963–4	4.3
1965	4.4
1966	4.5
1967	4.4
1968	4.5
1969	4.6
1970	4.7
1971	4.8
1972–3	4.9
1974	5.0
1975–84	5.1

Data from 1955 to the third quarter of 1983, are taken from de Leeuw and Holloway (1982) and the *Survey of Current Business* (*SCB*) November 1983. The US Department of Commerce now uses a 6 per cent unemployment rate in estimating the high employment surplus, which is presented periodically in the *SCB*. The series based on a 5.1 per cent rate is extrapolated through 1984 on the basis of the following equation:

$$\text{HES}(5.1)_{t,j} = \text{HES}(6)_{t,j} + \text{HEGNP}_t[\text{HES}(5.1)_{83.3}$$
$$- \text{HES}(6)_{83.3}]/\text{HEGNP}_{83.3}$$

$$t = 83.3 \text{ to } 84.4.$$

where

HES(5.1) = high employment surplus estimated for 5.1 per cent unemployment
HES(6) = high employment surplus estimated for 6 per cent unemployment
HEGNP = nominal high employment GNP for 6 per cent unemployment and the numerical subscripts refer to year and quarter.

5 Monetary Base

The data source for the monetary base, non-borrowed reserves and total reserves is the Federal Reserve Board's 'Reserves of Depository Institutions'. All monetary aggregates are seasonally adjusted and adjusted for changes in reserve requirements. The monetary variables used in the regressions are defined as the change in end of period real stocks divided by real GNP. Thus, for annual data

$$MCH_t = 100\left[\left(\frac{M^e_t}{P^e_t} - \frac{M^e_{t-1}}{P^e_{t-1}}\right)/GNP72_{t-1}\right],$$

where

MCH = change in real money stock (either the monetary base, non-borrowed reserves or total reserves) as a percentage of real GNP
M^e = nominal money stock at the end of period, taken to be the last week of the period
P^e = end of period GNP implicit price deflator
$GNP72$ = gross national product in US 1972 dollars.

The quarterly monetary variable is defined in the same manner except the change in real stocks is multiplied by 400.

6 Gross National Product

Data for GNP and its components are from the *National Income and Product Accounts, 1929–76*, the July 1982 *Survey of Current Business* and the 1985 *Economic Report of the President*. The dependent variable in the annual GNP regressions is the percentage change in real GNP (1972 US dollars). The dependent variable in the quarterly GNP regressions is the quarterly growth in real GNP, expressed as an annual rate. This is defined as

$$GNPCH_t = \left[\left(\frac{GNP72_t}{GNP72_{t-1}}\right)^4 - 1.\right]*100.$$

7 Unemployment

The unemployment variable is the percentage point change in the unemployment rate, defined as

$$UNCH_t = 100\left[\frac{UN_t}{UN_t + CIV_t} - \frac{UN_{t-1}}{UN_{t-1} + CIV_{t-1}}\right],$$

where

$UNCH_t$ = percentage point change in the unemployment rate
UN_t = total unemployment
CIV_t = total civilian employment.

The quarterly change in the unemployment rate is multiplied by four to express as annual rate. Annual data are from the 1985 *Economic Report of the President*. Quarterly data are calculated by averaging the monthly totals from *Business Statistics 1982* and the 1985 *Economic Report of the President*.

Notes

The authors are vastly indebted for the assistance of Sang In Hwang.

1. The monetary base and unborrowed reserves, both essentially policy instruments of the Federal Reserve, seemed more appropriate than broader monetary aggregates subject to direct endogenous fluctuations with movements in the economy. Experiments with M1 and M2, however, indicate that their use as monetary variables would not alter the conclusions of our analysis of annual data.
2. Antecedents of this formulation may be found in Haberler (1941), Pigou (1943) and Patinkin (1948). Clearly, we reject the argument by Barro (1974) that government debt and deficits do not affect aggregate demand, the so-called 'Ricardian equivalence effect.'
3. Sources and methods and some basic data for these and subsequent tables are given in the Appendices.
4. The dual constant terms in effect proxy for differences in inflation corrections in the two periods. They contribute what may be viewed as a greater spurious component to the coefficient of determination (R^2) in the regressions including the official high employment surplus.
5. This is true for the monetary base and reserve variables but M1 and M2, unlike in the annual data, perform somewhat better as regressors with quarterly time series. We conjecture that this is due to their more endogenous character in short-term fluctuations. As output rises, increased transaction demand generates an increased supply of M1, and higher interest rates, at least in recent years, generate an increased demand and supply of M2.

6. The sums of the estimated parameters for components do not equal precisely the estimated parameters for the aggregates, of which these are part, because of our use of the Cochrane–Orcutt estimator, with different autoregressive corrections.
7. There are similar substantial improvements in fit when the two-year lagged interest effect is introduced into Table 1.9 equations for the 'fine components' of GNP. The coefficients of the price adjusted surplus ($PAHES_{t-1}$) remain generally robustly negative while coefficients of the monetary base variable are again reduced substantially.

References

Barro, Robert J. (1974) 'Are Government Bonds Net Wealth?', *Journal of Political Economy*, vol. 82, November/December, pp. 1095–117.
Cox, W. Michael (1985) *The Behaviour of Treasury Securities: Monthly, 1942–84*, Federal Reserve Bank of Dallas, February.
Eisner, Robert (1986) *How Real is the Federal Deficit* (New York: The Free Press).
Eisner, Robert and Pieper, Paul J. (1984) 'A New View of the Federal Debt and Budget Deficits', *The American Economic Review*, vol. 74, March, pp. 11–29.
Eisner, Robert and Pieper, Paul J. (1985) 'Measurement and Effects of Government Debt and Deficits', in *Studies in Banking and Finance*, vol. 2, (Amsterdam, North Holland), pp. 115–44.
Haberler, Gottfried (1941) *Prosperity and Depression*, 3rd ed (Geneva: League of Nations).
Lange, Oscar (1938) 'The Rate of Interest and The Optimal Propensity to Consume', *Economica*, vol. V, February, pp. 12–32. Reprinted in *Readings in Business Cycle Theory*, American Economic Association, (1944).
de Leeuw, Frank and Holloway, Thomas M. (1982) 'The High-Employment Budget: Revised Estimates and Automatic Inflation Effects', *Survey of Current Business*, April, pp. 21–33.
Lucas, Robert E., Jr. (1981) *Studies in Business Cycle Theory* (Cambridge, Mass.: MIT Press).
Lucas, Robert E. and Sargent, Thomas J. (1978) 'After Keynesian Economics', in *After the Phillips Curve: Persistence of High Inflation and High Unemployment*, Federal Reserve Bank of Boston Conference, series no. 19, reprinted in Lucas, Robert E. Jr. and Sargent, Thomas J. (eds), *Rational Expectations and Economic Practice* (Minneapolis: University of Minnesota Press, 1981), pp. 295–319.
Patinkin, Don (1948) 'Price Flexibility and Full Employment', *The American Economic Review*, vol. 38, September, pp. 543–64.
Pigou, Arthur C. (1943) 'The Classical Stationary State', *Economic Journal*, vol. 53, December pp. 343–51.

DISCUSSION

This paper is a continuation of other work done by Eisner and Pieper. The basic premise is that conventional measures of fiscal deficits and debt (both actual and high employment) are fundamentally flawed. Eisner and Pieper correct for changes in the market value of government debt due to changes in interest rates and changes in the real value due to inflation. In earlier work, the authors show that these adjusted deficit figures are strongly related to economic activity. This paper studies the effects of the adjusted figures and selected monetary aggregates on changes in overall economic activity and on components of GNP.

Principal conclusions are that (1) the introduction of monetary aggregates does not mitigate the explanatory power of fiscal variables, (2) adjusted deficits are positively related to consumption and investment; that is, deficits 'crowd in' investment, (3) adjusted deficits are negatively related to net exports, (4) the evidence is strongly supportive of standard Keynesian propositions. Followers of other doctrines 'might all take pause'.

The regressions use annual data for 1960–84, with series on the high employment surplus, non-borrowed reserves, and the monetary base. The basic format is a linear regression of the change in economic activity on once lagged high employment surplus and the change in a monetary figure.

Professor John Taylor agreed that the adjusted deficits are, in principle, better measures than conventionally reported deficits. His main reservation was that the concept of an adjusted deficit may be abused in countries where deficits are financed largely by money creation.

Taylor interpreted the basic regression format as an aggregate demand equation, and noted that the paper could be interpreted as a rejuvenation of the Ando–Modigliani/Friedman–Meiselman debate on the relative strength of monetary and fiscal policy. He finds this 'contest' to be unsatisfactory, for several reasons. First, he objects to the use of narrow monetary figures that do not include deposits. He suggested M1 or M2 as alternatives.[1] Moreover, there is no demonstration that other lags do not matter. A vector autoregression would be more reasonable as a reduced form, and a structural model would be even more interesting.

The 'crowding in' result occurs, Taylor believes, because price adjustment is ignored. Deficits crowd out net exports because a fiscal stimulus raises both output and interest rates. Both effects reduce net exports. Finally, Taylor does not 'take pause' at the results, because the major issues, as he sees them, relate to price adjustment and aggregate supply, whereas the authors have focused on aggregate demand.

Professor Eisner responded that M1 and M2 were thought to be too endogenous to be useful. He agreed that structural modelling is an important next step. He is not a fan of vector autoregressions, but does not think that his models unduly restrict parameter values. To him, the fundamental issue is whether aggregate demand is important. He interprets the results as showing that aggregate demand has proved relevant for economic fluctuations.

Professor Pieper pointed out that the regressions used net debt: total financial assets minus financial liabilities.

Professor Marc Robinson suggested it may be useful to separate the components of net debt in the study. Moreover, the changing constant term (before and after 1967) suggests some structural changes.

Professor Bert Hickman objected to the treatment of prices as exogenous. The division of nominal income changes into price and output changes is critical. *Professor Michael Boskin* suggested it may be difficult to study the effect of fiscal policy on net exports without correcting for the change from fixed and floating exchange rates.

Dr Vito Tanzi noted that the authors adjusted the public debt for inflation, but not the private debt. He had difficulty accepting the idea that individuals are as rational as the model required them to be. Finally, he questioned whether there was double counting in the deficit adjustment since high inflation brings about high interest rates.

Professor Eisner responded that the market value adjustments induced by interest rates and real value adjustments induced by inflation were conceptually different. At a constant inflation and interest rate, the real value erodes. If interest rates then changed, with inflation constant, this would induce a further change in the market value of the debt.

Professor Kleiman suggested that the debt position *vis-à-vis* the rest of the world should be considered. *Professor Joseph Stiglitz* suggested that the unanticipated deficits should matter. *Professor Kenneth Arrow* pointed out that investment has exogenous components, so that it also should be included in the regressions.

Note

1. A note on this point has been added to the revised version of the paper with one or two other minor alterations.

2 On the Relevance or Irrelevance of Public Financial Policy

Joseph E. Stiglitz
PRINCETON UNIVERSITY

1 INTRODUCTION

There is a long-standing belief that while the money supply affects the price level, 'real' variables are determined independently. This proposition is generally referred to as the classical dichotomy. Variants of this belief in the inefficacy of monetary policy, its inability to effect anything real, have regained strength with the emergence of the new classical economists. This belief, however, is far from universal, with some economists maintaining that government deficits, while inflationary, displace private investment, while other, more traditional Keynesian economists claim that government deficits and monetary expansion can have real effects without at the same time inducing inflation.

The object of this paper is to establish a set of propositions concerning the circumstances under which

1. public financial policy is irrelevant: it has neither real nor inflationary effects;
2. public financial policy has price effects, but no real effects (as in the classical dichotomy); and
3. public financial policy has real effects.

Two basic premises underlie the analysis: that the effects of all the financial policies of the government – both its debt and tax policies – need to be taken into account simultaneously; and that these effects can only be analysed within intertemporal models with explicit assumptions about the formation of expectations by individuals and about the impact of the financial policy on the intertemporal distribution of income.

In Section 2, the Basic Irrelevance Theorem is presented, establishing that if the government's debt-cum-tax policy does not involve any intergenerational redistribution, government financial policy not only has no effect on any real variable in the economy, but it also has no effect on any financial variable (including the price level). The increase in the supply of debt (accompanying the decrease in taxes) leads to a precisely identical increase in the demand for government debt. (Accordingly, I shall sometimes refer to this result as Say's Law of Government Deficits.)

This result is in sharp contrast to the implication of deficits in the portfolio balance approach (e.g. of Tobin), though like Tobin (and unlike much of the recent literature in the new classical macroeconomics) we have explicitly assumed that all individuals are risk averse. In the portfolio balance models, the increase in government debt has real effects because individuals will not hold the additional government debt unless the return to debt relative to equities change; but in these models, individuals are myopic – they fail to take into account future tax liabilities,[1] and when they do so, their optimal portfolio turns out to require an increase in government debt just equal to the current increase in supply.

The model of Section 2 involves a single, infinitely-lived generation.[2] In contrast, in the remainder of the paper we focus our attention on models with overlapping generations (and without bequests). In Section 3 we show that there exist some financial policies (in particular, an increase in the nominal interest rate paid on government debt, financed by the issuance of additional debt) which have no real effects, including no effect on the intergenerational distribution of income; at the same time, this policy does have an effect on the rate of inflation. As a result, I sometimes refer to this Second Irrelevance Theorem as establishing the *neutrality of inflation*.[3] (It should be emphasised that not all inflation is of the 'pure' form described in Section 3. There are often other, accompanying changes in policy which have real effects.)

Most changes in public financial policy do, however, have consequences for the intertemporal distribution of income, and in Sections 4 and 5, I show that when the government's financial policy does involve intergenerational redistribution, then (even restricting ourselves to policies with the same expected rate of inflation) it has real effects on the economy, except in certain limiting cases. It is easy to see why alternative financial policies have an important effect on the intertemporal distribution of income. If the government should decide at some date to increase the supply of government bonds more than it had previously planned, it will increase the price level; owners of debt (the 'old' in the typical life-cycle model) become worse off; similarly, if it decides to decrease the debt, the price level falls, making the older generation better off, at the expense of the younger generation. In this sense, there is a close link between debt policy on the one hand, and social security policy on the other (a link which was extensively discussed in Atkinson and Stiglitz (1980) for non-stochastic models). These redistribution effects of debt policy will, in general, have a real effect on the patterns of capital accumulation; only if the demand for capital were independent of wealth would there be no such effect, a possible but implausible case.

That there is a close relationship between debt policy and capital accumulation can be seen from a slightly different perspective. It is well known, from the literature on money, debt and growth, that, in the absence of uncertainty, debt policy has a significant effect on capital accumulation.[4]

There, debt policy (the rate of change in the money or debt supply) has real effects, because individuals substitute government debt for capital in their portfolios. In those models, since there was no uncertainty, the real return on money had to equal the real return on capital,[5] and this asset equilibrium (or portfolio balance) condition determined the rate of change of prices. In the analysis here alternative debt policies change the probability distribution of the returns to financial assets (relative to, say, capital), and thus again there is a substitution between capital and government debt. Only if individuals are risk neutral – and so are indifferent among financial policies which generate the same mean rate of inflation – can such changes in policy have no effect.

It is important to realise, however, that this is just an intuitive argument: it would appear to be equally valid for the overlapping generations (life-cycle savings) model as it would for the model with long-lived individuals; yet for the latter, we establish in Section 2 that changes in *financial* policy of the government (without redistributive effects) have no real effects; the reason for this is in fact that they have no effects on prices. The price distribution is clearly endogenous, and whether it is or is not affected by a particular financial policy is the central question with which we are concerned.

Having established that, in general, public financial policy does matter, the next natural question is, what do optimal public financial policies look like? Section 6 characterises the optimal policy of intertemporal risk-sharing and income distribution, and shows that this policy can be implemented by means of a simple set of public financial policies. In Section 7 we expand the set of financial policies considered so far to include debt instruments of varying maturity. We show that, in our simple model of identical individuals, the additional instruments are redundant. If, however, there are restrictions on the set of admissible taxes and individuals differ, then the additional instruments may not be redundant. Section 8 summarises several directions in which the analysis may be extended.

Before beginning our formal analysis, I should mention two *caveats* concerning what I mean by public financial policy. First, throughout the analysis, I keep the level of real government expenditure at each date fixed. Financial policy is simply concerned with the manner in which those real expenditures are financed (and with the inseparable question of how income is redistributed among individuals). Secondly, I am not concerned here with those issues arising from there being both interest and non-interest bearing short-term financial assets in the economy at the same time. (I have dealt with those issues extensively elsewhere (Stiglitz, 1983)). I shall focus extensively on the demand for financial assets as a store of value.[7]

A standard question that is often raised at this juncture, in our argument that public financial policy is[8] relevant, is what can the government do that the private sector cannot do (or undo)? Within the life-cycle model, there are two answers: first, the government can engage in intergenerational redistribution, which the private sector cannot undo; secondly, by the very structure of the model, there cannot exist a full set of Arrow–Debreu securities in such an economy: there is no way that individuals at date t can trade the risks which they face with individuals at date 0. Government financial policy can provide risk-sharing opportunities which the private market cannot provide.

2 THE FIRST IRRELEVANCE PROPOSITION: SAY'S LAW OF GOVERNMENT DEFICITS

In this section, a simple model is developed in which debt policy has neither real nor financial effects. An economy with infinitely-lived individuals is considered, with wages at time t in state $\theta(t)$ of $w_i(t,\theta)$, lump sum taxes or transfers of[9] $T_i(t,\theta)$, consumption of $C_i(t,\theta)$, labour supply of $L_i(t,\theta)$, holdings of capital[10] of $K_i(t+1,\theta(t))$, and holdings of the single, interest bearing financial asset of $B_i(t,\theta)$. In the absence of uncertainty $\{L_i,C_i,K_i,B_i\}$ are chosen to maximise the individual's lifetime expected utility, which can be expressed simply as a function of the vectors $\{L_i, C_i\}$:

$$U_i = \{U_i, L_i, C_i\},$$

subject to the lifetime budget constraints.[11]

For simplicity, consumption is taken as our numeraire; it is assumed that the price ratio of capital goods to consumption goods is fixed at unity (this, like the assumption of a single consumption good, is a simplifying assumption which can easily be removed). Let $v(t, \theta)$ be the price of bonds in terms of consumption goods; $p(t, \theta) \equiv (1/v(t, \theta))$ is the price of goods in terms of the financial asset. p will be referred to as the price level. Let $\rho(t, \theta)$ be the real rate of return on a financial asset. In general, this consists of two parts, an interest payment and a capital gain (or loss). If $i(t, \theta(t))$ is the interest paid at date $t+1$ on a bond purchased at date t in state $\theta(t)$,[9] then

$$\rho(t, \theta(t), \theta(t+1)) = \frac{i(t, \theta(t))}{v(t, \theta(t))} + \frac{v(t+1, \theta(t+1))}{v(t, \theta(t))} - 1. \quad (2.1)$$

Clearly, in the absence of uncertainty, in the *marginal* transactions value of the financial asset is zero,[13] and η is the real rate of return on capital,[14]

$$\eta(t) = \rho(t) \quad (2.2)$$

the real return on bonds must equal the real return on capital.

The value A_i (in real terms) of the individual's assets at time t in state $\theta(t+1)$ is

$$A_i(t, \theta(t)) = K_i(t, \theta(t-1))(1 + \eta(t, \theta(t))) \quad (2.3)$$
$$+ B_i(t-1, \theta(t-1))[v(t, \theta(t)) + i(t-1, \theta(t-1))]$$
$$+ w_i(t, \theta(t))L_i(t, \theta(t)) - T_i(t, \theta(t))$$

i.e. the capital he had at the end of the last period, plus the return on that capital, plus the value of his bonds, plus the interest payments and wage payments, minus lump-sum taxes. This wealth can be used to purchase goods or assets,[15] i.e.

$$A_i(t, \theta(t)) = C_i(t, \theta(t)) + K_i(t+1, \theta(t)) + v(t, \theta(t))B_i(t, \theta(t)). \quad (2.4)$$

We assume a neoclassical production function of the usual form,

$$F(K, L, \theta) = C + \Delta K + G, \quad (2.5)$$

where G is expenditure on public goods, K is aggregate capital, C is aggregate consumption, L aggregate labour supply:

$$K = \Sigma K_i \quad (2.6a)$$

$$L = \Sigma L_i \quad (2.6b)$$

$$C = \Sigma C_i. \quad (2.6c)$$

Market equilibrium requires, in addition, that if $B^*(t, \theta)$ is the outstanding government debt at time t

$$B^*(t, \theta) = \Sigma B_i(t, \theta). \quad (2.7)$$

The demand for bonds must equal the supply of bonds. Moreover, we require real government revenues (taxes plus revenues from the issue of new bonds) to equal real government expenditures (interest payments plus purchases of public goods).[16]

$$i(t-1, \theta(t-1))B^*(t-1), \theta(t-1)) + G(t, \theta(t))$$
$$= v(t, \theta(t))[B^*(t, \theta(t)) - B^*(t-1, \theta(t-1))] + \Sigma T_i(t, \theta(t)). \quad (2.8)$$

Equation (2.8) is the government budget constraint.

We now establish, in this simple context, the debt neutrality proposition. Assume at t_1 the government increases $B^*(t_1)$ by one bond and (to keep the government budget constraint satisfied) decreases $\Sigma T_i(t_1)$ by $v(t_1)$. Now assume that at some later date, t_2, the government restores the debt to its previous level; again, if government expenditures remain unchanged, this necessitates an increase in taxes by $v(t_2, \theta)$. At interevening dates, to keep (2.8) satisfied,[17]

$$\Sigma \Delta T_i(t, \theta) = i(t, \theta).$$

Finally, let us assume that the taxes are imposed in such a way as to have no redistributive effect, i.e.

$$\frac{\Delta T_i(t,\theta)}{\Sigma \Delta T_j(t,\theta)} = \frac{\Delta T_i(t_1)}{\Sigma \Delta T_j(t_1)} \quad \text{all } t, i, \text{ and } \theta. \tag{2.9}$$

Corresponding to this new tax-debt policy, there exists a new equilibrium in the private sector. Denote by a single caret the original equilibrium values, and by a double caret the new equilibrium values. Then

$$\hat{\hat{C}}_i(t,\theta) = \hat{C}_i(t,\theta)$$

$$\hat{\hat{L}}_i(t,\theta) = \hat{L}_i(t,\theta)$$

$$\hat{\hat{K}}_i(t,\theta) = \hat{K}_i(t,\theta)$$

$$\hat{\hat{v}}_i(t,\theta) = \hat{v}_i(t,\theta) \quad \text{or, equivalently,} \quad \hat{\hat{\rho}}(t,\theta) = \hat{\rho}(t,\theta) \tag{2.10}$$

$$\hat{\hat{B}}_i(t,\theta) = \hat{B}_i(t,\theta) \quad \text{for} \quad t < t_1 \quad \text{and} \quad t > t_2$$

$$\hat{\hat{B}}(t,\theta) = \hat{B}_i(t,\theta) - \frac{\Delta T_i(t_1)}{v(t_1)} \quad \text{for} \quad t_1 \leqslant t \leqslant t_2.$$

To see this, assume that all aggregate variables other than $B^*(t,\theta)$ remain unchanged.[18]
From (2.3) and (2.4)

$$\hat{C}_i(t,\theta(t)) = K_i(t,\theta(t-1))(1 + \eta(t,\theta(t)))$$

$$+ \hat{B}_i(t-1,\theta(t-1))[\hat{v}(t,\theta(t)) + \hat{i}(t-1,\theta(t-1))]$$

$$+ \hat{w}_i(t,\theta(t))\hat{L}_i(t,\theta(t)) - \hat{T}_i(t,\theta(t)) \tag{2.11}$$

$$- \hat{K}_i(t+1,\theta(t)) - \hat{v}(t,\theta(t))\hat{B}_i(t,\theta(t)).$$

It is apparent from (2.9) and (2.10) that the policy described by (2.10) is feasible, and yields exactly the same consumption profile over time as did the original equilibrium. In fact, the feasible set of consumptions for each individual in the new situation is identical to that in the old,[19] and hence each individual will choose exactly the same values of consumption, capital holdings, and labour supply in each state and at each date, and will only alter his bond holdings in the manner indicated.

But, if they do this, the increase in the demand for bonds will precisely equal the increase in the supply of bonds. Hence, if all markets cleared before, they do now. *Debt policy has no effects on either the real economy or on the price level.*

The proof that has been employed is a straightforward extension of the proof I used earlier to establish the irrelevance of corporate financial policy (Stiglitz, 1969, 1974).[20,21] The critical assumption in that analysis was that of no bankruptcy. Here, bankruptcy is not an issue,[22] since the government can always impose taxes to pay back the bonds. What is critical here is the assumption that the bonds will eventually be redeemed, that there are no distributive implications of the tax changes (equation (2.9)), and that there are no binding constraints on individual borrowing.

Note that in obtaining this result we did not specify how the bonds were distributed by the government to the private sector. The changes in taxes that the government must undertake, if it is, at the same time to issue more bonds while keeping real expenditures fixed, in conjunction with the anticipated increases in taxes at some later date associated with the subsequent retirement of the new bonds, generate precisely the requisite demand for bonds. The only direct action of the government is to change taxes and to change the supply of bonds publicly offered. The market takes care of the rest. (Thus, this result is quite different from that associated with 'money rain' or, in this context, 'bond rain'.)

Note too that although it has been assumed that the bonds will be retired at a particular date t_2, the retirement date itself can be a policy variable, a function of θ. So long as individuals anticipate that the current deficits will eventually be retired by the imposition of taxes in the future, debt policy has no real effects and is non-inflationary.[23]

One might be tempted to argue that if nothing real changed, as has been asserted, then individuals will want to allocate their portfolios in the same ratios between bonds and capital (if, say, the individual had constant relative risk aversion) as before; but since the relative supply of bonds has increased, this implies that the market could not be in equilibrium with real variables unchanged. This argument ignores the nature of the tax liability which the individual anticipates will be imposed on him in the future. The individual hedges this particular risk by holding on to bonds (since he knows that the magnitude of the tax liability will be related to the price of the bonds by the basic government budget constraint). There is a simple moral to this story: traditional portfolio theory, based on myopic risk analysis, may be seriously misleading when analysing intertemporal equilibrium.[24]

This section is summarised in *Proposition I* (*the General Irrelevance Theorem, or Say's Law of Government Deficits*). *An increase in the government deficit has neither real nor inflationary effects so long as the associated changes in taxes are distribution neutral and so long as the debt will eventually be reduced to its original level.*

3 THE SECOND IRREVELANCE PROPOSITION: THE NEUTRALITY OF INFLATION

In this section a second irrelevance proposition is proved. Proposition II is established. *A change in the interest rate paid (in any state of nature, at any date) financed by an increase in debt has an effect on the price level, but not on any real variables.* In particular, the real value of debt (Bv) at all subsequent dates and states remains unchanged.

This proposition is true not only in models with infinitely-lived individuals, but also in life-cycle models. An immediate corollary of this proposition, then, is that such a financial policy has no intergenerational distributive implications.

Since in the subsequent sections of this paper attention will be focused on the life-cycle model, the proposition is established in that context. The modifications required to establish the proposition for the economy analysed in the previous section are straightforward.

Individuals are assumed to live for two periods, working in the first, and saving part of their wage income for the second, their retirement. In the subsequent discussion, all variables are functions of t and the state of nature, but for notational simplicity the dependence on the state of nature will be suppressed except where it would give rise to ambiguities. To simplify the analysis further, it is assumed that labour is inelastically supplied, with L normalised at unity. A constant population is assumed, which is also normalised at unity.

For simplicity, individuals' utility functions are assumed to be separable.[25,26]

$$U = u_1(C_1(t)) + \beta u_2(C_2(t)) \tag{2.12}$$

where $C_1(t)$ is the consumption the first period of those born at date t, $C_2(t)$ is the consumption the second period of those born at date t[27] and where β is the discount factor by which future utility is discounted.

The individual maximises his expected utility

$$\max Eu(C_1(t)) + \beta u(C_2(t)) \tag{2.13}$$

subject to this budget constraint, which can be written in parametric form as

$$C_2(t) = K(t+1)(1 + \eta(t+1)) + B(t)(v(t+1) + i(t)) - T_2(t) \tag{2.14}$$

$$K(t) + B(t)v(t) = w(t) - T_1(t) - C_1(t) \tag{2.15}$$

where

$T_1(t) =$ lump-sum taxes on young individuals at date t, and
$T_2(t) =$ lump-sum taxes on old individuals at date $t+1$.

Equation (2.15) simply says that the individual takes the resources available to him at date t (his wages minus lump sum taxes), and either consumes them or saves them; and if he saves them, he saves them either in the form of bonds or in the form of capital (equities). Equation (2.14) says that the individual's consumption the second period of his life consists of his return on capital and bonds, minus any lump sum taxes, plus what he can sell his capital bonds for to the younger generation. (These are just equations (2.3) and (2.4) rewritten for this simple case.)

Individuals form expectations concerning future prices and are assumed to know the probability distribution of the return on equities. They are also assumed to know the probability distribution of the real lump sum transfers that they will receive when they are old. This yields, in a straightforward way, individuals' optimal consumption and investment decisions:[28]

$$C_1(t) = C_{1t}(w(t) + T_1(t), \tilde{\rho}(t), \tilde{\eta}(t+1), \tilde{T}_2(t)) \tag{2.16a}$$

$$K(t+1) = K_{t+1}(w(t) + T_1(t), \tilde{\rho}(t), \tilde{\eta}(t+1), \tilde{T}_2(t)) \tag{2.16b}$$

$$v(t)B(t) = B_{t+1}(w(t) + T_1(t), \tilde{\rho}(t), \tilde{\eta}(t+1), \tilde{T}_2(t)) \tag{2.16c}$$

(Equations (2.16a), (2.16b), and (2.16c) are, of course, not all independent; from the budget constraint, knowing $C_1(t)$ and $K(t)$ it can be inferred what $B(t)$ must be. Equation (2.16c) shows the important property that the real demand for bonds (vB) depends on the real rates of return on the different assets.)

Assume that initially there is an equilibrium, with the values of all (market clearing) variables denoted by a single caret. Assume now that at t_1 the government increases $\hat{i}$ to $\hat{\hat{i}}$ and finances the increased interest payments by issuing more bonds. Then, there exists a new equilibrium to the economy with all real variables unchanged, but with (denoting the new equilibrium values by double carets):

$$\frac{\hat{\hat{v}}(t+1) + \hat{\hat{i}}(t)}{\hat{\hat{v}}(t)} = \frac{\hat{v}(t+1) + \hat{i}(t)}{\hat{v}(t)} = \rho(t) + 1 \quad \text{for all} \quad t \geq t_1.$$

(2.17)

$$\hat{\hat{v}}(t) = \hat{v}(t) \quad \text{for} \quad t < t_1,$$

i.e. the rate of inflation will adjust to keep the real return on debt the same (in every state of nature) and at every date. Moreover,

$$\hat{\hat{v}}(t)\hat{\hat{B}}(t) = \hat{v}(t)\hat{B}(t) \quad \text{for all} \quad t. \tag{2.18}$$

Since the real returns on all assets are unchanged, and taxes are unchanged, demands for capital, 'real' bonds (vB) and consumption are unchanged. If all markets cleared in the initial situation, they still do.

To confirm that the government budget constraint is satisfied, equation (2.8) is rewritten using (2.1):

$$G(t, \theta(t)) = \Sigma T_i(t, \theta(t)) \tag{2.19}$$

$$+ v(t, \theta(t))B^*(t, \theta(t)) - v(t-1, \theta(t-1))B^*(t-1, \theta(t-1))$$

$$+ \rho(t, \theta(t), \theta(t-1))v(t-1, \theta(t-1))B^*(t-1, \theta(t-1)).$$

So long as vB and ρ remain unchanged, the government's budget constraint will be satisfied at each date, in every state. It immediately follows that any *sequence* of such changes (such as a permanent change in the interest rate) also has no effect on the economy.

4 THE FUNDAMENTAL RELEVANCE THEOREM

In the preceding two sections, two general sets of conditions were provided under which government financial policy would not matter;

in Proposition I, it had neither real nor financial (price) effects, while in Proposition II, it had no real effects, but there were effects on the price of bonds (relative to consumption goods). In this section, it is shown that changes in financial structure – other than those described in the preceding two propositions – always have a real effect on the economy.

Not surprisingly, it makes a difference to the analysis whether the change in financial policy is announced (or anticipated) or unannounced (unanticipated). First, the effects of perfectly anticipated policy changes is considered. Assume that the government announces that at some date, t_1, in the future, it will increase its debt, and at the same time changes T_1 and T_2 to keep the budget constraints of the government satisfied. At some subsequent date, $t_2(t_2 > t_2 + 2)$, it will decrease the outstanding debt and increase taxes in a corresponding way. In intervening periods, it increases bonds to pay the additional interest costs. (This is the kind of policy change considered in Section 2, but there, the individuals were infinitely-lived, so there was no intergenerational distributive effect of the change.) Such a change obviously affects the consumption of different individuals. The question is, under what conditions will the change in debt policy have no real aggregate effects, e.g. on the level of capital accumulation?[29]

There is one special case that will be focused on, that will be helpful in developing our intuition concerning the nature of the equilibrium. Assume that there is no risk, or that individuals are risk neutral. Clearly, as was noted earlier, bonds and capital must yield the same return and they will then be perfect substitutes.

The argument that the financial change described above will have real effects is simple. Either the price of bonds on the new path is the same as on the old path, or it is not. Assume the prices are the same. Then, clearly, real returns at each date are unchanged, for this to be an equilibrium, individuals at all dates from t_1 on must be willing to hold the larger (real) bond supply. But an individual born at any date after t_1 and dying at any date before t_2 finds his budget constraint unaffected, and thus has his wage income, lump-sum transfers, and savings unaffected. If real capital accumulation is to be unchanged, therefore, his holdings of real bonds must be unchanged, contradicting our assumption that the real bond supply has increased.

Suppose now that prices change. For simplicity, assume i is unchanged. (The Second Irrelevance Theorem implies that this makes no difference.) Rewriting (2.15):

$$B(t)v(t) = [w(t) - C_1(t) - K(t+1)] - T_1(t).$$

Stiglitz: Public Financial Policy 53

This implies that if the policy change is to have no effects on $K(t)$[30]

$$\hat{v}(t) \equiv \hat{\hat{v}}(t) \quad \text{for} \quad t < t_1 - 1, t > t_2 + 1$$

and

$$\hat{v}(t)\hat{B}(t) \equiv \hat{\hat{v}}(t)\hat{\hat{B}}(t) \quad \text{for} \quad t_1 + 1 \leq t < t_2 - 1.$$

This implies that over the interval $(t_1 - 2, t_1 + 1)$ the average rate of return on bonds must have been less than that on capital, and hence this could not be an equilibrium.

There are two conditions imposed on the equilibrium; one relating to the equality of the returns between financial assets and capital assets, the other that investment must be equal to savings minus holdings of financial assets. It is impossible, within the life-cycle model, to change the supply of bonds in such a way as to have no real effects. Only if the bond supply is increased at t_1 and retired at $t_1 + 1$, and the additional revenues generated at t_1 are used to finance a lump-sum subsidy to the young, while a lump-sum tax is levied on the old at $t_1 + 1$ to retire the debt, is the financial policy neutral. But then, the financial policy affects only the t_1 generation, i.e. it is completely described by Proposition I.

It should be clear that the assumptions of risk neutrality or no risk, though they simplified our exposition, were not critical to the results. Even if the increase in the government debt at t is unanticipated, the policy change will have a real effect unless it is anticipated that there will be no subsequent reduction in the government debt. So long as an unanticipated change gives rise to anticipations of further changes, the previous analysis (*mutatis mutandis*) applies.

This analysis has one interesting corollary. Assume for simplicity that the single financial asset is non-interest bearing ($i = 0$). Assume, moreover, that the government announces that it will increase the bond (money) supply by a given percentage. It is sometimes supposed that equilibrium will be restored simply by an equi-percentage reduction in the price of bonds (so that the real bond supply remains unchanged). But if this change were anticipated, it would have had effects on the demand for bonds in preceding periods. Only if individuals completely ignore the asset return will such a change be neutral. Moreover, if it is believed that the increase in the bond supply is temporary, with it returning to the previous level the next period, with prices at subsequent dates unaffected, individuals will now anticipate a larger return to holding the bond than they obtained previously, and this will induce them to hold more bonds, again contradicting the assumption of no real effects. On the other hand, if it is believed that the increase in the bond supply is permanent, unless in the previous situation the bond supply at all future dates were fixed, then the fixed increase in bond supply represents a variable proportionate increase. Thus, for the real bond supply to be fixed at every date requires the return to the bond to vary from date to date. Finally, even if it is believed that there will be an equi-proportionate increase in the bond supply at every date, so that if the price of bonds fell by a given percentage, the real bond supply at each date would be unchanged, there will be real effects. If it were anticipated, of course, it would have had real effects in previous periods. But even if it is unanticipated, it will have real effects, through the government's budget constraint. The equi-proportionate fall in the price of bonds is equivalent to a lump-sum levy on the present owners of bonds. Only if the extra revenue generated by this 'tax' is spent on the old (the owners of the bonds) will there be no distributive effects of the change (and hence will there be no real effects).

The results of this section on Proposition III can be summarised as follows. *Any anticipated changes in financial action other than those described in Propositions I and II have real and financial effects on the economy.*

Any unanticipated change has no real effects on the economy only if (a) it does not give rise to anticipations of further changes (i.e. it does not change individuals' subjective probability distributions concerning future government actions); *and (b) increases in debt are used to provide lump sum subsidies to current owners of the financial asset* (the aged).

These results should not be surprising: it is well known that in this form of the simple life-cycle model there are simple equivalency relationships between debt policy and social security policy; they induce equivalent intergenerational redistributions of income and will, in general, have real effects (see Atkinson and Stiglitz, 1980). This theme will be returned to in Section 6.

5 SECOND RELEVANCE PROPOSITION

So far, the effect of a change in the financial structure of the government at two points of time has been considered. It was seen how any such changes would have real effects. It is now asked, are there *combinations* of such changes, with offsetting real effects? In particular, we now consider the effect of financial policies, i.e. rules that specify what the government will do under each contingency. In the simple model provided, the government controls four variables; the bond supply, the interest it pays on government debt, and the lump sum transfers to the young and to the old. It can make these variables a function of all observable variables, i.e. letting

$$x(t) = \{K(t), L(t), C_1(t), C_2(t-1), \psi(t), v(t)\}$$

where $\psi(t)$ is the vector $\{\eta(t), w(t)\}$, the *exogenous* variables describing the state of the economy at any time, and

$$x^*(t) = \{x(t), x(t-1), \ldots\}$$

i.e. the entire history of the observable variables up to and including their values at date t, then a government financial policy is a sequence of functions[31] of the form

$$T_1(t) = T_{1t}(x^*(t)) \tag{2.20}$$

$$T_2(t) = T_{2t}(x^*(t))$$

$$B(t) = B_t^s(x^*(t))$$

$$i(t) = i_t(x^*(t))$$

which satisfy the government's budget constraints. Thus, future government *actions* are unknown, simply because the events on which they will be based are unknown; but the policies are assumed to be known. As soon as the events on which they depend become known, the government action is well specified.

A *rational expectations equilibrium* can now be easily defined (for each set of feasible policy functions). For each public financial policy (set of functions (2.20)), and for each set of expectations about the price distribution

$$v^e(t) = v^e(x^*(t-1), \eta(t), w(t))$$

(prices next period are a function of the entire history of observables up to and including their values at $t-1$ and the realisation of the exogenous variables η and w), there will be a demand for bonds $B_t^d(x^*(t))$. Equilibrium requires that this demand for bonds equal the supply

$$B_t^d(x^*(t)) = B_t^s(x^*(t)) \quad \text{for all} \quad x^*(t). \tag{2.21}$$

Rational expectations requires an addition that given the assumed known probability distributions of η and w, and the policy functions (2.20), expectations are realised

$$v^e(x^*(t)-1), \eta(t), w(t)) \equiv v(x^*(t-1), \eta(t), w(t)). \tag{2.22}$$

A simple policy, for instance, would be to increase the bond supply by x per cent if the return to capital exceeds its average value, decrease it by x per cent if the return to capital is less than its average value. This kind of rule makes little sense. In Stiglitz, 1983, the consequences of several simple but more reasonable rules are considered.[32] For now, we wish to show that, even if the government restricts itself to policies which are functions of current exogenous variables, and confines itself to policies which, in any state, have the same expected rate of inflation, i.e. $E\hat{\rho} = E\hat{\rho}$, changes in financial policy have real effects.

The government, for instance, announces that if, at t, $w(t) = w_1$, it will increase the bond supply more than it had planned to do under the original financial policy while if $w(t) = w_2$, it will increase the bond supply less. The two changes are chosen so that, in the rational expectations equilibrium, the *expected* rate of change in the price level is unchanged.

Consider first the case where individuals are risk neutral. By our earlier analysis we can, without loss of generality, restrict ourselves to economies in which government bonds pay no interest, so in equilibrium[33]

$$Ev(t+1) = v(t)(1+\bar{\eta}). \tag{2.23}$$

Two cases are investigated: that where the changes in bonds are accompanied by changes in taxes on the young, and that in which they are accompanied by changes in taxes on the old. In the latter case, since $T_1(t_1)$ is unchanged, if $K(t)$ were unchanged for all t, vB would be unchanged for all t. This follows from substituting the government's budget constraint into the individual's budget constraint, to obtain

$$v(t)B(t) + T_1(t) = w(t) - C_1(t) - K(t+1) \tag{2.24}$$

If $T_1(t)$ is unchanged, individuals' opportunity sets are unchanged,[34] and hence $C_1(t)$ is unchanged. But this implies that $T_2(t_1 - 1)$ must be increased. Rewriting the government's budget constraint for this case, from (2.8) can be obtained

$$G(t, \theta(t)) = v(t, \theta(t))B(t, \theta(t)) - \frac{v(t, \theta(t))}{v(t-1, \theta(t-1))} x \quad (2.25)$$

$$v(t-1, \theta(t-1))B(t-1, \theta(t-1)) + T_2(t-1, \theta(t))$$

Hence, if $B(t_1, \hat{\theta}(t_1))$ is changed for some $\hat{\theta}(t_1)$, $v(t_1, \hat{\theta}(t_1))$ must have changed, and hence $T_2(t_1 - 1, \hat{\theta}(t_1))$ must have changed. If, however, the expected value of $v(t_1)$ is unchanged (i.e. (2.23) is satisfied), the expected value of $T_2(t_1 - 1)$ is unchanged, and if individuals' behaviour only depends on their expected taxes next period, this change has no effect on capital accumulation at dates prior to t_1. Under these circumstances, then, this change in financial policy has no aggregate real effects. (By the same token, a sequence of such changes, e.g. changes in the financial rules at every date, or at the same date in more states, will have no real effects.)

But this is, essentially, the only circumstance in which a change in financial policy has no real effects. Consider, by contrast, what happens if the change in the debt is accompanied by a change in T_1. From the government's budget constraint, it is clear that an increase in the return on government bonds in some state O accompanied by a tax on the young is equivalent to a transfer of resources in that state from the young to the old. But the marginal propensity to consume of the old is unity; the marginal propensity to consume of the young is, in general, less than unity; and hence the total demand for consumption goods increases. But then it is impossible for the level of capital accumulation in that state to remain unchanged.

Moreover, even if the government accompanies changes in the returns to government bonds by changes in the taxes of the old, these changes will not be neutral if individuals are not risk neutral. For our earlier analysis showed that if $v(t_1)B(t_1)$ remains unchanged, in all states, C_2 will remain unchanged. But then individuals at t_2 will not be in portfolio equilibrium, except if the marginal utility of consumption in the two states for which ρ is altered are the same (see equations (2.26) and (2.27) in note 35).[35] This establishes that the previous argument for the neutrality of financial policy cannot be extended to the case of risk averse individuals.[36]

The results of this section are summarised in Proposition IV. *Mean preserving changes in financial policy have no real effects if and only if the individual is risk neutral and changes in the level of debt are offset by changes in lump-sum taxes/subsidies for the aged.*

6 IMPLEMENTABILITY OF OPTIMAL INTERTEMPORAL RISK REDISTRIBUTION SCHEMES THROUGH FINANCIAL POLICIES WITH CONSTANT PRICE LEVELS

We have stressed in the preceding two sections that alternative government financial policies have real effects, largely because they generate changes in the intertemporal distribution of risk and wealth. Because individuals of different generations cannot get together to trade risks, the only way such risks can be exchanged is through governmental action. Any financial policy has implications for the intergenerational distribution of risk bearing, and changes in the financial policy thus benefit some generations at the expense of others. The government needs to take this into account when designing its financial policies.

In this section, we characterise the optimal intergenerational distribution of risk bearing and show that this policy can be implemented by means of a financial policy with constant prices, provided that the government's ability to levy lump-sum taxes on the young and the old is sufficiently flexible.

The problem of the optimal intertemporal allocation of resources can be easily formulated; for simplicity, an additive social welfare function is assumed of the standard form

$$E\sum_{t}\frac{u^{t}}{(1+\delta)^{t}} \qquad (2.28)$$

where u^t denotes the utility of the tth generation, given by

$$u^t = u_1(C_1(t)) + \beta u_2(C_2(t))$$

where $1/1 + \delta$ is the social rate of discount. Equation (2.28) will be maximised subject to the resource constraints of the economy. For simplicity, it is assumed that labour is fixed ($L = 1$) and that capital (like rabbits) can be eaten, so that the resources available at date t are given by:[37]

$$S(t) = w(t) + K(t)(1 + \eta(t)) \tag{2.29}$$

while

$$K(t + 1) = S(t) - C_1(t) - C_2(t - 1). \tag{2.30}$$

In addition, there is a natural non-negativity constraint on $K(t)$:

$$K(t) \geq 0. \tag{2.31}$$

Formulated in this way, the problem has been converted into a standard optimal savings problem with random wages and returns on capital, with the standard non-negativity constraints on capital. This can be solved using dynamic programming techniques.[38] Our interest here, however, is not in characterising the solution so much as in providing an analysis of the implementation of the optimal intertemporal redistribution of income through financial and tax policy. Hence, it is simply asserted that the solution yields consumption and capital accumulation functions of the form[39]

$$C_1(t) = C_1^*(S(t)) \tag{2.32}$$

$$C_2(t - 1) = C_{2t-1}^*(S(t)) \tag{2.33}$$

and

$$K(t + 1) = K_{t+1}^*(S(t)). \tag{2.34}$$

The assumptions that wages and the return on capital, at each date, are identically distributed independent random variables are essential in obtaining this simplification. If, for instance, wages were described by a random walk, then w itself would be a state variable.

How this optimal solution can be implemented in a market economy with a single financial instrument is now considered. To implement any policy, it must control, at each date, and each state, three variables; C_1, C_2, and K. The government has four instruments, T_1, T_2, i and B. This suggests a redundancy of instruments, and indeed, Proposition II showed that there was such a redundancy. We could change i and change the bond supply in such a way as to keep the government's budget balanced, and have no real effects; such a policy would, however, have an effect on the price level (v).

The four instruments are not independent, since they are linked together by the government's budget constraint. There are thus three independent instruments. On the other hand, the three variables C_1, C_2, and K are also not independent; they are linked together by the individual's budget constraint, or, equivalently, by the national income constraint:

$$C_1(t) + C_2(t-1) + K(t+1) = w(t) + (1 + \eta(t))K(t). \tag{2.35}$$

If these constraints are taken into account, there are three independent variables controlling two independent equations. It would seem apparent that we could easily implement any desired intertemporal allocation of risk bearing, including the optimal one we have just derived. In fact, a slightly stronger result is established: this policy can be implemented through a financial policy involving constant prices, i.e.

$$v_t = v_{t+1} = vt_{t+\tau} = 1 \quad \text{(without loss of generality)}. \tag{2.36}$$

To see this, and to help develop our intuition, we begin with the case where there is no risk. Then, (2.36) together with the equilibrium requirement of equality of returns, implies that we set

$$i(t) = \eta(t) \quad \text{all } t. \tag{2.37}$$

In this situation, individuals are indifferent to holding bonds or capital in their portfolio.

To induce any generation to consume the correct amount, T_1 is increased or decreased. So long as the marginal propensity to consume is not zero, this will lead to a change in C_1. Next, B is increased or decreased so that the desired amount of capital accumulation occurs. (Since the two are perfect substitutes, an increase in B induces a dollar-for-dollar decrease in K.) If C_1 and K are set at their correct levels, C_2 must be at its desired level (by (2.35)). Similarly, any deficit is financed by lump sum taxes on the aged and any surplus is distributed to the aged.

Formally, the optimal policy is found by solving the set of equations.[40]

$$C_1^*(S(t)) = C_{1t}(w(t) + T_1(t), \eta, T_2(t+1)) \tag{2.38a}$$

$$K^*(S(t)) = w(t) - C_1^*(S(t)) - B(t) - T_1(t) \tag{2.38b}$$

$$T_1(t) + T_2(t) + B(t) - B(t-1) = G + i(t-1)B(t-1). \tag{2.38c}$$

Essentially the same argument holds if η is random; now, however, individuals are not indifferent as to the form in which they hold assets. Changing T_1 alters the level of consumption and savings the first period. Now, however, the fraction of this savings that they wish to hold in the form of capital is not indeterminate. To induce individuals to hold more capital, the return on capital has to be made more attractive relative to money. This can be done by lowering i. By this means it can be ensured that C_1 and K_t are 'correct' for each S. But this (through the national income identities) assures that $C_2(t-1)$ is also correct.

Proposition V has thus been established. *The optimal intertemporal distribution of income can be implemented by means of a financial policy with a constant price level, provided there is a sufficient flexibility in the imposition of lump-sum taxes/subsidies on the young and the old.*

7 THE ROLE OF ADDITIONAL FINANCIAL INSTRUMENTS

Since it has been shown that the optimal intertemporal distribution of income can be obtained with a single financial asset, is there any role to be played by the introduction of additional financial assets, e.g. government bonds of differing maturities? It is now shown that if there is complete flexibility in the imposition of lump-sum taxes and subsidies, such an additional financial asset has no effect, but if there are restrictions, say, on the variability of lump-sum payments to the aged, then an additional financial instrument can be used to achieve the optimal intertemporal distribution of income.

For simplicity, let the second financial asset be a long-term bond, a perpetuity, paying $1 every period. The price, q, of these bonds is, however, random, so that the net yield r_t is a random variable. Government policy again entails a *rule* for the increase or decrease in the supply of these financial instruments, as a function of the state (and possibly history) of the economy.

It is obvious that, in the case where η is not random, and v_t is constant, such a financial instrument is completely redundant. For since i is constant, the price, q, of this security is fixed, and it is no different from a short-term bond.

In the case where η is random, however, such a security is different from a short-term bond. To show that it is still redundant, the government's budget constraint needs to be rewritten:

$$T_1 + T_2 + q(t)(D(t) - D(t-1)) + v(t)(B(t) - B(t-1))$$
$$= G + i(t-1)B(t-1) + D(t-1) \tag{2.39}$$

where $D(t)$ is the number of long-term bonds outstanding at date t. Thus, assume that the government were to fix T_2 at zero (or at any other arbitrary fixed level). Assume the government set T_1 at its previous level, and set

$$\hat{v}\hat{\hat{B}} + \hat{\hat{q}}\hat{\hat{D}} = \hat{v}\hat{B} \qquad \text{for all dates and states,} \tag{2.40}$$

i.e. made the total value of outstanding government securities the same. It can easily be verified that, taking the government budget constraint into account, the value of second period consumption is

$$K(t+1)(1+\eta(t+1)) + T_1 - G + q(t+1)D(t+1)$$
$$+ v(t+1)B(t+1), \tag{2.41}$$

which is identical to what it would have been had the government had a single financial asset. (Compare (2.41) and (2.25), using (2.40).)

Thus, the individual's first-order condition for savings (first period consumption) is still satisfied (equation (2.24)) at the original value of C_1; and since savings are unchanged, and the value of financial assets is unchanged, capital accumulation is unchanged. By the national income identity (2.35), C_2 must be unchanged.[41,42]

The analysis so far has assumed that there is a single type of individual. Is the second financial instrument redundant if individuals differ?

First best optimality would necessitate the government imposing a different set of lump-sum taxes/subsidies on each type of individual. It is assumed that that is not feasible. The addition of a second risky asset may have two effects: it may affect the ability of the economy to share risks efficiently within a generation; and it may affect the intra- and intergenerational distribution of income. In order to abstract from the first effect, let it be assumed that there is initially a complete set of intragenerational Arrow–Debreu securities markets, so that the marginal rate of substitution between consumption in two different states is the same for all individuals alive contemporaneously. Still, the addition of a second financial asset will, in general, have real effects. If it is assumed not to be the case, then it must be that the Arrow–Debreu prices are unaffected by the changes in financial policy;

but the change in financial policy does result in a change in T_2, and hence in the value of the individual's endowments. But this change in the value of endowment, at fixed Arrow–Debreu prices, will have real effects, both on C_1 and C_2. In general, then, adding an additional financial asset will have real effects.

The basic intuition behind this result is that policies which affect aggregate consumption, say, in the second period, in the same way, may have different effects on different individuals. Paying an effectively higher return on long-term bonds, but lowering social security payments, may, on average, have no effect on the consumption of the aged. But the old who are less risk averse and buy risky, long-term bonds are better off under such a policy, and those who do not speculate, and rely on their social security payments, are relatively worse off. But these intragenerational distributional changes have, in turn, real effects on the economy.

Note that for any particular specification of the financial policy of the government, the term structure of interest rates, the relationship between the expected return on the long-term bond and the return on the short-term bond can be calculated; though the normal presumption is that, since the long-term bonds are riskier, they have to yield an expected return which exceeds that on the short-term bond. Since the equilibrium, the yield on the long-term bonds is related to $S(t+1)$, as is $T_2(t)$, it is conceivable that just the opposite result obtains.

It is easy for the government to create additional financial instruments. Assume that the government announces a long-term bond, which when the state is $S(t)$, will yield (in the following period) a return $i(S)$; such a perpetuity will (with the appropriate financial policy) yield a variable return, which will not, in general, be a linear function of the return on short-term bonds and long-term perpetuitites with fixed payments. So long as such instruments represent real additions to the set of assets, and so long as there are fewer such instruments than there are types of individuals in the economy, then these additional instruments will not be redundant.

The basic insight behind the results of this section can be put fairly simply. When all individuals are identical, to 'control' the economy, all one needs to do is to control $C_1(t)$ and $K(t+1)$. This requires two instruments, and the availability of age specific lump-sum payments and short-term bonds provides all the instruments needed. But when individuals are not identical, and the age specific lump-sum payments cannot be varied from individual to individual, there are more 'objects' which need to be controlled than there are instruments; i.e. we would like to control $C_1^j(t)$, $C_2^j(t)$, and $K(t)$. Increasing the set of financial instruments, then, does in general increase the real opportunity set of the economy.

The results of this section are summarised in *Proposition VI. With a single type of individual, and full flexibility in the imposition of lump-sum taxes and subsidies, additional financial instruments (such as long-term bonds) are redundant. When there are more types of individuals, or when there are restrictions on the flexibility of lump-sum taxes and subsidies, additional financial instruments are not redundant. The maturity structure of the government debt then has real effects.*

8 EXTENSIONS AND CONCLUDING REMARKS

The object of this paper has been to develop a framework within which alternative financial policies of the government may be analysed. It is our contention that any meaningful analysis of public financial policy requires the integration of all the important aspects of debt, tax and social security policy within a single framework, and in particular, requires an intertemporal, stochastic model. There are some circumstances in which it has been shown that changes in public financial policy (such as changes in corporate financial policy) have neither real nor financial effects (i.e. all prices remain unchanged). An increase in the supply of bonds gives rise to an exactly equal increase in the demand for bonds. There are other circumstances in which changes in public financial policy have effects on prices, but no real effects. Thus public financial policy affects the rate of inflation, but the rate of inflation has no real consequences. In general, however, public financial policy has real consequences for the intertemporal distribution of risk bearing, and thus for the intertemporal distribution of welfare. Even restricting the government to financial policies with the same expected rate of inflation, and the same expected return to financial assets, changes in financial policy have important real effects on the economy. Indeed, it was shown how an appropriately designed public financial policy could be used to implement the first best intertemporal allocation of resources. To do this required, however, complete flexibility in the imposition of lump-sum taxes and subsidies on the young and the old. When, for instance, social security payments were not allowed to vary from year to year and from state to state, the first best intertemporal allocation of resources could only be implemented through public financial policy if there was an additional financial instrument.

It should be noticed that in the model we have constructed all individuals have fully rational expectations concerning the nature of future government policies. Yet, in general, in spite of the rational expectations, public financial policy does have real effects. Those models which have concluded that with rational expectations government financial policy is irrelevant reach their conclusions not because of their assumptions concerning how expectations are formed, but rather from the specific structural assumptions of their models. One such assumption which has been extensively criticised is their assumption of complete price flexibility (see Taylor, 1980; Neary and Stiglitz, forthcoming); results concerning full employment (and hence the inefficacy of monetary policy) are perhaps not surprising in a world with perfect price flexibility, and could be established under a variety of assumptions concerning how expectations are formulated. Here, it has been established that even with perfect price flexibility, changes in public financial policy will in general have real effects.

8.1 Interpretation of Results

One of the uses to which this model can be put is to help clarify our understanding of the mechanisms by which public financial policy affects the economy. A consideration of the situations in which each of the assumptions underlying the *irrelevance* result no long holds provides a taxonomy of the possible ways in which public financial policies may have real effects. As has been emphasised, it then becomes easy to construct models in which public financial policy is in fact relevant, in which it has real effects. The question then becomes one of the magnitude of the effects.

For instance, changes in the intergenerational distribution of income, or intergenerational risk sharing, will have real effects. But are these the effects which we believe account for the potency of public financial policy?[43] Elsewhere, (Stiglitz, 1981, 1983) I have argued that the effects that public financial policy may have though its effects on the supply of the medium of exchange (on the costs of transactions) are too slight to be of quantitative importance. Changes in the intertemporal distribution of the distortions associated with levying non-lump-sum taxes again have real effects, but are unlikely to provide a convincing explanation of why it is that public financial policy has real effects.

There are, I think, two critical assumptions. The first is that concerning rational, or perhaps I should say, consistent expectations.[44] It is not obvious to me that when individuals' taxes are reduced and debt is increased, they fully integrate those future financial obligations into their calculations. I suspect that they do not fully see through the *public veil*. The evidence, in other contexts, that individuals do not see through the public veil seems to me to be sufficiently compelling that I see no reason why we should expect them to do so here. More generally, evidence concerning how individuals form their expectations, and how they justify *ex post* the actions which they have undertaken should at least make us sceptical about models requiring the sophisticated kind of expectations formation required by our irrelevance theorem. Many economists will find discomforting the fact that public financial policy may depend for its effect on a kind of irrationality. But our objective is to describe how individuals behave, and the consequences of that behaviour, however unsavoury that behaviour is, or inconsistent with our preconceptions concerning rational behaviour. In another world, where individuals have rational expectations, public financial policy may indeed be of limited potency.

The second critical assumption is the perfect capital market assumption. Elsewhere, we have argued that imperfect information results in credit rationing (Stiglitz and Weiss, 1981, 1983, 1986, 1987) and equity rationing (Stiglitz, 1983; Greenwald, Stiglitz and Weiss, 1984). Individuals and firms will not be able and or willing to offset fully the change in public financial policy.[45] Those who are against their credit constraint will respond to a reduction in their taxes by an increase in their expenditures. Firms which find that their 'equity' has been increased as a result of a tax reduction may be willing to undertake more investment (Greenwald and Stiglitz, 1987a, 1987b, 1988). Banks that find their deposits reduced as a result of an open market operation and have no excess reserves will have to restrict their loans. But because of information asymmetries, and the inability to transfer effectively, or in any case, costlessly, information, other intermediaries do not increase their lending in an offsetting way. Banks that find that their net worth has decreased (as a result of an increase in taxes, or an unexpected increase in the costs of obtaining funds) may decrease the amounts that they are willing to lend. Even in the absence of credit and equity rationing, so long as there is a probability of firm or individual bankruptcy, public financial policy will have real effects. To put the matter another way, a reduction in taxes today, followed by an increase in taxes next period, can be viewed as a loan from the government; but the conditions under which the government can collect the future payment are distinctly different from those in which a private lender could collect, and hence the government 'loan' and private loans are far from perfect substitutes.

I believe that it is largely through the mechanisms I have described in the last few paragraphs that public financial policy exercises what influence it does. Correspondingly, I would argue that a closer examination of the functioning of the capital market is the direction of research which is likely to yield the highest pay-offs.

8.2 Other Directions of Future Research

The analysis of this paper raises several further questions of interest. First, it has been assumed throughout that all taxes are lump sum. In practice, most taxes are distortionary. With lump-sum taxes, the intertemporal pattern of the imposition of taxes (on a single individual) makes no difference. When taxes are distortionary, it does. In the absence of uncertainty, for instance, with suitable symmetry and separability assumptions, it would be optimal to levy wage taxes at a constant rate throughout the individual's lifetime. This provides, then, a simple theory of the optimal size of the government debt: government debt simply serves as a 'buffer stock' between the optimal pattern of government expenditure and the optimal pattern of tax revenues. The analysis of optimal taxation in the presence of uncertainty is a far more complicated question, which we hope to pursue elsewhere.

Second, it is of interest to know the consequences of alternative simple financial rules. If the government must choose, say, between a rule which maintains prices fixed, and a rule which keeps the real value of the debt fixed, which is preferable?

Third, although we have provided a general result characterising the optimal pattern of the intertemporal distribution of resources under uncertainty, we have not provided many insights into its detailed structure; this will be required if we are to analyse the structure of optimal public financial policies.

Fourth, although we have discussed the role of additional financial instruments, there are two such securities that merit more detailed attention. We have ignored throughout the role of government debt in facilitating transactions; in particular, we have ignored the distinction between non-interest bearing short-term debt and interest bearing short-term debt. If we introduce money, and assume that it has transactions advantages over interest bearing short-term debt, how are our results affected? The results reported in Stiglitz (1982) suggest that, if anything, introducing debt strengthens the presumption that public financial policy does matter.

A second financial instrument which has received extensive attention in recent years is a government bond with a guaranteed real rate of return. Would the introduction of these indexed bonds make a difference? The analysis of this chapter (confirmed by the results in Stiglitz, 1982) suggests that if individuals are essentially identical, then this additional financial instrument is redundant; but that if they differ enough, then providing this extra instrument does expand the real opportunity set of the economy.

Finally, and perhaps most importantly, the analysis of this chapter has been conducted within a neoclassical framework, in which there is full employment every period. One of the central issues with which public financial policy has traditionally been concerned is the extent to which it can affect the level of employment and output. To address these questions requires the formulation of a macroeconomic model with unemployment. It is likely that at least some of the mechanisms by which public financial policy affects the economy in such circumstances are quite different from those portrayed here.

Notes

This paper represents a revision of results originally presented at a Conference on Indexation and Economic Stability in the World Economy, Fundaçao Getulio Vargas, Rio de Janeiro, Brazil, 16–17 December 1981, and at a conference at Rice University, April 1982. I have benefited greatly from conversations with John Taylor, Alan Blinder, P. Kyle, D. Bradford, R. Dornbusch, S. Fisher, Neil Wallace, Frank Hahn, J. M. Grandmont, and Dilip Abreu. Research support from the National Science Foundation is gratefully acknowledged. Any opinions expressed are those of the author.

1. Thus, the result can be viewed as an extension of the Ricardo–Barro approach to include uncertainty; obviously, in the absence of uncertainty, the form in which individuals hold their assets is not of much interest; all assets are perfect substitutes.
2. Or equivalently, families, all of whom have and care about their descendant(s), with descendants, all of whom have and care about their descendants, etc. (see Barro, 1974).
3. This result thus represents an extension and generalisation of an earlier result reported in Stiglitz (1981).
4. Though earlier studies of Tobin (1965) or Shell, Sidrauski and Stiglitz (1969) are open to the criticism that the individuals are not explicitly maximising their intertemporal utility, the studies of Cass and Yaari (1967) and Diamond (1965) made it clear that similar results also obtained in the life-cycle models (see also Atkinson and Stiglitz, 1980).

5. This is a slight simplification. While Tobin (1965), Johnson (1966) and Sidrauski (1967), for instance, did not explicitly introduce uncertainty into their analysis, they treated the two assets as imperfect substitutes, without formally explaining why this was so.
6. Recent developments in financial markets make it clear that the costs involved in providing transactions services associated with interest bearing bonds is not significant.
7. I shall occasionally refer to government policies with respect to the supply of short-term bonds (or more general financial policies) as 'monetary' policies.
8. With the minor exceptions previously noted.
9. For notational simplicity, θ for $\theta(t)$ will be written when there is no ambiguity.
10. $K_i(t+1, \theta(t))$ is the amount of capital purchased at time t, but used at date $t+1$.
11. It should be clear that nothing in this formulation requires us to restrict our analysis to preference orderings satisfying the expected utility axioms.
12. It makes no difference for the analysis whether the individual knows the interest which will be paid, i.e. $i = i(t, \theta(t))$ or does not, i.e. $i = i(t, \theta(t+1))$. It will be assumed, for simplicity, he does. i is a *real* interest payment, i.e. i is measured in terms of consumption goods. This assumption too is made for notational simplicity. It is more realistic if we let i be dominated in financial units, so

$$\rho(t, \theta(t), \theta(t+1)) = (1 + i(t, \theta(t))\frac{v(t+1, \theta(t+1))}{v(t, \theta(t))} - 1.$$

The requisite modifications to the analysis are straightforward. Even if i is measured in consumption goods, and is specified at t, ρ is uncertain because $v(t+1, \theta(t+1))$ is uncertain. In Stiglitz (1983) the analysis is extended to indexed bonds.
13. As is assumed throughout this paper; but see Stiglitz (1983).
14. η will, in general, depend on the capital: labour ratio. The individual, however, simply takes η as given, and hence in our notation, η is simply written as a function of t (and θ). Again, when there is no ambiguity; the dependence of variables is suppressed (such as ρ and η) on θ.
15. In a finite period model, there is a natural boundary

$$K_T = B_T = 0.$$

In the infinite period problem, a corresponding transversality condition needs to be imposed.
16. If all the other equilibrium conditions are satisfied, (2.8) must be satisfied.
17. Alternatively, the additional interest payments could be financed by additional bond issues; if these new bond issues are themselves retired at t_2, the analysis remains unchanged.
18. In the new situation, there may, of course, be more than one equilibrium, just as in the old situation there may be more than one equilibrium. The argument is only that corresponding to any equilibrium in the original

situation there exists an equilibrium in the new situation which is related to the original equilibrium by equation (2.10).
19. That is, any consumption-labour sequence which is feasible in the new situation is feasible in the original situation, and conversely. This ignores any non-negativity constraints (see below and Stiglitz, 1982).
20. See also Atkinson and Stiglitz (1980).
21. For another application of this kind of analysis, see Wallace (1981). His model differs in a number of important ways from that presented here. In particular, he employs a life-cycle model, and in his model there is a complete set of Arrow–Debreu securities. He focuses his attention on changes in financial policy which are accompanied by changes in government's holding of capital, and thus are not pure financial changes (as we have defined that term).
22. The reason that bankruptcy made a difference in the earlier analysis was that it resulted in the creation of a new security; in the absence of a complete set of Arrow–Debreu securities, this, of course, may have real effects. Similarly, public financial policy – the issuance of a new kind of bond – may result in the creation of a new security, in the absence of a complete set of Arrow–Debreu securities. But the simple kinds of financial policy considered in this section cannot have the effect (see, however, Section 7 below and Stiglitz, 1982).

There is a sense in which bankruptcy is relevant here too: as is noted below, the proof of the irrelevance proposition requires that as the individual borrows more, the interest rate he has to pay is unchanged. This will be the case only if there is no probability that the borrower defaults.
23. Some difficult problems arise if there is some probability that the government will never retire the bonds. Then the increase in the government debt is inflationary. To see this, assume that prices remain unchanged and that individuals' consumption, labour supply and capital holdings remained unchanged at each date and in each state. Then their bond holdings must have increased, and if the transversality condition held before, it no longer holds. Assume now that v falls in proportion to the increase in B, so that vB remains unchanged, and that the government reduces i proportionately at each date. Then, it is easy to show that nothing real has changed, and hence if we were initially in equilibrium, we will still be in equilibrium, with p increasing proportionately at each date and state. Now, if we move from this equilibrium to a new equilibrium where i remains at its original value, but the corresponding differences in government expenditure are reflected in changes in new issue of government bonds, then we again obtain an equilibrium in which all real variables remain unchanged, but the price level has changed (see Section 3).
24. Another area in which myopic portfolio analysis has recently been shown to be very misleading is in the analysis of the effect of capital gains taxation. A reduction in the tax rate on long-term capital gains might increase government revenue, but at the same time lead to an increase in consumption and a reduction of savings (since individuals' future tax liabilities have been reduced) (see Stiglitz, 1981).

25. This plays no role in this section, but has some interesting implications for the analysis of Section 6.
26. As in the standard life-cycle model, we assume away altruism: individuals do not care either for their antecedents or their descendants. If *all* individuals care about their children, and their children care about their children, then clearly, we obtain a derived utility function where consumption at all future dates enters into the individual's welfare function (see Barro, 1976). Though the fact that some individuals do intentionally leave bequests suggests that the assumption of no altruism is extreme, the assumption that everyone leaves a bequest, and adjusts fully for a change in government debt by a change in his bequest, is also extreme. The qualitative propositions presented in this section require only that there exist some individuals who leave no bequests, either because of a complete lack of altruism, or because they have no children. Since, in fact, a significant fraction of the population has no children, and with a non-zero probability, any individual will have only a finite number of descendants, we believe that the qualitative results presented here are of some relevance.
27. Thus, $C_2(t)$ occurs at date $t + 1$.
28. $C_2(t)$ is determined as a residual, from equation (2.14).
29. Or, if labour were elastically supplied, on the level of employment.
30. That is, for $t < t_1 - 1$ and $t > t_2 + 1$, $\hat{B} = \hat{\hat{B}}$ and $\hat{T}_1 = \hat{\hat{T}}_1$.
31. In this formulation, actions at date t depend on observables at t. Other formulations, with lags in observations, will work as well.
32. A specification of a financial policy requires specifying not only the circumstances under which, for instance, B is increased or decreased, but who is taxed or subsidised. We consider three alternative rules for deficits (keeping the bond supply constant, keeping prices constant, keeping the real bond supply, vB, constant) under the assumption that any resulting deficits (or surpluses) are financed by (distributed as) lump-sum taxes (subsidies) on, alternatively, the young or the old.
33. If we restrict ourselves to economies in which bonds pay an interest of $E\eta(t)$, so equilibrium requires

$$Ev(t + 1) = v(t),$$

i.e. the price level is a martingale.
34. It was required in addition that $T_2(t)$ be unchanged for $t \geqslant t_1$. But if vB and ρ at all subsequent dates (in all states) are unchanged, then the government's budget constraint will be satisfied, without the alteration in any taxes, and in particular, without the alteration in $T_2(t)$ for $t \geqslant t_1$.
35. Equilibrium portfolio allocation requires

$$Eu'_2(\rho - \eta) \qquad (2.26)$$

where

$$u'_2 = \frac{\delta u(C_2)}{\delta C_2}.$$

The condition for equilibrium savings

$$u'(C_1) = Eu'(C_2)\eta \qquad (2.27)$$

will be satisfied.

36. What this establishes is that if financial policy is to have no real effects at t_1, it must change $v(t_1)B(t_1)$. To establish that the change in financial policy must have real effects, it needs to be shown that it is not possible for there to be a sequence of changes in $v(t)B(t)$ for $t \geqslant t_1$, and associated changes in $T_2(t)$ (to keep the government's budget balance), such that the level of capital accumulation at each date is unchanged. The proof is not presented here.
37. Again, for simplicity, population growth has been ignored. This may easily be incorporated into the analysis.
38. The solution to this problem, ignoring the non-negativity constraints, is fairly straightforward. Taking these non-negativity constraints into account, however, complicates the problem in an essential way. Newbery and Stiglitz (1981) provide an extensive discussion of the solution of this problem for the special case where η_t is non-random.
39. The assumption of separability of the utility function was essential in arriving at this simplification in the structure of the solution. With a non-separable utility function, there are two state variables describing the economy at any date t, $S(t)$ and $C_1(t-1)$.
40. (2.38b) can easily be solved for the optimal sequence of $B(t) + T_1 \equiv z^*(t)$. Then, using (2.38c), (2.38a) can be rewritten:

$$C_1^*(S(t)) = C_{1t}(w(t) + T_1, \eta; z^*(t+1) + (1+\eta)(z^*(t) - T_1(t))) + G$$

which we can solve for $T_1^*(t)$, and hence for $B^*(t)$.
41. It is assumed $\{q,(t), i(t), v(t)\}$ adjust to whatever they have to in order for portfolio equilibrium to be established.
42. More formally, it is shown that the individual's opportunity set is unchanged. For simplicity, we normalise by letting $\hat{\hat{v}}(t) \equiv 1 = \hat{v}(t)$. If the individual sets

$$\hat{B}(t) = \hat{\hat{B}}(t) + \hat{\hat{q}}(t)\hat{\hat{D}}(t)$$

the government's budget constraint is satisfied with unchanged taxes if

$$\hat{i}(t)\hat{B}(t) + \hat{B}(t) = (q + \hat{\hat{i}})\hat{\hat{B}}(t) + \hat{\hat{D}}(t) + \hat{\hat{q}}(t)\hat{\hat{D}}(t)$$
$$+ \hat{B}(t-1) - \hat{\hat{B}}(t-1) - \hat{\hat{q}}(t)\hat{\hat{D}}(t-1)$$
$$= (1 + \hat{\hat{i}})\hat{\hat{B}}(t) + \hat{\hat{D}}(t) + \hat{\hat{q}}(t)\hat{\hat{D}}(t).$$

Clearly, any sequence of $\{\hat{C}_1, \hat{C}_2, \hat{K}\}$ which was initially feasible is still feasible (and conversely). Hence, the same $\{C_1, C_2, K\}$ will be chosen: nothing real has changed. This establishes that corresponding to any equilibrium with long-term bonds, there is a corresponding and essentially identical equilibrium without long-term bonds.

43. One does not have to agree with Barro that parents fully offset the effects of intergenerational transfers to believe that these effects are not large enough to be at the centre of a theory of the effectiveness of public financial policy. Similarly, when individuals live for many periods, there will be over-lapping periods in which some risk-sharing may occur. Still, as long as children cannot enter into insurance agreements with their parents before they are born (as they implicitly can in the Arrow–Debreu model), there is scope for public financial policy to improve the intergenerational distribution of risk.

44. For the analysis, fully rational expectations are not required, only that individuals 'rationally' calculate the *changes* in their tax liabilities as a result of a change in financial policy. We call these, 'consistent' expectations.

45. Part of the problem arises from the inability to collateralise future tax reductions. Assume the government increases taxes today, and individual's tax liabilities in the future are decreased. If those decreases could be collateralised (individuals could sell their future tax 'rebates') then the amount that banks would be willing to lend to the individual would increase by the amount of the tax increase, using the future tax rebate as collateral. But such is not the case.

In those cases where the government reduces taxes, individuals could buy an offsetting amount of government bonds. But even this would have real effects, if there is any probability that the individual will go bankrupt; for those bonds will be transferred to the individual's creditors in the event of bankruptcy, without a corresponding transfer of the future tax liability. Because of the asymmetric treatment of the bond and future tax liabilities, individuals will not, in general, wish to fully offset the tax reduction with increased purchases of government bonds.

References

Atkinson, A. B. and Stiglitz, J. E. (1980) *Lectures in Public Economics* (New York and London: McGraw-Hill).
Barro, R. (1974) 'Are Government Bonds Net Wealth?', *Journal of Political Economy*, vol 82 December, pp. 1095–1118.
Bryant, J. and Wallace, N. (1980) 'A Suggestion for Further Simplifying the Theory of Money' (mimeo) December.
Cass, D. and Yaari, I. E. (1967) 'Individual Savings, Aggregate Capital Accumulation and Efficient Growth' in Shell, K. (ed.), *Essays on the Theory of Optimal Economic Growth* (Cambridge, Mass.: MIT Press).
Diamond, P. A, (1965) 'National Debt in a Neoclassical Growth Model', *American Economic Review*, vol. 55, December, pp. 1125–50.
Fischer, S. (1979) 'Anticipations and the Nonneutrality of Money', *Journal of Political Economy*, vol. 87, April, pp. 225–352.
Greenwald, B., Stiglitz, J. E. and Weiss, A. (1984) 'Informational Imperfections in the Capital Market and Macroeconomic Fluctuations', *American Economic Review*, vol. 74, May, pp. 194–9.
Greenwald, B. and Stiglitz, J. E. (1987a) 'Imperfect Information, Credit Markets

and Unemployment', *European Economic Review*, vol. 31, pp. 444–56.
Greenwald, B. and Stiglitz, J. E. (1987b) 'Keynesian, New Keynesian and New Classical Economics', *Oxford Economic Papers*, vol. 39, pp. 119–33.
Greenwald, B. and Stiglitz, J. E. (1988) 'Information, Finance Constraints and Business Fluctuations', in Kohn, M. and Tsiang, S. C. (eds), *Studies in Monetary Economics* (Oxford: Oxford University Press).
Johnson, H. (1966) 'The Neo-classical One-sector Growth Model: A Geometrical Exposition and Extension to a Monetary Economy', *Economica*, vol. 33, August, pp. 265–87.
Neary, J. P. and Stiglitz, J. E. (forthcoming) 'Towards a Reconstruction of Keynesian Economics: Expectations and Constrained Equilibria', *Quarterly Journal of Economics*.
Newbery, D. and Stiglitz, J. E. (1981) *The Theory of Commodity Price Stabilization* (Oxford: Oxford University Press).
Newbery, D. and Stiglitz, J. E. (1982) 'The Choice of Techniques and the Optimality of Market Equilibrium with Rational Expectations', *Journal of Political Economy*, vol. 90, April, pp. 223–46.
Shell, K., Sidrauski, M. and Stiglitz, J. E. (1969) 'Capital Gains, Income and Savings', *Review of Economic Studies*, vol. 36, pp. 15–26.
Sidrauski, M. (1967) 'Inflation and Economic Growth', *Journal of Political Economy*, vol. 75, December, pp. 296–810.
Sidrauski, M. (1967) 'Rational Choice and Patterns of Growth in a Monetary Economy', *American Economic Review*, vol. 58, May, pp. 534–44.
Stiglitz, J. E. (1969) 'A Re-examination of the Modigliani-Miller Theorem', *American Economic Review*, vol. 59, December, pp. 784–93.
Stiglitz, J. E. (1974) 'On the Irrelevance of Corporate Financial Theory', *American Economic Review*, vol. 64, December, pp. 853–66.
Stiglitz, J. E. (1977) 'Lectures in Macroeconomics', mimeo, Oxford University.
Stiglitz, J. E. (1981) 'On the Almost Neutrality of Inflation: Notes on Taxation and the Welfare Costs of Inflation', in Flanders, K. J. and Razin, A. (eds), *Development in an Inflationary World* (New York: Academic Press), pp. 419–57.
Stiglitz, J. E. (1983) 'On the Relevance or Irrelevance of Public Financial Policy: Indexation, Price Rigidities and Optimal Monetary Policy', in Dornbusch, R. and Simonsen, M. (eds), *Inflation, Debt, and Indexation* (Cambridge, Mass.: MIT Press), pp. 183–222.
Stiglitz, J. E. and Weiss, A. (1981) 'Credit Rationing in Markets with Imperfect Information', *American Economic Review*, vol. 71, June, pp. 393–410.
Stiglitz, J. E. and Weiss, A. (1983) 'Incentive Effects of Terminations: Applications to the Credit and Labor Markets', *American Economic Review*, vol. 172, December, pp. 912–27.
Stiglitz, J. E. and Weiss, A. (1986) 'Credit Rationing and Collateral', in Edwards, J., Franks, J., Mayer, C. and Schaefer, S. (eds), *Recent Developments in Corporate Finance* (Cambridge: Cambridge University Press) pp. 101–35.
Stiglitz, J. E. and Weiss, A. (1987) 'Credit Rationing and Macro-economic Equilibrium', New York: NBER Discussion Paper.
Taylor, J. B. (1980) 'Aggregate Dynamics and Staggered Contracts', *Journal of Political Economy*, vol. 88, February, pp. 1–23.

Tobin, J. (1965) 'Money and Economic Growth', *Econometrica*, vol. 33, October, pp. 671–84.

Wallace, N. (1981) 'A Modigliani-Miller Theorem for Open Market Operations', *American Economic Review*, vol. 71, June, pp. 267–74.

DISCUSSION

This paper presents a framework in which it is possible to analyse irrelevancy propositions concerning public financial policy. Two basic premises are that (1) all financial policies need to be taken account of simultaneously, and (2) the effects can only be analysed within intertemporal models with explicit assumptions about expectation formation.

In the basic irrelevance proposition (Say's Law of Government Deficits), the issuance of government debt creates an identical demand for itself, because individuals know they will have to pay higher taxes in the future. A second irrelevancy result is that a change in the rate of interest paid on debt, if financed by issuing more of that debt, has price effects, but no real effects. The Fundamental Relevance Theorem is that any other policy has real results.

Finally, prescriptive results are presented. Optimal intergenerational risk redistribution can be obtained with a constant price level and, if the government has unlimited tax and transfer powers, one financial instrument is sufficient to obtain optimal risk sharing.

Professor Douglas Bernheim commended the explicit treatment of risk and uncertainty, the treatment of both real and nominal effects, the examination of economies with and without intergenerational linkages, and the prescriptive policy analysis. The key to relevance, he pointed out, was the intergenerational redistribution of risk. Since generations could not trade with each other, government policies in this paper generally have real effects. However, he thought that this channel of policy was overemphasised, for several reasons. First, if linkages do exist, then intergenerational pooling is already accomplished. Moreover, even if only some families are dynastic, the private market can carry out optimal risk sharing by trading with those families. Even if no families are dynastic, but people live three periods, trading can occur between any two periods, so private markets would still efficiently pool risks. Furthermore, Bernheim suggested that intergenerational issues may not be paramount in the analysis of monetary or fiscal policies. He supports the view that deficits have effects through capital market imperfections, liquid constraints in particular.

Say's Law of Government Deficits only holds if liquidity constraints never bind, and if there is no uncertainty about who will pay future taxes. Moreover, multiple equilibria are likely to exist. Finally, the relevance results do not provide much useful information, since no one believes in exact neutrality anyway.

Professor Stiglitz stressed that the purpose of the irrelevancy results is simply to set up the extreme case and then ask 'which assumption is inappropriate'. He believes that the important imperfection is the existence of liquidity constraints. Rigorous analysis of endogenous liquidity constraints would be a useful next step.

Professor Mordecai Kurz, citing evidence in a paper by Mervyn King, argued that liquidity constraints hold for only a small part of the population. Stiglitz responded that he is also interested in credit constraints on firms. Moreover, the possibility of liquidity constraints can affect behaviour even when they do not currently bind.

Professor Bernheim interpreted King's results as showing that most people are forward looking in consumption, which does not imply the lack of constraints.

Professor Stiglitz noted further that capitalisation of future tax liabilities apparently does not occur in simple cases, such as future local property taxes. There is, therefore, no reason to expect full capitalisation to occur in more complicated situations in the real world.

3 Concepts and Measures of Federal Deficits and Debt and Their Impact on Economic Activity

Michael J. Boskin
STANFORD UNIVERSITY AND NBER

1 INTRODUCTION

The relationship between budget deficits or public debt and real economic activity has sparked a tremendous debate. For example, various strands of thought argue that deficits are (1) inflationary, (2) expansionary, (3) alter the composition of output away from investment and net exports, or (4) do not matter. The mechanisms by which these effects occur are also widely debated.

The purpose of this chapter is two-fold. First, drawing on a major research project that I have been engaged in for the last few years, on a more comprehensive and comprehensible set of accounts for the federal government of the United States, I wish to highlight movements in various components of spending, deficits and debt, including items which are excluded in the traditional figures. I will also discuss how various major excluded items may affect real economic activity, evaluating the evidence (where it exists), and discussing the avenues by which real activity may be affected. In fact, it is likely that examining deficits or debt, as traditionally measured,[1] can be quite misleading, whether or not one views the private sector as seeing through 'the government veil'.

Secondly, some new evidence will be presented on the likely impact of deficits and debt, and alternative measures of them, on real economic activity, primarily consumption and the composition of output.

Toward this end, Section 2 will present a cursory review of the discussion of the economic effects of deficits and debt. It is not meant to be exhaustive, but merely illustrative of the theoretical and empirical research in recent years on the subject. We find Barro's Ricardian equivalence conjecture, while an important caveat to the traditional treatment, to rest on several assumptions which are likely to be violated in the real world, for example, non-distortionary taxation and equal rates of discount in the private and public sectors. Further, a recent careful test by Boskin and Kotlikoff (1985) strongly rejects an implication of the debt neutrality hypothesis, namely that the age distribution of resources does not affect aggregate consumption.

However, most studies (with a few important exceptions) focus on officially reported nominal budget deficits. These would closely resemble the difference between real accrued government spending and real accrued government revenue only by accident. Various adjustments ranging from correction for the endogeneity of income and the inflation erosion of the real value of the previously issued national debt, to the inclusion of a substantial number of excluded items in the official accounts, to distinguishing between government investment and government consumption, are likely to lead to major problems in interpreting the effects of deficits. For example, Japan has had substantial budget deficits as a fraction of GNP for the last few years, but the fact is that the Japanese government is really a large net saver, i.e. government consumption in Japan is substantially less than revenues because the Japanese government is a large net investor. Thus, the conceptual experiments one has in mind in discussing the likely effects of deficits or debt on the level or composition of real economic activity must be carefully specified. Further, we have virtually no evidence on whether changes in the various components which comprise a sensibly measured deficit symmetrically affect consumption, investment or net exports.

Section 3 discusses the major adjustments that one might make. We remain agnostic as to whether there is a 'correct' budget deficit, or a 'correct' national debt, or a 'correct government net worth'. The nature of the budget deficit, debt or net worth measure one wishes to use depends heavily upon the types of questions that one may wish to ask, one's view of the nature of the economy under study, and on empirical information concerning the likely differential impacts of various components in a fully adjusted deficit or debt or net worth figure. This section highlights the difference between government consumption and investment, and therefore, the relationship between deficits and government saving or dissaving. High employment or income endogeneity adjusted measures of the deficit (as stressed by de Leeuw and Holloway (1985)), inflation adjustment (as stressed so forcefully by

Eisner and Pieper (1984) and Miller (1982)), social security unfunded liabilities (as stressed by Feldstein (1974) and others), government lending and guarantees (stressed by Boskin, Barham, Cone and Ozler (1987)), land and mineral rights (as developed by Boskin, Robinson, O'Reilly and Kumar (1985)), federal, and state and local, government investment in tangible capital (stressed by Boskin, Robinson and Roberts (1985), Boskin, Robinson and Huber (1987) and Eisner and Pieper (1984)), are also discussed. The vastly different measures of deficits, debt and the debt: GNP ratio or deficit: GNP ratio, often changing signs as well as varying amounts, under alternative concepts are discussed. Specific examples are presented from the United States.

Section 4 presents some preliminary empirical results on the effects of deficits, debt, and their components on real economic activity. It is concluded that government financial policy may well affect real economic activity in various ways.

2 A CURSORY LITERATURE REVIEW

2.1 Measurement and Analysis of Deficits and the National Debt

Before discussing the potential economic effects of deficits and the national debt, it is important to realise that measuring, let alone forecasting deficits and debt in the USA is not an easy task. For example, large numbers of items are excluded by law from the federal budget, various other federal government accounting procedures are not consistent with the general notion of accrual accounting, separate capital and current services accounting, and adjusting from par to market valuations (see Boskin 1982 and 1987a). Thus, for example, when the US had a large defence build-down under President Carter, it was partially disguised by the fact that new investment in military hardware was falling short of the depreciation and obsolescence of the existing capital stock. Or, note that in 1980 the $59 billion nominal federal government deficit was offset by a still larger decline in the inflation adjusted value of the previously issued national debt held by the public! Further, it is often the case that the combined state and local government sector of the United States runs a substantial surplus. Some recent attempts to measure these effects are discussed in Section 3.

Further, deficits do *not* measure government dissaving. Government saving, S_g, is the difference between tax (or other) revenue, T, and government consumption, C_g. Thus,

$$S_g = T - C_g. \tag{3.1}$$

If government consumption (including consumption of government fixed capital and durables) falls short of total government spending by a sufficient amount, government saving could be positive despite a deficit, e.g. there could be substantial net government investment. Indeed, in the world's second largest economy, Japan, which is also the largest supplier of capital to the world capital market, the government sector has been a large net saver despite large deficits for many years. Table 3.1 presents national saving, private saving, government saving, investment and deficits for the USA and Japan annually for 1970–84. These data are adjusted to include purchases of consumer durables and government capital as saving and the rental flow from these items as consumption and income. Even the USA occasionally has had a substantial level of government saving despite a large combined federal and state and local government deficit. What should we make of this? Clearly, *the economic impact of the current deficit depends heavily upon the nature of the substitutability or complementarity of private and public consumption and investment. Without a full specification of these factors, the impact of the deficit may range from increasing to decreasing private consumption, saving or investment.*[2]

2.2 A Simple Analysis

Ultimately, at full employment, large deficits, net of the interest component (the so-called primary deficit) run continuously for a very long period *must be inflationary*. To see this, the following equations indicate where the ratio of *privately* held national debt is headed given large deficits as a share of GNP (net of the interest component) and real interest rate and growth rate scenarios.

Let D represent the debt: GNP ratio, d the deficit (net of interest): GNP ratio, r the real interest rate, g growth of real GNP. Then, by definition

$$D_t = d_t + (r_t - g_t)dt, \tag{3.2}$$

for a fiscal programme with constant d, and constant r and g, D will evolve toward an equilibrium D_e (*if* $g > r$) of

$$D_e = \frac{d}{g - r}. \tag{3.3}$$

Table 3.1 Japan and USA, public and private net saving rates based on the net national savings concept, adjusted for consumer durables, government investment and appropriate rents

	Japan				
Year	National saving	Private saving	Government saving	Government investment	Deficit
1970	31.45	22.91	8.54	8.17	−0.37
1971	29.20	21.43	7.77	8.98	1.21
1972	28.54	21.65	6.89	9.57	2.69
1973	28.89	21.13	7.75	9.31	1.56
1974	26.68	19.54	7.14	8.16	1.03
1975	22.83	19.26	3.57	7.83	4.25
1976	23.03	20.80	2.23	7.35	5.12
1977	23.00	20.45	2.54	7.63	5.09
1978	23.39	21.83	1.56	8.45	6.88
1979	22.26	19.55	2.71	8.46	5.74
1980	21.31	18.40	2.91	7.84	4.93
1981	21.39	18.04	3.35	7.66	4.31
1982	19.90	16.68	3.22	6.89	3.67
1983	18.84	16.16	2.68	6.22	3.54
1984	19.89	17.37	2.52	5.36	2.85
1970–9	25.93	20.86	5.07	8.39	3.32

	United States				
Year	National saving	Private saving	Government saving	Government investment	Deficit
1970	9.97	9.18	0.80	1.94	1.15
1971	11.12	11.25	−0.13	1.81	1.94
1972	12.30	10.82	1.49	1.79	0.31
1973	14.39	12.12	2.27	1.63	−0.64
1974	10.73	9.42	1.30	1.67	0.36
1975	7.90	10.72	−2.81	1.67	4.48
1976	9.39	10.29	−0.90	1.11	1.01
1977	10.33	10.23	0.10	1.11	1.01
1978	11.72	10.27	1.44	1.40	−0.04
1979	11.15	9.17	1.98	1.34	−0.65
1980	7.58	7.60	−0.02	1.26	1.28
1981	8.57	8.66	−0.09	0.91	0.99
1982	4.80	7.79	−2.99	1.16	4.15
1983	5.65	8.93	−3.28	1.20	4.49
1984	8.37	10.94	−2.57	1.11	3.69
1970–9	10.90	10.35	0.55	1.58	1.02

Source: Boskin, M. and Roberts, J. 'A Closer Look at Saving Rates In the US and Japan', AEI (1986).

The ratio of the federal government debt to GNP evolves through time depending upon this primary deficit and the relation between the real rate of interest and the growth rate. For example, if we start out with a positive national debt, and the real interest paid on the national debt exceeds the growth rate, then the interest payments will grow more rapidly than the GNP, and if nothing else has changed, eventually the interest payments will consume all of the budget, then all of GNP, then all of national wealth in an explosive pattern. In the more usual case of the growth rate exceeding the rate of interest the ratio of debt to GNP will evolve according to the equation above.

Table 3.2 presents some estimates of two recent major fiscal episodes in the United States. First, we see the substantial increase in the equilibrium debt: GNP ratio toward which we were headed if fiscal policy had not been changed, in the 1975–9 period, a period generally regarded as the beginning of the increase of the ratio of debt to GNP after the substantial postwar decline in this ratio. The second, and more important for our purposes, is where we were headed in the early Reagan Administration years. We can see that under the 1983–4 projections, the ratio of debt to GNP was heading toward an equilibrium which is many times, not only current GNP, but the ratio of the entire value of the capital stock of the United States to GNP. This latter number is around 3, so it is clear that either the private sector would have to increase its wealth/income ratio by an enormous increase in saving, or

Table 3.2 Some US fiscal episodes

	1975–9	1984–9	
D_0	23.4%	37%	37%
		CBO baseline	Administration
d average	3.7	1.8	1.4
g average	3.5	3.8	4.0
i (net of monetisation)	6.0		
GNP deflator	7.2		
r	−1.2	3.6	2.4
$g-r$	4.7	0.2	1.6
D_e	79%	900%	88%

Note:
D_t declined steadily from The Second World War to 1974.

Source: Boskin, M. 'Conceptual and Measurement Issues in the Analysis of Deficits and Debt'. Paper presented at the NBER Taxation Program meeting, Palo Alto, CA, March, 1983.

the rest of the world will have to buy up Treasury bills, or if neither of these alternatives is available and current fiscal policies persist for the indefinite future, the Federal Reserve will have to buy up the bonds as the lender of last resort, thereby eventually inflating the economy. Can we reasonably expect foreigners to continue to finance our deficits *ad infinitum*? It would be imprudent to operate on the assumption that this was possible, let alone desirable. Eventually, foreign firms and individuals will have a progressively higher fraction of their wealth in dollar denominated assets, which will mean that further increases in dollar denominated assets will be even riskier for them. Thus, we can expect the flow of foreign capital into the United States, *ceteris paribus*, to slow down and real interest rates to rise. Nor is such a huge increase in our saving rate as to increase the capital:output ratio by such a large amount likely. In short, the recent fiscal policy was eventually either inflationary or unsustainable. Fortunately, in the last two budget cycles, substantial reductions have occurred in (primarily military) spending growth, and it is likely that the danger of an explosion in the debt:GNP ratio is over.[3]

Deficits or government debt may affect the real economy at less pernicious levels than just mentioned. While virtually all economists agree that an increase in government spending – at least if it is unanticipated – may affect real output and its composition,[4] the effects of a tax cut given government spending are more controversial. Certainly, the dampening effects of monetary feedbacks through higher real interest rates, reduced real money balances and changes in portfolio composition and also currency appreciation and net exports are by now well recognised (see, for example, Feldstein, 1982, 1986). However, recently, several economists have revived the notion that debt and taxes are equivalent and that government deficits therefore have no effect in aggregate demand. The argument is by now so well known that I will merely summarise it here. Each extra dollar of national debt must eventually be repaid or serviced by interest payments with a present value of a dollar. Thus, there is no change in the present value of tax liabilities and private net wealth, so real decisions are unaffected.

Public debt policy, or intergenerational transfers towards older generations, can be and has been conducted in quite subtle ways. The unfunded financing of the US Social Security System is by now a well understood, if none the less quite subtle, debt policy (Feldstein, 1974). Less well understood debt policies are changes in the tax structure that shift the burden of taxation from older to younger age groups (Summers, 1981; Auerbach and Kotlikoff, 1983a) and changes in tax provisions that raise market values of financial assets and, thereby, transfer resources to older age groups who are the primary owners of such assets (Summers, 1987). An example of the former type of policy is switching from income taxation to wage taxation. An example of the latter policy is reducing investment incentives (Auerbach and Kotlikoff, 1983b). Since investment incentives in the USA are effectively provided only to new investment, old capital, capital that has been fully or partially written off, sells at a discount reflecting the differential tax treatment. A reduction in investment incentives means a smaller discount and capital gain to owners of old capital. Younger and future generations are worse off as a result of such policies because they must now pay higher prices to acquire claims to the economy's capital stock.

In addition to these more subtle mechanisms of transferring to older generations, governments can engage in debt policies by reducing taxes levied on current generations and raising taxes levied on future generations. Intergenerational redistribution of this variety may eventuate in larger officially reported deficits. An example in which even this more obvious form of redistribution does not necessarily alter official calculations is when such tax cuts and tax increases are coincident, respectively, with equivalent reductions and increases in the level of government consumption.

The fact that very significant intergenerational redistribution can be run without its ever showing up on government books suggests that officially reported deficits are at best a very poor indicator of underlying public debt policies.[5] This proposition notwithstanding, there has been an enormous public interest, especially in recent years, in officially reported deficits. Curiously, public attention has focused only on a subset of official liabilities of the federal government and has essentially ignored both the official assets of the federal government and the official assets and liabilities of state and local governments. As discussed by Boskin (1982 and forthcoming 1988); Boskin, Robinson and Huber (1987); Eisner and Pieper (1984); and the *1982 Economic Report of the President*, the market value of the US federal government's official assets may currently equal if not exceed the market value of its official liabilities.

In light of the very significant if not overwhelming difficulties of gauging the extent of true debt policies from official reports, it seems safer to assess debt policy by asking the following question: were the lifetime budget constraints of older generations expanded significantly as a consequence of government policy at the expense of contracted budget constraints for young and future generations? One might point, in this context, to the enormous expansion of the social security system which greatly increased the budget opportunities of the elderly. The problem, however, with considering any one component of government policy is that it may have been instituted to offset some other component; i.e. the postwar redistribution through social security to the elderly may simply represent the government's way of compensating the elderly for higher income taxes over their lifetimes or for their contribution to the nation during the Second World War. Just as there is no single correct way to measure official deficits, there is no single correct way of posing counterfactuals about observed government transfer polifices. To put this point differently, intergenerational redistribution must always be assessed relative to some benchmark, and the choice of a benchmark seems inherently subjective. The implication of this point is that any calculation of the magnitude of intergenerational transfers will be somewhat arbitrary.

It is instructive to examine the likely effects of federal government deficits on the composition of GNP by examining the actual correlation between changes in the deficit and various components of GNP.

Since the federal government deficit is just the difference between federal government spending and taxes, it must equal the sum of private saving, and the state and local surplus, less domestic investment and net foreign investment. Simply put, if the level of GNP is held constant (the deficit may affect the level of GNP but we are concerned here with its composition) increases in the deficits must crowd out something. Will they lead to increased private saving or decreased domestic investment or less net foreign investment (i.e. more foreign capital inflows)? A provocative, but preliminary, analysis by Summers (1986) suggests that budget deficits call forth increased private saving of about 30 cents per dollar of deficit. This results from a combination of extra saving for future tax liabilities resulting from the deficits, the sensitivity of savings to higher real interest rates caused by deficits, and/or the crowding out of consumer durable expenditures due to higher interest rates. In addition, he estimates that deficits crowd out net exports by attracting foreign capital, in this case, about 25 cents on the dollar. He also estimates about a 5 cent increase per dollar of deficit in state and local surpluses, and a 40 cents per dollar decrease in net investment. Further, of course, the net business investment must be separated from residential investment which is crowded out at about 20 cents on the dollar. These estimates are highly preliminary and subject to many statistical problems.[6]

The two leading theories of private saving behaviour are the pure life cycle theory of Modigliani and Brumberg (1954) and Ando and Modigliani (1963) and the intergenerational altruism model of Barro (1974). In the former, government debt decreases private saving and in the latter it has no effect.

Various studies have attempted to demonstrate that life-cycle behaviour can explain several important phenomena concerning aggregate wealth accumulation in the United States (see Tobin, 1967). More recently, there has been an attack on the pure life-cycle model (no bequest, average propensity to consume over the lifetime of one) by a variety of authors. For example, Kotlikoff and Summers (1981) conclude that life-cycle saving can account for only about 20 per cent of the aggregate wealth in the United States. Unfortunately, a mathematical error in their derivation of the formulae is part of the explanation for their result, and corrected, the numbers would be about 50 per cent. This is still a telling indictment of the extreme version of the life-cycle hypothesis.

There have also been a number of studies attempting to examine the extent of dissaving after retirement. For example, Michael Darby (1979) demonstrated, using longitudinal household data, that there was surprisingly little dissaving post-retirement, and concluded these results were incompatible with the pure life-cycle hypothesis. Mirer (1979), David and Menchik (1980), and King and Dicks-Mireaux (1982) also find either no dissaving or too little dissaving after retirement to be consistent with the pure life cycle model.

In recent work, Bernheim (1984) and Diamond and Hausman (1984), using panel data, do observe dissaving after retirement. In an important study just completed, Hurd (1986) makes several methodological and data improvements (e.g. a ten-year longitudinal panel study rather than a cross-section or shorter panel), and his conclusion is that the dissaving pattern of the elderly is quite consistent with the pure life-cycle model. Further, tests for a bequest motive show no evidence of one.

Rejection of the pure form of the life-cycle model should not be taken to mean that there is no consumption smoothing over the life-cycle, or that the propensity to consume is independent of age. It is the rejection of the assumption that the average propensity to consume over the lifetime is one, and that there is no bequest motive (even accounting for the fact that an uncertain date of death may require very slow dissaving in the absence of actuarially fair annuities).

A variety of studies presume the pure form of the life-cycle theory in analyses of public policy. We shall comment on several below, but it is important to point out that one of the major conclusions from the pure life-cycle model is that public debt – explicit or implicit – crowds out private saving, and ultimately, therefore, capital formation. In an alternative model proposed by Barro (1974), extending work of Bailey (1962), and dating all the way back to Ricardo, a Say's law of public finance is developed in which increases in the supply of public debt call forth an increased demand for it.[7] The argument is simply that in a world where there are intergenerational altruism and operative bequest motives – as well as many other assumptions such as lump-sum finance, etc. – the private sector can undo the government's attempt to redistribute resources across generations. The assumptions for this result to hold are quite restrictive.[8] The two least reasonable assumptions required for the results to hold are non-distortionary taxation and equal discounting of public and private decision makers. The latter stems from the linking of all generations due to children's utility appearing as an argument in the parent's utility function. Thus, private decision makers act as if they are an infinitely-lived dynasty, ignoring the mortality probabilities which would normally be added to subjective discount rates.

Many studies have tried to analyse the effect of some measure of deficits or public debt on consumption (e.g. Kormendi, 1983; Feldstein, 1982; Barth, Iden and Russek 1984) and the studies cited therein) or of unfunded liabilities in social security on the consumption/saving choice (see Feldstein, 1974; Barro, 1978; Feldstein and Pellechio, 1979, among many). The conclusions are somewhat mixed. I believe that an accurate summary of the econometric literature is that Feldstein's original dollar-for-dollar estimate of the substitution of unfunded social security liabilities or public debt for private saving has been revised to 25 to 50 cents on the dollar and that the statistical evidence concerning the effects of deficits is mixed, but on balance suggests that (correctly measured) deficits do matter.

Since concepts such as deficits, public debt and unfunded social security liabilities are subject to vagaries of accounting procedures, more *direct tests* of the intergenerational altruism model are possible. To see this, note that in the intergenerational altruism model *aggregate* consumption depends only on *aggregate* resources, not on their age distribution. This forms the basis for the test developed by Boskin and Kotlikoff (1985). We develop a finite approximation to the intergenerational optimisation problem for Barro-type behaviour under earnings and rate of return uncertainty, and demographic change, for the US economy, and test whether, given the level of consumption predicted by this model, variables measuring the age distribution of resources influence actual consumption. Data on the age distribution of resources is obtained from the annual current population surveys. The results, presented in a variety of forms using various measures of the age distribution of resources, reject the hypothesis that aggregate consumption is independent of the age distribution of resources. They therefore cast considerable doubt on the pure intergenerational altruism model and on the contention that government debt policy – explicit or implicit – does not affect the consumption/saving choice.

Thus, neither the pure life-cycle model nor the pure intergenerational altruism model seems *sufficient* to explain aggregate saving behaviour or the effects of policy on saving. Undoubtedly, different people in the economy could be described in their saving behaviour by different models, including a Keynesian liquidity constraint consumption/saving model, and the convex combination that results in aggregate saving is some complicated combination of these models.

I do believe that it is important to realise, however, that there are substantial differences in the propensity to consume by age, some lifetime smoothing, and substantial bequests in aggregate capital formation. Thus, elements of both the bequest model and the original pure life-cycle model are important in explaining saving behaviour, despite the fact that each of the models in its most pure form is rejected in the data.

Finally, the results of Eisner and Pieper (1984) and Feldstein (1982) suggest that deficits, particularly when adjusted for measurement problems such as those due to inflation, lead to an increase in aggregate demand and real GNP. While I have mentioned above several caveats to this story limiting the likely size of the impact of a pro-deficit tax cut on real GNP, it is important to point out that some fiscal stimulus still remains after one has made all these adjustments. Further, it should be realised that the debt neutrality hypothesis assumes a given level of government spending. An increase in government expenditures is likely to raise total aggregate demand somewhat, (the extent depending upon the nature of monetary policy) and therefore can affect interest rates as well.

In summary, it should not be surprising that there are many avenues by which deficits, government spending and various forms of taxes can affect interest rates and the composition of GNP, as well as the level and growth rate of nominal GNP and its division into real and inflation components. However, the alleged 'bang-for-the-buck' in fiscal stimulus is undoutedly much less than had been supposed by the closed economy Keynesian fine-tuners who dominated economic policy making in the 1960s and 1970s.

3 THE POTENTIAL SIGNIFICANCE OF VARIOUS ADJUSTMENTS TO MEASURES OF FEDERAL AND STATE AND LOCAL GOVERNMENT DEFICITS, DEBT, AND/OR NET WORTH

As discussed above, the impact of government budget deficits or debt may well depend on the nature of the spending programmes (e.g. whether they are consumption or investment), revenues (especially the effective marginal tax rates on various factors of supply and commodity demands), and on items traditionally not measured in US government budgets, especially the federal budget. To repeat, few would argue with the proposition that changes in the real value of government purchases of goods and services may affect economic activity, especially if they are unanticipated. Even those working in the rational expectations tradition believe that a temporary increase in government spending above its expected or trend value will lead to a rise in interest rates, a postponement of consumption, and increased short-run supply. It is often the case that government investment is financed by borrowing, especially at the state and local level in the United States. However, the Ricardian equivalence theorem is most readily seen as applying to changes in the mix of tax and debt finance, given a certain level of government *consumption*, rather than government spending. This is because for a given level of government spending, changes in the mix between consumption and investment may send very different signals to the private sector concerning future income and tax liabilities. For example, a temporary public sector investment boom (such as the building of the interstate highway system in the United States) may signal increased productivity and a subsequent decline, *ceteris paribus*, in future taxes below what they otherwise would have been, if the investment is not financed completely by borrowing. Further, it is now widely recognised that government consumption may either be a substitute or a complement to private consumption, and through this mechanism may alter private consumption and saving (see, for example, Feldstein, 1982; Barro, 1985).

The purpose of this section is to discuss recent attempts to measure various components of a more complete balance sheet for the federal government, and various attempts to provide better measures of deficits, debt, assets, investment and consumption. The various attempts discussed here are only a subset of those that have been made. This is partly because some of the papers I will mention draw on data from the careful work of others. To economise on space, I will not go into detail on the latter, but these authors do not get the credit they deserve for attempting to rework the basic data more carefully.[9]

This section is divided into four parts. First, various issues in measuring government assets are discussed. Secondly, various attempts to get more comprehensive or economically meaningful measures of government deficits, debt, and net debt, and the potential problems as well as advantages thereof are discussed. Thirdly, present evidence on a net worth concept for the government sector is presented and discussed. It is unclear whether those who have attempted to generate greater information on government assets and liabilities really believe that a net worth variable is the appropriate one (whether adjusted for inflation or cyclical conditions) to enter as a measure of the government's economic impact. Eisner and Pieper (1984) tend to hint at this, but it is my opinion that such estimates are useful primarily to provide measures of national wealth and to place concern about government liabilities in better perspective.

Finally, the last subsection discusses reasons why addition across various types of spending, revenues, assets, or liabilities, may be inappropriate. Not only are different components subject to wide variations in their reliability, but fully rational forward looking behaviour would account for the differential riskiness of the various components with regard to expected future government consumption, impact on private productivity, and likely future tax liabilities in assessing real private permanent net-of-tax income. Nor is it correct that one should discount the various components by different risk-adjusted rates. This is correct only in cases where the differential risk involves mortality probabilities. Instead, a risk charge (or bonus if the riskiness is negatively correlated with other components of income) should be applied to the various components in each period before discounting. Perhaps this is harping since the degree of rationality and foresight involved is even less obviously reasonable than that attributable to the basic Ricardian equivalence proposition.

3.1 Government Assets

Various recent studies have attempted to document the quantitative importance of government assets (e.g. Hulten and Peterson, 1984; Boskin, Robinson and Roberts, 1985; Eisner and Pieper, 1984; Boskin, Robinson, O'Reilly and Kumar, 1985; Boskin, Robinson and Huber, 1987). Federal, and state and local, governments in the United States own substantial amounts of land, mineral rights, buildings, inventories, equipment, gold and other financial assets. The Federal Reserve Flow of Funds Division's National Balance Sheets for the United States estimate various components (Federal Reserve (1986)). The US Department of Commerce, Bureau of Economic Analysis publishes detailed estimates of federal, state and local government capital stocks, investment, and depreciation (BEA 1982). These data form the starting point for many attempts to expand upon or improve, these data. There are problems with these initial attempts to measure government assets, but they represent an important and under-utilised resource, and attempts to improve upon them should not lose sight of this fact. For example, the FED records the value of bonds (whether assets or liabilities) at par; the BEA uses depreciation methods which would only approximate economic depreciation by accident, etc. Whether using the FED or BEA numbers or attempts to improve upon them (such as in Boskin, Robinson, and Huber, 1987), the conclusion seems to be that, until recently, federal government assets substantially exceeded regular federal government liabilities (additional federal government liabilities will be discussed below). Table 3.3 provides some data from my work in this regard. It compares federal, state and local government tangible capital with their outstanding debt. The development of these estimates of federal, state and local net investment and net capital differs from the BEA estimates and attempts to incorporate improved measures of economic depreciation based on estimates of used asset prices. They are far from definitive, but in general, they exceed the BEA estimates

Table 3.3 Government tangible capital and federal debt held by public, selected years, in $1982 billions

Year	Tangible capital		Federal debt
	Federal	State and local	
1950	477.2	482.4	1,018.7
1960	662.9	753.6	721.0
1970	752.6	1,224.7	664.1
1980	810.2	1,542.8	825.8
1984	936.8	1,611.3	1,213.1
1985	999.2	1,634.7	1,353.0

Source: Tangible capital: Boskin, Robinson and Huber (1987). Debt: *Economic Report of the President*, selected years.

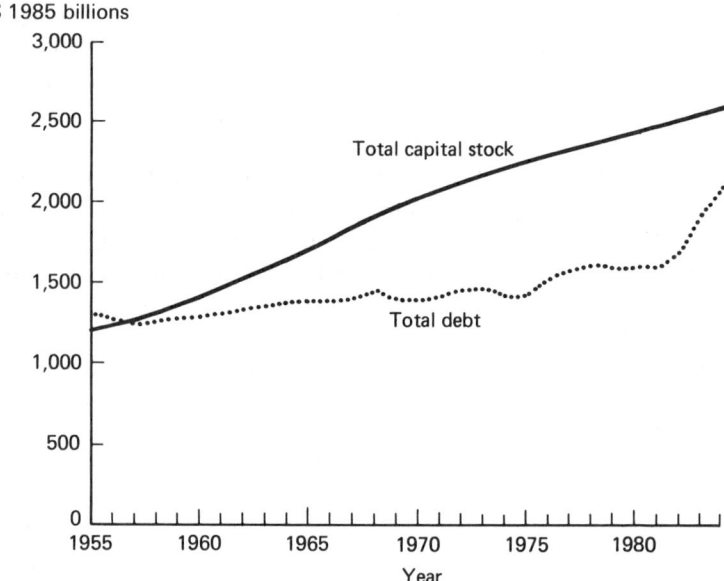

Figure 3.1 Total government debt and total government reproducible fixed net capital stock

Source: Boskin, M., Robinson, M. and Huber, A. (1987) *Government Saving, Capital Formation and Wealth in the United States 1947–1985* (New York: NBER).

by about 20 per cent. Figure 3.1 portrays pictorially that despite the recent explosion in federal government official debt, federal and state and local tangible capital apparently exceeds the corresponding official obligations by a substantial amount.

There are additional problems in measuring assets. Loans made by the government to the private sector are carried on the books as assets. But a very poor treatment of the market value of such loans is included. In fact, the budgetary process makes no attempt to reserve for bad loans, and hence, grossly overstates the market value of federal government accumulated loans (to be discussed further below).

One of the most important assets held by the federal government is the substantial amount of land and mineral rights. In a recent paper (Boskin *et al.*, 1985), I estimated the market value of the federal government's oil and natural gas rights to exceed $500 billion as of 1981. Of course, the federal government debt held by the public has doubled since then, and oil and gas prices have plummeted. Still, the value of these resources are substantial. Table 3.4 highlights that in

Table 3.4 Change in the value of federal oil and gas rights in billions of current dollars

Year	Change in value	Nominal federal deficit
1974	+43.7	6.1
1976	+16.1	53.2
1978	+11.8	59.2
1979	+60.8	40.2
1980	+131.5	73.8
1981	+142.5	78.9
1982	+27.9	127.9
1983	−16.5	207.8
1984	−12.3	185.3
1985	−28.8	212.3
1986	−156.7	220.7

Sources: Boskin et al., (1985); updated and corrected in Boskin, Robinson and Huber (1987); Economic Report of the President (1987).

several recent years the *change* in the value of oil and gas rights held by the federal government exceeded the nominal deficit.[10]

Federal government assets or changes in their value may affect the real economy in a variety of ways. A large increase in the value of mineral rights, for example, may imply substantial increases in future revenue from royalties and bonuses. This may signal either an increase in government investment or consumption, or that a tax decrease is in the offing. National wealth will have increased. It is unlikely, of course, that private consumers will respond instantaneously to changes in these values and in corresponding forecasts of expected future changes in fiscal variables. But eventually, there will be potential substantial changes in taxes due to swings in the value in mineral rights affecting private decision making. We are unused to thinking of this on the national level in the United States despite the fact that income from mineral rights is the second largest revenue source (after taxes) for the federal government. But the states of Alaska and Texas have had their state fiscal policies dominated by oil and gas revenues. Of course, there are several nations whose fiscal policy is primarily driven by oil revenues.

3.2 Debt and Deficits

A variety of adjustments should be made in examining debt and deficits, depending upon the use one wishes to make of these figures. Attempts to measure national wealth or the sectoral balance sheets for the federal government certainly should include an inflation and par to market adjustment of outstanding liabilities (Eisner and Pieper, 1984; Miller, 1982). While a standardised employment, high employment, or mid-expansion path adjusted deficit may be used to correct for the endogenenity of spending, and especially revenue, due to cyclical conditions (as discussed in de Leeuw and Holloway, 1985), the construction of such a series is subject to substantial disagreement concerning the appropriate employment benchmark. There can be no doubt that correcting for income endogeneity is potentially important, but the recent upward revision of the high employment rate to 6 per cent from slightly over 5 per cent suggests that even the government statisticians disagree on the exact formulation of the high employment concept.[11]

The use of an inflation adjusted deficit either by itself or in conjunction with a cyclically adjusted deficit to measure the short-run impact of fiscal policy on the real economy has been proposed and implemented, for example, by Eisner and Pieper (1984). While the inflation adjusted measures appear to provide a better explanation than the nominal figures, inflation adjusted deficits – the deficit less the decline in the real value of the previously issued national debt held by the public – presumes that consumers are rational and foresightful enough to calculate this decline in the real value of their wealth and respond to it in *exactly* the same way as other components of wealth changes. The effect of the decline in the real value of the previously issued debt on the real economy depends heavily upon the extent to which investors realise this decline and adjust to it completely by restoring their real portfolio positions (for mixed reactions to this proposition, see Cagan, 1981). I present some evidence on this issue below.

There are a variety of other items excluded from the official deficit and debt figures. For example, the federal government guarantees a substantial amount of lending and is subject to future payment to cover default. In either a market clearing or credit rationing regime, the likely effect of federal loans and guarantees on real investment depends upon the elasticity of the supply of funds into the system, the marginal source of finance, the nature and number of loan programmes, etc. (Gale, 1986). Table 3.5(b) presents some recent data on loans and loan guarantees outstanding and new commitments thereof. In previous work (Boskin, Barham, Cone and Ozler, 1987), we estimated that each dollar of new loan guarantee commitment carried with it an expected present value of future expenditures of about twleve cents.

Table 3.5 Some contingent and potential liabilities of the federal government

(a) Social Security (OASDI), Projected revenues, benefits and deficit as per cent of taxable payroll

Prior to 1983 amendments	25-year period			75-year period
	1982–2006	2007–31	2032–56	1982–2056
Income	12.01	12.40	12.40	12.27
Outgo	11.35	14.08	16.79	14.07
Surplus	0.66	−1.68	−4.39	−1.80
Post-1983 amendments	1983–2007	2008–32	2033–57	1983–2057
Income	12.50	12.95	13.15	12.94
Outgo	10.66	12.64	15.23	13.35
Surplus	1.83	0.32	−2.08	−0.41

(b) Loans and guarantees ($ billions)

	Direct loans		Loan guarantees		Federal sponsored enterprises
Year	New commitments	Total outstanding	New commitments	Total outstanding	Total outstanding
1966	7	33	24	99	19
1975	29	74	50	189	85
1983	41	223	97	364	309

Source: (a) Boskin (1986); (b) US budgets Special Analysis F.

Deposit insurance operates in a similar manner. While deposit insurance provides various types of benefits, the institutional arrangements in the United States generate a situation where banks have a put option on the FDIC (Federal Deposit Insurance Corporation) and excessive risk is probably incurred because of the lack of risk related premiums. A sensible forward looking budget document would treat deposit insurance (and by analogy, other types of loan guarantees and lending programmes) with a forward looking bad debt reserve (see Boskin, Barham, Cone and Ozler, 1987).

Perhaps the most important, if controversial, liabilities involve future unfunded expected benefits in social security and related retirement programmes, such as civil service retirement, military retirement, state and local government retirement, Medicare, etc. The excess of the present value of expected benefits over the expected present value of tax revenue under the social security administration actuaries intermediate assumptions over the next seventy-five years is presented in Table 3.5(a), as augmented in Boskin (1986). Clearly, these sums are enormous. Something will undoubtedly have to be done about social security and Medicare. The 1983 amendments to social security were a major step in this regard reducing by almost two trillion dollars the actuarial deficit in the retirement and disability part of the programme. Since then, the deficit has increased to about a quarter of its previous level based on changes in assumptions and events. But there is a much larger deficit in Medicare, amounting to several times the regular national debt. I know of no explicit tests of the likely impact of the Medicare programme on consumption and saving decisions, but there are certainly a variety of ways in which it could affect those decisions. Provision of such insurance may decrease the precautionary incentive to save, and Medicare provides insurance against the most important risk faced by the elderly – ill-health and substantial medical expenditures. In any event, as discussed above, the empirical evidence of the effects of social security on the consumption/saving choice is somewhat mixed, although I tend to side with those who contend social security's unfunded obligations have had about one-quarter to one-half dollar-per-dollar offset on private saving. Consider the 1983 social security amendments. These decreased the unfunded actuarial debt in social security retirement and disability programme by almost two trillion dollars. If it is true that social security wealth offsets private saving, we should have seen a substantial plunge in consumption and increase in saving pursuant to this enormous decline. But it is perhaps reasonable to expect that it will take years for people to understand fully that taxes will increase and benefits decrease via a gradual increase in the age of eligibility for full retirement benefits. Also, in the United States, we face the virtually unprecedented scenario of the retirement and disability programmes building up a trust fund from 1990 to 2020 which will approach the value of the regular national debt (see Boskin, 1986). While this is currently forecast, I do not know of anyone who really expects it to happen. It is likely that the social security retirement surplus will be used to bail out Medicare, to raise benefits, or to reduce taxes (see Boskin, 1987b, for a discussion of the potential impact of these financing alternatives on national saving). Thus, the signals are mixed, but the discrete change in the social security laws enacted in 1983 have far greater potential impact on the lifetime resources of persons below the age of 45 than the much more hotly debated tax reforms currently under consideration (see Boskin et al., 1987).

3.3 Net Worth

Government net worth is a concept that has been used to parallel the balance sheet for private companies. Certainly, the federal government accounting procedures would be illegal if used in the private sector and would produce some very strange results on private balance sheets and profit and loss statements. But governments are not firms. They can print money, borrow, and tax, in a manner that private firms cannot. While some people would argue these privileges can be abused and at times they have been, how does one value the right or option to exercise them? Further, while the government sector's net worth is a concept relevant to measures of national wealth, particularly in modern times when the government sector is a non-trivial fraction of the entire economy, it is unclear that any addition of assets and subtraction of all liabilities to get a net worth figure would leave one with a measure that has any significance for short- or long-term real economic activity.

There are a variety of problems with the net worth figure as a measure of the government's net economic impact or changes in net worth as a similar measure. As noted above, different components of assets and liabilities may affect the real economy differently. This may be because of differential risks involved in future revenues or consumption resulting from assets, payments resulting from liabilities, and the differential correlation of these components with other components of income in the private sector; the ability of the private sector to measure and analyse the fiscal signal that is being sent by various changes in the asset or liability side or correspondingly on the spending or revenue or borrowing side of the government budget. In fact, if we want to take it to its logical conclusion, rational consumers will be forming expectations not only on their future incomes, but also of the entire stream of future government consumption, investment, taxation and borrowing. Changes in government spending, taxes, transfers, borrowing, or the values of various assets and liabilities may change that subjective distribution and that change may be based on the entire previous history of these variables (contrary to some recent specifications of consumption behaviour). Thus, government net worth estimates, despite their measurement problems, appear to be most valuable to provide some indication of the relative importance of government debt and improved measures of national wealth. They are unlikely to replace deficit, debt, and/or their composition, or changes therein as sensible measures of fiscal impact.

3.4 Government Consumption and Investment

Finally, it is important to distinguish between government consumption and investment. Government consumption may substitute or complement private consumption and therefore, a dollar increase in government consumption, leading to a dollar increase in government deficit, may have opposite effects on private consumption, private saving, and national saving, depending upon the substitutability or complementarity of private consumption and government consumption. Government investment may be temporary, such as building an infrastructure (maintaining it should be much less costly than building it in the first place), and so on. This may signal a decline in future taxes if the government investment is not fully debt financed, or it may signal the early stages of an increased round of expanded government consumption. We really have very little evidence upon which to evaluate

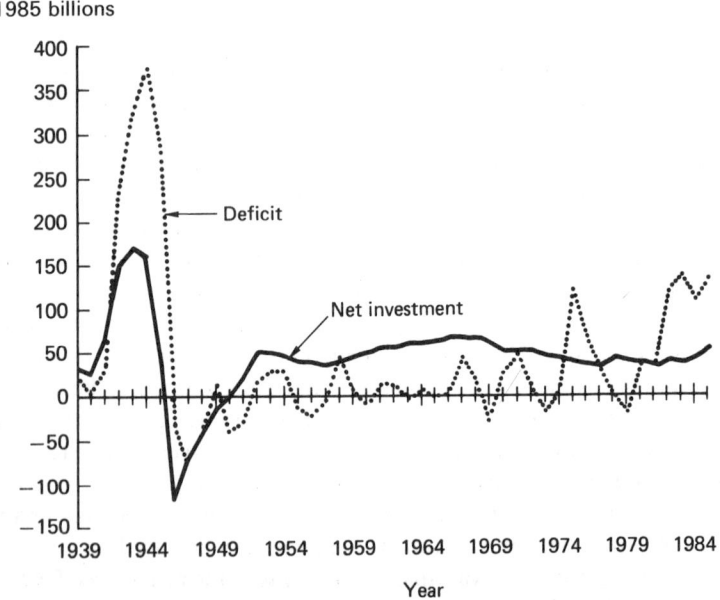

Figure 3.2 Total government net investment in fixed reproducible capital and NIPA total government budget deficit.

Source: Boskin, M., Robinson, M. and Huber, A. (1987) *Government Saving, Capital Formation and Wealth in the United States 1947–1985* (New York: NBER).

these matters, but the private sector's perception of them can be important with regard to how changes in government spending – especially unanticipated ones – affect the real economy. Figure 3.2 presents an interesting pictorial comparison of the recent history of the relationship between government net investment and deficits in the United States. As can be seen, the government sector in the United States is sometimes a net saver when it is running deficits, since its net investment exceeds the value of those deficits.

With these provisos, and the cursory survey of recent attempts to expand and improve measures of government financial statements and fiscal impacts in mind, let us turn to some new evidence concerning the impact of fiscal policy on the real economy.

4 NEW EMPIRICAL RESULTS ON THE EFFECTS OF GOVERNMENT DEFICITS AND DEBT ON REAL ECONOMIC ACTIVITY AND ITS COMPOSITION

This section reports new tests using updated, expanded and improved data to test alternative propositions concerning the impact of deficits and public debt on real activity and on the composition of GNP.

These tests go through several stages and incorporate several data improvements. Most important, we adjust private consumption and income to treat purchases of consumer durables as saving and the imputed rental flow from the durables as consumption and an analogous adjustment is made for treating the imputed flow of services from government capital as government consumption in addition to direct government consumption. Our results reported below with C^*, adjusted consumption, contain this expanded definition (and Y^* is the expanded definition of national income). For purposes of comparison, results are presented using NIPA consumer expenditures and standard national income account concepts.

Since various previous studies have estimated consumption functions using various measures of permanent income, using national income, disposable income, or labour income, and various lags thereof to proxy permanent income, we present in equations (1)–(4) what might be called traditional consumption functions. Equations (1), (2) and (4) present alternative specifications using our expanded definition of consumption and income, including the public's holding of government bonds. Equation (3) presents analogous results for NIPA (national income and product accounts) consumer expenditures. All of these equations, and those discussed below are estimated by ordinary least squares with first-order serial correlation adjustment.

Results in equations (1)–(4), estimated on the sample period 1947–84 are quite similar to typical results (see Table 3.6). The short-run marginal propensity to consume out of income varies from 0.6 to 0.8, depending upon the specification and measure of the variables. The marginal propensity to consume out of private wealth, including the public's holding of government bonds, ranges from about 0.02 to 0.04. Note that this would imply that a one dollar increase in outstanding government debt would increase consumption by 2 to 4 cents. No explicit test of debt neutrality or the efficacy of fiscal policy is conducted in this framework, since the specifications presume that the impact of changes in debt policy are identical to other changes in private wealth, i.e. that government bonds are part of private wealth. A one dollar tax cut would increase disposable income and therefore consumption by 60 to 80 cents in the short run, while decreasing private saving by a few cents eventually via the wealth effect. Since about 30 cents on the dollar out of the tax cut is saved, wealth will be increased and a dynamic process will continue until the wealth effect leads to further increases in consumption.

A new set of regressions, presented in Table 3.7, adds to the archetypical consumption functions just discussed various measures of the deficit. Regressions, such as these have been used by various authors (Kochin, 1974; Barro, 1978; Feldstein, 1982) in the debate over the effects of government deficits on real economic activity. Note first that in the various specifications the marginal propensity to consume out of disposable income is about 0.75, while the marginal propensity to consume out of private wealth is about 0.015. These estimates are quite precise. The equations perform quite well by the usual summary measures. The nominal deficit, presented in equation (5) appears to decrease consumption by 22 cents per dollar of deficit, holding disposable income constant. An alternative explanation of this result is that this is the impact of increased government spending on consumption since disposable income is being held constant. Alternatively, a one-dollar cut in taxes would have several effects. It would increase the deficit by a dollar and directly decrease consumer spending by 22 cents, but also raise disposable income sufficiently to increase consumption by 75 cents, increase saving substantially, and eventually increase consumption through the increased wealth. Of particular interest is the fact that alternative measures of the deficit, cyclically adjusted (6), the real deficit, accounting for the decline in the

Table 3.6 Private consumption functions

Eq^{no}	Dependent variable[a]	Constant	YN	YN(−1)	YD	YD(−1)	YL	YL(−1)	WPRIV(−1)	ρ	DW	SSR	R^2
1	C*	0.572 (0.111)	0.421 (0.044)	0.137 (0.053)					0.040 (0.008)	0.480 (0.146)	1.6	0.237	0.988
2	C*	0.701 (0.065)			0.485 (0.046)	0.281 (0.054)			0.0129 (0.0060)	0.320 (0.165)	1.9	0.142	0.996
3	CNIPA	0.183 (0.072)			0.597 (0.057)	0.191 (0.067)			0.0202 (0.0067)	0.255 (0.166)	1.8	0.206	0.995
4		0.779 (0.092)					0.627 (0.060)	0.057 (0.070)	0.0383 (0.0074)	0.472 (0.149)	1.6	0.182	0.991

Note:
[a] C* is adjusted consumption as described in the text. CNIPA is NIPA consumer expenditures. The income variables correspond to the consumption definition (adjusted and NIPA). The income variables refer to national (YN), disposable (YD) and labour (YL) income, respectively.

Table 3.7 Tests of the effect of deficits on consumption, alternative definitions of deficits

Eq^{no}	Constant	YD	YD(−1)	DEF	DEFC	RDEF	RDEFC	WPRIV(−1)	P	DW	SSR	R²
5	0.691 (0.073)	0.484 (0.047)	0.283 (0.055)	−0.219 (0.072)				0.0132 (0.0061)	0.314 (0.169)	1.9	0.141	0.996
6	0.831 (0.103)	0.457 (0.058)	0.286 (0.067)		−0.010 (0.133)			0.0154 (0.0064)	0.242 (0.196)	1.9	0.123	0.994
7	0.810 (0.093)	0.456 (0.058)	0.283 (0.067)			−0.045 (0.076)		0.0160 (0.0062)	0.215 (0.197)	1.9	0.121	0.995
8	0.816 (0.096)	0.455 (0.059)	0.288 (0.068)				0.014 (0.102)	0.0154 (0.0063)	0.240 (0.197)	1.9	0.123	0.994
9	2.27 (0.44)	YXG 0.449 (0.050)	YXG(−1) −0.023 (0.050)	0.327 (0.089)				0.053 (0.013)	0.964 (0.033)	1.7	0.188	0.859
10	2.72 (0.597)	0.402 (0.051)	0.006 (0.069)		0.340 (0.151)			0.046 (0.017)	0.976 (0.029)	1.4	0.162	0.891
11	1.73 (0.296)	0.516 (0.049)	0.089 (0.065)			0.403 (0.089)		0.038 (0.014)	0.859 (0.092)	1.8	0.126	0.969
12	2.49 (0.550)	0.403 (0.049)	0.044 (0.070)				0.342 (0.123)	0.046 (0.016)	0.970 (0.034)	1.5	0.151	0.909

Note:
All equations use adjusted consumption and income.
YXG = income less government consumption
DEF = nominal deficit
DEFC = cyclically adjusted deficit
RDEF = inflation adjusted deficit
RDEFC = inflation and cyclically adjusted deficit.

real value of the previously issued national debt (7) and the real cyclically adjusted (6), the real deficit, accounting for the decline in the coefficients which are extremely small and statistically insignificant. However, equations (9)–(12), probably the most important findings presented here, come to quite different conclusions. Here, rather than subtracting taxes from income as a measure of disposable income, government consumption is subtracted. This is much more in the spirit of the Ricardian equivalence hypothesis and we are basically asking: given the level of government consumption, what would a shift from tax to debt finance (or vice versa) do to consumption? With these improved measures of consumption and income, and the better specification of the income variables given the Ricardian equivalence proposition, all four measures of the deficit produced virtually identical results in their impact on consumption. The tax cut, holding government consumption constant unambiguously increases consumption substantially, about 30 to 40 cents on the dollar. Each of the equations performs quite well by traditional summary measures. The propensities to consume out of private wealth increase to about 0.04, whereas the propensity to consume out of expanded income less government consumption (a concept not usually mentioned nor directly comparable to that of disposable income) is about 0.5. The size, statistical significance, and robustness to alternative specifications of the deficits are a strong rejection of the proposition that government financial policy is irrelevant.

Table 3.8 presents alternative estimates of expanded fiscal impacts on consumer expenditures. Equation (13) nets out government bonds from private wealth, treating them in full accord with Ricardian equivalence as if they are not a part of private wealth and estimates a separate coefficient on government wealth holdings (note that since we keep a separate sectoral account for the government, these are treated as liabilities, and therefore their sign would be opposite to what one would normally expect). Once this is done, the estimated coefficients on the regular private wealth term and the government bond term are virtually identical, and while the former is quite statistically significant, the latter is marginally so. Again, it appears as if bonds are perceived as private wealth. The other features of the equations remain quite robust, with a marginal propensity to consume of about 0.7 out of short-run income and about 0.03 out of wealth.

Equation (14) tries to estimate the impact of social security wealth. Various authors have concluded that social security wealth offsets private saving dollar for dollar and should be treated like other

Table 3.8 Effects of augmented government and private wealth on consumption

Eq^{no}	Constant	Y	Y(−1)	WPRIV(−1)	SSW(−1)	WTOT(−1)	WGOV(−1)	NWGOV(−1)	Rho	DW	SSR	R^2
13.	1.46 (0.43)	0.443 (0.067)	0.257 (0.071)			0.027 (0.0077)	0.037 (0.062)		0.641 (0.129)	1.6	0.431	0.960
14.	1.15 (0.19)	0.572 (0.059)	0.022 (0.069)	0.036 (0.0085)	0.017 (0.0075)				0.592 (0.142)	1.5	0.160	0.988
15.	0.972 (0.103)	0.438 (0.046)	0.269 (0.048)			0.016 (0.0031)		0.046 (0.021)	0.046 (0.171)	2.0	0.104	0.998

Notes:
13. National income, government consumption.
14. Labour income.
15. Disposable income.

government obligations. The results reported here with our augmented definitions of income, including the substantial revisions in the social security wealth series pursuant to the 1983 amendments for the last couple of years in the sample, still leave us with a propensity to consume out of social security wealth of about 2 cents on the dollar, about half of that relative to private wealth. Thus, this is consistent with the notion that there is some offset to private saving caused by social security, but substantially less than dollar for dollar.

Finally, equation (15) reports an expanded definition of government capital. The potential impact on private consumption of the value of government tangible capital over government regular debt is examined. The propensity to consume out of what might be called net government explicit assets is about 0.04, quite similar to the propensity to consume out of private wealth found in other specifications, but slightly larger than the propensity to consume out of private wealth in this specification. This would suggest that government tangible assets, i.e. government saving, is a substitute for private saving and allows individuals to expand their consumption. The propensity to consume continues to hover around the 0.7 range.

Table 3.9 reports results examining the effects of deficits, variously defined, on the composition of GNP. From the national income identity, changes in the federal deficit must show up as changes in net foreign investment, domestic investment, private saving, or the state and local surplus. These equations regress these variables as shares of GNP on a constant, a measure of the federal deficit, and to control for the cycle, current and lagged capacity utilisation. The sample period is 1952–84, but in equations (5) and (10), separate coefficients are estimated on the deficits for the periods 1952–72 and 1973–84 to examine the impact of deficits on net foreign investment in the flexible exchange rate period. Each of the specifications suggests that deficits have powerful impacts on the composition of GNP given the level of GNP. Each $1 increase in the federal deficit appears to be associated with about a 30 cent increase in private saving, about a 35 cent decrease in domestic investment, and about a 25 cent decrease in net foreign investment. These results are similar to those reported by Summers (1986).

While this is a reduced form of a larger structural model, and the explanatory power of these results should not be overstated, they do suggest that the debt versus tax finance decision, and/or government spending decisions can substantially affect the composition of GNP.

Table 3.9 The effects of deficits on the composition of GNP

Dependent variable	C	DFED/GNP[a]	CAP[c]	CAP(−1)[c]	DW	R^2
(1) I/GNP	0.067 (0.048)	−0.357 (0.142)	1.64 (0.41)	0.43 (0.27)	1.64	0.85
(2) NFI/GNP	0.049 (0.033)	−0.269 (0.010)	−0.88 (0.29)	0.392 (0.210)	1.63	0.35
(3) SPG/GNP	0.137 (0.042)	0.310 (0.124)	0.359 (0.375)	−0.013 (0.261)	1.99	0.78
(4) SLDEF/GNP	0.016 (0.017)	−0.034 (0.047)	0.377 (0.137)	0.120 (0.090)	1.86	0.30
(5) NFI/GNP[d]	−0.045 (0.034)	−0.289 (0.118) −0.243 (0.115)	0.876 (0.301)	0.397 (0.218)	1.62	0.35
		DFED1/GNP[b]				
(6) I/GNP	0.054 (0.043)	−0.376 (0.132)	1.76 (0.35)	−0.32 (0.26)	1.63	0.85
(7) NFI/GNP	0.031 (0.031)	−0.226 (0.088)	−0.74 (0.27)	0.45 (0.21)	1.56	0.34
(8) SPG/GNP	0.167 (0.027)	0.398 (0.089)	−0.01 (0.25)	−0.05 (0.24)	2.08	0.75
(9) SLDEF/GNP	0.007 (0.014)	0.016 (0.054)	−0.33 (0.12)	0.17 (0.09)	2.08	0.75
(10) NFI/GNP[d]	0.031 (0.031)	−0.257 (0.116) −0.215 (0.093)	0.74 (0.28)	0.46 (0.22)	1.56	0.34

Notes:
Standard errors in parentheses. All equations estimated with first-order serial correlation adjustment. Sample period is 1952–84 except equations (5) and (10) which are estimated for 1973–84.
[a] Nominal federal deficit
[b] Inflation adjusted federal deficit
[c] Estimated coefficients and standard errors should be multiplied by 10^{-3}
[d] First set of coefficients and standard errors for 1952–72 period; second set for 1973–84.

5 CONCLUSION

Despite theoretical and empirical controversies and alternative interpretation of historical episodes, the analysis and results reported above tend to confirm that fiscal policy can affect real economic activity. We discussed numerous avenues by which these effects occur, and that broad aggregates, especially the officially reported nominal aggregates, may be quite misleading in measuring either short-run fiscal stimulus or long-run effects on the composition of output.

The major contribution of the chapter is to introduce extensions of the national income accounts to include a consistent treatment of consumer durables and government capital in the measure of consumption and income, updating the data (relative to previous studies) by several years, a period of substantial swings in the relevant variables, and explicitly testing alternative propositions concerning the effects of government financial policy on real economic activity. By far the most important conclusion is that holding government *consumption* constant, deficits appear to increase private consumption. Numerous explanations of this result are possible, and I do not distinguish among them, e.g. liquidity constraints, myopia, fiscal signals, etc. Further, the impact of increases in federal deficits on the composition of GNP, given GNP, is a modest increase in private saving and a substantial decrease in domestic investment and net foreign investment (i.e. increase in net inflow of capital).

Much of the work alluded to or briefly summarised in this chapter is still in progress. Indeed, the substantial attention being placed on improved measures of government fiscal activity attests to its potential importance.

Notes

This paper draws heavily on the material developed for my project on more comprehensive and comprehensible federal government financial statements. It is meant to give an overview of the issues involved, not to resolve them. I am grateful to John M. Roberts and Brad Barham for their valuable research assistance, and to participants at the IEA Conference for valuable comments and suggestions.

1. An exciting recent development is the attempt by various government agencies to provide more comprehensive data than that traditionally used.
2. These issues are recognised by researchers with mutually exclusive views on the impact of deficits and debt. See Barro (1985) and Feldstein (1982), as important examples.

3. This simple analysis is in the spirit of the more detailed models presented in Buiter (1983) and Sargent and Wallace (1981).
4. See Barro (1981) and Brunner (1985). Barro focuses on temporary increases in government spending above trend or permanent levels, increasing interest rates and signalling the private sector to consume less and produce more.
5. Boskin (1982) and Boskin and Kotlikoff (1985) provide extensive discussions of the failure of officially recorded debt to measure underlying redistribution to older generations. One might argue that zero intergenerational transfers is an objective benchmark. There are at least two problems with such a benchmark. First, distinguishing negative intergenerational transfers from taxes required to finance government consumption is inherently somewhat arbitrary. Secondly, past intergenerational transfers imply (require) offsetting current or future intergeneration transfers. Hence, taking zero intergenerational transfers as the benchmark requires considering a world in which intergenerational transfers in the past had always been zero.
6. Tanzi (1985) presents evidence of the effects of US fiscal deficits on interest rates which would support this effect on the composition of GNP.
7. Also see Kochin (1974) and Tanner (1979).
8. An excellent discussion of these points may be found Chapter 2.
9. See the references in Boskin, Robinson and Huber (1987), and Eisner and Pieper (1984) for examples.
10. The basic estimates in Boskin, Robinson, O'Reilly and Kumar (1985) are derived from a model of expected present value of bonuses and royalty payments on economically recoverable reserves as estimated by the US Geological Service, both on and off shore (see the paper for details).
11. Other problems with this concept exist. For example, the change in unemployment contemplated may bring with it a host of other changes (e.g. in inflation) that may affect the size of the deficit.

REFERENCES

Ando, Alberto and Modigliani, Franco (1963) "The 'Life Cycle' Hypothesis of Saving: Aggregate Implications and Tests" *American Economic Review* vol. 53, March, pp. 55–84.

Auerbach, A. J. and Kotlikoff, L. J. (1983a) 'National Savings, Economic Welfare, and the Structure of Taxation', in Feldstein, M. (ed.) *Behavioral Simulation Methods in Tax Policy Analysis*, (Chicago: University of Chicago Press), pp. 459–93.

Auerbach, A. J. and Kotlikoff, L. J. (1983b) 'Investment Versus Saving Incentives: The Biggest Bang for the Buck and the Potential for Self-Financing Business Tax Cuts', in Meyer, L. H. (ed.) *The Economic Consequences of Government Deficits* (Boston: Kluwer-Nijhoff Publishing), pp. 121–54.

Auerbach, A. J. and Kotlikoff, L. J. (1983c) 'An Examination of Empirical Tests of Social Security and Savings', in Helpman, E. *et al.* (ed.)

Social Policy Evaluation: An Economic Perspective (New York: Academic Press 1984).
Bailey, M. (1962) National Income and the Price Level (New York: McGraw-Hill).
Barro, R. (1974) 'Are Government Bonds Net Wealth?', Journal of Political Economy, vol. 82, no. 6, pp. 1095–117.
Barro, R. (1978) The Impact of Social Security on Private Sacings (Washington, DC, American Enterprise Institute).
Barro, R. (1981) 'Output Effects of Government Purchases', Journal of Political Economy, vol. 89, December, pp. 1086–121.
Barro, R. (1985) 'Government Spending, Interest rates, Prices and Budget Deficits in the United Kingdom, 1730–1918', Rochester Center for Economic Research Working Paper, No. 1.
Barro, R. and Sahasakul, C. (1983) 'Measuring the Average Marginal Tax Rate from the Individual Income Tax', Journal of Business, vol. 56, no. 4, pp. 419–52.
Barth, James R., Iden, George and Russek, Frank S. (1984) 'Do Federal Deficits Really Matter', Contemporary Policy Issues, vol. III, Fall, pp. 79–95.
Bernheim, D. (1984) 'Dissaving After Retirement', National Bureau of Economic Research Working Paper No. 1409, July (New York).
Blinder, A., Gordon, R. H. and Wise, D. E. (1980) 'Social Security, Bequests and the Life Cycle Theory of Savings: Cross-Sectional Tests', National Bureau of Economic Research Working Paper No. 619, (New York).
Blinder, A. and Solow, Robert M. (1973) 'Does Fiscal Policy Matter?', Journal of Public Economics, vol. 2, November, pp. 319–37.
Boskin, M. J. (1978) 'Taxation, Saving, and the Rate of Interest', Journal of Political Economy, vol. 86, no. 2, April, Part 2, pp. 3–27.
Boskin, M. (1982) 'Federal Government Deficits: Some Myths and Realities', American Economic Review, vol. 72, May, pp. 296–303.
Boskin, M. (1986) Too Many Promises: The Uncertain Future of Social Security (Homewood, IL: Dow Jones-Irwin).
Boskin, M. (forthcoming 1988) The Real Federal Budget, forthcoming Cambridge, Mass.: Harvard University Press).
Boskin, M. (1987) 'Future Social Security Financing Alternatives and National Saving', NBER Working Paper No. 2256, in S. Wachter (ed.) Financing Retirement in the 21st Century (D. C. Heath & Co.).
Boskin, M., Barham, B., Cone, K. and Ozler, S. (1987) 'The Federal Budget and Federal Insurance Programs', in Boskin, M. (ed.), Modern Developments in Public Finance (Oxford: Basil Blackwell).
Boskin, M. and Hurd, M. (1984) 'The Effect of Social Security on Retirement in the Early 1970s', Quarterly Journal of Economics, vol. 99, no. 4, November, pp. 67–90.
Boskin, M. and Kotlikoff, L. (1985) 'Public Debt and US Saving: A New Test of the Neutrality Hypothesis.' Carnegie-Rochester Conference Series, Summer.
Boskin, M. and Kotlikoff, L., Puffert, D. and Shoven, J. (1987) 'Social Security: A financial Appraisal Across and Within Generations', National Tax Journal, March, vol. 40, no. 1, pp. 19–34.
Boskin, M. and Robinson, M. (1987) 'The Value of Federal Mineral

Rights: Correction and Update', *American Economic Review*, December, pp. 1073-4.

Boskin, M., Robinson, M. and Huber, A. (1987) 'Government Saving, Capital Formation and Wealth in the United States, 1947-1985', NBER Working Paper, 1987, forthcoming in Lipsey, R. and Tice, H. S. (eds), *The Measurement of Saving, Investment and Wealth* (New York: NBER and University of Chicago Press).

Boskin, M., Robinson, M., O'Reilly, T. and Kumar, P. (1985) 'New Estimates of the Value of Federal Mineral Rights and Land', *American Economic Review*, December, vol. 75, no. 5, pp. 923-36.

Boskin, M., Robinson, M. and Roberts, J. (1985) 'New Estimates of Federal Government Tangible Capital and Net Investment', NBER Working Paper, No. 1774, (New York).

Brunner, K. (1985) 'Fiscal Policy in Macro Theory: A Survey and Evaluation', unpublished mimeo, University of Rochester.

Buiter, William H. (1983) 'Measurement of the Public Sector Deficit and Its Implications for Policy Evaluation and Design', IMF Staff Papers, June, 30, 306-49.

Buiter, William H. and James Tobin (1980) 'Debt Neutrality: A Brief Review of Doctrine and Evidience', in von Furstenberg, George M. (ed.) *Social Security versus Private Saving*, (Ballinger Publishing Co.), pp. 39-63.

Bureau of Economic Analysis (BEA), US Dept of Commerce (1982), 'Fixed Reproducible Tangible Wealth in the United States, 1925-79', (Washington, DC).

Cagan, P. (1981) 'The Real Federal Deficit and Financial Markets', *The AEI Economist*, November.

Darby, M. R. (1979) *The Effects of Social Security on Income and the Capital Stock* (Washington, DC, American Enterprise Institute).

David, M. and Menchik, P. (1980) 'The Effect of Income Distribution and Redistribution on Lifetime Saving and Bequests', University of Wisconsin Institute for Research on Poverty Discussion Paper No. 582.

de Leeuw, F. and Holloway, T. (1985) 'The Measurement and Significance of the Cyclically Adjusted Federal Budget and Debt', *Journal of Money, Credit and Banking*, vol. 17, May, pp. 232-42.

Diamond, P. and Hausman, J. (1984) 'Individual Retirement and Savings Behavior', *Journal of Public Economics*, vol. 23, pp. 81-114.

Eisner, R. (1986) *How Real Is the Federal Deficit?* (New York: Free Press).

Eisner, R. and Pieper, P. J. (1984) 'A New View of the Federal Debt and Budget Deficits', *American Economic Review*, vol. 74, March, pp. 11-20.

Federal Reserve, Board of Governors, Flow of Funds Division (1986) 'Balance Sheets for the US 1948-85' (Washington, DC).

Feldstein, M. (1986) 'Budget Deficits and the Dollar', NBER Working Paper.

Feldstein, M. (1982) 'Government Deficits and Aggregate Demand', *Journal of Monetary Economics*, vol. 9, January, pp. 1-20.

Feldstein, M. (1974) 'Social Security, Induced Retirement, and Aggregate Capital Accumulation', *Journal of Political Economy*, pp. 905-26.

Feldstein, M. and Pellechio, A. (1979) 'Social Security and Household Wealth Accumulation: New Microeconomic Evidence', *Review of Economics and Statistics*, vol. 61, pp. 361-8.

Gale, W. (1986) 'Federal Lending Policy and the Credit Market', preliminary.

Howrey, E. P. and Hymans, S. H. (1980) 'The Measurement and Determination of Loanable-Funds Saving', *Brookings Papers on Economic Activity 3*, 1978. Also in Pechman, J. A. (ed.) *What Should Be Taxed: Income or Expenditure?* (Washington, DC: The Brookings Institution).
Hulten, C. and Peterson, G. (1984) 'The Public Capital Stock: Needs, Trends, Performance', *American Economic Review*, vol. 74, May.
Hurd, M. (1986) 'Savings and Bequests', New York: NBER Working Paper No. 1826, January.
King, M. A. and Dicks-Mireaux, L. (1982) 'Asset Holdings and the Life Cycle', *Economic Journal*, vol. 92, no. 366, pp. 247–67.
Kochin, L. (1974) 'Are Future Taxes Anticipated by Consumers?', *Journal of Money, Credit and Banking*, vol. 6, pp. 385–94.
Kormendi, Roger C. (1983) 'Government Debt, Government Spending, and Private Sector Behavior', *American Economic Review*, vol. 73, December, pp. 994–1010.
Kotlikoff, L. J. (1979) 'Testing the Theory of Social Security and Life Cycle Accumulation', *American Economic Review*, vol. 69, June, pp. 396–410.
Kotlikoff, L. J. and Summers, L. (1981) 'The Role of Intergenerational Transfers in Aggregate Capital Accumulation', *Journal of Political Economy* vol. 89, no. 4, pp. 706–32.
Leimer, D. and Lesnoy, S. (1982) 'Social Security and Private Saving: New Time Series Evidence', *Journal of Political Economy*, vol. 90, pp. 606–29.
Miller, M. (1982) 'Inflation-Adjusting The Public Sector Financial Deficit', in Kay, J. (ed.), *The 1982 Budget* (Oxford: Blackwell).
Mirer, T. W. (1979) 'The Wealth-Age Relations Among the Aged', *American Economic Review*, vol. 69, June, pp. 435–43.
Modigliani, F. and Brumberg, R. (1954) 'Utility Analysis and the Consumption Function: An Interpretation of Cross-Section Data', in Kurihara, K. E. (ed.), *Post-Keynesian Economics* (New Brunswick, NJ: Rutgers University Press).
Modigliani, F. and Japelli, T. (1986) 'Fiscal Policy and Saving in Italy Since 1860', International Conference on Private Saving and Public Debt, in Boskin, M., Flemming, J. and Gorini, S. (eds), *Private Saving and Public Debt* (Oxford: Basil Blackwell).
Penner, R. (1981) 'Forecasting Budget Totals: Why Can't We Get It Right?', *AEI Economist*.
Sargent, Thomas J. and Wallace, Neil (1981) 'Some Unpleasant Monetarist Arithmetic', *Quarterly Review*, Federal Reserve Bank of Minneapolis, vol. 5, Fall, pp. 1–17.
Stiglitz, J. (1988) 'On the Relevance or Irrelevance of Public Finance Policy', in Arrow, K. and Boskin, M. (eds), *The Economics of Public Debt*, (London: Macmillan for the International Economics Association).
Summers, L. A. (1981) 'Capital Taxation and Accumulation in a Life Cycle Growth Model', *American Economic Review*, vol. 71, September, pp. 533–44.
Summers, L. A. (1985) 'The After Tax Return Does Affect Private Savings', *American Economics Association Meetings Papers and Proceedings*.
Summers, L. A. (1986) 'Issues in National Savings Policy', in Adams, G. and Wachter, S. (eds), *Saving and Capital Formation*, (Lexington: D. C. Heath).

Summers, L. A. (1987) 'The Asset Price Approach to the Analysis of Capital Income Taxation', in Boskin, M. (ed.), *Modern Developments in Public Finance* (Oxford: Basil Blackwell).

Tanner, J. (1979) 'Fiscal Policy and Consumer Behavior', *Review of Economics and Statistics*, vol. 61, no. 2, May, pp. 317–21.

Tanzi, V. (1985) 'Fiscal Deficits and Interest Rates in the United States: An Empirical Analysis, 1960–84', Fiscal Department of Affairs, IMF, August.

Tobin, J. (1967) 'Life Cycle Saving and Balanced Growth', in Fellner, W. (ed.), *Ten Essays in Honor of Irving Fisher* (New York: John Wiley).

US Department of Commerce, Bureau of Economic Analysis (1982) 'Fixed Reproducible Tangible Wealth in the United States 1925–79' (Washington, DC).

DISCUSSION

Professor Paul Pieper was the principal discussant of Michael Boskin's paper. Pieper's overall view was that there were many items that could be included in the government balance sheets, but that the criterion to be used varied with the application intended. Different times will have different effects on the economy, and so one must be careful of the way in which these items are included. Pieper then began a consideration of several items, which was not intended to be exhaustive. He began with land and mineral rights. He noted that these could be expected to affect future revenue needs, with royalties potentially offsetting the need for tax revenue. Pieper pointed out the analogy between land and mineral rights and gold. On tangible capital, Pieper suggested that a separate capital account would allow a proper consideration of the effect of government investment on future income and thus on future taxes, and on future government consumption.

Pieper next turned to contingent-type items. Loans made by the government should not be counted as assets at full value because of default risk. Pieper cites Boskin as saying that items should be valued at 88 cents on the dollar. Insurance commitments, such as those through the FDIC, are more problematical. While clearly not treated properly in the current system, it is difficult to decide on an appropriate expected value for these items.

Pieper suggested Feldstein's approach as one way of calculating social security wealth. He pointed out in this approach that what really matters is the public's perception of what social security is worth to them. An interesting case is the 1983 law changes. These changes led to an estimated two trillion dollar drop in social security wealth, and should have led to a large drop in consumption.

Pieper came to the conclusion that, depending on what one chose to include, one got very different views of the Federal financial picture. He was interested in knowing Boskin's view of the overall picture, in particular, wondering which elements Boskin was willing to aggregate. Pieper also wondered how one ought to treat the various uncertain claims, whether one would want to use certainty equivalents.

Turning to Boskin's empirical results, Pieper pointed first to Table 3.7, where it appeared that Boskin had provided additional evidence that tended to reject Ricardian equivalence. A rise in the deficit seemed to have the effect of leading to an increase in consumption, suggesting that the debt was considered to be net wealth. In Table 3.8, the results suggested that deficits did crowd out investment, contrary to Pieper's own results with Eisner. But Pieper point out that Boskin's regressions were run with the deficit itself, rather than with the cyclically adjusted deficit, so that Boskin may be capturing cyclical effects that do not reflect the long-run impact of deficits.

Professor Boskin began his response by noting that the official US federal budget is a poor guide to the government's actual wealth position. He noted that in 1982, at the trough of the recession and the onset of the international debt crisis, the FDIC was said to have made two billion dollars in profit simply because insurance premia in that year exceeded outlays. The calculations were in no way forward looking, so that no loss reserves were set aside, as they would have been in the private sector.

In response to Pieper's query as to whether he would be willing to add up to the various components, Boskin responded that he would not. Boskin noted Pieper's own observation that the various components have very different risk components, so that it would be inappropriate to add them up.

Boskin also noted that government actions that have no impact on the aggregate Federal financial position can have an impact on real variables. He cited his work with Kotlikoff (1985), which showed that changing the age distribution of assets can have an impact on aggregate consumption. As well as providing an additional test of the neutrality hypothesis, this exercise points to the importance of population heterogeneity, as emphasised by Professor Kurz. Boskin cited as another example the fact that although the impacts of inflation on mortgages do net in the private sector, inflation does have the effect of moving resources around and, because the borrowers and lenders are potentially systematically different, the shift in resources can have an impact.

Turning to his empirical results, Boskin focused on equations 9 through 12 of Table 3.7. Income net of government consumption rather than net of taxes comes close to what Barro might mean by permanent income net of permanent government consumption. Hence, the deficit in this case is capturing the effect of variation in taxes. Thus, increases in deficits do lead to higher consumption. Boskin notes that in a Barro world, we would expect the signs on the deficit to be -1. Instead we get 0.3.

Boskin noted that because of heterogeneity, each fiscal action of the government requires a close examination. One needs to consider what kinds of signals the private sector can get from government actions. For example, does a government capital build-up mean lower taxes on the future? Boskin concluded with a word of caution, noting that the view one takes of government net worth is dependent on what question one is trying to answer.

In the general discussion, *Professor Marc Robinson* remarked that he was willing to go a step further than Boskin in stating what he was willing to aggregate. As far as the asset side of the government balance sheet was concerned, Robinson felt that land and tangible capital should certainly be included, because leaving these out leads to a misstatement of national wealth. On the other hand, Robinson felt that less was lost by excluding loan and insurance commitments, since the effects of these were only distributional, and thus of second order importance on national wealth relative to land and tangible capital.

Professor Ephraim Kleiman felt that Boskin's work was useful in attempting to bring Goldsmith up to date, and in attempting to bring additional items into the national balance sheet. But Kleiman noted that many of Goldsmith's exclusions may have been made on the basis of the sensitivity of the excluded items to people's perceptions. Taking mineral rights as an example, Kleiman noted that rather than assuming that the future revenues meant lower taxes in the future, one should also consider the possibility that the government might spend the money.

Professor Stiglitz took exception to Kleiman's assumption that government consumption was of little value to consumers. He noted that some government consumption is a close substitute for private consumption. And, if we view contingencies only as redistributions, then we have to remember that these are commitments to redistribute in the future. A loan guarantee is a state-contingent commitment to redistribute income and different from an unfunded liability.

Professor Boskin suggested that Stiglitz ought to be sympathetic to the potential benefits of Federal government intervention in lending policy, citing the numerous works of Stiglitz on potential private market failures in lending policy.

Professor Richard Musgrave asked about the extent to which changes on the asset side of the government balance sheet were important. Robinson responded that in the 1980s, the falling value of land and mineral rights was compounding the large current account deficits of the Federal government, so that it appeared that the government had consumed something on the order of two trillion (2×10^9) dollars, not an insignificant amount.

Professor Mordecai Kurz asked how one was to use these numbers. He noted that the government is a monopolist with respect to many of its assets, and could determine the value of them by its own action. He noted that selling the national parks would raise their value relative to keeping them as natural preserves. The issue is thus not how to measure government wealth, but how to use these measures in a behavioural world.

Mr John Flemming suggested that the real interest rate might be an important variable to include in an empirical consumption function.

Professor Boskin, in his concluding remarks, said that he was quite sympathetic to the idea of including the real interest rate, noting that he himself had been among the first to introduce the real rate. He also acknowledged Mordecai Kurz's point, that the notion of net worth used depends on the question asked. He noted that this point was made several times in the text.

Boskin noted that loan guarantee commitments are worth hundreds of billions of dollars, and that to the extent that the recipients are liquidity constrained, which they should be to qualify for the guarantee, those guarantees ought to affect real behaviour. He also acknowledged his links with Goldsmith's work, and noted that, like Goldsmith, he was hesitant about adding certain components together. He also noted, though, that because of advances in several theoretical areas, such as natural resource economics, one was able to come to firmer conclusions about how certain items ought to be counted.

Boskin discussed the point, mentioned by Stiglitz earlier, about whether government consumption substitutes for or complements private consumption. He suggested that the effect depended on the particular government expenditure considered, whether roads or nursing homes.

Finally, Boskin raised the issue of the information conveyed by any particular government action about future government actions, and the respective roles of anticipated and unanticipated government actions.

4 Optimum Fiscal Policy when Monetary Policy is Bound by a Rule: Ramsey Redux

Edmund S. Phelps
COLUMBIA UNIVERSITY, NEW YORK

and Kumaraswamy Velupillai*
AALBORG UNIVERSITY CENTER

1 INTRODUCTION

The Keynesian revolution, whatever Keynes's own views, fostered the precept that fiscal policy – the determination of government spending and taxation – should be put at the service of employment stabilisation. This calls for 'functional finance', as its early proponent Abba Lerner (1944) dubbed it, and it became one of the essential tenets of paleo-Keynesian thought. Make the budget stimulative when the economy shows slack, said those Keynesians favouring automatic over-discretionary stabilisation. Make the budget stimulative when the economy shows signs of incipient slack in order to avert that slack, said those advocating discretionary stabilisation. On either view monetary policy was to play the role of keeping real interest rates low in order to hasten the day of full investment, to use Alvin Hansen's (1960) term for the golden rule state.

In the 1950s the group of young theorists who came to be called neo-Keynesians took the first step in their reevaluation of Keynesian doctrine by rebelling against functional finance.[1] A series of papers by Paul Samuelson (1951, 1953, 1956) articulated a counter-vision: let public expenditures be determined by neoclassical principles as begun by Pigou (1932) and Meade (1951), and let target tax revenue be governed equally neoclassically by the intertemporal optimum saving and investment considerations of Ramsey (1928) and Hotelling. The responsibility for stabilising employment could then be reassigned to the monetary authorities.[2] In retrospect, it appears that the differences between the old and new doctrines were a matter of means more than ends. The much-maligned Keynesians also had read Ramsey and valued optimum capital deepening. However, the neo-Keynesians were clearer in their formulation and right in their intuitive judgement that monetary policy had the comparative advantage (over fiscal policy) in performing the stabilisation function.

Then a certain sadness breaks into the story. The Keynes–Samuelson Camelot is criticised as unworkable and a dangerous model for the real world to apply. The old Austro–Hungarian notion that inflation (or an added amount of it) is ultimately incapable of 'buying' additional output and employment was finally formalised in terms of expectations so that Keynesians, old and new, could understand the claim and no longer ignore it. This meant that equilibrium, speaking loosely, is a sort of razor's edge: unless the stabilisation authorities happen to be attempting to stabilise employment around the true equilibrium level they in time generate hyperinflation or depression. Hence it is safer to stabilise some nominal variable such as the exchange rate, the price level, nominal income or expenditure, or the money supply. It came also to be argued, notably by the monetarists of the Chicago school, that the career ambitions of self-interested central bankers might cause them on occasion to diverge from the agreed stabilisation object if they have the discretionary powers to do so; it is better to require their adherence to an operational rule for monetary policy, such as a fixed money supply or fixed exchange rate, and to hold them accountable for any slippage from the standard. It is also worth something that the brave notion of a timeless monetary rule was congenial to the new econometric breed of macroeconomists who could quickly calculate the steady-state operating properties of rival rules in stationary stochastic models. For all these reasons, we have witnessed in recent years a tendency among Western countries for monetary policy to be more rule-bound, or at any rate more rule conscious, than early Keynesian thought envisioned – though the rules have sometimes changed and they have not always been observed.

If monetary policy is bound by a nominal rule, the rug is pulled out from under Samuelson's rationale for basing fiscal policy on the neoclassical principles of Ramsey and Pigou: fiscal policy will have Keynesian demand effects upon employment if the latter is not being stabilised (directly or indirectly) by the monetary authority. On the other hand, it is also hard to see any rationale for devoting fiscal policy singlemindedly to the stabilisation of output or employment – regardless of the decumulation of national wealth – as supply siders appear to favour.

The present paper briefly explores the possibilities of synthesising the optimum-stabilisation approach to fiscal policy and the optimum-growth approach in an economy in which monetary policy is tied up by a nominal rule. We begin with a discussion of the modelling decisions faced along the way and an unveiling of the chosen model. The chapter proceeds to an analysis of the properties of the optimum fiscal policy. Particular attention is paid to its comparison with the optimum policy in the Ramseyesque full employment at no cost case, adopting Ramsey's utilitarian optimality criterion so as not to make the two problems unnecessarily dissimilar. A 'second best' version of the model that heightens the tension between the Keynesian and neoclassical objectives is also taken up.

2 MODELLING THE PROBLEM OF INTERTEMPORALLY OPTIMAL FISCAL POLICY

We want a model of fiscal policy that has points of contact with the 1928 model of optimum national saving by Frank Ramsey and yet does not neglect excessively the conceptual advances that have occurred since. One of these advances, surely, is the representation (first implemented by Arrow and Kurz and by Mirrlees) of the micro-optimisation by households – their private saving decisions – 'inside' the macro-optimisation by the government – its public saving decision and public expenditure decision, taking account of their ramifications upon private decisions. This feature has been introduced nicely in Chapter 7, John Flemming, on the intertemporally optimum fiscal policy. But in that model a tax cut imparts no Keynesian demand effects, which is a feature we want here.

The difficulties of modelling the micro-optimisation of saving is circumvented by postulating that households in our model neither retire nor bequeath and over the entire range of circumstances arising in our analysis, they consume all of their income continuously over their lives. This *is* optimising behaviour if their rate of pure time preference always exceeds the relevant real rate of interest, and so they do not desire to exchange present for future consumption; we may suppose that credit rationing restrains their dissaving – from exchanging future for present consumption.

It follows that the national wealth of our hypothetical country, denoted S, is entirely in the hands of the government, being the product of past acts of public saving, that is, fiscal surpluses. The rate of national saving is

$$dS/dt = rS + p(T-G)$$

where S is measured in units of the capital good. G (Government expenditure) and T (taxes collected) are measured in units of the consumer good, whose relative price is p. Here r is the own interest rate and 'foreign real rate'.

The other state variable in our model is the nominal wage. As the underlying Keynesian imperfection we adopt the tradition and tractable assumption that there is some sluggishness in the adjustment of the average money wage, W. This feature is described by a Phillips Curve relation between the proportionate rate of wage change, or wage inflation rate, and the excess of employment, N, over its structural, or zero-wage-change level, N^*. Hence

$$dW/dt = W\phi.[N - N^*], \qquad \phi > 0.$$

Such a purportedly stable relation would be out of place in many other contexts, of course, but it is not inappropriate here.

The next problem is to conjure up an open economy so structured that fiscal stimulus, either in the form of increased public expenditure (of a certain kind at any rate) or a consumption-inducing tax cut, is effective in increasing aggregate demand and employment – given the sluggishness of the average money wage and given, also the nominal rule followed by the monetary authority. It might seem that the fixed exchange rate rule in conjunction with the structure of the Mundell–Fleming open economy model would nicely serve the purpose. However, that otherwise convenient case has the drawback that increased consumer demand springing from a tax cut (or any other cause) would not appear to provide any boost to demand for domestic output: the extra consumer goods, being tradable in that model, are obtainable through extra imports or reduced exports – a crowding out of net foreign investment – without entailing increased domestic employment and gross domestic product.[3] Moreover, one would prefer a model having only one consumer good so that 'consumption' and the 'real interest rate' are readily and simply interpreted.

A model better suiting our purposes has been devised here in consultation with Slobodan Djajic, whose suggestions and analyses have been most helpful. The key feature of the model given here is that there is a single consumer good and it is non-tradable – say, books in the local language. It requires for its production the importation of the services of some capital good or the importation of some intermediate good (a semi-finished, or unassembled, consumer good) or both; the world prices of this service and this intermediate good are given and (for simplicity) constant over time. In the tradable sector, capital and labour combine to produce another product for export, some raw material. Constant returns to scale, shiftability of capital to and from abroad, mobility of employed and unemployed labour, and pure competition prevail. To determine the scale of the export sector we carry over the Mundell–Fleming demand curve for exports, which asserts that there is something unusual about these exports, rather than introduce customer markets (hence another set of dynamics) or a third factor of production (hence rent income at home or else foreign ownership of all land). To minimise dynamics, the capital stocks in the two sectors are permitted to jump up or down. Other features of the model will become clear.

An increase of government expenditure, G, or decrease of taxes collected, T, generates an equal increase of demand for the output of the (non-tradable) consumer good. Under the rule of a fixed exchange rate, the effect will be a positive jump of capital and employment in the non-tradable sector in equal proportion, with no change occurring in the tradable (export) sector. The increased demand for money is matched by an equal increase of the supply to prevent appreciation of the currency. Note that the so-called capital widening in the non-tradable sector, an equi-proportionate increase of inputs and output that is caused by an increase of $G - T$ leaves p, which is the price of the consumer-good output there relative to the price of the capital-good input there, unchanged; p is invariant to $G - T$.

The effect of a change of W is more complicated, unfortunately. A decrease of W, in lowering prices in both the tradable and non-tradable sectors, increases real cash balances so that the money supply will support a larger level of output, which means an increased output of exports (since consumer demand, we are assuming, feels no Pigou effect). However, there is also a substitution away from capital toward labour in the consumer-good producing sector because the rental on capital goods does not decrease when W decreases. It follows that the money wage decreases relatively to the money price of the consumer good, so that the real wage, v, is seen to be an increasing function of the money wage: $v'(W) > 0$. Also, there is a fall of the price of the consumer good relative to the price of the capital good, which is our relative price p. Hence p is an increasing function of the money wage: $p'(W) > 0$. In the optimisation analysis that follows, however, v and p will be taken to be constants, thus neglecting the influence of W on them. (We therefore set p to equal to 1.) Hence, for private consumption we write

$$C = vN - T, \quad v = \text{constant} > 0$$

For employment we write the reduced-form equation

$$N = N(G - T, W), \quad N_G(= -N_T) > 0, \quad N_W < 0.$$

The variables N, C, and G completely determine utility, U.

Our Phillips Curve equation for the rate of wage inflation contains the equilibrium employment level, N^*. This may be taken to be a variable, like the quantity of labour supplied to the labour market, rather than a parameter. The function giving N^* differs from the labour supply function in subtracting from the latter the extent of job rationing, it may be supposed. If the amount of labour supplied is an *increasing* function of the after-tax wage rate, as many model builders regularly postulate, then N^* may also increase with the after-tax wage. For the sake of definiteness, and to make contact with supply side doctrine as well, it will be supposed that that is the case. Hence an increase of T in raising the tax rate on wage income causes N^* to fall. In principle, of course, what matters for N^* is T as a ratio to real wage income, $vN(G - T, W)$; hence increased G and decreased W cause N^* to rise by widening the tax base, and increased T has a doubly deleterious effect on N^*. But we shall suppose that these latter effects are not of sufficient importance to make a qualitative difference. We therefore have

$$N^* = N^*(T, N), \quad N_T^* < 0, \quad 0 < N_N^* < 1$$

and

$$dw/dt = \phi \cdot W[N(G - T, W) - N^*(T, N)] \equiv W\phi(T, G, W),$$

$$-\phi N_T^* = \Phi_G + \Phi_T > 0, \quad \Phi_G > 0, \quad \Phi_W < 0$$

We cannot put a sign to Φ_T; traditional Keynesians conceive it to be negative, at most zero, but it could be that N falls by less than N^* does when T is increased, so wage inflation, Φ, goes up. It will be seen that the borderline case $\Phi_T = 0$ is convenient.

Finally, we specify that the instantaneous rate of social (average) utility, U, is a function of public expenditure, G, consumption, C, and employment, N, with *positive* and *diminishing* marginal utilities. Adopting Ramsey's axiom of utility satiation we postulate that there is an upper bound to the rate of utility, the 'bliss' level denoted by B, which is reached only in the limit as G and C go to infinity; following recent convention B is usually set equal to zero, leaving U everywhere negative. In our notation,

$$U = U(G, vN(G - T, W) - T, N(G - T, W))$$

$$\equiv u(G, T, W), u_G > 0, u_T < 0, u_W\, 0.$$

Since the inclusion of employment, N, as an argument of the U function does not seem to add a crucial ingredient we often dispense with it, writing instead $U(G, vN - T)$ for the rate of utility.

Our problem is the analogue of Ramsey's:

$$\underset{\{G,T\}}{\text{Max}} \quad \int_0^\infty u(G, T, W) dt$$

subject to
$$dS/dt = rS + T - G$$
$$dW/dt = W\phi(G, T, W),$$

and given initial conditions S_o and W_o.

The Ramsey problem, translated to the present context, may be interpreted as treating the money wage as instantly self-adjusting or else costlessly accommodated by rule-free monetary policy and as neglecting the distortion from tax rates. It is:

$$\underset{\{G, T\}}{\text{Max}} \quad \int_0^\infty u(G, T) dt$$

subject to
$$dS/dt = rS + T - G$$

and given the initial condition S_o.

Our main interest is in comparing the solutions to these problems.

3 RESULTS FROM THE OPTIMUM FISCAL POLICY MODEL

Our optimisation problem and Ramsey's both seem to be well suited to the dynamic programming approach by Bellman so let us try to extract some findings with that approach to begin with. The Ramsey problem in its present translation gives the familiar Bellman equation

$$0 = \underset{G, T}{\text{Max}} [u(G, T) + (rS + T - G)f'(S)],$$

where $f(S)$ is the value of the maximised integral considered as a function of the initial (or currently available) national wealth, S. At the currently optimal G and T, therefore,

$$0 = u(G, T) + (rS + T - G)f'(S)$$

$$0 = u_G - f'(S)$$

$$0 = u_T + f'(S).$$

Solving for the unknown constant $f'(S)$ from the top equation we find

$$0 = -u(-1) + u_G dS/dt$$

$$0 = -u + u_T dS/dt.$$

These equations say essentially that marginal benefit (viewed intertemporally) equals marginal cost along the optimal path. They are recognisable as close analogues of the Ramsey–Meade expression for the optimum rate of saving.[4]

If T is assigned to controlling dS/dt, it may be concluded that:

$$0 = -u + u_T dS/dt \qquad \text{(Ramsey)}$$

$$u_G = -u_T \qquad \text{(Pigou)}$$

Neither Ramsey nor Pigou's principle need be compromised by considerations of wage dynamics.

The Bellman equation for our present problem, with its two control variables now controlling the motion of the two state variables S and

W, is a straightforward generalisation of the previous Bellman equation:

$$0 = \underset{G, T}{\text{Max}}[u(G, T, W) + f_S(S, W)dS/dt + f_W(S, W)dW/dt],$$

where $f(S, W)$ is the maximised overlife utility integral, an unknown function of the initial state S_o and W_o. Hence, at optimal G and T,

$$0 = u + (tS + T - G)f_S(S, W) + W\Phi(G, T, W)f_W(S, W)$$

$$0 = u_G - f_S(S, W) + W\Phi_G f_W(S, W)$$

$$0 = u_T + f_S(S, W) + W\Phi_T f_W(S, W)$$

The last two equations yield

$$f_S(S, W) = \frac{-u_T W\Phi_G + u_G W\Phi_T}{W(\Phi_G + \Phi_T)}, \quad f_W(S, W) = \frac{-u_G - u_T}{W(\Phi_G + \Phi_T)}.$$

Upon substituting these results into the first of the above trio of equations we obtain our analogue of the Ramsey–Keynes–Meade condition:

$$0 = u + \frac{-u_T W\Phi_G + u_G W\Phi_T}{W(\Phi_G + \Phi_T)}(dS/dt) + \frac{-u_G - u_T}{W(\Phi_G + \Phi_T)}(dW/dt)$$

This equation is trying to tell us something about the extent to which costly sacrifices through positive dS/dt and negative dW/dt should be borne for the sake of advancing the schedule for the climb of u toward the bliss level. But clearly we are one equation short for determining the separate motion of S and W. The method of dynamic programming seems to be inefficient, having somehow burned up information along the way to the last result. Before leaving this result, however, we note that the coefficient of dW/dt is proportional to the *net* marginal utility of an equal increase of G and T, and the coefficient of dS/dt is a weighted average of the marginal utility of G and the marginal utility of tax reduction (that is, the marginal utility of $-T$). This invites the interpretation that the variable $G - T$, called in public finance the primary (algebraic) budgetary surplus (as distinct from the total surplus which includes the net interest earned), is employed to control dS/dt, with the *mix* of expenditure cutback and tax increase such as to keep constant the other motion, dW/dt; then there is a constant surplus adjustment of G and T in equal amounts to produce the desired dW/dt.

To obtain the Euler first-order conditions we have gone back to our integrand and rewritten it in the canonical way:

$$U = U\{A(\dot{W}, W, \dot{S} - rS), vN(rS - \dot{S}, W)$$

$$- [\dot{S} - rS + A(\dot{W}, W, \dot{S} - rS)]\}$$

Here the employment variable has been omitted as a separate argument of the utility function, though it remains a factor in consumption. The dotted symbols are the rates of change of the variable under the dot, dS/dt and dW/dt. Finally, the function A gives the level of G necessary to achieve the specified dW/dt at a given W and given $\dot{S} - rS$, which is the primary surplus, $T - G$. Manipulation of the total differential of the dW/dt equation provides the following results regarding the A function:

$$A_{\dot{W}} = \frac{1}{W(\Phi_G + \Phi_T)}, \quad A_W = \frac{-(W\Phi_W + \Phi)}{W(\Phi_G + \Phi_T)}, \quad A_{\dot{S}} = \frac{-W\Phi_T}{W(\Phi_G + \Phi_T)}.$$

Recalling that a balanced budget increase of G and T worsens wage inflation through its supply-side shrinking of N^*, so the denominator in every case is positive (on our supply-side hypothesis), we see that the first of the above derivatives is unambiguously positive – the government can spend more if it can tolerate higher wage inflation – and the second also positive if we disregard the possibility that the current level of wage inflation is well above zero. Yet when $\dot{S}$ and hence T is increased we cannot say whether wage inflation is thus decreased and so G must be increased to achieve the specified rate of wage inflation or whether wage inflation is thus increased so that G must be decreased or whether neither is true so G must be unchanged. As hinted earlier, the last case is convenient.

Differentiation as required yields the Euler equations:

$$0 = \frac{\partial U}{\partial S} - \frac{d}{dt}\frac{\partial U}{\partial \dot{S}} = rU_C[1 + vN_{G-T} + A_{\dot{S}}] + rU_G(-A_{\dot{S}})$$

$$+ \frac{d}{dt}\{U_C[1 + vN_{G-T} + A_{\dot{S}}] + U_G(-A_{\dot{S}})\}$$

$$0 = \frac{\partial U}{\partial W} - \frac{d}{dt}\frac{\partial U}{\partial \dot{W}} = (U_G - U_C)A^W + U_C v N_W - \frac{d}{dt}\{(U_G - U_C)A_{\dot{W}}\}.$$

These two second-order differential equations in the rates of change of $\dot{S}$ and $\dot{W}$ together with terminal, or transversality, conditions may be conceived as determining the appropriate paths of $\dot{S}$ and $\dot{W}$ once the right initial rate of utility is specified, while the foregoing Ramsey–Keynes–Meade condition is needed to determine the right initial rate of utility.

To obtain a feel for the general solution to our problem a special (but not uninteresting) case will now be analysed, that in which $\Phi_T(G, T, W)$ and hence $A_{\dot{S}}$ are equal to zero. This is the case in which a tax change controls dS/dt without spilling over to dW/dt and thus necessitating a compensating change of G. Further, we take N_{G-T} to be a constant. The first of the two Euler equations then simplifies to

$$rU_C(G, C) + \frac{d}{dt}U_C(G, C) = 0,$$

which will be recognised as an old friend introduced to us by Fisher and Ramsey. Suppose we now simplify further by taking utility to be separable in G and C:

$$U = U_G(G) + U_C(C)$$

Then the first integral of the Fisher–Ramsey differential equation in the present context can be calculated to be

$$-[U_C(C) - U_C(vN - G)] = k + (rS + vN - G - C)U'_C(C)$$

in which k is a constant of integration. Its time derivative,

$$-U'_C\dot{C} + U'_C(v\dot{N} - \dot{G}) = -U'_C\dot{C} + (v\dot{N} - \dot{G})U'_C + \dot{S}rU'_C$$
$$+ \dot{S}\frac{d}{dt}U'_C,$$

can be seen (upon dividing the terms that do not cancel by $\dot{S}$) to give us back the Fisher–Ramsey differential equation in marginal utility.

Since the optimal path of consumption must increase without bound in our problem, in view of the positive rate of interest, so that $U'_C(C)$ vanishes in the limit, the constant k must equal the asymptotic value of the left-hand side of our equation. Taking the bliss level of $U_C(C)$ to be zero makes k the asymptotic value of $U_C(vN - G)$.

Two conclusions are in order. The first is that the Ramsey rule is brought back! Remarkably, national saving is increased to the point where if multiplied by the marginal utility of consumption the resulting product is just equal to the extra utility afforded by consuming some interest. Secondly, as has been just made apparent, optimum consumption exceeds wage income after netting out required government expenditure; equivalently, $C + G$ exceeds vN. With the help of Figure 4.1 it can be seen how our integral condition determines a positive volume of saving but less than interest income. There we take B to be positive. Other propositions are suggested by an examination of the figure. It appears that if v rose or if peace broke out, so that G fell, the resulting increase of available social income would induce a decrease of saving. But such results are perhaps too dependent upon the simplifying features of the present special case to be worth exploring.

To complete our analysis of the special case we may substitute the 'formula' for dS/dt presented by our integral condition into the foregoing Ramsey–Keynes–Meade equation in ds/dt and dW/dt. This gives an equation in which $T - G$ is determined in the manner of Figure 4.1 as a function of $vN - G$ and rS and which can be solved for G and hence dW/dt:

$$0 = U_G(G) + U_C(C) + \frac{W\Phi_G}{W(\Phi_G + \Phi_T)}[-U_C(C) - U_C(vMN - G)]$$

$$- \frac{u_G + u_T}{W(\Phi_G + \Phi_T)}(dW/dt)$$

This condition can presumably be rationalised along the lines suggested by Keynes – that increased wage deflation 'costs' in the present while it also has the benefit of advancing the scheduled rise of utility over the future.

There is, up to a point, an advantage to be gained from having a lower W in the future since the lower future W boosts future employment; hence $G + T$ need not be so repressed in relation to its Pigovian ($u_G = -u_T$) level. It is not clear to us what the asymptotic

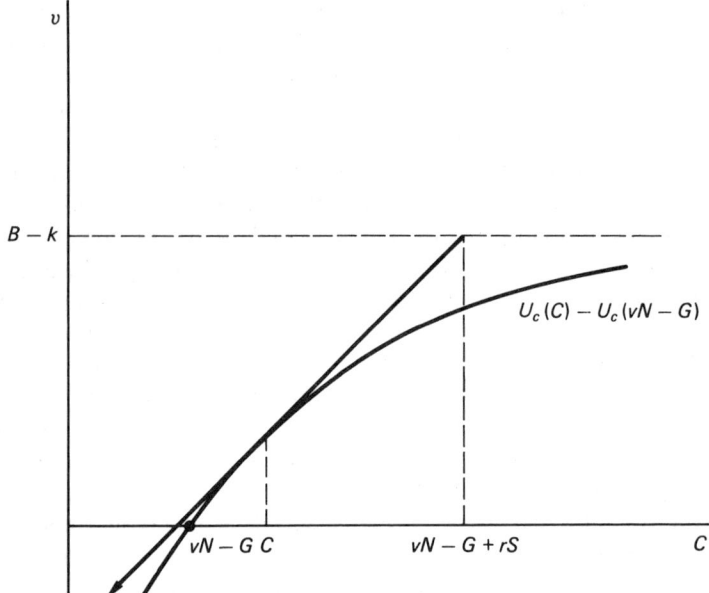

Figure 4.1 Optimum saving in the special case

behaviour of dW/dt may be; but the simplistic inflation mechanism used here does not justify attaching importance to that question.

4 FURTHER RESEARCH

Obviously we have only scratched the surface of this problem. Yet the problem and suitable extensions of it are important and give promise of a rich yield of results.

In the future we must return to the inflation mechanism, for if wage definition does not vanish in the limit we shall want to avoid the Phillipsian feature that the non-vanishing wage change is producing a non-vanishing benefit or cost in terms of employment.

We also want to turn our attention to what may be an equally important variant of the policy problem. It may be that, to put it over-strongly, public expenditure cannot be controlled with an eye to its effect on wages and employment – in short, it is exogenous. In this case we have just one control variable, T, with which to push on two state variables. We do not have controllability in the technical sense of the term. In this case, does it make sense (is it optimal) for the government to deviate from the Ramsey rule for the sake of the effect on the path of the wage? And if so, can we characterise the point to which this compromise is carried? Notwithstanding these needs for future research, it can be said that we the authors understand the problem of optimum fiscal policy subject to a monetary rule much better than when we began this work. In particular there seems to be a case for scaling up or down the size of public expenditure with a view to its wage and employment effects — without ever violating 'Ramsey'.

Notes

Our collaborative efforts could not be as intensive as planned, but we offer this chapter as a preliminary exploration. Special thanks go to Slobodan Djajic for some expert advice; Kevin Lancaster also gave helpful comments.

1. Later steps by this group, of course, included the incorporation of the neutrality of money into Keynesian models and the adoption of the Phillips curve in the analysis of inflation.
2. If they stay on their toes, Samuelson went on to suggest, a new economy will be synthesised that behaves as if it were classically frictionless, from full employment to marginal-cost prices! However, the more extreme claims for the counter doctrine are not our concern here.
3. If the country, though too small to have any effect on the interest rate in terms of the basket of consumer goods bought is *big* enough that its increased banana demand, in contracting its exports of bananas, appreciably raises the world price of bananas, then the resulting incipient currency appreciation entails an increase of the money supply to stabilise the exchange rate, which *expands* output and employment. But such a structure is too complicated to be appealing here.
4. As readers of the original Ramsey paper will recall, Keynes provided Ramsey with a brilliant intuitive explanation for Ramsey's famous equation. The marginal benefit from increased saving lay in the hastening of the march toward utility satiation and the marginal cost involved the marginal utility of consumption. Here the former is $-U$, and the latter is $-u_T \, dS/dt$.

References

Hansen, Alvin H. (1960) 'The Economics of the Soviet Challenge', *Economic Record*, vol. 36, March, pp. 5–12.

Lerner, Abba P. (1944) 'Functional Finance', in Lerner, A. P. (ed.), *The Economics of Control* (New York: Macmillan), pp. 302–22.

Meade, James E. (1951) *The Theory of Economic Policy* (London: Allen & Unwin).

Pigou, Arthur Cecil (1932) *The Economics of Welfare*, 4th edn, (London: Macmillan).

Ramsey, Frank P. (1928) 'A Mathematical Theory of Saving', *Economic Journal*, vol. 38, December, pp. 543–59.

Samuelson, Paul A. (1951) 'Principles and Rules in Modern Fiscal Policy: a Neoclassical Reformulation', in *Money, Trade and Economic Growth: Essays in Honor of John H. Williams* (New York: Macmillan), pp. 157–76.

Samuelson, Paul A. (1953) 'Full Employment versus Progress and Other Economic Goals', in Millikan, Max (ed.), *Income Stabilization for a Developing Democracy* (New Haven: Yale University Press).

Samuelson, Paul A. (1956) 'The New Look in Tax and Fiscal Policy', *Federal Tax Policy for Growth and Stability*, US Congress, (Washington, DC: GPO, pp. 229–34. Also in (1966) *Collected Economic Papers* (Cambridge, Mass.: MIT), ch. 100.

Part II
Public Debt and Equity

5 Public Debt and Intergeneration Equity

Richard A. Musgrave
UNIVERSITY OF CALIFORNIA

The role of debt finance and its bearing on future generations has been of longstanding concern to fiscal economists. Ricardo and Pigou in particular gave it their careful attention, advancing what may be called the classical doctrine of debt finance in a full-employment economy. The Keynesian model added a new perspective and the nature of debt burden once more became the subject of lively discussion during the 1960s.[1] As seen in the modern perspective, debt policy not only poses issues of intergeneration equity but also of demand management and of fiscal discipline. Moreover, debt finance may serve to even out swings in tax rates, thereby reducing dead-weight loss over time. The difficulty lies in simultaneously satisfying these various considerations.

1 INTERGENERATION EQUITY IN THE CLASSICAL MODEL[2]

The classical indictment of debt finance, as advanced by Ricardo and Pigou rested on the proposition that borrowing draws on savings while tax finance draws on consumption. Ricardo, in passing, noted the now famous equivalence theorem, i.e. that 'in economy' the effect of the two modes should be the same as the present value of future tax obligations (needed to meet debt service) equals that of initial tax finance. But he quickly rejects the equivalence as unrealistic. Rather, tax payers will reduce consumption ('save out of income') by the full amount under tax finance, but only by the amount of tax needed to finance interest charges under loan finance (Ricardo, 1957, 1962) Pigou, apparently independently and without reference to Ricardo, also visualised an 'imagined situation' where the two modes yield similar results, but again modifies this outcome when moving to the 'actual world'. But unlike Ricardo, he was reluctant to abandon the assumption of rational behaviour. Instead, he notes various factors which may lead to similar results. Lenders and taxpayers will not be the same people and the distribution of future tax burdens may be uncertain. Thus the debit side of the loan transaction tends to be overlooked, and lenders will find it less necessary to reduce consumption than do taxpayers.[3]

Debt finance, by reducing saving, thus impairs capital formation and retards growth, thereby imposing a negative inheritance on future generations. Debt finance of current outlays is hence unfair, but this structure does not apply for public investment. Debt finance of outlays which yield future benefits serves to spread the cost across future generations which share in the benefit stream. Thus, debt finance of public investment is considered sound, while current expenditures should be tax financed. The rationale is one of benefit taxation as applied across generations: since the benefits of today's public investment will be shared by tomorrow's consumers, intergeneration equity requires them to also share in the cost. According to the classical (Ricardo–Pigou) doctrine, debt finance accomplishes this because it leaves the future generation with less private capital, thereby offsetting the gain which it derives from an increased public capital stock. Thus intergeneration equity calls for the initial debt finance to be followed by debt amortisation over the useful life of the asset. This involves separation of the budget between a current and a capital part, with the former tax and the latter debt financed. On the outlay side of the current budget, interest and debt repayment is included, with amortisation timed in line with the using up of the asset.

There are, of course, some difficulties in implementing such a scheme. For one thing, the concept of public capital outlay has to be defined. What matters is not simply whether (in mistaken analogy to a private firm) government acquires title to public assets, e.g. buildings or highways, but whether the economy's capital stock, including human investment via health or education, has been increased. In principle, teacher's salaries as well as road construction should be included; and with it, the depreciation of human assets would also have to be allowed for under current outlays, a task which would be difficult to implement. Moreover, the benefit may not emanate from income-yielding assets, public or private, but take an intangible form. Thus, it may be argued that the cost of a war, fought by one generation, should be shared by the next, as the latter also shares in such benefits as may result.

This view of debt finance as a benefit rule implies that generation 2 should leave generation 3 with the same public capital stock which it has inherited from generation 1. But the problem of intergeneration equity may also be seen in terms of redistribution across generations. If per capita incomes rise over time, it may be appropriate for the present generation to impose a burden on the future. This may call for debt finance of current outlays and the amortisation schedule on public capital may be lengthened. Alternatively, if per capita income is expected to fall, tax finance of public investment or a shortened rate of amortisation may be appropriate. This broader issue of optimal distribution across generations need thus be distinguished from the distributionally neutral concept of benefit finance which underlies traditional discussion of whether or not debt finance is prudent.

We begin with the latter issue. Here intergeneration equity calls for each generation to pay for the benefits which it receives from public outlays. Debt finance of a productive public investment, be it a highway or a health programme, is viewed as a vehicle by which the incidence of its cost can be synchronised with the incidence of its benefits. To examine the mechanism by which this synchronisation occurs, the relationship between successive generations need be specified.

Model 1   No Overlap, No Heirs

Consider first a situation where there is no overlap among generations. The first generation G_1 living during period P_1 departs before the second generation G_2 living in P_2 arrives on the scene. Nor is there an indirect overlap via heirs. The welfare of G_2 does not enter into the utility function of G_1, thus ruling out an altruistic or selfish desire to leave G_2 with a positive or negative inheritance. In this case, G_2 will only install capital assets – be they public or private – whose useful life expires in P_1, as it has no concerns for what happens in the next period or P_2. Technology may be such as to call for assets whose useful life extends beyond that of G_1, thereby benefitting G_2, but this overlap would not enter into G_2's investment choice. By definition, this setting rules out the very problem of intergeneration equity as G_1 will dissave and consume its assets before G_2 arrives. This, of course, is an unrealistic setting, noted only as a point of departure.

Model 2   Overlap, No Heirs

We retain the assumption that there are no heirs, thus requiring G_2 to liquidate (and consume) its assets before departing. However, we now introduce overlap in the lifetime of successive generations. Suppose that the life of G_1 covers periods 1 and 2 while that of G_2 covers period 2 and 3, with overlap during period 2. The benefits of the investment made by G_1 in P_1 extend into P_2. A problem of intergeneration equity now arises. The benefits will accrue to G_2 only in P_1, but will be shared by G_2 in P_2. To simplify, we assume that half the benefits will accrue during P and the other half during P_1. G_2 should thus carry three-quarters of the cost while G_2 should carry one quarter.[4] The traditional argument has been that debt finance by reducing public investment provides such a burden transfer to G_2. But this is not what happens in the present case. Debt finance in the confines of Model 2 does indeed serve as a vehicle of burden transfer, but not via its impact on private capital formation.

Assuming taxes to fall on consumption, tax finance will place the entire burden on G_1, while G_2 enjoys a free ride when sharing in the benefit stream in P_2. The requirement of cost sharing is not met. Turning to debt finance, let us assume first that lending as well as taxation comes out of G_2 consumption, i.e. that the Ricardian equivalence holds. Considering a public investment of $100 financed by bond sales of $100, G_1 will reduce consumption by this amount. As distinct from tax finance this, however, is not the end of the story. G_1 is now given $100 of bonds which will be serviced and amortised during the life of the asset. With half the benefits accruing during P_2, $50 is amortised during that period. G_1 as taxpayer reduces consumption by that amount, but as recipient of the amortisation proceeds raises consumption accordingly. In P_2, taxes on $25 are imposed on G_1 and G_2 each, with each reducing consumption accordingly. At the same times, G_1 receives amortisation payments of $50 with a corresponding increase in consumption. In all, G_1 has reduced consumption by $75 while G_2 has suffered a reduction of $25. The cost of the investment is thus shared equitably by the two. This then is the mechanism by which G_2 compensates G_1 for its participation in the benefit stream. Both G_1 and G_2 will have traded private for public consumption and each carries its proper share in the cost. Note that debt finance has provided this mechanism even though it has been assumed that bond purchases are withdrawn from consumption thus leaving private investment unaffected. This reasoning, we add, holds even if we relax the assumption that the lives of public assets created in P_2 extend beyond P_2 and hence the life span of G_2. G_1 holders, before departing may then sell their remaining bonds to G_2 and consume the proceeds. If the benefits extend beyond P_2, G_2 in turn may sell its remaining holdings to G_3 and so forth.

Consider now the more realistic setting where we assume the bond purchases to fall on G_1 private investment rather than consumption. Effects during P_1 now involve a reduction in private investment by $100, a tax-induced cut in G_1 consumption of $50, and an increase in private investment (out of amortisation payments) of $50. During P_2, we find both G_1 and G_2 consumption to fall by $25 in response to taxation, while G_1 consumption rises by $50 in response to amortisation proceeds. In addition, G_1 consumption out of wealth liquidation is reduced by $50, the amount by which its private investment was reduced in P_1. In all, G_1 consumption has again fallen by $75 while that of G_2 has declined by $25, once more in line with their benefit shares and the requirement of intergeneration equity. Provided that amortisation matches the benefit stream, debt finance thus meets the norm whether drawn from consumption or investment.

This conclusion, needs some qualification. Loan finance, if withdrawn from private investment, leaves the P_2 economy with a reduced private capital stock. As a result, the capital income of G_1 investors is reduced. While G_2 users pay a lower return to C_1 owners, this is no gain to them since they also find their services reduced. There is, however, a further effect on G_2 because the reduction in capital stock, due to the decline in G_1 investment also bears on G_2 owned factor earnings. Thus wage rates will fall and G_2 wage income will be reduced, while returns on G_2 held capital will rise. As G_2 suffers a net loss in factor earnings, sharing in the resulting decline in income, it thus suffers an additional burden. Since G_2, as noted previously already compensates G_2 via its tax contribution to debt repayment, G_2 is no longer left whole. Such at least is the case if the benefit rule is defined so as to require compensation for loss of rental income. In that case partial tax finance will be needed to achieve an equitable result.[5]

Viewed more realistically, loan finance will not fall entirely on capital, nor will tax finance fall entirely on consumption. To the extent that loan finance falls on consumption, the impact on rental income is lessened and the required share of tax finance will be reduced. Contrary to the classical assumption that debt finance results in burden transfer because it falls on investment, debt finance in Model 2 does best if it equals tax finance and falls on consumption.

Model 3 Heirs, No Overlap

We now turn to an alternative setting, where generations do not overlap, but provision for heirs is allowed for. Suppose again that G_1, living in P_1 undertakes a public investment which produces benefits divided equally between P_1 and P_2. G_2, living P_2, thus partakes in these benefits, and should carry half the cost. But in the absence of overlap, G_1 can no longer recover a G_2 contribution via the amortisation process. The mechanism of burden transfer, operating in Model 2 no longer applies. Instead, a reduction in G_1 private capital formation now burdens G_2 as it will inherit a reduced capital stock.

Tax finance, if assumed to fall on G_1 consumption, again leaves G_1 with the entire burden, and G_2 once more enjoys a free ride. Turning to loan finance, we begin again with the assumption that lending as well falls on consumption. G_1 consumption then falls by $100 in P_1 when making the loan, and by $50 when paying the amortisation tax, while it rises by $50 when receiving the amortisation payment. G_1 consumption is reduced by $100, thus defraying the entire cost of the investment. G_2 in P_2 will reduce consumption by $50 when paying the amortisation tax and raise consumption by $50 when receiving the amortisation payment. G renders the amortisation to itself and suffers so net burden in the process.[6] The entire burden, as with tax finance now stays with G_1.

Such is no longer the case, however, once we let debt finance be drawn from investment. G_1 and P_2 will now reduce private investment by $100, reduce consumption by $50 in response to the amortisation tax and increase investment by $50 when receiving the amortisation proceeds. Since bequests may now be left, G_1 no longer dissaves and consumes at the end of its stay as was the case in Model 2, but its bequest left to G_2 is reduced by the fall in investment or $50. G_2 in P_2 will similarly reduce consumption by $50 in response to the tax and invest $50 in response to the proceeds. Both G_1 and G_2 have shared in the cost by reducing consumption by $50.

Debt finance again generates burden transfer but the mechanism by which this occurs has changed. In Model 2 recoupment was provided via G_2 participation in debt amortisation, with effects on G_1 private investment of secondary importance. In Model 2, amortisation becomes an intrageneration transfer only, with intergeneration transfer provided by reducing the bequest (in private capital) which G_2 receives. The classical thesis, that debt finance burdens future generations by reducing the capital stock via reduced bequests now holds. Provided that lending falls on private investment whereas taxation falls on consumption, loan finance of public investment now leaves the total (public plus private) capital endowment of future generations unchanged, thus meeting the benefit rule of intergeneration equity. All this, however, assumes that

G_1 identifies with its heirs in G_2 so that its approaching departure will not affect its consumption-saving behaviour at the close of P_1. To the extent that liquidation of assets and consumption occurs in expectation of death, the inheritance mechanism ceases to apply and, in the absence of overlap, the entire burden stays with G_1.

Model 4   The General Case

It remains to consider the general case, with both overlap and inheritance allowed for. Suppose again that the life of G_1 extends over P_2 and P_2 while that of G_2 extends over P_2 and P_3. A public investment of $100 is undertaken in P_1, with benefits spread equally over P_1 and P_2. The project is debt financed and amortised in line with the benefit stream. G_1 should thus contribute $50 in P_1, with both G_1 and G_2 contributing $25 in P_2. Now consider the following four possibilities: (1) borrowing is drawn from consumption, taxes fall on consumption and amortisation payments flow into consumption; (2) the situation is similar except that amortisation payments flow into private investment; (3) both borrowing and taxes draw on consumption while amortisation also flows into consumption; (4) the situation is similar except that amortisation payments flow into investment.

In case (1) we find that private investment falls by $100 and G consumption (over both P_1 and P_2) rises by $25. Since there should have been a decline of $75, G_1 is left with a net gain of $100. G_2 in turn suffers a decline in consumption of $25. Adding thereto the loss of inheritance (equal to the decline in private investment), its total cost is $125. Compared to the appropriate payment of $25, its net loss or overcharge equals $100. In case (4) the opposite holds, with G_1 now suffering a fall in consumption of $175, or an overcharge of $100. G_2 in turn reduces consumption by $25 but also enjoys a gain in inheritance (equal to the rise in investment) of $100. Debt finance in the general case may thus yield the equitable result or it may overcharge either G_1 or G_2, depending on how borrowing is withdrawn and on how amortisation payments are used.

Throughout these pages we have made the crucial assumption that debt finance of a public project will be followed by amortisation in line with the accrual of the benefit stream. If amortisation is delayed, the future generation will be burdened, be it under Models 2 or 3, just as more rapid amortisation will place an excessive share of the burden on the initial generation.

1.5 Further Issues

The preceding discussion has focused on the main features of the three models and may be supplemented by brief reference to certain further issues.

1. The argument has proceeded as if each generation consisted of one individual only, i.e. individuals comprising any one generation have been dealt with as a group. This may miss important aspects of the problem. It thus becomes necessary to distinguish between intergeneration equity as applied to entire generations of groups of individuals and the equitable treatment of particular individuals within such groups.[7] The two applications may differ since the distribution of benefits across individuals may not be matched by the distribution of the tax burden needed to service the debt. As Pigou noted, this may affect the way in which individuals respond to loan finance, as well as the implementation of interindividual equity.[8] To secure the latter not only must the debt be amortised in line with the benefit stream, but amortisation taxes would have to be assessed in line with individual benefit shares therein. Such may be feasible where the public investment is in the nature of a private good, thus permitting fee finance, but not in the case of public goods where fee finance is inapplicable and inefficient. Here the political process has to be relied upon to secure an approximation to inter-individual equity via Lindahl taxes.

2. Debt finance may also serve to secure a more equitable distribution of the burden among individuals within the same generation. This essentially was the purpose of Keynes' proposal for financing the Second World War by a compulsory loan. During the war, it would be necessary to release resources and to restrain purchasing power by massive drafts on the working classes, but by using a forced lending scheme, this could then be corrected for subsequently by repaying such loans out of a capital levy.[9]

3. The preceding discussion was directed at central finance, with $G_1, G_2 \ldots$ reflecting successive generations of age groups. An argument essentially similar to that of Model 2 may be applied also to the case of local finance (Musgrave, 1959). Here capital expenditures are made in P_1 in a particular locality, and $R_2, R_2 \ldots$ are successive generations of residents. By use of debt finance, R_1 may then collect from R_2 during P_2, when R_2 by moving into the locality assumes its tax obligations. R_2, when leaving the location may collect debt service from R_3 and so forth. Unlike the Model 2 case, no overlap (or inheritance) is required since the life of any one R does not expire when leaving the location.

4. So far we have assumed that finance is drawn within the benefit region, but a similar argument also applies to the case of foreign borrowing. By borrowing abroad, the need for immediate domestic resource release, be it from consumption or investment is postponed. Returning to the overlap case of Model 2, G_1 now pays $50 in tax in P_1 and $25 in P_2, reducing consumption accordingly. G_2 pays taxes of $25 in P_2 with a corresponding cut in consumption. Domestic investment is not affected in either period as amortisation payments flow to abroad. Turning to Model 3, G_1 pays $50 of tax during P_1 and reduces consumption by that amount, with the tax proceeds used to amortise half the debt. The remaining $50 of foreign debt are left to G as a negative inheritance. Amortisation of this debt is now no longer an internal transfer but burdens G_2 since payments are made to the outside. The effects of reduced private investment on the earnings of G_2 held factors (noted in our earlier discussion of Model 3) are now avoided, as domestic investment does not fall.

5. The question may be raised whether the introduction of inheritance in Model 3 still fits the conceptual framework of intergeneration equity as defined by the benefit or *quid pro quo* rule. Assuming rational behaviour, the leaving of bequests implies that testators derive satisfaction from the well-being of their heirs. This means, in effect, that their anticipated utility stream extends across generations, giving them a more or less infinite life span. But if this is the case, the concept of benefit finance across successive user groups (which postulates distinct generations) may be taken to dissolve. Each generation will consume or invest (with the appropriate mix of public and private investment) depending on its own time preference, covering a time horizon which extends to infinity via heir-based reincarnation. The financing of public investment then loses its specific feature, as it is no longer necessary for any one generation to collect from the next so as to 'remain whole'. Debt finance of public investment simply becomes a diversion of saving from private investment, while debt finance of public consumption merely reflects a decision to reduce saving and increase the rate of total (and specifically public) consumption. By reducing the capital stock, the present generation curtails its future consumption stream, defined to include not only its own consumption but also the discounted value of consumption by its heirs. Viewed this way, the choice between tax and debt finance is no longer one of fiscal prudence in relation to intergeneration equity. If an effect there exists only one generation, the problem becomes merely one of timing 'its' consumption in an optimal fashion, including the appropriate mix

between private and public investment.

This reasoning would be compelling if each generation in fact consisted of a single individual. But it does not. Individual members of any one generation differ in their valuation of future benefits, yet provision for the future via public investment involves collective choice. Policy decisions regarding the time pattern of consumption thus come to be based on a political process. Moreover, society may wish to adjust the distribution of income across generations, e.g. in response to changing per capita income. The problem of intergeneration equity thus enters into the social welfare function.

Most important, individual members of G_1 may be concerned with those members of G_2 who are their individual heirs, but be indifferent regarding others. The politics of redistribution, not surprisingly, extends over age cohorts as well as across income groups. The debate over how to finance old-age security is a case in point. It is not surprising, therefore, that the issue of intergeneration equity should remain a lively topic, be it in its narrower (and distributionally neutral) sense of benefit finance, or in the broader frame of temporal redistribution.

2 DEBT FINANCE IN THE NEO-CLASSICAL MODEL

As we leave the classical setting, the issue of debt finance can no longer be viewed in terms of intergeneration equity only. Given the context of an extreme Keynesian model, with unemployed resources and inelastic private investment, debt finance of public services becomes costless and indeed carries a negative cost via its multiplier and accelerator effect. The setting changes as we turn to a neoclassical model, defined here as a setting where (1) there may be a need for policy action to set a proper level of aggregate demand, be it to secure full employment or to check inflation; (2) aggregate demand is affected by both the state of balance in the total (current plus capital) budget and the degree of monetary ease; and (3) alternative policy mixes generate different growth rates in the private sector, with tight budget-monetary ease more favourable to capital formation and growth. Debt policy at the national level (where responsibility for stabilisation rests) now faces the additional or even primary task of maintaining the proper level of aggregate demand and of adjusting the economy's rate of growth. The latter is no longer set automatically by market forces, and has to be determined by the political process. Growth thus becomes an additional policy target.

In this setting, the argument would seem to run as follows: suppose first that the size of the budget and its composition between current and capital outlays is determined. The benefit rule of intergeneration equity then tells us what the state of balance is to be. This in turn sets the degree of monetary ease or tightness needed to secure the proper level of aggregate demand. That monetary policy, however, may leave the growth rate in the private sector higher or lower than desired. With the state of budgetary balance determined by the level of public capital expenditures (given that intergeneration equity is to be net) monetary policy cannot provide for both the correct level of aggregate demand (as required for stabilisation) and the consumption-investment mix needed to meet target growth. The problem might be resolved by addition of a third policy instrument, such as a tax subsidy scheme by which to control the consumption-investment mix in the private sector, but not without adding complexity to the policy design.

This reasoning, however, gives a misleading picture. Suppose policy provides for a fiscal and monetary mix which (1) secures a full employment level of demand at current prices, and (2) yields an investment-consumption mix in the private sector which (given the level of public investment) results in the desired growth. The issue of intergeneration equity has then been faced already. The future generation benefits from higher growth by inheriting a larger capital stock, independent of whether this growth takes the form of private or public capital formation. Setting the growth target involves *total* capital formation, with the private and public shares therein to be determined so as to equate their returns at the margin. Intergeneration equity as applied to the public budget in particular thus drops out as a separate policy consideration, permitting the fiscal-monetary mix and with it the state of balance in the total budget to be set so as to satisfy the requirements of aggregate demand control and to meet the desired rate of growth. Setting specific financing rules for the capital budget in particular thus becomes meaningless.[10]

This, however, does not apply to debt finance at lower levels of government, where there is no primary responsibility for macro policy. The role of the capital budget, therefore, is similar to that of the classical setting. Resulting patterns of tax and loan finance at the lower levels then enter as an input into the determination of national policy, implementation of which covers all levels of government.

But even at the national level, where a fully-fledged capital budget becomes inapplicable, a rigorous system of accounting for capital costs is still in order. While such charges do not enter into cash outlays (current or capital) in determining the appropriate balance (deficit or surplus) in the total budget, they nevertheless enter along with current cash outlays to indicate the overall cost of public services during the budget year.

3 DEBT FINANCE AND FISCAL DISCIPLINE

So far, how debt finance *should be* conducted as an instrument of correct policy design has been considered. It remains to note a quite different perspective on debt finance, i.e. how to avoid its abuse. Debt finance is seen to make for excessive budgets, and does so precisely because voters do not act in line with the Ricardian equivalence. Far from equating the present value of their future debt service with that of immediate tax finance, voters are taken to overlook future liabilities and to assume that debt-financed public services come for free. The availability of deficit finance may thus join with other forces (such as bureaucratic aggrandisement or voting bias) to generate excess budgets. In my view, debt finance has not been the (and hardly a) major cause of the rising budget share in GNP which Western countries have experienced over the last half-century. Structural factors, such as the rise of defence costs, demographic changes, and changes in social climate have been much the major factors, thus raising the question of how 'excessive' should be defined (Musgrave, 1985). Nevertheless the availability of deficit finance may weaken fiscal discipline and thus deserves consideration in the present context.

In a setting where all public expenditures are current and where there is no need for stabilisation, the entire budget should indeed be tax financed. Short of drastic fluctuations in the level of current expenditures, this would then be sound policy. But not all public outlays are of the current type, so that intergeneration equity calls for departure from that rule. In the absence of stabilisation needs, this may not pose too serious a conflict, Where capital expenditures tend to remain fairly constant over time, a 'pay as you go' approach may be used, with each generation (apart from the first and last) may be taken to tax finance its own outlays while servicing the debt of the preceding one.

The conflict deepens, however, as requirements of stabilisation policy are allowed for. A discipline based requirement that the budget be held in continuous balance now involves a heavy cost in terms of stabilisation needs. Even if aggregate demand could be controlled by monetary policy alone, the resulting growth rate may not be what is desired.

A perfect solution satisfying all these objectives will hardly be available so that some compromise has to be resorted to. This is not to be found in a rigid requirement of balance such as proposed by S. J. Resolution 58.[11] Moreover, approaches, such as an expenditure limitation in relation to GNP, stricter voting rules (requiring a more than absolute majority if such a limit is to be exceeded) offer better techniques, provided that restraining action is needed. Reflecting my long-standing distinction between the three major 'branches' of the budget (Musgrave, 1959), a good case may also be made for a closer linkage between tax and expenditure votes on particular service items (e.g. a defence tax), while dealing with distributional adjustments via a separate tax-transfer set.

Notes

1. See Ferguson (1964) and also Harris (1947) especially ch. IV where the history of doctrine is traced.
2. I am indebted to Carl Shoup and James Ferguson for helpful comments on an earlier version of this section.
3. See Pigou (1940a and b).
4. Where the public investment provides for a social good, with per capita benefits independent of the number of consumers, G_1 will be required to pay for two-thirds of the benefits, with G_2 paying for one-third only. Note also that our discussion throughout focuses on the role of debt amortisation, its finance and use, rather than on interest payments. This does not affect the central problem, as it is largely through the amortisation mechanism that burden transfer occurs.
5. This reasoning involves the somewhat asymmetrical assumption that private investment is in the form of producer goods, whereas public investment provides durable consumer goods. If the latter is also in producer goods, the effect of reduced private investment on factor earnings will be neutralised by increased public investment. Such at least is the case if we consider the combined effects of introducing a public investment and its financing, but not if we consider the effects of substituting loan for tax finance of a given public investment.
6. This disregards the potential efficiency cost of taxation. See Pigou (1928).
7. For emphasis on this point, see also Buchanan (1964).
8. See note 3 above.
9. See Keynes (1978); 'There would be perfect efficiency in this', he argues, as 'the people would enjoy the compensation to which their war efforts had entitled them, at a time when this would cost the community nothing, since the resources required would otherwise have been running to waste' (pp. 49, 121). After the war the debt could be paid off by a capital levy drawing on 'redundant savings' available in the post war slump (p. 121). Considerations of intergeneration equity are thus joined neatly with the Keynesian macro model.

10. But suppose that generations G_1 and G_2 are each divided into two groups, A and B, and that an investment made in P_1 will yield benefits in P_1 and P_2 but will benefit the A groups only. Taking G_1 and G_2 to overlap in P_2, benefit finance requires that the debt be serviced and retired from selective taxes to be paid by G_{A1} in P_1 and by G_{A1} in P_2. To maintain the overall fiscal-monetary mix as required by stabilisation policy, this calls for offsetting adjustments in debt finance elsewhere in the budget. Such general debt, however, is to be serviced by both the A and B groups, and not by the A groups only. The capital budget thus retains a function. While it will have no bearing on the overall level of debt finance in the budget as a whole, the capital budget may thus serve to secure benefit financing (with the use of differentiating taxes) of public investments which benefit particular groups in successive generations.
11. For discussion of this resolution and similar proposals see Congressional Budget Office (1982) p. 68.

References

Buchanan, J. (1964) 'Concerning Future Generations' in Ferguson, James E. (ed.), *Public Debt and Future Generations* (Chapel Hill: University of North Carolina Press).
Congressional Budget Office (1982) *Balancing the Federal Budget*, September.
Ferguson, James E. (ed.) (1964) *Public Debt and Future Generations* (Chapel Hill; University of North Carolina Press).
Harris, S. (1947) *National Debt and the New Economics* (Newark, NJ: McGraw-Hill).
Keynes, J. M. (1978) 'How to Pay for the War', in Moggridge, D. (ed.), *J. M. Keynes Collected Works, Vol. xxii* (London: Macmillan).
Musgrave, R. A. (1959) *The Theory of Public Finance* (Newark: McGraw-Hill) reprinted as Internal Debt in the Classical System in Ferguson (1964).
Musgrave, R. A. (1985) 'Excess Bias and the Nature of Budget Growth', *Journal of Public Economics*, vol. 28, no. 3, December, pp. 287–308.
Pigou, A. C. (1928) *A Study in Public Finance* (London: Macmillan).
Pigou, A. C. (1940a) *A Study in Public Finance*, 2nd edn (London: Macmillan).
Pigou, A. C. (1940b) *The Political Economy of War* (London: Macmillan)
Ricardo, David (1957) *Principles of Political Economy*, Vol. I, Sraffa, P. (ed.) (Cambridge: Cambridge University Press).
Ricardo, David (1962) 'Funding System', Vol. IV, *The Works and Correspondence of David Ricardo*, Sraffa, P. (ed.) (Cambridge: Cambridge University Press), pp. 186–7.

DISCUSSION

This paper[1] examines the appropriate role of debt finance in a variety of models and circumstances. The underlying view is that debt finance is part of the allocation function of government and allows the intertemporal synchronisation of the costs and benefits of public investment. Intergenerational equity (IGE) occurs if each generation pays the same share of the costs as it receives in benefits.

In the 'classical' model, issues in debt policy are posed in terms of IGE only. Musgrave examines three such models:

1. *No overlap between generations, no heirs.* This is used as a starting point only, as IGE has no rule here.
2. *Overlap, no heirs.* In this case, IGE occurs through debt financing. It is unimportant whether the debt crowds consumption or investment.
3. *Overlap, with heirs.* Now individuals have an infinite horizon, so IGE ceases to be an issue.

In the 'neo-classical' model, government, by assumption, is concerned about and can affect aggregate demand, overall growth, and IGE. However, setting a growth rate is equivalent to solving the IGE issue. Finally, the paper examines debt and fiscal discipline, concluding that in general there will be no ideal solution that satisfies fiscal discipline, aggregate demand, and growth objectives.

Professor Marc Robinson pointed out that in Model 2, using debt for consumption loans would Pareto dominate using debt for IGE only. Moreover, he thought that whether debt crowded out consumption or investment did matter, because pecuniary externalities may exist – namely, that wages will be a function of the capital stock. Therefore the current 'young' will be affected by the investment decisions of the old. He noted that Ricardian equivalence holds in Model 2 only because negative bequests have been implicitly ruled out.

Mr John Flemming noted that one way to avoid the pecuniary externality problem would be to posit an international capital market, which supplied an exogenous interest rate to the economy. He also emphasised that the existence of bequests, in Model 3, does not guarantee that individuals act as if they are infinitely-lived, because of heterogeneity in the population. Professor Michael Boskin commented that rising consumption over time could also inhibit bequests.

Professor Vito Tanzi thought that many intergenerational transfers, such as education, occur while both parties are alive, not through bequests. He also stressed the importance of, and the complications involved by, unintended bequests. *Sir Austin Robinson* suggested that IGE is difficult to define because of diversity within each generation.

Professor Ephraim Kleiman said that in Model 2 the older generation could finance capital by user fees, or, if the government used the capital, by lower spending and lower taxes. Government investments are not necessarily for public goods.

Professor Boskin suggested that many policies are age specific, often in subtle ways. For example, the investment tax credit benefits the holders of new capital relative to holders of old capital. Moreover, it is not clear what the norm should be in intergenerational transfers. Finally, he noted that it is difficult to consider IGE without explicit consideration of economic growth, for in the long run, the government can change the growth rate only changing the rate of technical progress.

Professor Robert Eisner stressed that public investment tends to be longer-lived than private investment.

Professor Musgrave agreed the points regarding pecuniary externalities and longevity of public investment.

Note

1. Some modifications have been made in the text as a result of the discussion.

6 Debt and Burden and Intergeneration Equity

Toshihiro Ihori
OSAKA UNIVERSITY

1 THE DEBT BURDEN

This chapter investigates an important aspect of the debt problem, namely the proposition that debt finance burdens future generations. If so, this can be both a critique of borrowing (since it may be abused by burdening future generations with the cost of services which are enjoyed currently) and an argument for borrowing (since it may be used to secure intergeneration equity by passing on part of the cast of capital outlays to the future).

The primary question, however, is: does such a burden transfer in fact occur, and if so, how? It is an old and recurrent question in economics. It seems that the answer to the question depends upon the definition of the burden of debt. In this chapter, we define the burden of debt to be a decrease in utility level of future generations which would not exist if the government debt were not issued and instead taxes were collected.

Modigliani (1961) argues that a permanent increase in government debt will displace the same amount of capital from private portfolio in the long run. According to his analysis the decrease in net investment shows up in the long run as a decrease in the stock in capital. Modigliani refers to this negative effect on the capital stock as a burden of the public debt. That is, each generation 'burdens' the next one by bequeathing them a smaller aggregate stock of capital. However, his argument is confined within stationary states only and the effect of debt finance on each generation's utility during the transitional growth process is not explicitly analysed.

Diamond (1965), using Samuelson's (1958) generation-overlapping framework, shows that at least in certain circumstances an increase in government debt will decrease the long-run utility level of consumers but also that these equilibria are stable. There are two points which we wish to emphasise. First, Diamond considers an economy where the amount of tax is controlled so that the per capita government debt is held constant, and pure debt finance is not analysed. Such a formulation is sometimes against our intuition. That is, the tax instruments are subject to congressional approval and are seldom altered, whereas government issues debt to finance budgetary deficit whenever necessary. Secondly, he ignores the effect of debt finance on the welfare of earlier generations alive during the economy's transition to its steady state.

In a model without capital, i.e. in consumption-loan models, Gale (1973) shows that the long-run competitive equilibrium without government debt (or social contrivance of money) is stable but Pareto inefficient while the long-run equilibrium with debt is efficient but unstable if the economy is in what he calls the 'Samuelsonian case'. In this regard, the stability question of equilibria à la Diamond must be investigated more carefully. The stability question is important also from the viewpoint of distribution between generations. Okuno (1983) and Burbridge (1983) examine the stability property of long-run equilibria with respect to capital when the tax rate is predetermined and the government debt issue is endogenously determined by budgetary deficits. However, as in the previous papers they do not compare the welfare effect of debt finance on each generation with that of tax finance during the transitional growth process. When considering the intertemporal distribution, it is necessary to look beyond simply the changes in steady-state utility. Hence it remains unsettled whether the burden of debt may exist in the sense that the economy may be unstable and debt issue may decrease private capital forever. It remains also unsettled how the burden of debt is placed on each generation in the transition. The second point is important even if the per capita government deficit is held constant and hence the system is stable. Analogous to the differential view of tax incidence, the problem is to see how the current and the successive generations would be affected by alternative methods of finance while holding government expenditures constant It is important to explore the relative burden of debt and taxation on each generation during the transition.

The first question considered in this chapter is the following: does debt finance of current expenditures place an undue burden on the future? Barro (1974) shows that when inheritance is allowed and each consumer cares for the welfare of his descendants, the issuance of government debt will have no effect whatsoever on the real aspects of the economy. As is well known, the conditions for this perfect debt neutrality are quite restrictive – no wealth constraints, equal borrowing and lending rates, no childless families, and so on – and may not be fully met. On the other hand, if no consumer is concerned with the welfare of his descendants at all, debt neutrality does not hold at all. We do not follow Barro's line of argument because the purpose of this paper is to examine how debt burden relates to intergeneration equity. If debt neutrality holds perfectly, it makes no sense to investigate this topic. In fact, it is plausible to conjecture that behaviour in the real world may fall between these extremes. Less extreme behaviour by economic agents would produce estimated coefficients that were intermediate between those predicted by the extreme cases. Therefore, it is useful to investigate the following question in Section 2: to what extent is the debt neutrality hypothesis relevant to the real economy?

Section 3 investigates the case where taxes are predetermined and government debt issuance is endogenously determined by budgetary deficits. In particular, the issue of intergeneration equity is examined in a finite horizon model from the viewpoint of the so-called chain-letter mechanism of debt finance.

The implication of the chain-letter paradox in a finite horizon setting would be important in a following sense. It is the assumption of a finite horizon that is crucial for debt burden to be transferred to future generations. However, if the bond issuance policy is permanently maintained, then taxes will never have to be levied on any generations so the relevance of debt burden transfer on future generations with finite horizons is unclear. Is it always possible to avoid debt burden by issuing debt permanently? Section 3 clarifies the notion of sustainability of deficits and considers its determinants and hence provides both the theoretical rationale for the critique of borrowing and an argument for borrowing. Since the use of capital outlays will extend over a long period, it is fair to spread the burden among the successive generations which will benefit from the service. We re-examine the rationale for the principle of tax finance of current and debt finance of capital outlays.

Finally Section 4 investigates the case where government debt issue is predetermined and taxes are determined by budgetary needs. We consider the effect of debt-tax reform on intergeneration incidence. It is now well recognised (see Diamond, 1965; and Ihori, 1978) that public debt can be regarded as a device which is used to redistribute income between the younger and the older generations. Similarly, tax reforms among distortionary taxes may be investigated from the viewpoint of the timing of tax payments. Thus, it is natural to analyse the debt-tax reform within the same framework. We clarify theoretically the effect of timing of effective tax payments (including debt issuance) on the welfare of earlier generations during the transition process.

2 THE DEGREE OF DEBT NEUTRALITY

2.1 Introduction

This section is an investigation of the degree of debt neutrality in the Japanese economy. Primitive empirical evidence is brought to bear on the following questions. To what extent is consumption sensitive to the choice of tax versus debt financing of current government expenditure? To what extent is public debt treated as net wealth?

The debt neutrality question has stimulated a considerable amount of research since Barro's (1974) revival of the 'Ricardian neutrality' proposition, that is, as a first approximation, that the choice between current taxation and debt issuance to finance a given government expenditure stream is irrelevant to the determination of the level of aggregate demand. Most of the literature examines empirically the question of whether or not the debt neutrality proposition holds. Among others Kochin (1974), Tanner (1979), Kormendi (1983) and Aschauer (1985) obtain empirical results favourable to the debt neutrality proposition. On the other hand, Feldstein (1982) rejects some of the assumptions adopted in the empirical specifications of Kochin, Barro and Tanner and comes to the conclusion that debt neutrality is contradicted by the data. Boskin and Kotlikoff (1985) cast doubt on the contention that government debt policy does not affect consumption and saving. As for the Japanese economy, Ihori (1985) and Homma *et al.* (1986) obtain empirical results which do not necessarily reject debt neutrality. However, the degree of debt neutrality has been little investigated.[1]

Even if the data cannot reject debt neutrality, it does not necessarily imply that the extreme debt neutrality proposition holds. Therefore, it is useful to investigate the following question: to what extent is the debt neutrality proposition relevant to the real economy?

This section examines the degree of debt neutrality for the Japanese economy. In subsection 2.2 the degree of debt neutrality is theoretically defined within the framework of Blanchard's (1985) 'uncertain lifetime' approach. In subsection 2.3 the consumption function is estimated for the Japanese economy, and the degree of debt neutrality is calculated. Finally, subsection 2.4 concludes this section.

2.2 Theoretical Considerations

As is well known there are several ways by which a 'fully rational' model can incorporate the feature that debt burden matters. In order to define the index of the degree of debt neutrality, we develop a finite horizon model of identical individuals that contains the essential of Blanchard's work. Each agent throughout his life faces a constant probability of death, p. At any instant of time a large cohort, whose size is normalised to be p, is born. If the probability of death is constant, the expected remaining life for an agent for any age is given by p^{-1}. As p goes to zero, p^{-1} goes to infinity: agents have infinite horizons when $p = 0$.

Under the assumption that instantaneous utility is logarithmic, as shown by Blanchard aggregate consumption is given by

$$C = (p + e)(H + W). \tag{6.1}$$

Aggregate consumption C is a linear function of aggregate human and non-human wealth, $H + W$. e is the rate of time preference.

Human wealth is the present value of future labour income accruing to those currently alive.

$$H = (YW - T)/(r + p) \tag{6.2}$$

where YW is permanent labour income, T is permanent taxes and r is the constant rate of interest. If agents have finite horizons (if $p > 0$), then the discount rate on non-interest income $YW - T$, $(t + p)$, exceeds the interest rate (r).

The government spends on goods G that do not affect the marginal utility of private consumption and finances spending either by lump-sum taxes T or debt issuance D. Its dynamic budget constraint is $\dot{D} = rD + G - T$. When G and T are permanently fixed, its budget constraint is in the long run

$$rD + G = T. \tag{6.3}$$

Under the transversality condition (6.3) is equivalent to the statement that the level of debt is equal to the present discounted value of future surpluses $((G - T)/r)$.

The case of a small open economy is considered where the interest rate is given by the world interest rate r, at which consumers can freely borrow and lend. For simplicity, there is no real capital and the only private assets are therefore the net holdings of foreign assets F and government debt D. Therefore, we have

$$\dot{F} = rF + YW - C - G. \tag{6.4}$$

Equation (6.4) is regarded as the equilibrium condition for the goods market. $\dot{F}$ is a surplus of the current account, and $\dot{F} - rF$ is the trade balance.

From (6.1)–(6.3) we have

$$C = (p+e)\left(\frac{YW-G}{r+p} + \frac{p}{r+p}D + F\right). \tag{6.5}$$

An increase in taxes and debt ($dT = rdD > 0$) does not affect income but leads agents to feel wealthier by an amount $p/(p+r)dD$. This leads then to an increase in consumption and to a decumulation of foreign assets. $p/(p+r)$ is the wealth effect of debt. If $p = 0$ (the infinite horizon case), $p/(p+r)$ is zero; debt will not be regarded as net wealth. The choice between current taxation and debt issuance to finance a given government expenditure stream is irrelevant to the determination of the level of aggregate demand. We have the extreme debt neutrality case. On the other hand, if $p = 1$, $p/(r+p)$ is approximately equal to one; debt will be regarded as being perfectly substitutable with foreign assets. We have the extreme Keynesian case.

Therefore it is natural to denote by $x \equiv 1 - [p/(r+p)]$ the degree of debt neutrality. If $p = 0$ then $x = 1$, and if $p = 1$ then $x = r/(1+r)$. The index $1 - x$ indicates to what extent public debt will be regarded as net wealth. In other words x shows the extent to which private consumption is insensitive to the choice of tax versus debt financing of government expenditure, and hence x may be regarded as the degree of debt neutrality.

There are several remarks to be made as to the plausibility of index x. First, x is dependent on r and x increases with r. Even if p remains constant, any change in r will alter index x. For example, if $r = 0$, then $x = 0$ for any $p > 0$. If the rate of interest is zero, we have the extreme Keynesian case, irrespective of the level of p. Secondly, x may not be the only candidate for the index of the degree of debt neutrality. From (6.4) and (6.5) in the steady state we have

$$F = \{(r-e)(YW-G) - (p+e)pD\}/(p+e-r)(r+p). \tag{6.6}$$

Equation (6.6) implies that government debt displaces foreign assets in agents' wealth. The displacement is almost one for one if $p = 1$. On the other hand, in the infinite horizon case ($p = 0$) the level of debt has no effect on the steady-state level of F. Hence an alternative candidate for the index of the degree of debt neutrality would be $z \equiv 1 - (1 - x)(p + e)/(p + e - r)$. $1 - z$ shows the extent to which government debt displaces foreign assets in agents wealth, and hence reflects the degree of substitution of government deficits and current accounts. However, as for the degree of debt neutrality z is less plausible than x. If $r > e$, then z is negative, z may not be between 0 and 1 for plausible values of p, e, and r. It is desirable to normalise the degree of debt neutrality between 0 and 1. Therefore, this section adopts x as the index of the degree of debt neutrality.

2.3 Empirical Results

This subsection presents preliminary time-series evidence for the Japanese economy on the degree of debt neutrality. A private sector consumption function based on the uncertain lifetime approach is estimated. Some evidence of the degree of debt neutrality for the Japanese economy is presented.

Consider as an empirical specification of the private sector consumption function the following modified version of equation (6.5).

$$C_t = a_0 + a_1(Y_t - G_t) + a_2 D_t + a_3 F_t + u_t \qquad (6.7)$$

where Y is NNP (net national product), G is government spending on goods and services, D is government debt, and F is net foreign assets.

There is a difference between (6.5) and (6.7). In (6.5) income is labour income YW, while in (6.7) NNP is used for income. The difference is capital income rK. In this section, following Kormendi (1983), a simple version of the permanent income hypothesis is used in order to focus on the issues of how the private sector responds to government fiscal policy. If capital income is explicitly considered, (6.5) will be altered to:

$$C = (p + e)\{(YW - G)/(r + p) + [p/(r + p)]D + F + K\}. \qquad (6.5)'$$

Substituting $Y = YW + rK$, we have

$$C = (p + e)\{(Y - G)/(r + p) + [p/(r + p)](D + K) + F\}. \qquad (6.5)''$$

Because of the unavailability of the quarterly data on real capital, we use (6.7) in place of (6.5)''.[2]

Theoretical considerations imply positive coefficients for $Y-G$, D, and $F(a_1, a_2, a_3 > 0)$ and it is expected that the coefficient for F is greater than the coefficient for $D(a_3 > a_2)$. The index of the degree of debt neutrality x is given by $1 - a_2/a_3$.

Table 6.1 reports the results of estimating (6.7) over the period first quarter 1970 to fourth quarter 1983 in two forms; ordinary least squares (OLS) in the first differences, and OLS in the ratios divided by Y. A quick inspection of Table 6.1 reveals that the coefficient estimates are similar across the two forms of equations, which indicates that the results may not suffer from spurious regression problems. The results on the individual coefficients in Table 6.1 conform to the implications of the uncertain lifetime approach quite well. The coefficient on $Y-G$ is of reasonable magnitude and t-statistics is significantly large. The coefficient on D is positive and smaller than the coefficient on F. The index of the degree of debt neutrality x is calculated as 82 and 73 per cent. Therefore, Table 6.1 suggests that x would be in the range of 70 to 80 per cent.

Recently, Seater and Mariano (1985) have estimated a version of the

Table 6.1

	Constant	$Y-G$	D	F	R^2	DW	X
(1)	2582 (3.27)	0.45 (6.22)	0.03 (2.24)	0.17 (6.36)	0.63	1.25	0.82
(2)	−0.03 (−0.24)	0.66 (6.30)	0.03 (7.69)	0.11 (3.11)	0.54	1.59	0.73

Notes: t-statistics are shown in parentheses. All variables are stated as real per capita amounts. DW is the Durbin–Watson statistic: (1) reports OLS in the first differences, and (2) OLS in the ratios divided by Y.
C = private consumer expenditure
Y = net national product
Y^* = normal values for Y computed according to the Beveridge–Nelson method.
G = expenditures of general government
G^* = normal values of G computed according to the Beveridge–Nelson method.
D = cumulative deficits of general government
F = net holdings of foreign assets.
All variables are stated as real per capita amounts.

Table 6.2

	Constant	Y*−G*	D	F	R^2	DW	X
(1)	6261	0.55	0.035	0.149	0.57	1.42	0.76
	(7.14)	(4.28)	(0.05)	(4.26)			
(2)	−0.086	0.70	0.031	0.11	0.57	1.57	0.72
	(−1.03)	(10.10)	(7.76)	(2.57)			

Notes: See Table 6.1.

Source: All variables are taken from the Annual Report of National Account (Economic Planning Agency).

permanent income consumption function by using Beveridge and Nelson's (1981) method to conduct series on permanent income. The procedure is to estimate an ARIMA model for Y and then compute the stochastic steady state values of Y for each period t. These steady state values are the normal levels, denoted Y^*. Normal government spending G^* is estimated by using the Beveridge–Nelson method as well.

Table 6.2 reports the results of estimating (6.7) where $Y^* - G^*$ in place of $Y - G$ is used in two forms; OLS in the first differences and OLS in the ratios. Comparing the estimates in Table 6.2 with those in Table 6.1 reveals the coefficients to be stable. Table 6.2 suggests that the degree of debt neutrality would be in the range of 72 per cent to 76 per cent.[3]

2.4 Comment

It is well known that the general government's budgets in Japan were generally in balance or in surplus until 1974. From 1975 the deficit:GNP ratio continued to rise to 5.5 per cent in 1978. In 1979 an introduction of general consumption taxation became a big political issue. It is plausible to think that individuals recognise the future tax obligations implicit in current debt issuance more fully when the government deficits are at the higher levels of the late 1970s.

Ihori (1985) and Homma et al. (1986) suggest that it is more likely in recent years that the data are incapable of rejecting debt neutrality. However, the degree of debt neutrality has not been estimated. The present preliminary results show that the degree of debt neutrality would be in the range of 70 to 80 per cent.[4]

No empirical study is without its caveats and this section is no exception as it has not considered many aspects of reality. The estimated values of the structural parameters should be regarded as giving a rough idea about the empirical magnitudes, rather than as exact values. We should not overstate the explanatory power of these results. It would be useful to estimate the degree of debt neutrality by using micro data.

The neoclassical school of macroeconomic policy stresses the real effects of government spending rather than the method by which such spending is financed. The empirical results of this section suggest that the debt neutrality view of the effects of fiscal policy actions on the economy deserves at least some credibility for the Japanese economy. The empirical results also suggest that debt neutrality does not hold perfectly. The standard Keynesian approach to modelling private consumption behaviour deserves at least some credibility as well. This set of results, taken as a whole, is inconsistent with both the perfect debt neutrality hypothesis and the more traditional hypothesis. The results suggest that reality lies between these extremes. As the conditions for perfect debt neutrality are quite restrictive, our results are intuitively appealing. Therefore, from now on Barro's line of argument is not followed. Allowance is made for the possibility that public debt will place at least some burden on the future. For purposes of analytical tractability the formulation developed in Diamond (1965) and Samuelson (1958) is adopted.

3 THE CHAIN-LETTER MECHANISM OF GOVERNMENT DEBT

3.1 Introduction

As inflation recedes, fiscal deficits are becoming the major source of concern for economic policy. Concern that present levels of budget deficits are abnormal and undesirable is reflected in the fact that a majority of OECD countries have been following budget strategies which aim to reduce, or eliminate, their deficits in the medium-term. In Europe and Japan, the large current deficits are inhibiting the use of further, even temporary, fiscal expansion; indeed at the bottom of a recession, many governments are attempting to reduce spending and increase tax revenues. In the United States, on the other hand, current deficits are large and anticipated deficits much larger. It is argued that the current deficits are not sustainable, that governments in those countries will be forced in effect to repudiate their debt, either explicitly or through inflation depreciation. The purpose of this section is to clarify the notion of sustainability of deficits and to think about its determinants from the viewpoint of the chain-letter mechanism of debt finance.

The chain-letter mechanism is briefly described as the one in which individuals would be willing to hold ever-expanding amounts of public debt without regard to the government's limited capacity to raise revenue for debt payment. The chain-letter mechanism is associated with the case of a permanent deficit, financed by infinitely continuing issuance of bonds. In that case, as the deficit continues, the outstanding bond stock continues to grow. So, accordingly, does the interest that must be paid each period on the outstanding stock.

The chain-letter mechanism has been investigated in a maximising model that incorporates the crucial components of the Ricardian view, namely, agents of infinite lives who correctly take account of the government budget constraint. Under these circumstances Barro (1976) argues that the value of the outstanding stock of debt at any point in time is bounded by the government's present value of future taxing capacity and consequently that the mechanism is unlikely to exist. Sargent and Wallace (1981) argue that the chain-letter mechanism cannot go on forever, since the demand for bonds places an upper limit on the stock of bonds relative to the size of the economy. McCallum (1984) counteracts Barro and Sargent-Wallace by arguing that if the bond issuance policy is permanently maintained, then taxes will never have to be collected and that under the Ricardian view government bonds are not regarded as net wealth to the private sector. McCallum shows that permanently maintained, positive per capita deficit is feasible if the deficit is measured as inclusive of interest payments but is not feasible if the deficit is measured exclusive of interest payments. Kanaya (1984) shows that the chain-letter mechanism of debt finance is inconsistent with economic agents' income maximising behaviour.

It seems that there has been little work examining the chain-letter mechanism in a finite horizon setting. As stated in the previous section, the finite-horizon formulation developed in Diamond (1965) and Samuelson (1958) is adopted.

It is well recognised that the assumption of a finite horizon is crucial for debt burden to be transferred to future generations. If the bond issuance policy is permanently maintained, then taxes will never have to be levied on any generation so the relevance of debt burden transfer on future generations with finite horizons is unclear. Is it always possible to avoid debt burden within a finite horizon framework by issuing debt permanently?

The outline of this section is as follows. Subsection 3.2 develops an analytical framework. Subsection 3.3 examines the feasibility of the chain-letter mechanism of debt finance. Subsection 3.4 investigates the welfare aspect of the mechanism from the viewpoint of intergeneration equity. Finally, subsection 3.5 provides some remarks on the principle of tax finance of current and debt finance of capital outlays.

3.2 Analytical Framework

We develop an overlapping generations growth model of identical individuals that contains the essentials of both Diamond (1965) and Gale's (1973) work extending Samuelson's consumption-loans model. In the first period of his life an individual works, consumes and saves. Savings are done in the form of durable goods. In the second period he retires and consumes the fruits of his first-period savings plus the accumulated interest. The number of young consumers or labour force in period t, L_t, is assumed to grow exponentially, i.e. $L_t = (1+n)^t L_0$, where n is the rate of population growth. Here, superscript t means generation t and subscript t means period t.

When the matter of justification for burden transfer among generations is concerned, it is best to separate this problem from the expenditure issue. It is assumed that in every period the government expends a constant required quantity of the consumption good (g) per labour force and collects a constant required quantity (τ) per labour force by means of lump-sum taxation. τ is not necessarily equal to g. Furthermore, in period 0 the government is assumed to expend an extra quantity of the consumption good (g_0) per worker. The resulting deficit will be financed by means of bond issuance. In this section tax τ is predetermined and government debt issue b is determined by budgetary deficits.

Consider a young person in period 0. He has a standard utility function.

$$u^0 = u(c_1^0, C_2^0) \tag{6.8}$$

when c_1^0 is his first-period consumption and c_2^0 is his second-period consumption. His consumption and saving programmes are restricted by the following first- and second-period budget constraints.

$$c_1^0 = w_0 - s_0 - \tau - b_0 \tag{6.9}$$

$$c_2^0 = (1 + r_1)(s_0 + b_0) \tag{6.10}$$

where w_0 is real wage in period 0. s_0 is his savings of real capital (excluding public debt holdings). τ is lump-sum tax levied on him, b_0 is per-capita debt issuance to generation 0 and r_1 is real rate of interest in period 1.

Therefore, his saving function can be expressed as

$$s_0 = \alpha(w_0 - \tau) - b_0. \tag{6.11}$$

The sign of $\partial s/\partial r_1$ depends on the relative magnitude of income and substitution effects. For simplicity the propensity to save α is assumed to be constant.[5]

The government budget constraint in period 0 is simply

$$g + g_0 = \tau + b_0. \tag{6.12}$$

The case of $g = \tau$ and hence $g_0 = b_0$ may be called pure debt finance of the extra expenditure.

Since s_0 is used for production in period 1 as capital,

$$s_0 = (1 + n)k_1 \tag{6.13}$$

where k_1 is the capital-labour ratio in period 1.

The optimising behaviour of an individual of generation t $(t \geqslant 1)$ is the same as that of generation 0. His saving function is given by the same form as (6.11). The government budget constraint in period t is

$$L_t g + (1 + r_t)b_{t-1}L_{t-1} = L_t \tau + L_t b_t \tag{6.14}$$

or

$$g + \frac{1 + r_t}{1 + n} b_{t-1} = \tau + b_t.$$

Production will use both capital and labour, resulting in a constant return to scale production function. Based on cost minimising behaviour, the factor-price frontier is given by

$$w_t = w(r_t), \qquad w' = -k_t. \tag{6.15}$$

Hence, this economy may be summarised by the following two equations where r_0 and b_0 are initially given.

$$b_{t+1} = (1 + r_{t+1})b_t/(1+n) + (g - \tau) \tag{6.16}$$

$$\alpha w(r_t) = -(1+n)w'(r_{t+1}) + b_t + \alpha\tau \qquad (t \geq 0). \tag{6.17}$$

3.3 The Chain-Letter Mechanism

Tax Finance

First of all, it is useful to explore the dynamic property of tax finance. As stated in Section 1, the burden of debt is defined to be a decrease in utility level of future generations which would not exist if the government debt were not issued and instead taxes were collected. Therefore, the purpose of this subsection is to explore the welfare aspect of taxation and debt finance on the current and the successive generations. Under tax finance $g_0 + g = \tau + \tau_0$, where τ_0 is extra taxes in period 0. For future generation t $(t \geq 1)$ $g = \tau$, and hence the government's budget is always balanced.

Thus, the economy may be summarised by the following two equations, where r_0 and g_0 are initially given.

$$\alpha w(r_0) = -(1+n)w'(r_1) + \alpha(g_0 + g) \tag{6.18}$$

$$\alpha w(r_t) = -(1+n)w'(r_{t+1}) + \alpha g \qquad (t \geq 1). \tag{6.19}$$

In order to analyse the welfare aspect of tax finance on each generation, it will be useful to explore dynamic properties of the economy. The stability condition for this economy is

$$0 < -\frac{\alpha w'}{(1+n)w''} < 1. \tag{6.20}$$

From now on we assume (6.20). (6.20) may be reduced to $(1+n)w'' + \alpha w' > 0$, which is likely to hold when the elasticity of substitution between capital and labour is large. This is essentially what Diamond assumes for the stability of his model. In order to make it meaningful to compare with debt finance, the system is assumed to be stable in tax finance. Under (6.20) r will monotonically converge to the long-run equilibrium level, r^*.

Debt Finance

In order to analyse the welfare aspect of the chain-letter mechanism on each generation, it will be useful to explore dynamic properties of the economy. Let us investigate dynamic properties of this economy using a phase diagram.[6] To analyse the behaviour of b_t, we first find the locus of (b, r) where $b_{t+1} = b_t$. We call this locus the bb curve. From (6.16) this locus is given by

$$b(n - r) = (g - \tau)(1 + n). \tag{6.21}$$

If $g = \tau$, this locus, illustrated in Figure 6.1, is given by $r = n$ and $b = 0$. If $g < \tau$, this locus is the rectangular hyperbola, illustrated in Figure 6.2. If $g > \tau$, this locus is the rectangular hyperbola, illustrated in Figure 6.3. By differentiating (6.16) partially with respect to r_t,

$$\frac{\partial b_{t+1}}{\partial r_t} = \frac{1}{1+n} b_t > 0 \quad \text{(if } b > 0\text{)}. \tag{6.22}$$

Hence if $b > 0$ on the right-hand side of the bb curve, $b_{t+1} > b_t$, and on the left-hand side of the bb curve, $b_{t+1} < b_t$. If r were not changed, on the right (left) hand side of the bb curve b will increase (decrease).

On the other hand the locus of $r_t = r_{t+1}$ is determined by analysing (6.17). We call this locus the rr curve. Substituting $r = r_{t+1} = r$ into (6.17), and totally differentiating (6.17), we have the slope of the rr curve as

$$\frac{db}{dr} = (1 + n)w'' + \alpha w' \tag{6.23}$$

which is likely to be positive when the elasticity of substitution between capital and labour is large. This is essentially the stability condition under pure tax finance. Denote r at $b = 0$ by r^*. Then the rr curve is given by an upward-sloping curve from r^*. Note that r^* is the same as the long-run equilibrium r in pure tax finance. By differentiating (6.17) partially with respect to b_t,

$$\frac{\partial r_{t+1}}{\partial b_t} = \frac{1}{(1+n)w''} > 0. \tag{6.24}$$

Hence, above the rr curve $r_{t+1} > r_t$, and below this locus $r_{t+1} < r_t$. If b were not changed, above (below) this locus r will increase (decrease).

For given tastes and technology there are two kinds of steady states which we labelled as E_A and E_B. Here 'A' subscripts denote variables in a Gale type-A equilibrium and 'B' subscripts denote variables in a Gale type-B equilibrium. From stability viewpoint, type A equilibrium is always a saddlepoint and hence unstable except only one path aa. Above this borderline (the aa curve), the economy eventually goes bankrupt; b and r will eventually approach to the infinite. As b increases, savings of real capital (excluding public debt holdings) will be reduced. Sooner or later, savings of real capital turn to be negative. However, because of the non-negative constraint of real capital, the system would not work in such a case. We may call such a situation bankruptcy of the economy.

It may be that b is negative. However, since we are concerned with debt burden and the chain-letter mechanism, we will concentrate on the case of $b > 0$. We have three possibilities; $g = \tau$, $g < \tau$, and $g > \tau$. In Figure 6.1, where the narrowly defined government budget is balanced ($g = \tau$), there are two kinds of steady states. Figure 6.1(a) corresponds to the 'Samuelson' case of $r^* < n$, and Figure 6.1(b) corresponds to the 'classical' case of $r^* < n$. In Figure 6.1(a) there are two types of equilibrium E_A and E_B. At E_A $r = n$ and at E_B $b = 0$. In Figure 6.1(b) there exists only one type of equilibrium E_A. In Figure 6.1(b) the economy will go bankrupt eventually. The chain-letter mechanism is

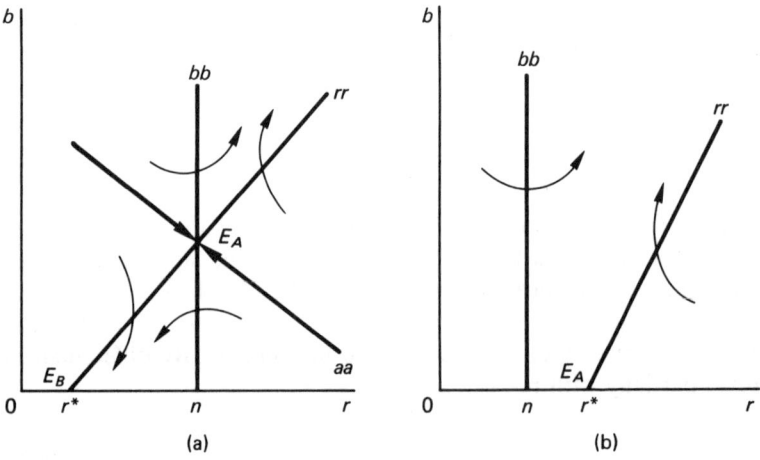

Figure 6.1

not feasible in the long run. In Figure 6.1(a), on the other hand, if the initial condition (b_0, r_0) is below the aa curve, the economy eventually approaches to r^*. The chain-letter mechanism is feasible in the long run. Which case is more relevant to the real economy, the 'Samuelson' case of $r^* < n$ (Figure 6.1(a)) or the 'classical' case of $r^* > n$ (Figure 6.1(b))? As an example, consider an economy with Cobb–Douglas production and utility functions.

$$u(c_1, c_2) = (1 - \alpha)\log c_1 + \alpha \log c_2$$

$$f(k) = k^\beta$$

Then, the long-run equilibrium r under $b = 0$ (r^*) is given by

$$r^* = \frac{\beta(1+n)}{\alpha(1-\beta)}. \tag{6.25}$$

Let n^* denote the critical growth rate that satisfies

$$r^* = n$$

or

$$n^* = \frac{\beta}{\alpha(1-\beta) - \beta}.$$

Therefore, if $n > n^*$, we have the 'Samuelson' case of $r^* < n$ (Figure 6.1(a)), and if $n^* > n$, we have the 'classical' case of $r^* > n$ (Figure 6.1(b)). Suppose $\alpha < \frac{1}{2}$ and $\beta > \frac{1}{3}$. Then, $n^* < 0 < n$; we have the classical case. It seems that it is more likely to have the classical case than the Samuelson case for plausible values of α and β. Hence, the chain-letter mechanism may not be feasible in the long run in the case of $\tau = g$.

In Figure 6.2, where the narrowly defined government budget is in surplus ($g < \tau$), there exists only one type of equilibrium E_A irrespective of the sign of $r^* - n$. Above the aa curve the economy eventually goes bankrupt. Below the aa curve a permanently maintained, positive per capita deficit is feasible in the long run.

In Figure 6.3, where the narrowly defined government budget is in deficit ($g > \tau$), there may not exist an equilibrium at all. In Figure 6.3(a), where r^* is significantly small compared with n, there are two types of equilibria, E_A and E_B. In Figure 6.3(b), where r^* is relatively large,

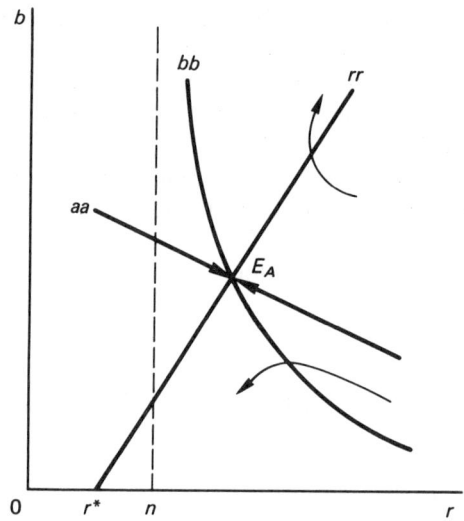

Figure 6.2

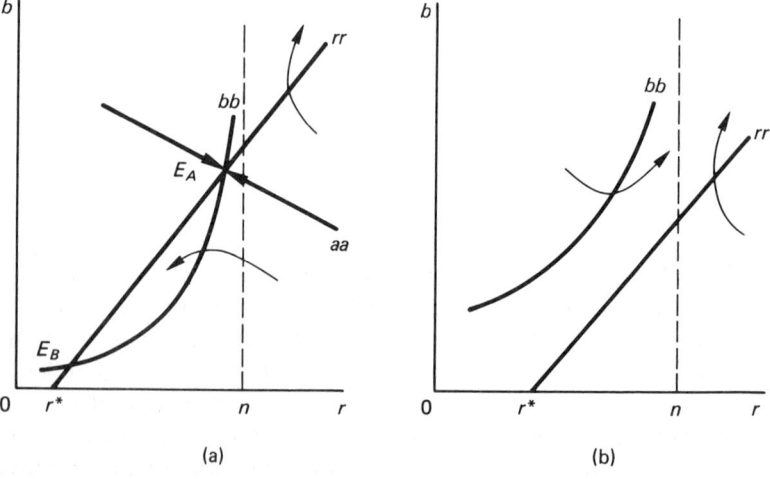

Figure 6.3

there is no equilibrium at all. If $r^* > n$, we always have the case of Figure 6.3(b). In Figure 6.3(b) the economy eventually goes bankrupt; b and r will eventually approach to the infinite.

We have investigated dynamic properties of this economy using a phase diagram.[7] If the economy eventually converges to the long-run equilibrium, we could say that the chain-letter mechanism is feasible in the long-run. A permanently maintained positive per capita deficit is feasible in the long-run. If the economy will not converge to the long-run equilibrium, the economy eventually goes bankrupt. The chain-letter mechanism of debt finance is inconsistent with economic agents' utility maximising behaviour in such a case.

Dynamic properties of this economy suggest that the chain-letter mechanism is likely to be feasible in the following cases. First, for given values of g and τ, the initial extra government spending (g_0) and the corresponding initial bond issue (b_0) are relatively small. In such a case the economy is likely to be below the borderline (the aa curve). It is intuitively plausible that a large extra government spending financed by debt issuance may well be inconsistent with the sustainability of deficits.

Second, the long-run equilibrium r under $b = 0$, r^*, is relatively small. The smaller is r^*, the more likely it is to have the case of Figure 6.1(a) or Figure 6.3(a), and to have equilibrium E_B. In the case of Cobb–Douglas production and utility functions, if the saving propensity (α) is large and if the relative share of capital income (β) is small, r^* is small. In such a case the chain-letter mechanism of debt finance is likely feasible.

Third, the steady state level of $g - \tau$ is relatively small. The economy is more likely to be below the aa curve in Figure 6.2 ($g < \tau$) than in Figure 6.3 ($g > \tau$). The primary deficit $g - \tau$ is the narrowly defined

Table 6.3 General government financial balances net of interest payments surplus or deficit ($-$) as percentage of nominal GDP at market prices

Major seven countries	1977	1978	1979	1980	1981	1982
United States	0.3	1.3	1.8	0.1	0.8	-1.8
Japan	-1.9	-3.3	-2.1	-1.3	-0.4	0.2
West Germany	-0.7	-0.8	-1.0	-1.2	-1.7	-1.2
France	0.5	-0.4	0.9	1.9	0.3	-0.5
United Kingdom	1.2	0.3	1.5	1.7	2.8	3.4
Italy	-3.0	-3.9	-3.7	-1.8	-4.5	-3.6
Canada	1.8	1.8	3.3	3.4	4.7	1.7
Total	-0.2	-0.2	0.5	0.0	0.3	-0.8

Source: National Accounts Statistics of OECD countries.

deficit, i.e. the permanently maintained deficit measured exclusive of interest payments.

Table 6.3 shows general government financial balances net of interest payments for major seven countries. As for Italy the primary deficit $g - \tau$ is large. For total major seven countries, $g - \tau$ is almost balanced. Thus sustainability might indeed be an issue in Italy: it appears to be less so in other countries.

In an infinite horizon setting McCallum (1984) shows that if the deficit is measured exclusive of interest payments a constant noninflationary per capita deficit is not feasible. The present result is consistent with McCallum. In such a case this section shows that the chain-letter mechanism is unlikely to be feasible in a finite horizon setting as well. However, excluding interest payments in the deficit is not the only determinant of the infeasible mechanism. As Figure 6.3(a) shows, it is still possible to have the feasible chain-letter mechanism if b_0 is small and r^* is small.

3.4 Intergeneration Equity

In this subsection we explore the relative burden of debt and taxation on each generation. First of all, we analyse the welfare effect of tax finance and debt finance during the growth process, respectively.

Tax Finance

Let us examine the effect of tax finance on the utility of each generation t, $u^t(t \geqslant 1)$. u^t is dependent on r_t. As shown in the Appendix, $du^t/dr_t < 0$ if $w' + (1 + r_{t+1})w''$ is positive and large. Thus, if the elasticity of substitution between capital and labour is large, which is consistent with the stability condition (6.20), higher capital endowment given to any generation makes its lifetime utility u^t higher. An increase in k_t raises w_t and lowers r_{t+1}. The former effect will increase u^t, while the latter effect will decrease u^t. If the elasticity of substitution is large, a decrease in r_t raises w_t substantially. The net effect is likely to increase u^t under the stability condition.[8] Therefore, on the growth process where capital accumulation is monotonically increased, each generation's lifetime utility is monotonically increased. Note that r^* is independent of g_0. The government intervention in period 0 will not affect long-run utility (u^*) at all. u^* is independent of g_0.

Debt Finance

Let us examine the welfare of each generation in the chain-letter mechanism. u^t is dependent on b_t and r_t. The Appendix shows that the effect of r_t on u^t is negative if the elasticity of substitution between capital and labour is large.

Secondly, the effect of b_t on u^t is considered. As shown in the Appendix, if the elasticity of substitution between capital and labour is large, an increase in b_t will raise u^t. From (6.24) an increase in b_t will raise r_{t+1}, which will enlarge its consumption possibilities for given r_t and w_t. From the properties of these partial derivatives if r_t decreases and b_t increases, u^t will increase. When b_t and r_t change in a same direction, the net effect on u^t is ambiguous, dependent on the magnitude of both effects. However, when b_t is large, an increase in b_t will not raise u^t any more. The Appendix also shows that when the economy goes bankrupt, utility will eventually drop to the minimum level.

Intergeneration Equity

It should be stressed that when considering the intergeneration equity, it is necessary to look beyond simply the changes in steady state utility. We now investigate the welfare effect of government policy during the growth process. First of all, let us investigate the welfare of the present generation 0. In the case of pure debt finance ($g = \tau$ and $G_0 = b_0$) it is easy to show $du^0/dg_0 > 0$. It is because from (6.24) an increase in b_0 will raise r_1 and hence u^0. At the given level of r_0, an increase in r_1 is beneficial for generation 0.

How are the successive generations affected by the extra government expenditure (g_0) in period 0? It is useful to distinguish between future generations close to the present generation 0 (the near future generation) and future generations far from the present generation 0 (the distant future generation). We pick up generation 1 representing future generations close to the present generation (the near future generation). In the case of pure debt finance ($g_0 = b_0$) an increase in g_0 may well raise u^1. We now explore this aspect using the indirect utility function.

Let us denote the indirect utility function of generation 1 derived from consumption stream as $u(w(r_1) - \tau, r_2)$ with the familiar properties that

$$u_1 = \gamma \quad \text{and} \quad u_2 = \gamma c_2/(1 + r_2) \qquad (6.26)$$

where $u_1 = \partial u/\partial w$, and $u_2 = \partial u/\partial r$. Here γ indicates the marginal utility of lifetime income. Considering (6.16) and (6.17), we have

$$\frac{dr_1}{db_0} = \frac{1}{(1+n)w''(r_1)} \tag{6.27}$$

$$\frac{dr_2}{db_0} = -\frac{1}{(1+n)w''(r_2)}\left[\alpha w'(r_1)\frac{dr_1}{db_0} - \frac{1+r_1}{1+n}\right] \quad \text{(when } b_0 = 0\text{)}. \tag{6.28}$$

Therefore, we have

$$\frac{du^1}{db_0} = \gamma w''(r_1)\frac{dr_1}{db_0} + \gamma \frac{c_2}{1+r_2}\frac{dr_2}{db_0} \tag{6.29}$$

$$= \frac{\gamma}{(1+n)w''(r_1)w''(r_2)}[w'(r_1)w''(r_2) - w'(r_2)w''(r_1)(1+r_1)$$

$$+ w'(r_2)w'(r_1)\alpha].$$

As $w'(r_1)w''(r_2)$ is approximately equal to $w'(r_2)w''(r_1)$, du^1/db_0 is likely to be positive. Therefore, debt finance is attractive for generation 1 as well as generation 0. In other words, for future generations close to the present generation their utility levels are likely to be increasing with bond issuance in period 0.[9]

The welfare aspect of debt finance in the long run is now analysed. Welfare of the distant future generation may be represented by the long-run equilibrium utility.

The nature of long-run equilibrium is dependent on the level of the initial bond issue b_0. It is useful to consider the following three possibilities as to the magnitude of b_0.

1. b_0 is on curve aa (see Figure 6.1(a), Figure 6.2, and Figure 6.3(a)).

We call this level of $b_0\tilde{b}_0$. The economy will approach to E_A. In Figure 6.1 ($\tau = g$), this is the golden rule path. As utility on the golden rule path ($\tilde{u}$) is the highest among steady state utility levels, it is higher than utility at E_B. In Figure 6.2 or Figure 6.3(a) E_A is not associated with the golden rule path. However, utility at E_A is higher than utility at E_B in Figure 6.3(a). The chain-letter mechanism on curve aa is consistent with utility maximising behaviour. Hence, in this case the relative burden of debt will not occur in the long run.

2. b_0 is below curve aa (see Figure 6.1(a), Figure 6.2, and Figure 6.3(a)).

When b_0 is below $\bar{b}_0$, the economy will approach to E_B. In Figure 6.1(a) in the long run u^t will approach u^*, which is associated with the case of pure tax finance. In Figure 6.2 in the long-run b is negative, so the chain-letter mechanism of debt issuance will disappear in the long run. In Figure 6.3(a) the long-run equilibrium b is positive, so the chain-letter mechanism is feasible in the long-run. As long as b_0 is below curve aa, the long-run utility is independent of whether the initial extra expenditure is financed by debt issuance or taxes. Hence, the relative burden of debt will not occur in the long-run. The chain-letter mechanism below curve aa is consistent with utility maximising behaviour.

3. b_0 is above curve aa (see Figure 6.1(a), Figure 6.2, and Figure 6.3(a)), $r^* > n$ (Figure 6.1(b)), or there is no equilibrium at all (Figure 6.3(b)).

In this case the economy will approach a catastrophe. In the long run debt outstanding will increase at the expense of private capital decumulation. Capital decumulation will lower utility of future generations. Thus, the relative burden of debt will occur in the long run. Eventually private capital turns to be negative; the economy goes bankrupt. The chain-letter mechanism above curve aa is inconsistent with utility maximising behaviour.

In order to explore the policy implications, it is necessary to specify individuals' preferences, and such utility functions should be used for welfare evaluations. Although the objective function may take several forms, our analysis suggests the following. It is useful to divide the future into two parts – the near future and the distant future. When the economy eventually goes bankrupt, the chain-letter mechanism of debt finance is undesirable as long as the government is concerned with the welfare of the distant future generation. If the government is solely concerned with the welfare of the present and near future generations, the chain-letter mechanism of debt finance could be a reality. From the point of view of intergeneration equity, it seems that the infeasible chain-letter mechanism will be undesirable.

If the economy does not approach a catastrophe, the relative burden of debt will not be transferred in the long run. The chain-letter mechanism of debt finance may well be desirable for the near and distant future generations. Here the chain-letter mechanisms of debt finance may be

3.5 Comment

It has been argued in the conventional textbook (see, for example, Musgrave and Musgrave, 1977) that the principle of tax finance of current and debt finance of capital outlays is in line with intergeneration equity. The rationale for this argument is that each generation should pay for its own share in the benefits received. Thus, since the use of capital outlays will extend over long years, it is fair to spread the burden among the successive generations which will benefit from the service.

Our analysis has shown that this argument is not necessarily valid once the whole path of economic growth is considered. Debt finance will not place an extra burden on the future if the economy converges to the long-run equilibrium. In this case debt finance may well be desirable even if the benefits of the government expenditure will not extend into the future. If the economy eventually goes bankrupt, debt finance will place an extra burden on the future. It does not, however, imply that capital outlays should be financed by debt issuance. This case is so catastrophic in the long run that the benefits of capital outlays to the future cannot be considered as an important factor. In this case debt finance will be undesirable from the viewpoint of the distant future generation even if the benefits of the government expenditure extend into the future.

So far public production has not been considered and it is therefore useful finally to introduce public production explicitly. For simplicity, government investment is assumed to be perfectly substitutable with private investment. Suppose in period 0 γg_0 is expended for public capital. As before g is expended for public consumption in every period. Without loss of generality $g = \tau$ is assumed. Then the government budget constraint will be

$$(1 + r_{t+1})b_t L_t = b_{t+1} L_{t+1} + \varepsilon \gamma r_{t+1} b_0 L_0 \tag{6.30}$$

where ε means the degree of marketability for public capital outlays. $\varepsilon \gamma r_{t+1} b_0 L_0$ means government revenues in period $t+1$ from public capital that was installed in period 0. If $\varepsilon = 1$, the market for the product of public capital is perfect; the government can collect all the return on public capital. If, in addition, $\gamma = 1$, then (6.30) may be reduced to

$$b_{t+1} = \frac{1}{1+n} b_t. \tag{6.31}$$

Hence, in the long run b_t will converge to zero; u^t will approach to u^*, which is associated with pure tax finance. $\gamma = 1$ means that all capital outlays are financed by debt issuance. In this sense the principle of 'tax finance of current and debt finance of capital outlays' will be justified.

If $\varepsilon < 1$, (6.30) may be reduced to

$$b_{t+1} = \frac{1}{1+n}b_t + (1-\varepsilon\gamma)b_0 r_0 \cdot \frac{r_1}{1+\eta} \cdot \frac{r_2}{1+\eta} \cdots \frac{r_{t+1}}{1+\eta}. \qquad (6.32)$$

Hence, the chain-letter mechanism of debt finance is unlikely to be feasible for lower values of ε and γ. In other words, if a larger portion of the government expenditure is used for public production and if the government collects a larger portion of the return on public capital, then it is more likely to have the feasible chain-letter mechanism. It is intuitively plausible that debt finance of capital outlays is in line with the sustainability of deficits when the marketability of the product of public capital is high.

We have employed a two-period overlapping-generations growth model to study the chain-letter mechanism of debt finance. This section has explored possibilities that the chain-letter mechanism may lead to a catastrophe. Namely, if (1) the magnitude of the initial government expenditure is large, (2) a permanently maintained positive per capita deficit is measured exclusive of interest payments (3) the saving propensity is low, and (4) the marketability of the product of public capital outlays is low, then the sustainability of the chain-letter mechanism may indeed be an issue within a finite horizon setting.

Moreover, it should be stressed that the chain-letter mechanism of debt finance will have different impacts among the future generations. In order to explore welfare implications, it is necessary to clarify how each generation is affected by debt finance. This section has shown how and why debt finance is desirable for the near future generation but not desirable for the distant future generation. This section has cleared up some of the conceptual and theoretical issues in the problem of the chain-letter mechanism of debt finance.

4 TAX REFORM AND DEBT FINANCE

4.1 Introduction

This section investigates the effects of a once-for-all change in debt finance on intergeneration incidence during the transition. Contrary to the previous section an economy is considered where the amount of tax is adjusted so that the per capita government debt is a policy variable. We call such a policy debt reform.

The effect of dynamic tax reform on intergeneration incidence is the subject of increasing interest among academic economists and economic policy makers. The effect of debt reform may be analysed in a similar way. This section seeks to contribute the comparison of debt finance and consumption, income and wage taxes. It presents a simple analytical framework for understanding intergeneration incidence from debt finance and tax reform along the transitional growth path of life-cycle economies. The principal findings of this study concern the implications of changing the timing of effective tax payments (including debt issuance) for intergeneration incidence.

Both the measurement of excess burden and the calculation of optimal tax schedules have been extended recently to the intertemporal issues surrounding the taxation of capital income. One useful framework for comparing alternative taxes is a growth model in which identical consumers optimise over their life-cycles. Feldstein (1978) presents efficiency calculations based on a two-period model in which an individual supplies labour in the first period and consumes in both periods. An alternative to the static, two-period model is the dynamic two-period model introduced by Diamond (1965). Auerbach (1979), King (1980), Atkinson and Sandmo (1980), and Ihori (1981, 1984) characterise tax structures that maximise the utility of individuals in the steady state of such an economy. For purposes of analytical tractability, these papers ignore the effect of the tax structure on the welfare of earlier generations alive during the economy's transition to its steady state. It is possible to improve the utility of steady state generations by switching from one efficient tax system to another by imposing a greater fraction of the economy's long-run tax burden on earlier, pre-steady state generations. Therefore, the implications of dynamic debt-tax reform will be relevant for the real economy.

As the incentive effects are complicated and sensitive to parametric structure, theory alone cannot provide a clear-cut guidance to efficient dynamic tax structures. With a numerical simulation model Summers (1981) compares steady state utility for a model with fixed labour supply, but a more realistic, multi-period description of life-cycle consumption behaviour. Auerbach, Kotlikoff and Skinner (1983) investigate the effects of switching from a proportional income tax with average rates similar to those in the USA to either a proportional tax on consumption or a proportional tax on labour income. As is stressed by Evans (1983), such simulation analysis, while instructive as to the behaviour of the class of models examined and as to the critical channels of influence, does not yield a theoretical presumption in favour of cutting taxes on income from capital as a means of stimulating capital formation. Such analysis can be instructive as the key theoretical influences, but cannot substitute for empirical research. In general, this type of simulation exercise is seen to be sensitive to parametric structure and to what factors are included or excluded.

By analysing the incentive effects of taxes, previous studies may give the impression that the impact on intergeneration incidence depends solely on the difference in such incentive effects on the representative person. In a two-class, disposable income growth model that eliminates the incentive effects of distortionary taxes, Seidman and Maurer (1982) show that tax reform may alter capital intensity by shifting disposable income from low to high savers. The present section employs an alternative approach that eliminates the incentive effects. Namely, within the framework of lump-sum taxation, this paper intends to analyse theoretically the effect of timing of effective tax payments (considering debt finance) on the welfare of earlier generations during the transition process.

The rationale for this approach is not that we believe that such incentive effects of distortionary taxes are unimportant. Instead, the aim is to demonstrate that even if there were no incentive effects, debt finance and taxes would generate different intergeneration incidence because consumers differ in their timing of payments. An important advantage of this approach is that the effect of debt finance and tax reform on intergeneration incidence may be investigated within the same analytical framework. Debt finance can be regarded as a device which is used to redistribute income between generations. This point is worth demonstrating because much of the literature comparing distortionary taxes may led the reader to believe that the impact on intergeneration incidence depends solely on the differing incentives on a representative person,[10] and hence the similarity between debt finance and these taxes is not well clarified.

For a constant level of revenues, it is pointed out that the consumption tax combines a one-time undistortionary lump-sum tax with a wage tax. Auerbach, Kotlikoff and Skinner stress that it is this element of lump-sum taxation, and not the exemption from taxation of capital income *per se* that is crucial to the achievement of efficient tax reform. If so, is the consumption tax always more efficient than the labour income tax? It is useful to analyse the implications of lump sum taxation for intergeneration incidence more fully. Note that public debt can be regarded as a lump sum device which is used to redistribute income between generations. Essentially, if the rate of interest is greater than the rate of population growth, the effect of a consumption tax is to reduce the lifetime present value of taxation by postponing tax payments to later in life. The tax postponement effect will be applied to debt finance as well. Does this tax postponement effect mean that during the transition some cohorts suffer significant reductions in welfare?[11] This section theoretically investigates under what circumstances the tax postponement effect would be relevant and how the timing of effective tax payments would affect intergeneration incidence. By doing so, it explores the similarity between debt finance and taxes. If budget deficits are to be controlled, government debt issue is predetermined and taxes are determined by budgetary needs. This section, therefore, is intended as a complement to the previous section where taxes are predetermined and government debt issue is determined by budgetary deficit.

4.2 Analytical Framework

The analytical framework is almost the same as in the previous section. An overlapping generations growth model of identical individuals is developed that contains the essential of Diamond's work. An individual's consumption and saving programmes are now restricted by the following first- and second-period budget constraints.

$$c_1^t = w_t - s^t - \theta_1^t - b_t \tag{6.33}$$

$$c_2^t = (1 + r_{t+1})s^t - \theta_2^t + (1 + r_{t+1})b_t \tag{6.34}$$

where w_t is real wage rate in period t, s^t is his savings of real capital, θ_1^t is lump sum tax levied in the first period, b_t is per capita debt issuance to generation t, r_t is real rate of interest in period t, and θ_2^t is lump-sum tax levied in the second period.

From (6.33) and (6.34), we have the lifetime budget constraint.

$$c_1^t + \frac{1}{1 + r_{t+1}} c_2^t = w_t - \tau^t \tag{6.35}$$

where

$$\tau^t \equiv \tau_1^t + \frac{1}{1 + r_{t+1}} \tau_2^t. \tag{6.35a}$$

$$\tau_1^t \equiv b_t + \theta_1^t \tag{6.35b}$$

$$\tau_2^t \equiv -(1+r_{t+1})b_t + \theta_2^t. \tag{6.35c}$$

We now use the concept of effective tax payments in each period which includes bond issuance as well as taxes. τ^t is his lifetime tax payments, τ_1^t is his effective tax payments in the first period, and τ_2^t is his effective tax payments in the second period. Therefore, his saving function can be expressed as

$$s^t = s(w_t, \tau_1^t, \tau^t, r_{t+1}). \tag{6.36}$$

Assuming consumption to be normal, $0 < s_w \equiv \partial s/\partial w_t < 1$, $0 > s_\tau \equiv \partial s/\partial \tau_1^t = -1$, and $0 < s_\tau \equiv \partial s/\partial \tau^t < 1$. However, the sign of $\partial s/\partial r_{t+1}$ depends on the relative magnitude of income and substitution effects. For simplicity as before the propensity to save α is assumed to be independent of r_{t+1}.

The government is assumed to expend a required quantity of the consumption good (gL_t). Its expenditure is financed by means of lump sum taxation and debt issuance. The government budget constraint for period t is simply

$$\tau_1^t + \frac{1}{1+n}\tau_2^{t-1} = g. \tag{6.37}$$

From (6.35a) and (6.37), we have

$$\tau^t = \frac{r_{t+1}-n}{1+r_{t+1}}\tau_1^t + \frac{1+n}{1+r_{t+1}}g + \frac{1}{1+r_{t+1}}(\tau_2^t - \tau_2^{t-1}). \tag{6.38}$$

Obviously, $\tau_1^t = \tau_1^{t-1} = \tau_1$ and $\tau_2^t = \tau_2^{t-1} = \tau_2$ under the same tax structure and the same per capita debt issuance in steady states. $\tau_2^t = \tau_2^{t-1}$ and the third term appears only when the effective tax structure is changed, and hence the economy diverges from the steady state.

As in the previous section, since s^t is used for production in period $t+1$ as capital, we have

$$s^t = (1+n)k_{t+1}.$$

Factor price frontier is given by (6.15)

$$w_t = w(r_t), \ w' = -k_t.$$

Hence, the economy may be summarised by the following equation, where τ_1^t and τ_2^t are policy variables.

$$\alpha(w_t - \tau^t) = (1+n)k_{t+1} - \alpha\tau_1^t \qquad (6.39)$$

In order to analyse the welfare aspect of effective tax reform on each generation, it will be useful to explore dynamic properties of the economy. The stability condition for this economy is

$$0 < \frac{\alpha w'}{(1+n)w'' - \alpha\dfrac{\tau_2}{(1+r)^2}} < 1 \qquad (6.40)$$

From now on, we assume (6.40). (6.40) may be reduced to $(1+\eta)w'' + s_w w' - \alpha\tau_2/(1+r)^2 > 0$, which is likely to hold when the elasticity of substitution between capital and labour is large. This is essentially stability condition (6.20) in the previous section. Under (6.40) r will monotonically converge to the long-run equilibrium level, r^*.

4.3 Effective Tax Reform in Period 0

The debt-tax reform may be investigated by considering the effect of changes in effective lump sum taxes τ_1 and τ_2. Any effects of the government debt may be neutralised by the appropriate combination of lump sum taxes and transfers. The burden of debt can only be relevant if the government is constrained in its use of lump-sum taxes. As for the existence of constraints on tax policy, let us assume that lump-sum tax in the first period θ_1 is exogenously given.

Suppose that the government will change the combination of effective taxes (τ_1, τ_2) in period 0. τ_2 is raised, and τ_1 is reduced. Namely, $\tau_2^{-2} < \tau_2^{-1} = \tau_2^0 = \tau_2$ and $\tau_1^{-1} > \tau_1^0 = \tau_1^1 = \tau_1$. Actually debt issuance in period 0, b_0, is reduced. Since lump-sum tax in the first period, θ_1, is kept constant, lump-sum tax in the second period, θ_2, is adjusted so as to meet the budgetary needs. In period 0, θ_2^{-1} therefore must be raised. In future periods $i(i = 1, 2, \ldots)$ θ_2 may also be raised. If $r > n$, however, θ_2 may be reduced since the reduction of debt issuance will reduce future government deficits. In any case as τ_1 is reduced, τ_2 must be raised so as to satisfy the government budget constraint. Note that a new level of debt issuance $b_0 = b_1 = b < b_{-1}$ will be maintained by adjustments of θ_2. In this sense government debt issue is predetermined and taxes are determined by budgetary needs. This effective tax reform may be regarded as a combination of a decrease in debt issuance and an increase in the second-period consumption tax.

For the future generations i ($i = 1, 2, \ldots$) (6.38) means that the present value of effective tax payments τ decreases if and only if $r > n$. If $r > n$, postponing effective tax payments to later in life ($\tau_1 \to \tau_2$) means a reduction of the lifetime present value of payments. This is called the tax postponement effect, which gives an extra benefit to the future generation. On the other hand, if $r < n$, the tax postponement effect is unfavourable for the future generation. Note that the tax postponement effect is relevant to the steady state as well as the transition process.[12] For the existing younger generation 0, the tax postponement effect works in the same way as in the case of the future generation. For the existing older generation -1, τ_2^{-1} is increased, while τ_1^{-1} is not reduced. Therefore, the lifetime present value of payments τ^{-1} is raised. This corresponds to the third term of (6.38). This gives an extra burden to generation -1. During the transition the earlier generation may suffer significant reductions in welfare by the effective tax reform. Note that this effect works, irrespectively of whether r is greater than n or not. In this sense, this effect should be distinguished from the tax postponement effect.

Let us investigate the impact of effective tax reform on savings. A reduction of τ_1 directly increases an individual's savings. However, if $r > n$, the decrease in τ_1 will increase τ and hence indirectly decrease his savings. From (6.38), we have

$$\frac{\Delta s}{\Delta \tau_1} = -\alpha + \frac{r-n}{1+r}\alpha = -\alpha \frac{1+n}{1+r} < 0. \tag{6.41}$$

Hence, the direct effect of τ_1 is always greater than the indirect effect of τ_1; an individual's saving is raised, irrespectively of the sign of $r - n$. The effective tax reform ($\tau_1 \to \tau_2$) will increase saving of the existing younger generation 0 and the future generation. This may be called the permanent capital accumulation effect.

The impact of this effective tax reform on generation -1's saving is dependent on whether a member of generation -1 anticipates this effective tax reform in period -1 or not. If an individual of generation -1 does not anticipate, his saving is unaffected by the effective tax reform. If he does anticipate, an increase in τ_2^{-1} will raise τ^{-1} and hence increase s^{-1}.

It is now useful to analyse the impact of effective tax reform on capital

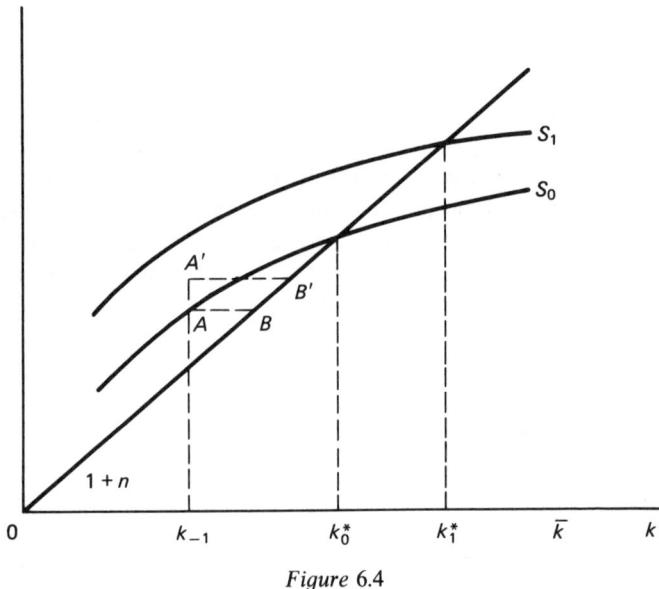

Figure 6.4

accumulation in Figure 6.4. Curve S_0 represents the initial saving function before the effective tax reform and curve S_1 represents the new saving function after the effective tax reform. Suppose the capital:labour ratio in period -1, k_{-1}, is less than the golden rule capital:labour ratio, $\bar{k}$, and the long-run equilibrium capital:labour ratio under the initial tax structure k_0^* is between k_{-1} and $\bar{k}$. By the effective tax reform the saving function of future generations will shift upwards. Hence, the effective tax reform stimulates capital accumulation during the transition path. The new long-run equilibrium capital:labour ratio k_1^* is greater than k_0^*. Namely, if $r > n$, the tax reform ($\tau_1 \to \tau_2$) will stimulate capital accumulation in the long run. If a member of generation -1 anticipates the effective tax reform, generation -1's saving is greater than the level indicated by the initial saving function. This extra saving is represented by AA' in Figure 6.4. This will lead to an extra initial endowment to generation 0, which is denoted by BB'. Therefore, generation -1's extra saving will stimulate capital accumulation during the earlier transition process. Note that this effect will disappear in the long run. In this sense, this effect may be called the temporary capital accumulation effect.

The welfare aspect of effective tax reform during the growth process is now explored. Let us examine the effect of effective tax reform on utility of each generation i, u^i ($i = -1, 0, 1, 2, ...$). If the tax reform is to increase τ_2 and to reduce τ_1 from period 0 on, u^{-1} will definitely be reduced. Moreover, if a member of generation -1 does not anticipate the effective tax reform, u^{-1} will be reduced more. The effect on the future generation i ($i = 1, 2, ...$) depends on the tax postponement effect and the temporary and permanent capital accumulation effects. If $r > n$, the tax postponement effect is favourable for the future generation. As for the temporary capital accumulation effect, it is useful to divide future generations into the near future generation and the distant future generation. As shown in the Appendix, higher capital endowment given to a generation makes its lifetime utility u^i higher. Therefore, on the growth process where capital accumulation is monotonically increased, each generation's lifetime utility is monotonically increased. Note that this capital accumulation effect works, irrespectively of the sign of $r - n$. Therefore, generation -1's extra saving will be favourable for the near future generation who are close to generation -1. Generation -1's extra saving is not important for the distant future generation. Utility of the distant future generation is dependent on whether the long-run equilibrium is closer to the golden rule by the effective tax reform than before. Hence, if $r > n$, the effective tax reform ($\tau_1 \to \tau_2$) is favourable for the distant future generation from the viewpoint of the tax postponement effect and the permanent capital accumulation effect.

The effect of debt finance and tax reform on intergeneration incidence is summarised in Table 6.4. Table 6.4 shows that if $r > n$, effective tax reform has different impacts on the existing older generation and the existing younger and future generations. Thus, the effective tax reform ($\tau_1 \to \tau_2$) hurts the existing older generation and benefits the future generation. On the other hand, the effective tax reform ($\tau_1 \to \tau_2$) benefits the existing older generation and hurts the future generation. There is a trade-off relationship between the existing older generation's welfare and the future generation's welfare. The effective tax reform ($\tau_1 \to \tau_2$) is associated with a reduction of debt issuance, and the effective tax reform ($\tau_1 \to \tau_2$) is associated with an increase in debt issuance. Therefore, debt finance benefits the existing older generation and hurts the future generation. The burden of debt will be placed on the future generation. Remember that under the chain-letter mechanism the burden of debt will not be placed on the near future generation but on the distant future generation. The effect of debt finance on intergeneration equity depends on how the government budget is satisfied. The growth path may be called efficient in the sense that no generation is better off unless some generations are worse off. If $r < n$,

182 Public Debt and Equity

Table 6.4 Effect of debt finance and tax reform of intergeneration incidence

Tax reform	Generation-1	Near future generation	Distance future generation
(1) $\tau_1 \to \tau_2$ $r > n$	$(-)$	TPP$(+)$ TCA$(+)$	TPP$(+)$ PCA$(+)$
(2) $\tau_1 \to \tau_2$ $r < n$	$(-)$	TPP$(-)$ TCA$(+)$	TPP$(-)$ PCA$(-)$
(3) $\tau_1 \leftarrow \tau_2$ $r > n$	$(+)$	TPP$(-)$ TCA$(-)$	TPP$(-)$ PCA$(-)$
(4) $\tau_1 \leftarrow \tau_2$ $r < n$	$(+)$	TPP$(+)$ TCA$(-)$	TPP$(+)$ PCA$(+)$

Notes:
$(+)$ = a favourable effect
$(-)$ = an unfavourable effect
TPP = the tax postponement effect
TCA = the temporary capital accumulation effect
PCA = the permanent capital accumulation effect.

tax reform will affect welfare of the existing older generation and the distant future generation in the same direction. The corresponding growth path may be called inefficient. In this case the burden of debt will not necessarily be placed on the future generation. Furthermore, if a member of the existing older generation anticipates the effective tax reform, the temporary capital accumulation effect will product 'externality' to the near future generation.

4.4 Comment

A 'pay as you go' (or just 'pay-go') social security programme is defined to be a programme in which social security tax revenues equal benefits in each period. Consider the introduction of a pay-go plan in the context of the model in subsection 4.2. The only modification of the subsection 4.2 model is to assume $g = 0$. The introduction of a pay-go plan in period 0 means $\tau_1^0 = \tau_1^1 = \tau_1 > 0$ and $t_2^{-1} = \tau_2^0 = \tau_2 < 0$. Therefore, the introduction of a pay-go plan corresponds to the tax reform $(\tau_2 \to \tau_1)$. As summarised in Table 6.4, the existing older generation is better off, and the future generation gets benefits if the growth path is inefficient. Let us now investigate the impact of social security on private saving.

Social security may reduce private saving in two ways. First, if a member of generation -1 anticipates the introduction of a pay-go plan, generation -1's saving will be reduced. Secondly, if $r > n$, by the tax postponement effect the future generation's saving will be reduced. Our analysis suggests that an introduction of the social security has very similar impacts on the economy as the effective tax reform ($\tau_2 \to \tau_1$). Both debt finance and social security provide the similar means whereby income can be redistributed between generations.

So far the case where taxes are lump sum has been considered. Our analysis suggests that the tax postponement effect, the temporal capital accumulation effect, and the permanent capital accumulation effect are important for the evaluation of effective tax reform. When taxes are distortionary, how would the results of this section be affected? As for the timing of tax payments, a wage tax corresponds to θ_1 and a capital tax corresponds to θ_2. A consumption tax may be regarded as a combination of θ_1 and θ_2. Among the three taxes, an individual pays wage taxes earliest in life within the conventional two-period framework. In this sense, converting a wage tax to a consumption tax is associated with the tax reform ($\tau_1 \to \tau_2$). As far as the income effect is concerned, the implication of distortionary tax reform would be the same as in this section. Namely, the tax postponement effect, the temporary capital accumulation effect, and the permanent capital accumulation effect work in the similar way as in this section. It is well known that the difference between consumption and labour income taxation is not the exemption from taxation of capital income or the incentive effect but the different timing of tax payments. Therefore, the tax reform concerning consumption and labour income taxation may be evaluated within the framework of lump-sum tax reform.[13] Moreover, the effective tax reform concerning debt finance and consumption taxation (or labour income taxation) is analysed in the previous subsection.[14]

In a multi-period setting how would the main results be maintained? The main results of this section would be qualitatively valid. Of course, the existing older generations do not consist of a single cohort. Many cohorts would suffer significant reduction in welfare by the effective tax reform from earlier payments to later payments in life. Therefore the temporary capital accumulation effect would be more important during the transition than in a two-period setting.

The lump-sum tax reform model developed in this section is better suited to explore qualitatively the consequences of differing timing of effective tax payments, an aspect of reality that has not been systematically analysed in most of the literature comparing debt finance, consumption, wage and income taxes. An increase in debt issuance has the similar timing of payments effect as an increase in wage taxes and a decrease in consumption taxes. Debt finance under the debt-tax reform regime will place a burden on the future generation if r is greater than n.

5 CONCLUSION

This chapter has investigated an important aspect of the debt problem, namely, the question whether financing government expenditure by borrowing rather than taxation imposes a greater burden on future generations. The primary question is: does such a burden transfer in fact occur, and if so, how? Our main results may be summarised as follows.

The preliminary empirical results for the Japanese economy in Section 2 are inconsistent with both the perfect debt neutrality hypothesis and the more traditional Keynesian hypothesis. The results suggest that reality lies between these extremes. Therefore, the view that public debt will place at least some burden on the future deserves credibility for the real economy. This section's contribution is, hopefully, not only to test a particular formation of the debt neutrality hypothesis, but to stimulate additional research that directly tests the degree of debt neutrality.

In Sections 3 and 4 analysed how debt burden relates to intergeneration equity by using a two-period overlapping generations growth model. Section 3 explored possibilities that the chain-letter mechanism may lead to a catastrophe. Section 4 explored possibilities that the debt-tax reform may place an undue burden on the future. In a finite horizon setting at least in certain circumstances such a burden transfer may in fact occur. However, how such a transfer will occur depends upon the behaviour of government. Under the chain-letter mechanism of debt finance the magnitude of the initial government expenditure is a key variable, and the near future generation may transfer his burden to the distant future generation. Under the debt-tax reform the magnitude of the initial capital accumulation is a key variable, and the existing younger generation may be affected in a similar way as the future generation. If budget deficits are to be controlled, government debt issue is predetermined and taxes are determined by budgetary needs. If, on the other hand, taxes are predetermined, government debt issue is determined by budgetary deficit. This paper has shown that the behaviour of government is crucial for how debt burden relates to intergeneration equity.

APPENDIX

Tax Finance

In order to analyse the welfare of each generation explicitly, it is useful to employ the expenditure function approach. The system of tax finance in Section 3 will be summarised by

$$E\left(\frac{1}{1+r_{t+1}}, u^t\right) = w(r_t) - \tau \qquad (6.A1)$$

$$E_2\left(\frac{1}{1+r_{t+1}}, u^t\right) = -(1+n)(1+r_{t+1})w'(r_{t+1}) \qquad (6.A2)$$

where $E(\ )$ denotes the expenditure function and $E_2(\ )$ denotes the compensated demand function for the second-period consumption. Differentiating totally (6.A1) and (6.A2), we have

$$\begin{bmatrix} E_u, E_2 \dfrac{-1}{(1+r_{t+1})^2} \\ E_{2u}, E_{22}\dfrac{-1}{(1+r_{t+1})^2} + (1+n)(w' + (1+r_{t+1})w'') \end{bmatrix} \begin{bmatrix} du^t \\ dr_{t+1} \end{bmatrix} = \begin{bmatrix} w' \\ 0 \end{bmatrix} dr^t \qquad (6.A3)$$

where

$$E_u = \frac{\partial E}{\partial u^t}, \quad E_{2u} = \frac{\partial E_2}{\partial u^t}, \quad \text{and} \quad F_{22} = \frac{\partial E_2}{\partial \left(\dfrac{1}{1+r_{t+1}}\right)}.$$

Hence,

$$\frac{du^t}{dr_t} = \frac{w'}{\Delta}\left[E_{22}\frac{1}{(1+r_{t+1})^2} + (1+n)(w' + (1+r_{t+1})w'')\right] \qquad (6.A4)$$

where Δ is the determinant of the matrix of LHS of (6.A3). And, we have

$$\frac{dr_{t+1}}{dr_t} = -\frac{E_{2u}w'}{\Delta}. \qquad (6.A5)$$

Under the stability condition (6.20), $0 < dr_{t+1}/dr_t < 1$. Hence, $\Delta > 0$. The sign of [ ] will be positive if the elasticity of substitution between labour and capital is large.

Debt Finance

The system of debt finance in Section 3 will be summarised by

$$E\left(\frac{1}{1+r_{t+1}}, u^t\right) = w(r_t) - \tau \qquad (6.A6)$$

$$E_2\left(\frac{1}{1+r_{t+1}}, u^t\right) = -(1+n)(1+r_{t+1})w'(r_{t+1}) + b_t(1+r_{t+1}) \qquad (6.A7)$$

where $E(\ )$ denotes the expenditure function and $E_2(\ )$ denotes the compensated demand function for the second-period consumption.

Totally differentiating (6.A6) and (6.A7), we have

$$\begin{bmatrix} E_u, & E_2\dfrac{1}{(1+r_{t+1})^2} \\ E_{2u}, & E_{22}\dfrac{1}{(1+r_{t+1})^2} + (1+n)(w' + (1+r_{t+1})w'') - b^t \end{bmatrix} \begin{bmatrix} du^t \\ dr_{t+1} \end{bmatrix}$$

$$= \begin{bmatrix} 0 \\ 1+r_{t+1} \end{bmatrix} db_t + \begin{bmatrix} w' \\ 0 \end{bmatrix} dr_t$$

where

$$E_u = \frac{\partial E}{\partial u^t}, \quad E_{2u} = \frac{\partial E_2}{\partial u^t}, \quad \text{and} \quad E_{22} = \frac{\partial E_2}{\partial \left(\dfrac{1}{1+r_{t+1}}\right)}$$

Hence

$$\frac{\partial u}{\partial b_t} = \frac{1}{\Delta} \frac{E_2}{1+r_{t+1}} \qquad (6.A9)$$

where Δ is the determinant of the matrix of LHS of (6.A8). And, we have

$$\frac{dr_{t+1}}{dr_t} = -\frac{E_{2u}w'}{\Delta}. \qquad (6.A10)$$

Under the stability condition, $0 < \dfrac{dr_{t+1}}{dr_t} < 1$. Hence, $\Delta > 0$. Thus, the sign of (6.A9) is likely to be positive.

$$\frac{\partial u^t}{\partial r^t} = \frac{w'}{\Delta}\left[E_{22}\frac{-1}{(1+r_{t+1})^2} + (1+n)(w' + (1+r_{t+1})w'') - b_t\right]. \quad (6.A11)$$

The sign of (6.A11) is negative if the elasticity of substitution between capital and labour is large.

Moreover, if b_t is large, $\Delta < 0$. The stability condition under bond finance is not satisfied. We have therefore $\partial u^t/\partial b_t < 0$ and $\partial u^t/\partial r_t < 0$. The chain-letter mechanism is in such a case infeasible. When the chain-letter mechanism is infeasible, b^t and r^t will increase to the infinite, and the economy will approach a catastrophe: u^t will eventually drop to the minimum level.

Debt-Tax Reform

The system of debt-tax reform in Section 4 will be summarised by

$$E\left(\frac{1}{1+r_{t+1}}, u^t\right) = w(r_t) - \tau^t \quad (6.A12)$$

$$E_2\left(\frac{1}{1+r_{t+1}}, u^t\right) = -(1+n)(1+r_{t+1})w'(r_{t+1}) - \tau_2^t. \quad (6.A13)$$

Therefore, it is easy to show that du^t/dr_t is positive if the elasticity of substitution between labour and capital is large.

Notes

1. Seater (1982) examines empirically the degree of debt neutrality by estimating financial asset demand functions for the US economy. However, he draws no conclusion from the regression concerning the degree of debt neutrality.
2. The actual government budget is in deficit in recent years. However, if the private sector recognises the long-run government budget constraint (6.3), private consumption will be determined by (6.5). Put in another way, if the government budget satisfies the transversality condition, the level of debt is equal to the present value of future surpluses. And if in addition taxes and government expenditures are perceived as constant, (6.3) may be regarded as the dynamic budget constraint together with the transversality condition.
3. Alternatively, the index of the degree of debt neutrality x may be calculated by estimating a trade balance function. From (6.4) and (6.5) the trade balance function. From (6.4) and (6.5) the trade balance $NX(\dot{F} - rF)$ may be given by

$$NX = \frac{r-e}{r+p}(YW - G) - \frac{(r+e)p}{r+p}D - (r+e)F.$$

Therefore, an empirical specification of the trade balance equation will be

$$NX_t = b_0 + b_1(Y_t - G_t) + b_2 D_t + b_3 F_t + v_t$$

The index x is then given by $1-b_2/b_3$. The estimates for x over the period first quarter 1970 to 1983 fourth quarter are 0.71–0.81 and virtually the same as those estimated in Tables 6.1 and 6.2.

4. Boskin reports in Chapter 3 new empirical results on the effects of government deficits and debt on real economic activity. He estimates similar consumption equations as (6.7) but includes current government deficits as an additional explanatory variable. Following Boskin (Chapter 3) I estimate a modified version of (6.7) where the government deficits are also included. The estimates suggest that the tax cut, holding government spending constant increases consumption rather moderately about 10 to 13 cents on the dollar for the Japanese economy. The results are consistent with the finding that the degree of debt neutrality is about 70 per cent.

5. If the utility function is homothetic, α is dependent on r. This would not change our results qualitatively.

6. Since our dynamic model is characterised by difference equations, strictly speaking, our analysis with the aid of a phase diagram is not appropriate and should be considered as a first order approximation.

7. The local stability of the equilibria can be analysed mathematically. From (6.16) and (6.17), we obtain at the neighbourhood of an equilibrium

$$\begin{bmatrix} d\hat{r}_{t+1} \\ d\hat{b}_{t+1} \end{bmatrix} = \begin{bmatrix} A & B \\ C & D \end{bmatrix} \begin{bmatrix} d\hat{r}_t \\ d\hat{b}_t \end{bmatrix}$$

where $d\hat{r}_t = r_t - r^*$, $db_t = b_t - b^*$, and (r^*, g^*) is an equilibrium. In the above expression

$$A \equiv -\frac{\alpha w'}{(1+n)w''} > 0 \quad (0 < A < 1)$$

$$B \equiv \frac{1}{(1+n)w''} > 0$$

$$C \equiv A \frac{b}{1+n}$$

$$D \equiv \frac{1+r}{1+n} + B \frac{b}{1+n}.$$

In order to find the property of the characteristic roots of $\begin{pmatrix} A & B \\ C & D \end{pmatrix}$, define the characteristic equation

$$\psi(\lambda) = \lambda^2 - (A+D)\lambda + AD - BC.$$

When $r > n$, it can be easily shown that $\psi(1) < 0$ and $\psi(-1) > 0$. Hence one of the roots is real and larger than unity while the other root has

absolute value less than unity. Namely, any equilibrium with $r > n$ is a saddle point.
When $r < n$, the equilibrium is locally stable if and only if

$$(1+A)\left(1+\frac{1+r}{1+n}\right) < B\frac{b}{1+n} < (1-A)\frac{n-r}{1+n}.$$

8. An increase in w_t has the same effect as an increase in lump-sum transfer to him in the first period. Hence, it is plausible to raise u^t. Calvo (1979) pointed out that conditions under which capital deepening implies increasing welfare are dependent on the stability of the system and the elasticity of substitution in production.
9. Atkinson and Stiglitz (1980, p. 255) suggest that u^1 declines as the next generation 1 face a lower wage and in addition have to finance the interest on the debt. Our analysis has shown that under the chain-letter mechanism u^1 may well increase as the interest on debt will be financed by new debt issuance to generation 2.
10. Boskin (1978) and Summers (1981) stress that the interest elasticity of the saving rate is the key parameter in the analysis of these issues. Evans (1983) shows that the lower is the intertemporal elasticity of substitution of consumption, the lower is the interest elasticity, and the larger is the time preference rate, the higher is the interest elasticity of saving. Auerbach, Kotlikoff and Skinner (1983) conduct sensitivity tests of the intertemporal elasticity of substitution between goods and leisure, the intertemporal elasticity of substitution, and the elasticity of technical substitution between capital and labour.
11. The tax postponement effect is pointed out by Summers (1981) and Evans (1983). However, as their main interest is the interest elasticity of the saving rate, they do not clarify the full implication of the timing of tax payments for intergeneration incidence.
12. Note that the tax postponement effect is relevant to the existing younger generation and the future generation, not to the existing older generation.
13. If $r > n$, the tax reform of converting the labour income tax to the consumption tax is always desirable for the existing younger and future generations. This result is consistent with simulation results of Summers (1981) and Evans (1983).
14. As far as the income effect is concerned, if the tax reform $(\tau_1 \to \tau_2)$ is desirable, then a capital tax is better than a wage or consumption tax. However, a change in the tax rate on capital income would have an incentive effect. If the interest elasticity of saving is large, a reduction of the capital tax is desirable during the efficient growth process. If $r > n$, converting the capital income tax to either the consumption tax or the labour income tax will produce an unfavourable tax postponement effect to the existing younger and the future generations. Evans (1983) and Auerbach, Kotlikoff and Skinner (1983) explore the possibility that converting the income tax to the labour income tax is not desirable. Our analysis suggests that in such a case the tax postponement effect and the permanent capital accumulation effect outweigh the incentive effect of the interest elasticity of saving.

References

Aschauer, D. A. (1985) 'Fiscal Policy and Aggregate Demand', *American Economic Review*, vol. 75, pp. 117–27.

Atkinson, A. B. and Sandmo, A. (1980) 'Welfare Implications of the Taxation of Savings', *Economic Journal*, vol. 90, September, pp. 529–49.

Atkinson, A. B. and Stiglitz, J. E. (1980) *Lectures on Public Economics* (New York: McGraw-Hill).

Auerbach, A. J. (1979) 'The Optimal Taxation of Heterogeneous Capital', *Quarterly Journal of Economics*, vol. 93, November, pp. 589–612.

Auerbach, A. J., Kotlikoff, L. J. and Skinner, J. (1983) 'The Efficiency Gains from Dynamic Tax Reform', *International Economic Review*, vol. 24, February, pp. 81–100.

Barro, R. J. (1974) 'Are Government Bonds Net Wealth?', *Journal of Political Economy*, vol. 82, pp. 1095–115.

Barro, R. J. (1976) 'Reply to Feldstein and Buchanan', *Journal of Political Economy*, vol. 84, pp. 343–39.

Beveridge, S. and Nelson, C. R. (1981) 'A New Approach to Decomposition of Economic Time Series into Permanent and Transitory Components with Particular Attention to Measurement of the "Business Cycle"', *Journal of Monetary Economics*, vol. 7, pp. 151–74.

Blanchard, O. J. (1985) 'Debt, Deficits, and Finite Horizons', *Journal of Political Economy*, vol. 73, pp. 223–47.

Boskin, M. J. (1978) 'Taxation, Saving and the Rate of Interest', *Journal of Political Economy*, vol. 86, April, pp. s3–s27.

Boskin, M. J. and Kotlikoff, L. J. (1985) 'Public Debt and US Saving: A New Test of the Neutrality Hypothesis', New York: NBER Working Paper, No. 1646.

Burbidge, J. B. (1983) 'Social Security and Savings Plans in Overlapping-Generations Models', *Journal of Public Economics*, vol. 21, pp. 79–92.

Calvo, G. A. (1979) 'Capital Accumulation and Welfare: A Note', *Economics Letters*, vol. 4, pp. 135–9.

Diamond, P. A. (1965) 'National Debt in a Neoclassical Growth Model', *American Economic Review*, vol. 55, December, pp. 1126–50.

Evans, O. J. (1983) 'Tax Policy, the Interest Elasticity of Saving and Capital Accumulation: Numerical Analysis of Theoretical Models', *American Economic Review*, vol. 73, June, pp. 398–410.

Feldstein, M. S. (1978) The Welfare Cost of Capital Income Taxation', *Journal of Political Economy*, vol. 86, April, pp. s29–s51.

Feldstein, M. (1982) 'Government Deficits and Aggregate Demand', *Journal of Monetary Economics*, vol. 9, pp. 1–20.

Gale, D. (1973) 'Pure Exchange Equilibrium of Dynamic Economic Models', *Journal of Economic Theory*, pp. 12–36.

Homma, M., Abe, H., Atoda, N., Ihori, T., Kandori, M. and Mutoh, M. (1986) 'The Debt Neutrality Hypothesis: Theoretical and Empirical Analyses for the Japanese Economy', (in Japanese), Economic Planning Agency,

Ihori, T. (1978) 'The Golden Rule and the Role of Government in a Life Cycle Growth Model', *American Economic Review*, vol. 68, June, pp. 389–96.

Ihori, T. (1981) 'The Golden Rule and the Ramsey Rule at a Second Best Solution', *Economics Letters*, vol. 8, pp. 89–93.
Ihori, T. (1984) 'Partial Welfare Improvements and Capital Income Taxation', *Journal of Public Economics*, vol. 24, no. 1, pp. 101–9.
Ihori, T. (1985) 'Budget Deficits, Government Spending, and Aggregate Demand', *mimeo*.
Kanaya, S. (1984) 'On the Chain-Letter Paradox of Government Debt Finance'. *mimeo*.
King, M. (1980) 'Savings and Taxation', in Hughes, G. A. and Heal, G. M. (eds), *Public Policy and the Tax System* (London: Allen Unwin).
Kochin, L. (1974) 'Are Future Taxes Anticipated by Consumers?', *Journal of Money, Credit, and Banking*, vol. 6, pp. 383–94.
Kormendi, R. C. (1983) 'Goverment Debt, Government Spending, and Private Sector Behaviour', *American Economic Review*, vol. 73, pp. 994–1010.
McCallum, B. T. (1984) 'Are Bond Financed Deficits Inflationary? A Ricardian Analysis', *Journal of Political Economy*, vol. 92, February, pp. 123–35.
Modigliani, F. (1961) 'Long-run Implications of Alternative Fiscal Policies and the Burden of the National Debt', *Economic Journal*, vol. 71, pp. 730–55.
Musgrave, R. A. and Musgrave, P. B. (1977) *Public Finance in Theory and Practice* (New York: McGraw-Hill).
Okuno, M. (1983) 'The Burden of Debt and Intergenerational Distribution', *Keizai Kenkyu*, vol. 34, pp. 203–15.
Samuelson, P. A. (1958) 'An Exact Consumption-Loan Model of Interest with or without the Social Contrivance of Money', *Journal of Political Economy*, vol. 66, pp. 467–82.
Sargent, T. J. and Wallace, N. (1981) 'Some Unpleasant Monetarist Arithmetic', *Federal Reserve Bank of Minneapolis Quarterly Review*, vol. 5, pp. 1–17.
Seater, J. J. (1982) 'Are Future Taxes Discounted?', *Journal of Money, Credit, and Banking*, vol. 4, pp. 376–89.
Seater, J. J. and Mariano, R. S. (1985) 'New Test of the Life Cycle and Tax Discounting Hypothesis', *Journal of Monetary Economics*, vol. 15, pp. 195–215.
Seidman, L. S. and Maurer, S. B. (1982) 'Taxes and Capital Intensity in a Two-Class Disposable Income Growth Model', *Journal of Public Economics*, vol. 19, November, pp. 243–60.
Summers, L. H. (1981) 'Capital Taxation and Accumulation in a Life Cycle Growth Model', *American Economic Review*, vol. 71, September, pp. 533–44.
Tanner, J. E. (1979) 'An Empirical Investigation of Tax Discounting', *Journal of Money, Credit, and Banking*, vol. 11, pp. 214–18.
Yaari, M. E. (1965) 'Uncertain Lifetime, Life Insurance and the Theory of the Consumer', *Review of Economic Studies*, vol. 32, pp. 137–50.

DISCUSSION

Professor Mordecai Kurz was the principal discussant of Professor Ihori's paper. Kurz's comments focused on two points, one empirical and the other theoretical. His empirical point was that he was not convinced by Ihori's finding that debt was non-neutral. Kurz noted the similarity between Ihori's work and that of Barro and Feldstein on the impact of social security on consumption but pointed out that Barro and Feldstein were able to come to opposite conclusions from the same set of data and suggested that no consensus existed in the profession about the question of debt neutrality.

Kurz summarised Ihori's empirical model as being an application of Blanchard's model, with a fixed probability of dying, p. Thus p is an 'index' of the horizon agents use: $1/p$ is the life expectancy, $p = 0$ implies an infinite horizon, and $p = 1$ complete myopia.

With an implicit assumption of log utility, consumption is assumed to follow the permanent income hypothesis:

$$C = (p + e)(H + W),$$

where C is consumption, H is human wealth, W is nonhuman wealth, and e is the discount rate.

The government budget is assumed to have always a balanced budget. The government budget constraint is $rD + G = T$, where D is government debt, r is the rate of interest, G is government expenditure and T is taxes. Unlike the government, trade is allowed to be out of balance.

The equation that Ihori estimates is

$$C = (p + e)\left(\frac{YW - G}{r + p} + \frac{P}{r + p}D + F\right),$$

where YW is labour income and F is net holdings of foreign assets. The degree of debt neutrality is labelled X, and $X \times 1 - p/r + p$. The empirical results obtained are that $X = 0.82$, which is statistically different from both 0 and 1, so that there is neither pure neutrality nor pure myopia.

Kurz pointed out that the government budget is frequently not in balance, so that the government budget constraint should be

$$rD + G = T + \Delta D.$$

Also, the capital stock was erroneously omitted, so that the estimated equation should be

$$C + (p + e)\left(\frac{YW - G - S}{r + p} + \frac{p}{r + p}(D + K) + F\right),$$

where S is the budget surplus. At this, point the regression begins to resemble those of Barro and Feldstein. When Barro ran this regression, he obtained an estimate of 0.75 on the income variable, which is similar to Ihori's result. But his coefficient on S was only 0.2. In this model, it has been constrained to be -0.75. Kurz thus concludes that Ihori's specification is rejected by the data. Kurz noted here that the consensus in the profession was that the issue of debt neutrality could not be settled with time series data. Kurz thus concluded that the empirical work did not support Ihori's decision to use a model that assumes non-neutrality in his theoretical work.

Kurz then turned to his discussion of Ihori's theoretical model. Ihori's model was a two-period life-cycle model. It differed from Diamond's original analysis by allowing for a permanent budget deficit or surplus. The model reduces to a two equation difference equation system, the dynamics of which are analysed in Figures 6.1, 6.2, and 6.3:

$$b_{t+1} = (1 + r_{t+1})\frac{b_t}{1+n} + (g - \tau)$$

$$\alpha w(r_t) = -(1-n)w'(r_{t+1}) + b_t + \alpha\tau.$$

All quantity variables are per capita. b_t is government debt, n is the rate of population growth, g is government expenditures, τ is lump sum taxes and w is the wage. α is the marginal propensity to save out of net assets, and is assumed to be independent of the rate of return. Kurz said that the Diamond stability conditions were assumed.

In Ihori's Figure 6.1, $g = \tau$. When there is no debt, there is a stable equilibrium at r^*. Ihori then 'perturbs' the system by allowing there to be initial debt. In Figure 6.1(a), there are two stable equilibria.

Ihori characterised divergence, when b and r both approach infinity, as a 'catastrophe'. Kurz felt that instead, one ought to be concerned with the transversality conditions. In particular, one could eliminate such equilibria to the extent that they were not consistent with utility maximisation.

In Figure 6.2, $g < \tau$, so that there is always a budget surplus. In this case, there is a saddle point equilibrium at E_A. But Kurz pointed out that there was also an equilibrium with $b < 0$ and $r = 0$. Kurz was concerned about why equilibria with $b < 0$ were ruled out. He pointed out that these have a very natural interpretation, namely, that the government owns private capital, rather than being in debt to the private sector.

The case of continual deficits, $g > \tau$, was considered in Figure 6.3. Here there are two cases: either supply and demand for bonds intersect, or they do not. When they do not, the economy diverges. Kurz pointed out again the need to lay out explicit transversital conditions.

Kurz then briefly mentioned the subjects of the remainder of the paper. These included the allocation of utility across generations and the welfare implications of tax reform.

Kurz concluded by reiterating the points that the empirical time series treatment of the debt neutrality issue did not give compelling conclusions, and that therefore it cannot be said that the empirical part of the paper motivates the theoretical part. Kurz felt, though, that the theoretical section was a nice, fully dynamic treatment in its own right.

Professor Ihori began his response by addressing Professor Kurz's points on the empirical work. Ihori said that in future research, he might want to include the deficit and capital income in his regression equations. He was not sure, however, whether the inclusion of the deficit would be theoretically consistent, since the derivation of the regression equation assumed long-run equilibrium.

On the theoretical side, Ihori acknowledged that $b < 0$ was possible, but that he had not considered it in detail. On the question of transversality conditions, Ihori pointed out that in the two-period framework, individual utilising maximising behaviour would not concern itself with the infinite horizon transversality problem. Only the maximising behaviour of the central government would involve concern for the transversality problem. Ihori pointed out that the discussion behind Figures 6.1, 6.2 and 6.3 treated government behaviour mechanistically, and that optimising government behaviour was treated in a later section, which Kurz did not discuss in detail.

Ihori then mentioned that in this latter section, the deficit is analysed as a control variable. He stated his conclusion, that the specification of the maximising behaviour of the government was crucial in determining the consequences for the path of debt.

Professor Michael Boskin felt that Professor Ihori's work was useful in bridging the gap between the empirical and theoretical work on the neutrality of debt. Boskin suggested that in future work, Ihori might want to use government consumption in place of expenditures, and government saving instead of the deficit, citing Boskin and Roberts' (1986) observation that in Japan, government investment exceeds the deficit. On the theoretical side, Boskin noted that although governments do not run budget deficits for limited periods that would imply eventual debt burdens that could exceed GNP if extrapolated, it is unlikely that such conditions could exist indefinitely. He noted Sargent and Wallace's point that the monetary authorities would most likely monetise a debt that became too large. He acknowledged that it may be difficult to model the transition.

Boskin also noted that for many governments, assets did exceed liabilities, so that this case should not be rule out *a priori*.

Professor Eisner addressed Professor Kurz's remarks. Eisner's view was that both Barro and Feldstein were wrong. Feldstein's errors stemmed from the fact that the public did not take its social security wealth seriously, at least in part, because that wealth was difficult to measure. Eisner had found in his own estimates that social security wealth did not affect consumption.

Eisner emphasised that the fundamental point is to analyse what will happen when debt continues to rise. He pointed to Boskin's earlier remarks that debt projections can lead to absurd consequences, such as the interest on the debt exceeding GNP. Eisner made the point that this was unlikely to happen, with an analogy to the Keynesian story about the response of the economy to a monetary stimulus. Just as prices eventually rise to eliminate the initial stimulus of an increase in the money supply, so will an increase in prices eventually follow an ongoing increase in debt. Eisner cited Patinkin as making the argument in the early 1960s.

Eisner points out that the existence of unemployment can introduce a source of deficit non-neutrality.

Professor Joseph Stiglitz pointed out the usefulness of Ihori's theoretical results despite some objections. He felt that the predictions of a life cycle model such as Ihori analyses should be thought of as a thought experiment, rather than as a forecast. It provides a set of consistency conditions, and answers to 'what if' sorts of questions. In this sense, transversality conditions are not important to such an exercise. Debt becoming infinite is not consistent with the model, since people would never hold beliefs such that this could happen.

Stiglitz pointed out that many of the perverse potential outcomes of the Diamond-type model are eliminated when land or other natural resources are introduced. In particular, the possibility that the rate of interest could be less than the rate of growth is ruled out when there is a resource constraint. Stiglitz illustrated this point by noting that if $r \leqslant n = 0$, then the value of land would be infinite.

Stiglitz suggested that although a positive government net worth might be worth looking at, government as a net debtor was the more interesting and relevant case.

Sir Austin Robinson was puzzled as to what the model was assuming about inflation. Intergenerational equity was often irrelevant to the actual issue. In Europe both in the 1920s and 1930s, and again in the late 1940s and 1950s the burden of debt was largely liquidated by inflation. He raised the question whether intergenerational equity meant that rentiers had a right to be paid. He argued against this, reminding the conference of Keynes's comments on the euthanasia of the rentier. Because of the importance of the possibility of such liquidation, Sir Austin felt that inflation should be a part of the model. *Professor Ihori* acknowledged that his model had no monetary aspect. *John Flemming* felt that it was not clear how much difference inflation would make. He agreed with Joe Stiglitz, that the discussion of such models is valid as a 'what if' exercise. The important point is that expectations are not falsified. Indexed debt might be a way of ensuring that this is the case. *Professor Stiglitz* suggested that interest bearing money, backed by government bonds as has recently been introduced, would eliminate the possibility of inflationary liquidations of debt.

Mr John Flemming reiterated the point made by earlier speakers, that positive net wealth holding by the government should not be ruled out. He noted that even when financial debt is large, government net worth can be positive, citing Great Britain as an example, where, until recently, assets exceeded liabilities. He brought up the example of unfunded social security obligations, noting that under the assumption of unchanged benefits, changing demographics can lead to large debts, which can be altered by changing current tax rates.

Professor Boskin pointed out that social security is not analogous to other debt. In particular, it alters the behaviour of people close to retirement more than that of others. He asked Flemming whether varying tax rates might not be netted in a Barro-esque fashion.

Professor Mordecai Kurz addressed Bob Eisner's earlier remarks by stating that he (Kurz) was not a Barro-ite, but rather that be believed that there was a great deal of heterogeneity in the population, which means that the aggregates will reflect this heterogeneity, so that a simple life-cycle model was not adequate to capture the effects of debt policy. Rather than being a Barro-ite, Kurz said he was just pointing out that Ihori was analysing essentially the Barro model, and, in common with that model, time series were not adequate to resolve the issue of debt neutrality.

Kurz also noted that the Diamond model was not identical with non-neutrality of the debt. In particular, it is the case that other models can lead to debt non-neutrality, and that debt can be neutral in a life-cycle world.

Professor Bentzel reiterated the point that ignoring unemployment seemed an odd thing to do in a model designed to explore fiscal policy. He felt that this was abstracting from an important problem. *Professor Richard Musgrave* brought up the point of what was meant by the term 'neutrality'. Kurz said that in his discussion, he meant by non-neutrality that real variables in the economy were altered. He noted that non-neutrality does not necessarily entail a burden. *Marc Robinson* noted that Ihori defined the burden of the debt in his introduction to mean a reduction in the utility of future generations as a consequence of the issuance of debt.

Dr Christophe Chamley noted that Auerbach and Kotlikoff, in an exercise with synthetic time series data, were able to obtain whatever results they wished as to the neutrality of debt, suggesting that the actual time series data are incapable of discriminating among competing hypotheses.

Professor Kenneth Arrow cited Abba Lerner's views on debt. Lerner said that if you ran a deficit now in order to fight unemployment, you would have to make greater interest payments in the future. Lerner suggested that these larger interest payments could be met by running deficits in the future. But Arrow pointed out that if debt were large enough, then everyone would earn sufficient interest that they would have no incentive to work. He cited Meade in this regard. The upshot of this is that, in Ihori's Section 3, it is not that the unstable solutions are normatively bad, but rather that they will never come to pass.

Arrow's comments began a general discussion which concluded the session. *Professor Eisner* felt that Abba Lerner was right, that there was an upper bound on real debt. But *Professor Arrow* countered that inflation was not adequate to enforce that upper bound, since this would require the ex-post falsification of expectations.

Reference

Boskin, M. and Roberts, J. (1986) 'A Closer Look at Saving Rates in the US and Japan', AEI.

Part III
Aspects of Public Debt Theory and Practice

7 Debt and Taxes in War and Peace: The Closed Economy Case

J. S. Flemming
BANK OF ENGLAND

1 INTRODUCTION

This paper examines the role of budget deficits and surpluses in smoothing tax rates in stochastic world. A previous paper considered this problem in the case of an open economy in which factor prices were given by trade or capital mobility (Flemming, 1987). The earlier treatment is summarised in Section 2 below.

The extention of the endogenous factor prices of a closed economy is required not only for completeness but also because, in principle, the perfect world capital market offers perfect insurance against the publicly observable shifts in the relevant stochastic variables. The consequences of closing the model, which are more fully explored in Section 3, include the introduction of a maturity structure of the return on capital as it is bid up (or down) in the process of adjustment. Thus in the open economy the government has a choice of maturity at which to finance, or deploy, its surpluses or deficits. We consider the relative merits of spot (bill) and bond ('consol') financing.

Section 4 presents the formal analysis of the first best policy in the closed economy model with a single production sector producing both the public and the private consumption good. Second-, or third-best policies involving a single tax are also presented here. Section 5 introduces contingent bonds which pay different coupons depending on the state of the world. This section also considers an alternative interpretation of the model in which the preferences of citizen/consumers never change but they are ruled alternatively by high and low spending/taxing governments. Some of the details are changed by this interpretation but the general characterisation of the role of debt in tax rate smoothing survives.

Suppose that either the demand for a public good (which enters individual utility functions additively and separably) or the terms of trade, and thus the real consumption wage, is subject to random transition between two states: how do private consumption and wage income compare as tax bases? And to what extent should tax revenue changes match those of public expenditure on a change of state? Clearly if the match is not perfect one state will be associated with budget surpluses and the other with deficits, that is, rising and falling debt will play a key role in smoothing tax rates.

The proposition that debt should be used to smooth distorting tax rates has been advanced by Barro (1979). Our model differs from the one that he used there in that both the level of public expenditure and the size of the tax base are endogenised. Lucas and Stokey (1983) and Persson and Svensson (1984–5) have extended Barro's approach emphasising problems of time consistency. These problems are even more acute in the presence of both consumption and wage taxation as the former can be raised to confiscate existing private wealth while the latter is lowered to offset any distortion of future labour supply. Our model is, however, essentially stochastic so that we may be able to rely on the arguments of Currie and Levine (1985) that in that context the authorities' reputation is sufficiently valuable in inspiring confidence in their response to future shocks that they will behave as if committed to potentially time-inconsistent policies.

The issue is not merely of time consistency. If private wealth were large enough, relative to the present value of future public expenditure, a combination of proportional taxes would enable the first best allocation to be achieved at all times. The consumption tax would transfer resources to the government, the effect on labour supply would be offset by an equal wage subsidy and if the tax/subsidy rate were liable to change, for example, on a change of state the associated intertemporal distortion could be offset by an interest tax or subsidy.[1]

In what follows it will be assumed that this solution is not available, either because wealth is inadequate or because the necessary combination of taxes and subsidies is unfeasible. We do, however, get fairly close to such solutions when contingent bands are introduced in Section 5.

2 AN OPEN ECONOMY MODEL

In a previous paper I considered these equations in the case of a small open economy facing a perfect world capital market but restricted to distorting proportional taxation at home. The perfect world capital market offers perfect insurance to a small open economy, which could, for instance, issue state-contingent bonds. Whether the insurance is bought (or contingent bonds are issued) by the public or private sector depends on the source of the random shocks. If it is the demand for public goods, and the associated level of public expenditure, which is liable to jump in a random way, it is the government that issues the contingent bonds. These would be so designed that the difference between coupon payments in the two states exactly equalled the difference in public expenditures; these expenditure levels would be the (second best) optimum levels given the uniform tax rate applicable under both states. This tax rate would suffice to service the initial debt as well as the suitably averaged discounted value of exhaustive expenditures.

Where the wage is stochastic private agents will (in the model) buy insurance, smoothing their income and their demand for both the public and private goods, so that a constant tax rate applied to private consumption (or to adjusted labour income) yields a constant revenue to finance constant public expenditure without unbalancing the budget.

These results, which as summarised depend on the (effective) equality of the interest rate and pure time preference rate, highlight the importance of relaxing the assumption of a perfect world capital market, which eliminates most of the potentially interesting features of the problem. In the previous paper I did, nevertheless, consider the (third best) optimum policies if the insurance potential of the world capital market were not exploited. This might be rationalised if the relevant state were observable only to residents of the country concerned, the asymmetry of information precluding efficient insurance. I offer no rationalisation for the resort to distorting taxes in a world of identical consumers, a problem shared by much 'optimal taxation' literature (see Mirrlees, 1971; Hahn, 1973). Nor should the fact that the agents here live forever be taken to imply acceptance of Barro's argument that for practical purposes they do. The intention is to examine the role of debt in the stochastic version of a model in which distorting taxes are sufficient to undermine 'Ricardian equivalence'.

The main results followed from an argument that the optimum taxes could be expressed as functions of shadow prices of the state variables (private wealth, public debt, national capital) and that the shadow prices would not be expected to change given the equality of interest and time preference rates. This suffices to make the *unconditional* expectation of the future optimum tax rate equal (to a first approximation) to today's optimum rate. Much of the role of debt follows immediately from this proposition, which also ensures that although there are *ex post* tax rate changes behaviour is never affected by anticipation of change.

Consumer/taxpayers may save in 'good' (low tax) states, providing a stock to be drawn down in the event of a 'bad' (high tax) state occurring, but anticipated tax rate changes do not have the dramatic intertemporal substitution effects of which expected changes are capable; indeed the argument reflects the fact that such temporal substitution effects involve welfare losses.

Consider a point in time at which the economy has just switched from a good to a bad state; at unchanged tax rates revenue will have fallen relative to expenditure; and at a positive interest rate this will also be true of their present values. Thus to restore expected present value budget balance, which must always hold, and assuming that revenues are not already maximal, tax rates must rise discretely. This is consistent with unconditional expectations, prior to the shock, that the tax rate would be unchanged, if tax rates would have fallen had the shock not occured. This in turn is consistent if in the good state the budget was in surplus so that the debt would have fallen. The arguments for tax rate smoothing imply that the step rise in the tax rate on the adverse transition may not be sufficient to prevent the budget moving from surplus to deficit. As a result of the deficit, debt, and the tax rate, must rise throughout the duration of the 'bad' state; as the marginal cost of revenue rises with the tax rate in this model, the optimal provision of the public good will fall through 'bad' states and rise through 'good' ones. Thus by the end of a long 'war' the level of public expenditure may have fallen below that at the end of the preceding peace – but it will fall further on a return to peacetime conditions.

I also argued that, in the stochastic world, consumption offered a better tax base than did wage income – even though in a static world they were equivalent. Consider first the case in which the demand for public goods is stochastic, and assume that private property income is positive. When the demand for public goods increases, as it might on the outbreak of war, the level of public expenditure, and, at a positive discount rate, its present value, rises. The tax rate must therefore also rise (if not already at the revenue maximising level). If the difference between public and private goods were to disappear, as in a single member society, we know that the shift in demand would be associated with additional labour supply. A labour supply response in the second-best world qualitatively similar to that in the first-best case is clearly more likely if the consumption tax rises than if the wage tax rises.

The argument is more straightforward, and perhaps more convincing, when it is the wage that is stochastic. In this case it is not clear that the rate of consumption taxation would have to vary between states. Both optimum public and private consumption are related to permanent labour income which changes on a change of state. If they change in the same proportion a constant tax rate on the one will suffice to finance the other. Clearly, the relevant elasticity need not be unity, and the result is also affected by initial public debt and private wealth levels, but the consumption tax rate is not likely to have to vary much compared to the wage tax alternative. In this latter case the tax base is likely to fall much more when the wage rate falls than does public expenditure. The necessary rise in the tax rate will aggravate the contraction of the base. If the tax rate is more sensitive to the state, we know, from its unconditional constancy, that it must also rise and fall more rapidly within each state.

Although this is not an adequate index of expected welfare losses it is suggestive of a superiority of a consumption base for taxation when either the demand for public goods or the wage is stochastic.

The arguments just presented suffer from the disadvantage that they depend on an unexplained refusal to take full advantage of the insurance possibilities offered by a perfect world capital market. In this chapter a closed economy is considered – the rest of the world and its capital market no longer exist. This immediately renders the real wage endogenous and thus a less appropriate subject for exogenous shocks. I therefore consider shocks only to the demand for public goods. The question to be addressed is whether the results obtained as third best in an open economy do indeed carry over as second best in a closed one.

In a closed economy the marginal product of capital (and real rate of interest) is endogenous and not constant. Expectations of its future course give rise to a yield curve; variation of yields with maturity presents the government with a choice of maturities at which to finance its deficits or deploy its surpluses. Thus in addition to examining the role of debt and the optimum dynamics of debt and taxes in the model, two questions are also asked: is consumption or wage income the better tax base, and are (spot) bills or (perpetual) bonds the better financing instrument?

3 THE CLOSED ECONOMY MODEL

Closing the economy makes factor prices endogenous so the production structure has to be specified. It is assumed that the production function is linearly homogenous and convex in its two arguments labour L and capital K. Thus both the real rate of return (interest) r and the pre-tax real wage w are unique functions of the capital labour ratio (K/L). Convexity implies that the interest rate r moves in the same direction as labour supply L (and in the opposite direction to the real wage w) when L changes for a given K as, for instance, on a change of state.

Since r is endogenous it can no longer always be equal to the constant rate of pure time preference ρ. The closed economy is thus less static than an open one in which r is fixed and equal to ρ. If, as we assume or assert, intertemporal choice is undistorted, when r exceeds ρ in a deterministic world capital is accumulated and the economy evolves towards a stationary state in which the marginal product of capital $X_k = r = \rho$.

As r tends towards ρ long rates will be closer to ρ than are short rates. Defining c as the yield on a perpetuity or consol paying one unit of consumption per period, we have $c - \dot{c}/c = r$ as well as the proposition in a deterministic world, that $\dot{r} \gtrless 0$ as $r \lessgtr \rho$. These two conditions enable us to construct the phase diagram (Figure 7.1) from which we can

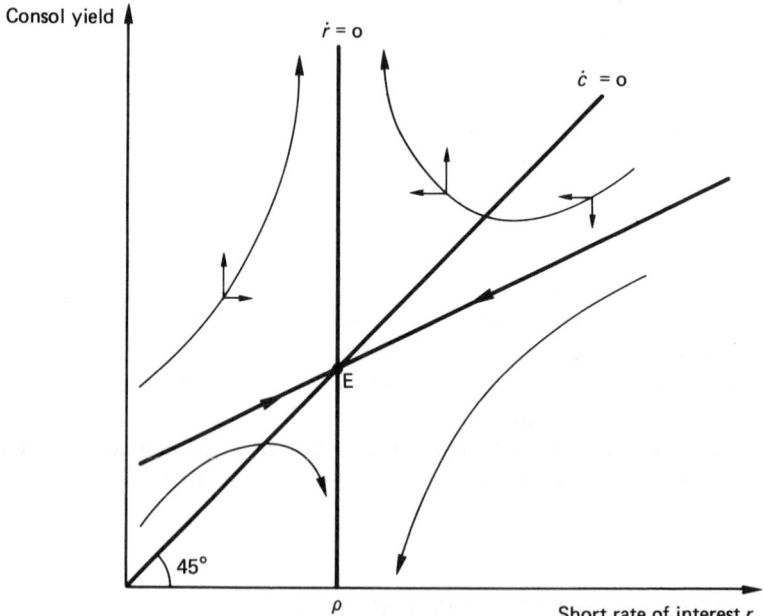

Figure 7.1 The relationship between instantaneous (r) and perpetuity yields (c) in the absence of shocks

infer that *either* $\rho > c > r$ and $\dot{c} > 0$ and $\dot{r} > 0$ *or* $r > c > \rho$ and $\dot{c} < 0$ and $\dot{r} < 0$.

In our stochastic world the analysis is modified in two ways. First $r \gtreqless \rho$ is no longer a sufficient condition for capital accumulation/decumulation. In the good state capital will be accumulated beyond the point at which $X_k = r = \rho$ in order to provide a fund to be drawn down in the bad state when capital will be decumulated beyond the critical value. This is explored more fully in Section 4 below (see also Figure 7.4). Secondly, the levels of both L and K at future dates may depend on the state then ruling and in the interim. Thus future short rates are uncertain and this could give rise to a risk premium element in the term structure.

Despite these qualifications the difference between long and short rates (c and r) does present the government with a choice of financing any deficit by issuing bonds (consols with coupon c) or short bills yielding r. Consols have some of the features of a contingent bond in that their value, if not their coupon, is liable to jump on a change of state. No other kind of contingent bond or insurance contract is considered until Section 4.

Before considering the role of debt in our two-state stochastic model there are two prior questions to address after setting up the model: what role, if any, would debt have in the absence of shocks, and why have we chosen the particular Markovian state-switching representation of uncertainty?

The model consists of five basic equations. The representative consumer's additively separable utility function

$$W = \int_0^\infty e^{-\rho t} \quad (U(C, L) + \tilde{s}P(G))dt \tag{7.1}$$

where C is private consumption, L is labour supply, G is public expenditure and $\tilde{s}$ is the random parameter which shifts demand for the public good. Given the separability of the public good the consumer maximises $U(C, L)$ subject to

$$\dot{F} = rF + (1-\tau)wL - (1+\theta)C \tag{7.2}$$

where F is his non-human wealth consisting of capital K and net claims D on the government, τ is the wage tax rate and θ the consumption tax rate.

National income

$$X = X(K, L),$$

and

$$X = X_K K + X_L L = rK + wL \tag{7.3}$$

and the capital stock K evolves as

$$\dot{K} = X - C - G$$
$$= rK + wL - C - G. \tag{7.4}$$

If the debt consists of bills earning the current rate r we have

$$D_b = b = F - K$$

and

$$\dot{D}_b = \dot{b} = rb + G - wL - C. \tag{7.5a}$$

Alternatively if it consists of N consols each paying one consumption unit per unit time their value is $D_c = N/c = F - K$ and

$$\dot{N} = c(N + G - \tau wL - \theta C)$$

whence

$$\dot{D}_c = N\left(1 - \frac{\dot{c}}{c}\right) + G - \tau wL - \theta C \tag{7.5b}$$

In the open economy case $r \neq \rho$ implied indefinite growth and, in general, growth of public expenditure, private consumption and wage income at different rates. This gives rise to a very clear, indeed ultimately dominating, role for debt – assuming that a strictly constant tax rate is optimal – which asymptotically either absorbs all tax revenue (if the growth of expenditure is less than that of the tax base) or (being negative) finances all expenditure (if the inequality is reversed).

In the present case all the relevant growth rates converge on zero as r converges on ρ. Figure 7.2 assumes that $K_o < K^*$, its asymptotic

209

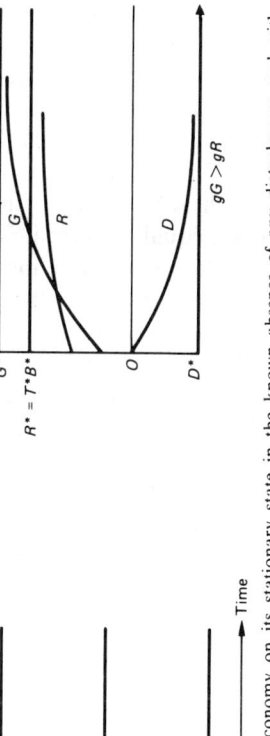
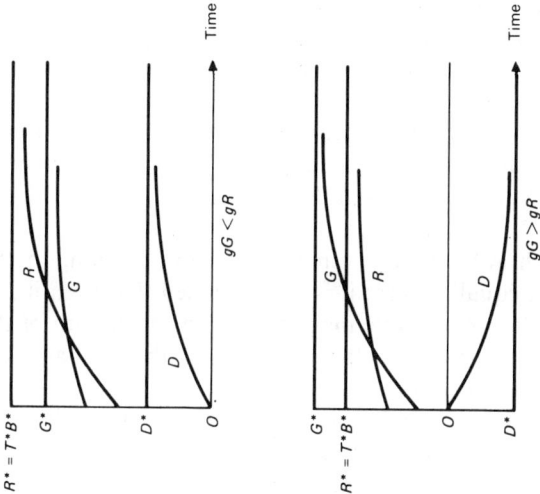

Figure 7.2 Convergence of the economy on its stationary state in the known absence of any disturbances and with initial capital stock below its equilibrium value

(a) Convergence of the economy on its stationary state in the known absence of any disturbance – with initial capital stock below its equilibrium value ($Ko < K^*$), and with no initial debt ($Do = O$), when the optimal tax rate is constant.

(b) The dynamics of debt (D), revenue (R) and exhaustive government expenditure G when (b) the tax base (and therefore revenue R) grows faster than G (so that the steady state Debt (D^*) is positive) and (c) when G grows faster than B so that D^* is negative.

steady state level at which $X_K(K^*, L^*) = \rho$. r_o is thus initially greater than ρ and $\dot{r} < 0$. This implies $(\dot{L}/K) < 0$ but is consistent with either increasing or falling labour supply depending on the income and substitution effects of the rising net wage and rising capital income, as long as $\dot{L}/L < \dot{K}/K$. $\dot{L}/LO$ is the more probable case chosen for illustration by solid lines.

The steady state to which the model tends is not independent of the starting point. Given K_o a higher initial debt D_o implies a higher private wealth $(F_o = D_o + K_o)$, lower initial labour supply L_o and higher constant tax rate T^*. The higher tax rate is likely to affect the steady state values of both K^* and L^* – in the same proportion. In the illustration D_o is set equal to zero; it is also assumed that even if $\dot{L}/L$ is negative it is smaller in absolute magnitude than the growth of the (net) real wage $\dot{w}/w(>0)$ so that the growth g_B of the tax base B is positive (for $r_o > \rho$) whether B is consumption or wage income.

Thus we see that the deterministic version of the model has the property that if launched from arbitrary initial conditions debt plays a role in smoothing the transition to the static optimum in which a positive or negative constant debt will persist indefinitely.

More interesting questions for both debt and taxes arise if the variation in expenditure and revenue are less than perfectly predictable; as mentioned above attention here is restricted to the random preference for public goods represented by the parameter $\tilde{s}$.

Not all random variations of $\tilde{s}$ lead to interesting results. Suppose that it is generated by a 'white noise' process, i.e. the value in each period is drawn from the same distribution. Even if the drawing is made before taxes and expenditures are set the optimum will be associated with a random deviation of the budget deficit or surplus from that previously planned. The next period's problem differs from that previously expected only by the larger or smaller debt and capital stock resulting from the previous period's realisation, and the solution will differ only to the extent that it depends on these two state variables which now follow some form of random walk – as also will the deviation of optimal taxes and public expenditures from their previously planned path. For small real interest rates the variance of the tax rate process will be small relative to that of the white noise processes generating $\tilde{s}$; and that of the expenditure deviation will be dominated by its direct reaction to shocks to $\tilde{s}$.

Secondly, suppose that s itself follows a random walk; in this case the best guess about the future is that it will be like the present. To a first approximation taxes and expenditures should thus be based on assuming that s will permanently retain its present value.

The tax rate, previously assumed broadly constant, and the previously planned profile of expenditure, is thus liable to small permanent random shifts with no (first order) implications for the path of the debt. The tax rate in fact follows a (possibly modified) random walk with a variance of the same order as that of $\tilde{s}$.

To generate more interesting results requires that shocks be in some way serially correlated – though not cumulating as in a random walk. In this sense they must follow stochastic 'cycles'. This will ensure a substantial role for debt. Note, however, that though the shocks may be cyclical the economy is one in which all markets clear continuously: there are no Keynesian cycles of alternating 'boom' and 'slump' in economic activity.

As the treatment of a general specification of such shocks is intractable, in this chapter I consider cases in which the economy switches between two states according to a Markov process. That is the probability, per unit time, of moving to the other state is constant – though it will generally differ between the two states. Thus the shift in demand for public goods might represent the discrete transition from peace to war – which I assume to be characterised by a greater demand for public goods (the analogy is not close, the probability of transition to peace is unaffected by expenditure, the end of the world is no nigher).

The government's problem is to select four functions $T_i(K, D)$, $G_i(K, D)$ where i indexes the state and $T = \tau, \theta$ depending on the tax base chosen. The government's choice is conditioned by the behaviour of private agents who also choose four functions $C_i(F, T, r)$, $L_i(F, T, r)$ in the knowledge of the government's tax rules and the yield curve for which the current short rate r is, given the state i and the constant ρ, a sufficient statistic.

Given the separability assumption public expenditure does not affect private decisions. Expectations of both parties are rational in the sense that the identity of the stochastic variable, which is generally observable, and the parameters of the process by which it is generated, are generally known; the government knows the consumers' optimising response to taxes and the consumers know the government's tax rules.

In the deterministic context of Figure 7.2 above we would expect greater initial debt to increase the tax rate whether applied to consumption or earnings. The direct effect of the requirement for additional revenue to service the debt is only partially offset by reduced expenditure and is reinforced, in the case of wage taxation, by the wealth effect of greater debt on labour supply. In the case of consumption taxation this wealth effect enlarges consumption and the tax base but the revenue gained at an unchanged tax rate necessarily falls short of the additional interest due. The effect of higher capital on the tax rate is, for both bases, ambiguous. The richer community will want more of a normal public good, more leisure, and more consumption: it will also have a higher wage for given labour supply. The first of these four effects tends to raise the required tax rate; the second and fourth pull the wage tax rate in opposite directions while the third could offset the need for a higher consumption tax rate.

4 ELABORATIONS

Before illustrating these second-best effects more fully it is useful to establish the first-best response to the oscillations in s in the context, for example, of a single-member society. These responses may act as a bench-mark by which to assess alternative second-best policies.

4.1 First Best

In bad, high s states private consumption is lower than in good states; its marginal utility is therefore higher (given $U_{cc} < O$) and capital (which in this case is indistinguishable from wealth) will therefore be accumulated in good states and run down in bad ones. Thus in good states capital, and consumption of both C and G, rise if they are normal goods, and labour supply falls if leisure is normal (and responds only weakly to the rising real wage) – and *vice versa* in bad states. This is illustrated in Figure 7.3, where two alternative paths are shown for labour supply, that in brackets applying where the income effect on labour supply is stronger. It is assumed that the initial capital stock is fairly close to its optimum in the sense that r (line four) is assumed to oscillate symmetrically, though stochastically, about ρ. For the reasons given its asymptote in low $\tilde{s}$ states is below ρ and in high $\tilde{s}$ states above.

As already mentioned the dynamics of capital accumulation are complicated in the stochastic model by the fact that K^* is state-dependent in two different and conflicting ways. In a static deterministic model a higher $\tilde{s}$ raises labour supply and thus, for given ρ, the steady state K^*. On the other hand in this model when $\tilde{s}$ is low capital is accumulated beyond the point at which $X_K = \rho$ to provide for consumption particularly, public, when $\tilde{s}$ rises. Thus K has an asymptote in low $\tilde{s}$ periods which is above that in high s periods as shown in the second line of Figure 7.3.

The issue can also be considered algebraically. Consider the indirect

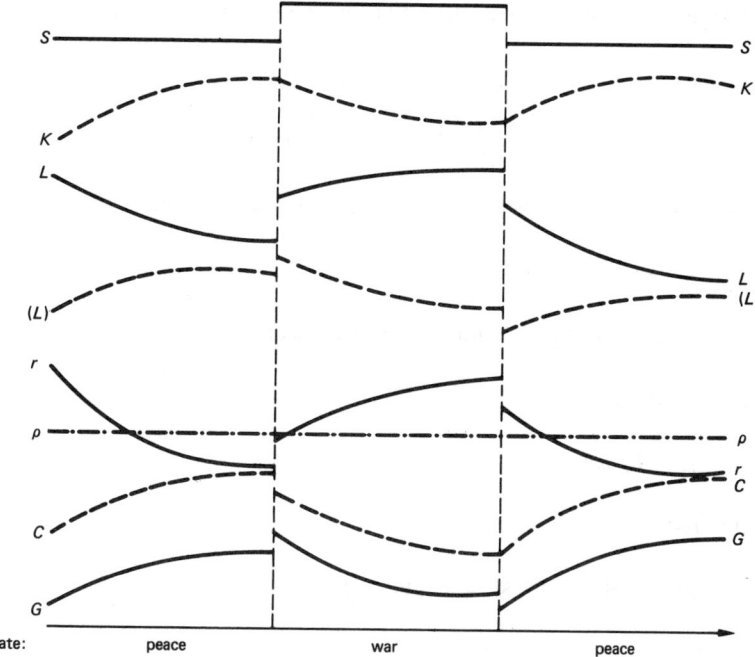

Figure 7.3 Movement of different variables in a single member economy as the preference for 'public' goods ($\tilde{s}$) shifts between peace and war

Key:
$\tilde{s}$ = demand preference for public goods
K = capital
L = labour
(L) = labour with a strong income effect on labour
r = rate of interest
ρ = constant rate of pure time preference
C = private consumption
G = public expenditure.

utility functions $V_i(K)$ where i indexes the state $1 =$ low $\tilde{s}$ (peace), $2 =$ high $\tilde{s}$ (war). We know that:

$$\rho V_i(K) = U(C, L) + s_1.P(G) + V'_1(\dot{K}_1) + \pi_2(V_2(K) - V_1(K)) \tag{7.6}$$

where π_2 is the probability of transition to state 2 and

$$\dot{K}_1 = X(L, K) - C - G \tag{7.7}$$

Using (7.7) and differentiating (7.6) with respect to K gives

$$\rho V'_1 = U_c.C_K + U_L.L_K + s_1.P'.G_K + V_1''.(K_1)$$
$$+ V_1'.(X_L L_K + X_K - C_K - G_K) + \pi_2(V_2' - V_1') \qquad (7.8)$$

which can be simplified by using the first-order conditions

$$U_c = s.P' = V'$$

$$-U_L = V'X_L \quad \text{and} \quad r = X_K(L,K),$$

and noting that

$$L_i = L_i(K)$$

this reduces to

$$\rho V_1' = rV_1' + V''.K_1 + \pi_2(V_2' - V_1')$$

whence

$$\frac{\dot{K}_1}{K_1} = r_1 \frac{(K) - \rho + \pi_2(V'_2/V'_1) - 1)}{-KV''_1/V'_1}. \qquad (7.9)$$

The denominator of the right-hand side of (7.9) is the coefficient of relative risk aversion of the indirect utility function: call it R_1, which might be constant. $((V_2'(K)/V_1'(K)) - 1)$ is also positive and might be constant; call it S_1.

We then have

$$\frac{\dot{K}_1}{K_1} = r_1 \frac{(K) - \rho + \pi_2 S_1}{R_1} \qquad (7.10)$$

and the dynamics of r and K are as illustrated below in Figure 7.4 (note that $S_2 < o$).

Where $r_1(K)$ lies below $r_2(K)$ because labour supply is higher in wartime in the first best case (the corresponding arguments are less straightforward in the second best case). Note that U_{cc}, P'', U_{LL} and V''' negative ensures that C, L and G move monotonically with K as shown in Figure 7.3.

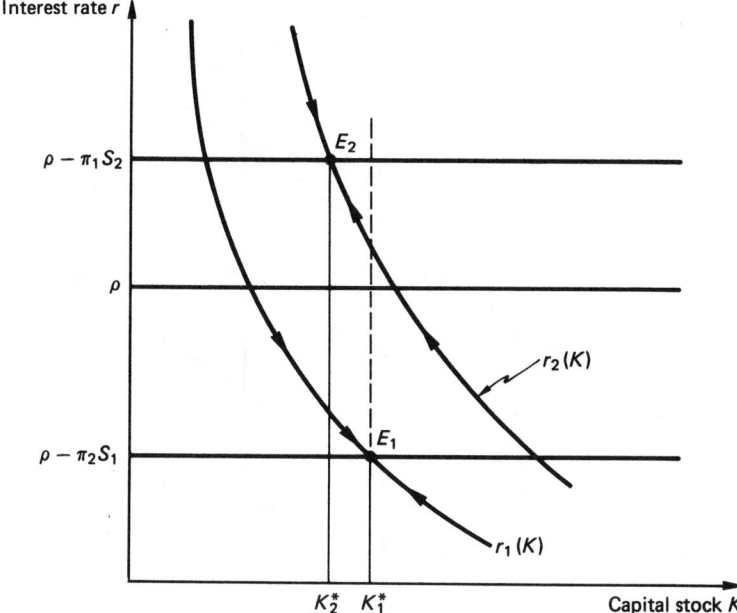

Figure 7.4 Dynamics of capital and short-term interest in the presence of shocks to the single member economy

What happens to the consol rate in this stochastic world? Equating the expected yield on bonds to the current spot rate gives two conditions

$$r_1 = c_1 - (1-\pi_2)\frac{\dot{c}_1}{c_1} - \pi_2\left(\frac{1}{2} - \frac{1}{c_1}\right)$$

$$r_2 = c_2 - (1-\pi_1)\frac{\dot{c}_2}{c_2} - \pi_2\left(\frac{1}{c_1} - \frac{1}{c_2}\right).$$

(7.11)

It is plausible that the last term in these two equations should be roughly constant. On that basis the $\dot{c}_1 = 0$ lines are as in Figure 7.5.

Thus the path of the consol rate corresponding to that of the interest rate in Figure 7.3 is as shown in the dotted line in Figure 7.6 although this relates to a single member society, and the capital market is therefore entirely hypothetical, the shadow prices are real enough.

4.2 Second Best

Returning to the second best world we have four possible policy regimes

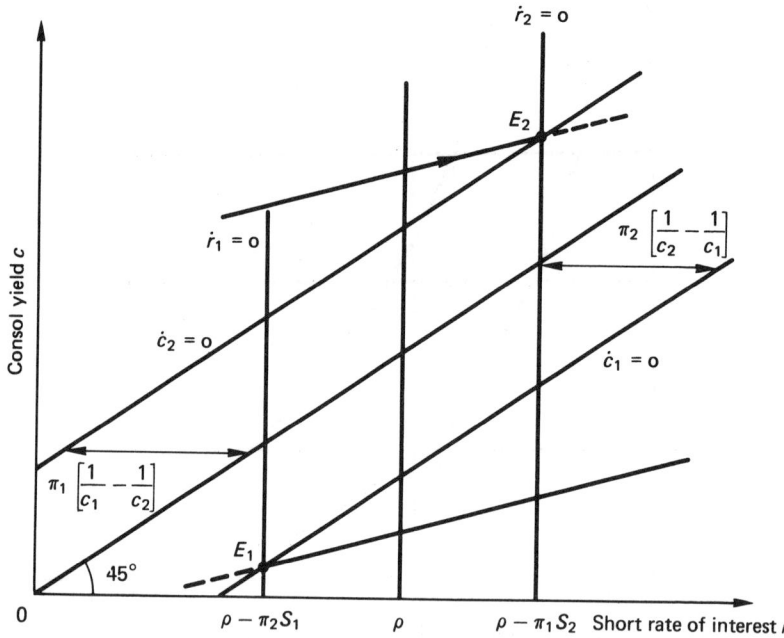

Figure 7.5 Dynamics of long and short interest rates in the presence of shocks to the single member economy

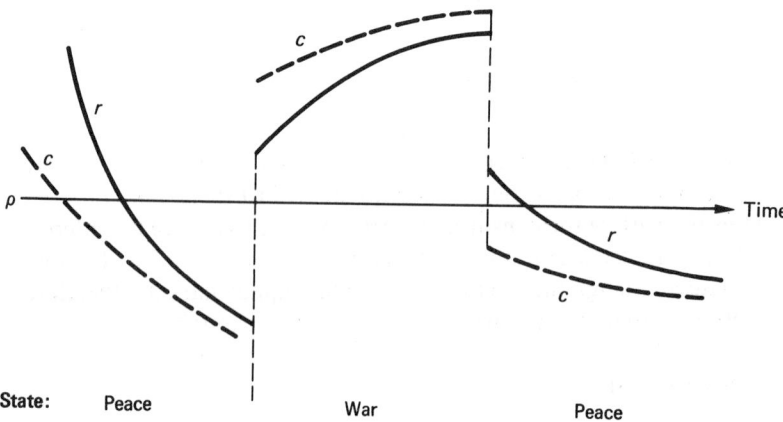

Figure 7.6 Illustrative time path of long and short interest rates in the stochastic single member economy

as consumption or wage taxation is combined with either bond or bill finance of fiscal deficits/surpluses. We also had two qualitatively different behavioural regimes in the first-best world depending on whether capital accumulation was associated with rising or falling labour supply. This ambiguity carries over to the second-best case where it is joined by an ambiguity in the step response of labour supply to the tax change, and, under bond financing, the wealth change on a change of state. Thus conceivably we might have sixteen cases to analyse as the four regimes intersect with four labour supply patterns.

A positive jump in L and c on a switch from low to high $\tilde{s}$ are mutually reinforcing: a rise in L raises r, and c; the latter lowers wealth held in bonds which increases labour supply, at least relative to the bill-financing case (in which wealth is unchanged and non-wage income rises). It is under these circumstances that a government would find bond financing attractive. We therefore confine bond financing to cases in which L rises with $\tilde{s}$, which is more likely under the consumption tax; and bill financing to cases in which L falls as $\tilde{s}$ rises, which is more likely under the wage tax.

With r endogenous the *ex ante* constancy of tax rates is relatively unlikely to hold exactly: it would hold exactly if $U(C, L) = U_1(C) + U_2(L)$ and $U_1(C)$, $U_2(L)$ and $P(G)$ are all isoelastic. More generally, however, the departures from $E(\Delta T) = 0$ are unlikely to be large. On this basis we again have the proposition that in high $\tilde{s}$, high tax, states there is a budget deficit and rising taxes and *vice versa*. We thus have two cases as shown in Figure 7.7.

I conclude that the expenditure tax base is likely to prove the more advantageous and that bond (consol) financing is likely to be preferable provided that labour supply responds positively to an increase in the expenditure tax rate.

In the open economy model with perfect international mobility of capital the question of the structure of domestic production did not arise. In the closed economy we need to face the possibility that the production functions of public and private goods differ. Assuming that both factors are perfectly mobile between the sectors the effect of a change of $\tilde{s}$ on the interest rate r will now depend not only on concomitant changes in labour supply L (and thus on the average factor ratio L/K) but also on the relative capital intensity of the two sectors.

If the public good is the less capital intensive, a rise in s might lower r even if aggregate labour supply were actually increased. Thus the sufficient condition for the superiority of the consumption tax has to be restated in terms of the net effect of aggregate labour supply, relative output demands, and factor intensities, on the interest rate.

218

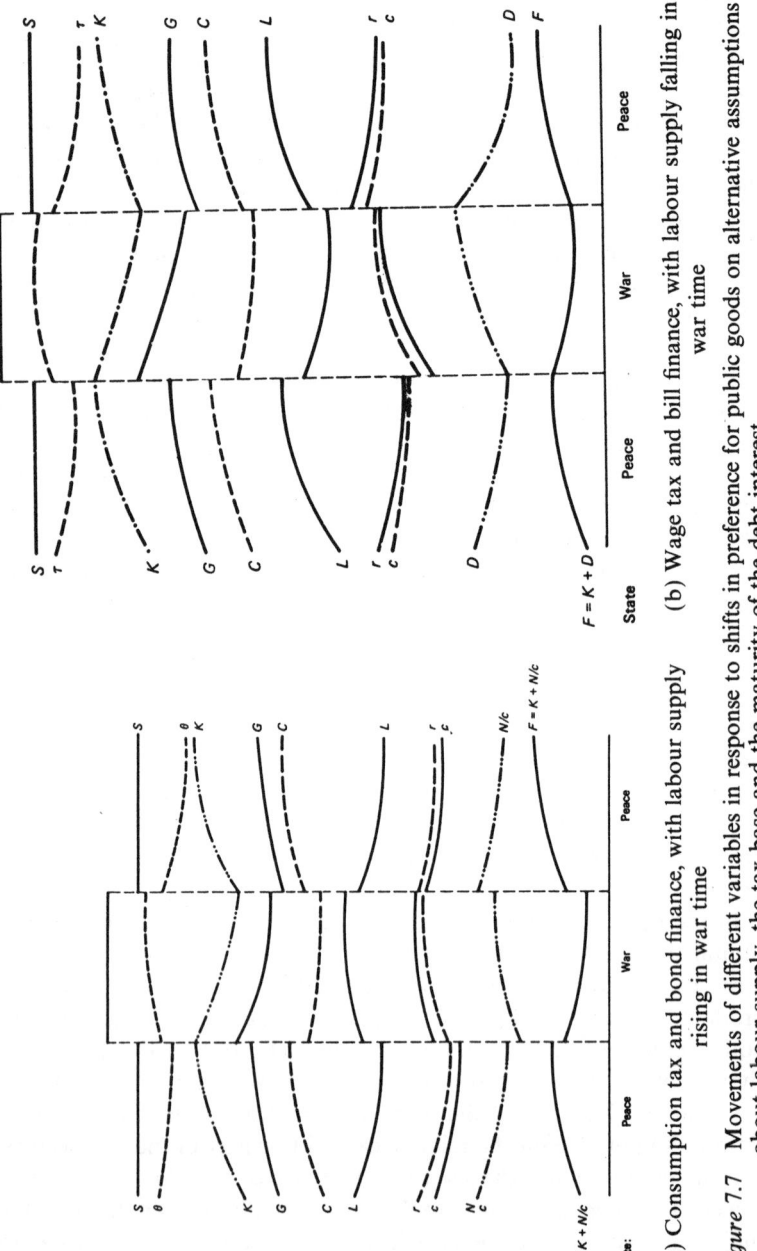

(a) Consumption tax and bond finance, with labour supply rising in war time

(b) Wage tax and bill finance, with labour supply falling in war time

Figure 7.7 Movements of different variables in response to shifts in preference for public goods on alternative assumptions about labour supply, the tax base and the maturity of the debt interest.

Figure 7.7 continued from page 218

Key:
$\tilde{s}$ = demand preference for public goods
θ = consumption rate tax
τ = wage tax rate
K = capital stock
L = labour sources
G = public expenditure
C = private consumption
r = instantaneous rate of interest
c = yield of consols
N = number of consols
F = consumers non-human wealth
D = consumers net claims on the government.

5 EXTENSIONS TO THE MODEL

In this section two extensions to the basic analysis of the previous section are considered. First, the implications of contingent bonds and secondly, the interpretation of the model not in terms of swings between states in which the representative citizen demands different quantities of public goods but swings between governments of different parties supplying them in different quantities.

5.1 Contingent Bonds

In an open economy a simple contingent bond could provide both perfect perfect insurance and full stabilisation of the tax rate. If the initial debt was not large enough this bond would carry a negative coupon in the bad state which could give rise to problems of enforcement but we abstracted from them.

In the closed economy insurance is impossible, the population is homogeneous and there is no one else to whom the risk can be shifted. Moreover, only a rather complex coupon structure could fully stabilise the tax rate. To achieve this the number of perpetual debt certificates outstanding must not change. Thus the coupon $c_i(K)$ will depend both on the state i and the capital stock K.

On the outbreak of war the coupon payment falls by the sum

(difference) of the amount by which exhaustive public expenditure rises and revenue falls, in the consumption tax case (rises in the wage tax case), the rise in public expenditure being that appropriate to the unchanged tax rate T^*. Private consumption, labour supply and the interest rate, however, will all change – in contrast to the open economy case. The fall in household coupon receipts would, at an unchanged interest rate, reduce wealth and consumption while increasing labour supply; but the interest rate would rise with the labour:capital ratio, reinforcing the fall in the bond price and consumption, and the increased supply of labour.

If the wartime coupon and tax rate were constant the private problem would be as in the first-best case, in which it was seen (Figure 7.3) that both public and private consumption, and the capital stock, fall, while labour supply and the interest rate rise further. Thus, if no additional debt certificates are to be bought or sold, the coupon on the bond may rise or fall as the war progresses depending on the relative movement of revenue, which falls under the consumption tax but rises under the wage tax, and public expenditure, which falls. Note, however, that as the interest rate rises the sign of the change in the value of the debt is uncertain even if the coupon rises. If, instead of a varying coupon, debt were issued or retired, the tax rate would have to change with the number of certificates outstanding.

Such a bond, with state and capital contingent coupon, would minimise the deadweight burden of the distorting tax. Although the tax rate is constant the two tax bases may not obviously be equivalent. As has been seen the difference in the coupon payable on the contingent bond is greater under the consumption tax, where revenue, at a constant tax rate, falls on the outbreak of war, than under a wage tax, when it rises. Both cash flows and relative prices are, however, identical, so that behaviour and welfare are identical under the two tax sytems.

Suppose that this full contingency is unfeasible, only state contingency being allowed. Even if the differential were such that the government's cash flow were not immediately disturbed by a change of state, we have seen that this could not last. Either debt would have to start being issued or retired, or the tax rate would have to change – or, in fact most likely, both. The changing tax rate is liable to set up intertemporal distortions which require a step change on a change of state to offset them. We are back in the world of the previous section, although the scale of all the tax rate changes, and the issue/retirement of debt, could be substantially reduced (but not eliminated) by the relatively simple form of state contingent debt.

5.2 Constant Consumer Preferences and Government Change

The second extension, which applies equally to the open economy case, reflects the fact that there may be a temptation to interpret the model of this (and the previous) chapter in terms not of shifts in totally external factors (wars or ice ages) but the different preferences for public goods of different political parties alternating in power with the (stochastic) swing of the political pendulum. This interpretation presents several problems, the first being that the exogeneity of the change of state is probably even less acceptable in this case. A second problem is that if the representative citizen/consumers' preferences change there are difficulties in applying standard models of rationality (Radner/Hammond/McManus).

If we postulate a population of homogeneous individuals with unchanging preferences, power over which alternates stochastically between groups with high and low preferences respectively for public goods, we cannot appeal to the single consumer case to establish first-best properties. Instead we introduce lump-sum taxation and balanced budgets (or Ricardian equivalence).

The Government of party i chooses G to maximise

$$\rho\psi_{ii}(K) = U(C_i, L_i) + S_i P(Gi) + \psi'_{ii}(\dot{K}_i) + \pi_j(\psi_{ij} - \psi_{ii}) \qquad (7.12)$$

where ψ_{ii} is the valuation function of party i of the state of affairs when it is in power, $\psi_{ij}(K)$ is its valuation when party j is in power. Loss of power to j occurs with probability π_j per unit time. Expenditure G is financed by a uniform poll tax G/N (where N is the population size) on consumers who maximise

$$\rho\phi_i(K) = U(C, L) + \phi'_i \dot{K}_i + \pi_j(\phi_j - \phi_{ii}) \qquad (7.13)$$

subject to $\dot{K} = rK + wL - C - G/N$ by choice of C and L. Thus $U_c = \phi', U_L = w\phi'$ and if $r = \rho$

$$\dot{K}_i = \frac{\pi_j(\phi'_j - \phi'_i) - \phi'_i Gik/N}{-\phi''_i} \qquad (7.14)$$

If N is large enough saving is not deterred by the knowledge that as total capital rises so does optimal public expenditure and hence the individual's poll tax. Thus for large N capital is accumulated under low spending governments and run down under high spenders as shown

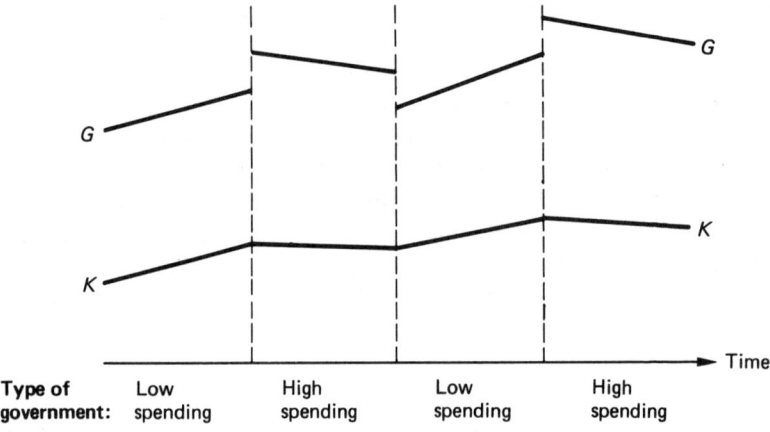

Figure 7.8 Government spending and private capital accumulation under governments of varying complexions.

in Figure 7.8. Where we turn to distorting taxes the previous argument relating to shadow prices under consistent (albeit stochastic) preferences break down. A qualitatively similar argument does, however, carry over.

Consider the low-sending/low-tax party, if when in power it behaved as though it expected to stay in power for ever, and as if it believed the citizens to share this illusion, it would, given $r = \rho$ choose a tax and expenditure rate it intended to maintain forever. Faced with a constant low-tax while this government lasted, and the prospect of a higher one under the alternative, consumers would save and the government would probably want to allow the growing private wealth to be reflected in higher public expenditure (which, under a wage tax, would also call for a rising tax rate). Moreover, the knowledge that the other party, if it behaved at all similarly, would, at some stage, come to power and raise taxes, would distort allocation decisions from those sought by the government which ignored its own mortality. Specifically, if the 'opposition' were thought likely to raise a consumption tax the *ex ante* return on savings would be depressed.

It would be in the interest of the low-tax government to offset this distortion, at least in part, either by subsidising interest or by levying a higher rate of tax initially, running a surplus and holding out the prospect of falling taxes as long as it remained in power. Thus, as in the previous cases, when taxes are low there is a budget surplus and the taxes fall further while the high tax party, when in power, may run a deficit and have rising tax rates.

The argument for this result suggests that the government which would prefer constant tax rates is unlikely to reduce the unconditional expectation of their change to zero. Notice also that the constraint imposed on government by the known preferences of the opposition includes a pattern of expenditure similar to that which would be achieved under lump-sum taxation. The relative inefficiency of proportional taxation must, of course, occur, and the lump-sum case itself cannot be described simply as first best given the postulated divergence between individual and 'party) preferences.

Note

1. I am grateful to Kenneth Arrow and Christophe Chamley for discussion of this case: see also Arrow and Kurz (1970).

References

Arrow, K. J. and Kurz, M. (1970) *Public Investment, the Rate of Return and Optimal Fiscal Policy* (Baltimore, MD: Johns Hopkins University Press).
Barro, R. J. (1979) 'On the Deterioration of the Public Debt', *Journal of Political Economy*, vol. 87, pp. 940–71.
Currie, D. A. and Levine, P. (1985) 'Credibility and Time Inconsistency in a Stochastic Model'. Queen Mary College, London, Research Paper, No. 36.
Flemming, J. S. (1987) 'Debt and Taxes in War and Peace: The Case of a Small Open Economy' in Boskin, M. J., Flemming, J. S. and Gorini, S. (eds). *Private Saving and Public Debt* (Oxford: Blackwells).
Hahn, F. H. (1973) 'On Optimum Taxation', *Journal of Economic Theory*, vol. 6, pp. 96–106.
Lucas, R. E. and Stokey, N. L. (1983) 'Optimal Fiscal and Monetary Policy in an Economy without Capital', *Journal of Monetary Economics*, vol. 12, pp. 55–94.
Mirrlees, J. A. (1971) 'An exploration in the theory of optimum income taxation', *Review of Economic Studies*, vol. 38, pp. 175–208.
Persson, T. and Svensson, L. E. O. (1984) 'Time Consistent Fiscal Policy and Government Cash Flow', *Journal of Monetary Economics*, vol. 14, no. 3, pp. 365–74.
Persson, T. and Svensson, L. E. O. (1985) 'International Borrowing and Time Consistent Fiscal Policy', *Scandinavian Journal of Economics*, vol. 14, pp. 365–74.

DISCUSSION

Professor Kenneth Arrow was the principal discussant of Mr John

Flemming's paper. Arrow characterised Flemming's paper as being a part of the literature in which debt is used to smooth out fluctuations in tax rates. Arrow illustrated the idea first in a determinant model, adding Flemming's uncertainty elements later. The model is an extension of one developed by Arrow and Kurz, with the addition of endogenous labour supply. We start by imagining a perfectly planned economy, in which the first best outcome is attainable. There is only one kind of output, produced by a production technology using capital and labour,

$$X = F(K, L).$$

Output can be used for any of three purposes: as private consumption, C; as government consumption, G; or as an addition to the capital stock, $\dot{K}$. Arrow appealed to Ramsey's result, that the first-best allocation is attainable through central planning. The question then is whether the optimum is attainable in decentralised economy.

Arrow considers a representative individual, in a population of identical people. Utility is separable in private and government consumption

$$U = U_1(C) + U_2(G).$$

The assumption of identical people means that social preferences can be expressed as

$$\int_0^\infty e^{-\rho t}[U_1(C) + U_2(G)]dt.$$

The government chooses its policy, and individuals make their choices on the basis of this policy. In this sense, this is a 'Stackleberg game'. If government chooses its policy correctly, though, individuals will desire the social optimum.

The individual maximises

$$\int_0^\infty e^{-\rho t} U_1(C) dt.$$

The social production constraint is

$$C + G + K = F(K, L).$$

The individual has private financial wealth which follows the equation of motion

$$\dot{F} = rF + X - T - C,$$

where T is taxes (not necessarily lump sum), r is the rate of return ($r = X_k$) and X is labour income.

$$F = K + D$$

where D is government debt. Its equation of motion is

$$\dot{D} = rD + G - T.$$

In this model, can government arrange tax policy to get one to the optimum? Yes, government can use a constant consumption tax, so that the present discounted value of tax collections equals to PDV (present discounted value) of government consumption, and individuals choose the optimum. The moral is that there is a role for debt in this model, with a consumption tax, and non-time-varying tax rate.

Now consider adding labour supply to the utility function. We then have

$$U = U_1(C, L) + U_2(G).$$

In this situation, a consumption tax alone will not be able to get us to a first best allocation. We will need to be able to tax

$$wL - C.$$

Whether or not the first best is attainable will depend on the available instruments.

In an earlier paper Flemming looked at a small open economy so that r is fixed, and, in this case, chosen so that $r = \rho$, where ρ is the rate of time preference. Flemming then adds uncertainty so that

$$U = U_1(C, L) + \tilde{s} U_2(G),$$

where $\tilde{s}$ is a random variable. The benefit from government consumption thus varies over time.

The process chosen for $\tilde{s}$ is very simple: it is a Markovian renewal process. $\tilde{s}$ can take on either of two states, s_1 or s_2 and there is a fixed transition probability each period of either changing states or staying in the initial state. Arrow points out that Flemming does not attempt to work out formally the second-best allocation.

There is a role here for debt. s_1 is chosen to be the period of high demand for the public good, and thus is the state of 'war' referred to in the title, and $s_1 > s_2$.

Arrow characterises Flemming's main result as a suggestion that expected tax rate changes should be zero. This implies that you do not go to war on a 'pay as you go' basis. Pigou and Ricardo had both argued that it did not matter.

Arrow then turned to the question, which he described as 'less interesting', of what we mean by bonds. Flemming does most of his analysis with very short-term securities but he also considers bonds. Arrow felt the analysis of bonds was heuristic and not convincing. He felt that a wider range of debt maturities should have been considered – perhaps a 'convex combination' of the two extremes. He also suggested that perhaps a convex combination of consumption and wage taxes should have been considered.

Professor Arrow noted in conclusion that Flemming failed to consider the possibility of contingent bonds,[1] that is, bonds contingent on the duration of the war. With such an instrument, the first-best optimum could be attained.

Mr John Flemming began his remarks by apologising for his 'overblown' title. He then noted that the English budget was currently running a surplus, properly measured. His paper suggested that this was appropriate behaviour in time of peace.

Flemming turned to three main points he wanted to make in response to Professor Arrow's remarks. The first was the allusion to the idea that some revenue could be obtained without distortionary taxation. Flemming noted that when one considered both a consumption and a wage tax, a time inconsistency problem was introduced whereby the government could fool people by switching from a wage to a consumption tax. He also questioned the scale upon which one could collect taxes in this way. The value of tax that could be collected in this way was limited to the current stock of capital, and this might not be sufficient to cover the present discounted value of future government spending.

Flemming's second point related to the question of the use of long-term bonds as opposed to short-term bills. Flemming said that the suggested superiority of bond finance was not general. It applied only when an increase in the relevant tax rate led to an increase in labour supply. In such situations he said, distortionary taxation could be reduced to the extent that the capital levy could be used.

The third point Flemming addressed was that of contingent bonds. He argued that state contingent bonds were not optimal, because the lump sum that is paid on transition between states introduces intertemporal distortion. A second alternative would involve selling a bond with a contingent coupon in the world market. If the rest of the world were risk neutral, the country could buy fair 'war insurance'.

The general discussion began with several questions from *Professor Joseph Stiglitz*. Stiglitz first asked how the results would differ if an overlapping generations model were used. He suggested that this would introduce a motive for smoothing for equity reasons. Stiglitz then brought up the question of controllability in an Arrow-type model. He pointed out that in the Arrow model without labour supply, the consumption tax amounts to a lump-sum tax. With labour supply endogenous, it is an interesting question whether the inflation tax can be used as a capital levy to fool people. In general, though, with both consumption and labour supply choice, one cannot achieve the first best.

Stiglitz pointed out, as did Flemming, that in a model with identical individuals, lump-sum taxes can be used, so that the introduction of distorting taxes is artificial. The assumption of intragenerational inequality is needed to motivate distortionary taxation. In that sort of framework, separability of consumption and leisure is sufficient to ensure the desirability of the consumption tax.

Stiglitz's final point was that in models similar to these, it is often optimal to use random tax policies in order to get greater labour supply. He contrasted this to Flemming's model, in which the environment was random.

Flemming addressed this last point by wondering whether a 'counter-randomisation' of tax policy might not be called for in a model with a random environment.

Dr Christophe Chamley suggested that a balanced budget could be maintained if the after-tax interest rate were varied with varying taxes. He also noted that the optimum can be achieved in the face of an endogenous labour supply if three particular tax instruments were available to the government. Counting instruments, however, would not be sufficient.

Professor Richard Musgrave also brought up the issue of intergenerational equity and the use of the life-cycle model.

Professor Michael Boskin mentioned in this regard that if a life-cycle framework were adopted, a switch from a wage tax to a consumption tax would imply double taxation of the income of retirees. Boskin also mentioned the fact that the assumption of separability had entered the analysis in a number of ways, for example, ensuring the independence of the choice of the consumer problem from the choice of government expenditures. *Professor Stiglitz* suggested that the problem had to be simplified in some respects to be understandable at all. *Dr Flemming* said that the assumption was both mathematically and politically convenient, since the question of the substitutability or complementary of public for private goods was a politically volatile one.

Dr Vito Tanzi suggested that since the benefits of a surprise change in tax regime are immediate, while distortions take time to reduce output, it might be acceptable to use the surprise instrument at the outbreak of the war, and hope that peace comes before the distortions become too onerous. In a similar vein, Tanzi suggested that because of sectoral shifts in wartime production, one could raise taxes on goods that have had curtailed production, such as cars and houses, with minimal distortionary effects.

Mr Flemming felt that such sectoral shift taxation went beyond the scope of the model, which had only one production sector. He did note, though, that government often limits housing construction during wartime, and hypothesised that this was mostly for equity and related moral reasons.

Professor John Taylor made two points, first, he was not clear how the time inconsistency problem, relating to the ability of the government to impose a capital levy by switching from wage to consumption taxation had been dealt with in the paper. His second remark presented the conjecture that tax rates ought to be random walk, so that the tax cuts in the first of the Reagan administration were in response to the 'news' that Reagan had been elected, which signalled that permanent government spending would be lower, even though the actual cuts had not yet been voted.

John Flemming responded to the second point first. He pointed out that in his paper, tax rates were a qualified random walk, jumping when there was new information, but then drifting systematically to keep expected tax rates fixed. He deliberately avoided the time inconsistency issue by assuming that the tax instrument could not be varied. Citing Currie and Levine, he argued that, in a stochastic world, the government must commit itself to a tax rate. *Taylor* suggested that

Flemming might want to address the time inconsistency problem directly by looking at a repeated game framework.

The final question was from *Sir Austin Robinson*. Sir Austin argued that in a war, governments try to depress consumption as much as possible. He suggested that one way of doing this was to encourage people to buy bonds, effectively shifting their consumption to the future.

Flemming acknowledged Austin Robinson's point. The war Flemming was modelling was not a real war. He noted the use in Britain of the 'postwar credit' during the Second World War. In conclusion Flemming said that this analysis hinged on the importance of intertemporal substitution. Many have argued that, empirically, intertemporal substitution effects are not important. This would suggest a very different analysis.

Note

1. Now addressed in subsection 5.1.

8 Public Debt and Fiscal Policy in Developing Countries*

Vito Tanzi and Mario I. Blejer
INTERNATIONAL MONETARY FUND

1 INTRODUCTION

Over the past decade the growth of public spending has generated large fiscal deficits in many countries, leading to increases in the share of public debt relative to gross domestic product (GDP). This happened in both industrial and developing countries. With the exception of a few, small countries such as Ireland and Denmark, the increase in public debt in industrial countries has been mostly domestic. In the developing countries, on the other hand, the public debt has been mostly external, although some countries, including Brazil and Mexico, have also accumulated sizeable domestic debts.

Public debt imposes constraints on economic policies in all countries. However, these constraints tend to be different depending on the maturity of the debt and on whether it is domestic or foreign. The share of concessionary debt in the total debt of a country is also of importance since concessionary debt carries lower servicing costs. A certain part of the debt of developing countries has concessionary elements while the debt of the industrial countries has been acquired generally on commercial terms.

This chapter is somewhat eclectic. It aims at providing a broad discussion of some debt-related issues of particular relevance to the developing countries and providing, in a consolidated manner, essential data to analyse the major issues. This information shows some surprising trends.

A study of developing countries must, by necessity, isolate a certain representative group as it would be difficult to deal with all of them. Several possible samples could have been chosen. However, we felt that in view of the importance attached to the Baker initiative in recent months, one obvious possibility was to concentrate on the fifteen countries mentioned in Secretary Baker's speech at the World Bank/IMF Annual Meetings of the Board of Governors in Seoul in October 1985. We shall refer to them as the fifteen Baker countries. This group includes the most highly indebted developing countries with good prospects for returning to spontaneous financial flows.[1]

Section 2 discusses the nature of the relationship between fiscal deficits and the accumulation of public debt. Section 3 deals with the constraints imposed by the presence of large public sector indebtedness on fiscal policies. Section 4 considers other macroeconomic effects of public debt. Section 5 reports the results of an econometric analysis of the determinants of changes in foreign debt and in interest charges on foreign liabilities for the fifteen Baker countries.

2 FISCAL DEFICIT AND PUBLIC DEBT

Fiscal deficits are prerequisites for the accumulation of public debt, since usually the issue of government liabilities arises from the need to finance the gap between ordinary revenues and total expenditures. However, the existence of fiscal deficits does not necessarily imply that the share of debt in GDP will grow over time. If a fiscal deficit is financed totally by foreign grants or by monetary expansion, then public debt will not grow, and may actually fall, in relation to GDP. Other variables are also important in that relationship; for example, the rate of growth of the economy and the real rate of interest on the existing public debt play a significant role. The time horizon is also relevant. If fiscal deficits are cyclical, in the sense that they turn into surpluses during boom years, there would no accumulation of debt and no expansion in the debt:GDP ratio over the cycle.

The first basic question to be asked in this context refers to the motivation of countries to allow the growth of public debt. Several answers could be given, some more important than others for developing countries. The main reasons or justifications that have traditionally been mentioned in the literature to explain or justify the growth of public debt are the following:

1. War Finance Wars require a sharp but transitory growth in public spending. Thus it makes sense to finance at least part of the increased spending through the sale of bonds rather than through taxation. Historically, in industrial countries this has been the main reason for the large accumulation of public debt as witnessed by the United

Kingdom during the Napoleonic wars and by the United States during the Civil War and the First and Second World Wars.

2. Development Finance The accumulation of public debt can arise from the need to finance a 'big push' in economic development. A country that at a given stage of its economic development engages in large expenditure on infrastructure would perhaps be justified in financing this through debt, provided that the expected rate of return of the development projects exceeds the cost of borrowing. In other words, if borrowed funds are invested efficiently, they can be expected to promote enough future growth so that the debt can be serviced, without difficulties, out of future higher incomes. Such reasoning is used to justify borrowing on the part of successful private corporations. It has also been used to justify large deficits and large borrowing on the part of some developing countries.

3. Availability of Cheap Credit Large borrowing by developing countries between 1974 and 1980 could be justified by the availability of cheap international credit. Given the low real rate of interest then prevailing in the international financial market, countries could borrow to finance the many projects with expected rates of return higher than the prevailing low real costs of borrowed funds. There were many projects that passed a benefit-cost test given the low real rates of interest.

4. Government Market Power Public sector borrowing by developing countries has at times been justified on the basis of the special position of the government as a borrower. It has been argued that the government can borrow abroad at lower rates than private borrowers since it carries a perceived lower risk and borrows larger amounts, thus reducing administrative costs. Private borrowers would pay higher rates if they borrowed directly. This arbitrage on the part of the government increase its *gross* debt while it may not increase immediately its *net* debt if the funds are, in turn, lent on to the rest of the economy. But, if the on-lending is done at subsidised rates, the gross debt of the government can also become, at least partially, a net debt. The fact that public as well as private enterprises obtain subsidised credit has, of course, made them less careful in project selection and has increased the role of political considerations in that selection.

5. Assumption of Private Sector Debt In a number of developing countries, particularly in Latin American, an important source for increases in the level of public debt has been the 'nationalisation' of private sector liabilities. In many countries governments have assumed the debt acquired by private sector enterprises, including financial institutions. In some cases, the private sector liabilities were originally guaranteed by the government, but in many other instances the government assumed the debt to avoid massive defaults that could have resulted in an extensive disruption for the domestic economy and a major loss of creditworthiness abroad.

6. Financing Current Expenditure In many instances governments borrowed for consumption purposes as they could score political gains in the short run by increasing subsidies or public employment without raising domestic revenues. The government obtained immediate political benefits by spending the proceeds of borrowing while the repayment of the debt was in the future and thus a successor government's problem. This public choice reason has certainly played a large role in the growth of public debt.

Some of the above reasons explain the emergence of large public debts. They do not explain, however, why industrial countries normally borrowed domestically while developing countries often borrowed abroad. To deal with this issue, we must review the different sources of financing available to governments to cover their expenditures. This issue highlights basic differences between industrial and developing countries. In all countries the most important source of financing public spending is obviously current revenue, a large proportion of which is made up of tax revenues. One would expect that taxes would cover a large share of public spending. However, there are many constraints on the level of taxation: political, structural, administrative, or purely social. These constraints tend to be much more inflexible in developing than in industrial countries. Therefore, the average tax ratio of developing countries tends to be much lower than the average tax ratio of industrial countries – generally less than half.

Experience indicates that it is very difficult to raise the tax level of developing countries significantly, at least in the short or medium run. There has been no experience among developing countries where the tax ratio has been raised by 10 or even 20 percentage points of GDP in a matter of one or two decades, or by several percentage points in a few years as has happened in industrial countries. In those developing countries where increases in the ratio of taxes to GDP have taken place, these increases have been relatively small. Moreover, in some of these countries, and particularly in those with high and increasing public debt, that ratio has fallen over time.

As in industrial countries, developing countries can try to tap domestic savings through the sale of bonds in the domestic market. This possibility, however, is very limited and only few developing countries have managed to finance a large proportion of their expenditure through increases in domestic debt.[2] In no case have developing countries been as successful on this score as industrial countries. The reasons for this outcome are (1) the small size of the domestic capital market and the limited role of financial intermediaries; (2) the high default and political risk perceived by potential bond buyers;[3] (3) the interest rates policies often pursued by these countries which have constrained the free market determination of the rates, sometimes resulting in negative real rates of return and, therefore, in lack of attractiveness for domestic financial investments; (4) the desire to limit the crowding out of the private sector from an already small financial market; and (5) the maintenance of overvalued exchange rates which create incentives for holding foreign currency denominated assets. In several cases where deficits have been financed with domestic debt, this has been done through some form of forced lending, which inevitably includes an element of taxation. Similarly, in many cases part of the fiscal deficit has been financed through the building up of domestic arrears. But although these arrears normally amount to an increase in government liabilities, they are excluded from the statistics of public debt. In any case, domestic arrears, although important in a particular year, cannot be accumulated to more than a few percentage points of GDP over time.

All the above sources of financing public expenditure are not directly inflationary, although this conclusion would need to be qualified in several ways. For example, tax increases may affect costs and prices and, if indexation mechanisms are in place, they may also affect the rate of inflation over time if accommodated by the monetary authorities. Arrears will tend to affect the prices at which suppliers make goods available. Domestic bonds may influence the rate of inflation if they become highly liquid and thus lead to a reduction in the demand for money.

Besides the above (and presumably non-inflationary) sources, public spending can be financed through monetary expansion, which will tend to have an inflationary impact.[4] Inflationary finance can provide the government with financial resources allowing it to purchase a certain quantity of goods and services, and it would seem to free it from the constraints imposed on spending by the inability to raise taxes or to sell bonds. However, there is a limit to the total amount of resources (expressed as a share of GDP) that the government can acquire through the inflation tax. If the government pushes the rate of inflation beyond it, it will actually end up with less real resources. This is well known (see Cagan, 1956). Less well known, however, is that the maximum amount of resources that can be acquired through inflationary finance is no indication of the *net* additional public spending that can be financed through this source (see Tanzi, 1978). The reason is that higher reliance on inflationary finance will normally reduce other revenue sources. This is very important for taxes but is also important for bond financing. Regarding taxes and recognising that (1) there are always collection lags, (2) that some taxes are levied with specific rates, and (3) that progressive income taxes represent only a small share of total tax revenue in developing countries (so that there is no significant fiscal drag), there is often a loss in real tax revenues associated with the acceleration of inflation[5] (see Tanzi, 1977). In addition, acceleration in the rate of inflation tends to increase the risk of holding financial assets (particularly if they are not fully indexed) and to lower the real demand for bonds.[6]

The above discussion has highlighted the motivations for debt financing and the particular importance that foreign sources acquire in developing countries, an importance that they do not often have in industrial countries given the availability of other sources. What have been the immediate consequences of external financing? Foreign financing can come in a variety of ways, including: (1) grants; (2) concessionary loans; (3) project loans; (4) suppliers' credit; and (5) commercial borrowing (see Tanzi, 1985, for more details). Grants and concessionary loans are very attractive but not costless. In both of these cases the costs are often political. Project loans and suppliers' credit may have concessionary elements but may also have hidden costs that make them less desirable than one would assume from the explicit cost. For example, they may force the countries to make purchases in markets where supplies are not cheaper or of desirable quality and they may tempt the countries to change the structure of their investment budgets because of the availability of financing for specific and often less profitable projects.

The most important source of foreign financing of public spending in recent years has been commercial borrowing. This borrowing has been done with varying maturities and with variable or fixed rates. Commercial borrowing played a major role in allowing developing countries to maintain levels of public spending higher than would have been possible through domestic sources. Thus, it probably contributed to the growth of the public sector in developing countries. The growth of commercial borrowing up to 1981 was phenomenal as will be shown in the empirical Section 5 of this chapter. Both supply and demand factors played a role in determining this growth.

In the 1970s the growth of debt financing from commercial banks was constrained mainly by demand considerations. OPEC surpluses made commercial banks very liquid, forcing them to compete among themselves to extend credit to the developing countries. In this period, it was not unusual for a finance minister of a developing country to be approached by the representatives of several foreign commercial banks and to be offered loans at terms that looked very attractive. This was a tremendous temptation as it made the financing of higher public spending seem almost costless. Mexico, Brazil, Venezuela and many other countries could get practically all the foreign credit that they wanted at very low real rates of interest. Public spending and foreign debt grew mainly in line with the demand for that credit by these countries. Foreign borrowing served the double purpose of financing the budgetary gap and the current account deficit in the balance of payments. There was, thus, a substantial net capital transfer from the industrial to the developing countries.

In the 1980s the situation changed dramatically. OPEC surpluses started to disappear, real interest rates rose, and the servicing costs on the public debt that had accumulated in the earlier period became extremely high, particularly for those countries with high ratios of debt to GDP.[7] In addition, prices of commodities, which represent a major share of developing countries' exports, declined strongly relative to industrial countries' export prices. Doubts about the ability of developing countries to service their debt started to emerge and the perceived risk associated with further exposure for private banks started to increase. The growth of foreign borrowing eventually came to be constrained by the supply of credit. Commercial banks became reluctant to keep increasing their lending to developing countries or even to agree to the automatic rolling over of the maturing debt. This, combined with the sharply higher real rate of interest, which also reflect increasing risk, reversed the direction of net capital flows. During this period developing countries have been faced with the need to generate substantial trade account surpluses to service their foreign obligations.

3 PUBLIC DEBT AND FISCAL POLICY CONSTRAINTS

Let us now turn our attention to the constraints that the presence of large public debt imposes on fiscal policy. We shall concentrate on fiscal policy but there are obvious constraints on other policies as well. In a detailed discussion of this issue, it would be desirable to discuss the policy constraints arising from four distinct situations: (1) all public debt is held domestically; (2) all public debt is held outside the country; (3) capital flight is an important concern; and (4) the citizens of the country already hold large assets in foreign countries which they could be encouraged to repatriate. Space limitations allow only a general discussion of these alternatives.

The first obvious fiscal policy constraint associated with the existence of a large public debt is a direct consequence of the need to service that debt. The government has to make payments that include interest and amortisation. For an unchanged level of government revenue and non-interest expenditure, the rise in interest payments associated with a rise in the public debt will increase the size of the fiscal deficit. This immediately raises an issue that has attracted some attention in recent writings: the need to make a distinction between nominal and real interest payments or, looking at it from a different angle, the need to distinguish a conventionally measured deficit from an inflation adjusted deficit. The higher the expected rate of inflation (and, therefore, the higher the nominal interest rate), and the higher the ratio of debt to GDP, the greater the spread between the conventional measure of the deficit and the inflation adjusted measure will tend to be.[8]

This is not the place to discuss the pros and cons of these two approaches to the measurement of the fiscal deficit. Writers have sharply separated themselves into those who would make no adjustment to the conventionally measured deficit and those who believe that only an inflation adjusted deficit provides a meaningful measure of the fiscal correction that a country needs.[9] In any case, the increase in nominal interest payments will tend to increase the financial resources needed to cover the fiscal gap, and when further borrowing is no longer a viable possibility it will force the country to either reduce non-interest public spending or to increase taxes. This is a major constraint that a large debt imposes on fiscal policy, a constraint that may have important implications for the potential growth of the economy.[10]

One problem observed in many countries that have been forced to reduce public expenditure is that the reduction in non-interest spending often does not follow efficiency considerations but rather political expediency. Thus, countries that have had to adjust their non-interest public spending have (1) reduced wages rather than public employment; (2) reduced capital rather than current expenditure; (3) reduced domestically financed investment while maintaining investment projects financed by foreign sources, even though these may have lower productivity; and (4) reduced maintenance costs rather than entitlements. The net result has been a structure of public spending less conducive to growth.

Countries have also attempted to accommodate the increased spending associated with higher interest payments by raising taxes but generally they have not been very successful. In any case, concern about capital flight has reduced the possibilities to increase taxes on income and wealth. Thus, countries have increased import duties, export taxes, indirect taxes, and especially excises and fuel taxes. Although the increase in indirect taxes is not necessarily damaging to the economy, the increase in foreign trade taxes often increases distortions and thus reduces the growth potential of the country.

The existence of large debt has also put pressures on governments to reduce the subsidies that central governments often pay to public enterprises. Here again the result has often been an increase in tariffs rather than a cut in employment or a greater concern with efficiency. As the problems of public enterprises are often due to excessive employment and to poor management, the increase in tariffs validates existing inefficiencies.

While it is considered that only interest payments contribute to the fiscal deficit, all the servicing of foreign debt, including both interest *and* amortisation, contribute to the total government outlay or to what is sometimes referred to as the public sector borrowing requirement. If amortisation payments could be fully refinanced through an equal borrowing obtained at similar conditions, those amortisation payments would not create difficulties for fiscal policy. However, when the financial climate is changing, either because of changes in the risk associated with lending to that particular country or because the international financial climate itself has changed, the cost of borrowing may go up so that borrowing to pay for amortisation or restructuring of the existing debt often increases interest costs. This is particularly true when the country is unable to pay even the interest due and, thus, it goes into arrears *vis-à-vis* interest payments. In this case the arrears are an automatic way of financing the unpaid interest part of the deficit. In the short run, however, these arrears are likely to reduce the availability of foreign financing thus reducing the country's growth potential. In the longer run, arrears are likely to increase the cost of borrowing thus raising deficits and putting even more of a squeeze on non-interest public expenditure.

4 MACROECONOMIC EFFECTS OF PUBLIC DEBT

The existence of a large stock of public debt has consequences not only for the management of fiscal policy but also for other areas of macroeconomic policy. These implications can be analysed better if we consider separately the effects of public debt on the external sector and on the domestic economy through the impact on the effectiveness of monetary policy and on the determination of key prices in the economy.

4.1 External Sector Implications

When most of the public debt is composed of liabilities to foreign countries, we are confronted with the double problem of assessing the impact of the outstanding debt not only on the fiscal budget but also on the balance of payments. A large volume of foreign debt usually requires an eventual trade surplus to generate the foreign exchange necessary to service the debt. This is particularly true when there are difficulties in rolling over the stock; in this case, in addition to interest payments, foreign resources must be generated to repay the principal.

Trade surpluses can be achieved through a number of means, such as (1) restrictions on imports, by imposing high import duties and/or quotas; (2) the implementation of an exchange rate policy conducive to such surpluses; (3) a reduction in the level of economic activity, which will compress the absolute level of imports; and (4) the encouragement of exports through export subsidies and export credits.

These alternatives are not costless for the economy. Although increasing exports may certainly be the preferred adjustment alternative, it may not be feasible in the short term and may involve considerable fiscal costs if it is achieved through subsidies.[11] If the adjustment takes the form of import reductions, the long-term consequences may be serious. Especially when a large proportion of imports constitute intermediate goods, capital goods, or other raw materials important to the production process, restrictions on imports inevitably result in a slowdown of investments and in a lower growth of the economy, thus leading to recession and unemployment. The adjustment that took place following the debt crisis of the early 1980s was predominantly of this

Table 8.1 External performance of the fifteen Baker countries, 1978–84

Year	Balance of trade	Exports	Imports	Interest payments/ exports
		($US millions)		(in per cent)
1978	−9,075.82	71,028.21	80,104.03	9.75
1979	−1,855.32	95,671.14	97,526.46	10.86
1980	4,194.34	124,103.62	119,909.28	12.20
1981	−6,550.43	124,509.28	131,059.71	14.34
1982	2,821.09	111,907.02	109,085.93	17.62
1983	27,578.58	108,053.92	80,475.34	17.32
1984	40,762.72	117,328.45	76,642.60	20.82

Sources: International Monetary Fund, *International Financial Statistics*, various issues; and Data Resources Incorporated, External Debt File.

sort. The external performance of the combined fifteen Baker countries since 1978 is shown in Table 8.1.

In these countries taken together, the balance of trade swung from a deficit of $7 billion in 1981 to a surplus of more than $40 billion in 1984. This resulted, however, from a 42 per cent contraction in imports from 1981 to 1984 coupled with a 5 per cent reduction in exports. The huge surplus of about $70 billion in the three most recent years was, therefore, mainly generated by sharply lower imports without a substantial improvement in export performance.[12] Moreover, the proportion of exports absorbed by interest payments more than doubled during the period. Thus, it is not surprising that the rates of growth in many of these high-debt countries have been relatively slow or even negative in recent years.

In addition to direct price intervention in import and export markets, maintaining substantial trade surpluses requires an exchange rate policy consistent with that objective, i.e. a real devaluation of the currency and continuous adjustments, particularly in the presence of inflation, so the real exchange rate does not deteriorate. But such policy also implies a higher domestic currency value of interest payments on the foreign debt and an additional budgetary burden. In other words, a real devaluation followed by a policy of maintaining purchasing power parity results in an automatic increase of the foreign debt stock in domestic currency, with the consequent increase in the ratio of budgetary outlays to receipts.

Another aspect of this problem arises from the government's need to serve as guarantor of the private sector in foreign capital markets. Following the large exchange rate depreciation needed to generate trade surpluses, the private sector will often no longer be able to service its obligations abroad,[13] so that the public sector will have to step in. Servicing the guaranteed debt imposes additional budgetary pressures, which in many cases result in monetisation and further inflationary effects.

4.2 Monetary Policy Implications

In cases where at least part of the debt is held domestically, the presence of a large public debt imposes a number of constraints on the ability to conduct monetary policy. The ability of the public sector to finance its deficit by borrowing from the domestic private sector is facilitated by its privileged position in the capital market. But the amount of debt that the private sector is willing to hold is constrained by the value of its wealth, alternative investment opportunities, its preference for present or future consumption, and its anticipation of future economic policy. In these circumstances, the ratio between domestic public debt and GNP is stable at best. Thus, in real terms, it may be feasible to expand debt financing only at a rate roughly close to the rate of growth of the economy. But, as argued earlier, the rate of growth is likely to have been reduced due to the fall of imports. The government can induce an increase in the debt:GNP ratio only by offering more attractive terms such as higher interest rates, greater liquidity and shorter maturities.[14]

It should be mentioned, however, that the constraint on monetary policy imposed by the need to maintain high real interest rates arises even when most of the public debt is not domestically held. This is so because in the presence of a large foreign debt, expectations of exchange rate devaluations will tend to create large capital outflows unless attractive rates on domestic savings are offered.[15]

High stocks of debt, domestic or foreign, are therefore generally coexistent with high interest rates. This situation creates political difficulties since high real interest rates must be maintained at a time when real wages must be reduced to facilitate the adjustment and the servicing of the debt. This clearly has social implications, as workers will perceive this policy as inequitable, and will make it difficult for the government to pursue it.

4.3 The Effect on Key Prices

The presence of a large public debt and the adjustments needed to service it result, as discussed above, in a clear impact on a number of key prices in the economy, including real interest rates, real wages, public utility rates, and exchange rates. What is characteristic of this impact is that the prices that emerge during the adjustment process are likely to be very different from their long-term equilibrium values. For example, if the surplus in the trade account needed to service the external debt is generated through a very depreciated exchange rate, this rate is likely to become lower in real terms than the long-term equilibrium real exchange rate that will emerge as the debt problem is resolved, and much lower than the rate that prevailed when the country was importing capital.

This has important implications for the determination of the optimal capital expenditures of the public sector and, in more general terms, for the investment budget of a country. For example, some investments that would be profitable at the long-run equilibrium rate would no longer be profitable at the present rates. This effect has, in fact, created difficulties for the investment budgets of many developing countries. While in the late 1970s investment budgets were swelled given the very low real rate of interest and the overvalued exchange rates which reduced the real cost of imported capital equipment, in the 1980s they have been sharply reduced due to the very high real interest rates and the undervalued exchange rates resulting from the high public debt levels. Investments that easily passed the test of profitability in the earlier period became highly unprofitable in the 1980s.[16] This raises questions about the standards or criteria to be used to determine whether a large number of investment programmes are worth being carried out or not and, for those already initiated, to determine whether they should be continued as originally planned.

5 EMPIRICAL ISSUES ON FOREIGN PUBLIC DEBT OF DEVELOPING COUNTRIES

The purpose of this section is to consider a number of stylised facts regarding the evolution of the external public debt, to analyse the burden that such debt is imposing on their economies, and to present some empirical results that confirm the discussion of the previous sections regarding the relative importance of fiscal deficits on the determination of different measures related to the burden of foreign debt. With the purpose of gaining a longer-term perspective on the subject, some trends and developments on external indebtedness for the fifteen Baker countries during the period 1970-84 are analysed. This is a period that includes important changes in the world economic environment in general as well as in the internal economic performance of the debtor countries.

5.1 Stylised Facts About the Evolution of Foreign Debt

Table 8.2 shows the evolution of total debt outstanding and disbursed for the fifteen Baker countries, distinguishing between private and official creditors.[17] The table shows the evolution of yearly gross disbursements, both from private and official sources.

Table 8.2 Public debt statistics: fifteen developing countries, 1970-84 (in $US millions)

Year	Debt outstanding and disbursed			Yearly disbursements		
	Total	Private creditors	Official creditors	Total	Private creditors	Official creditors
1970	17,420.00	7,947.50	9,472.50	3,910.70	2,308.50	1,602.20
1971	20,018.90	9,460.80	10,558.10	4,175.00	2,594.50	1,580.50
1972	24,444.00	12,317.70	12,126.30	6,498.20	4,423.90	2,074.30
1973	30,375.10	16,683.00	13,692.10	8,193.00	5,811.00	2,382.00
1974	39,900.90	23,247.60	16,653.30	11,719.00	8,285.80	3,433.20
1975	48,217.50	29.072.70	19,144.80	13,229.90	9,437.40	3,792.50
1976	62,190.50	40,930.60	21,259.90	18,314.80	14,970.20	3,344.60
1977	79,549.80	54,828.70	24,721.10	22,233.00	17,776.80	4,456.20
1978	104,603.30	75,348.20	29,255.10	33,473.60	28,906.50	4,567.10
1979	124,639.30	93,102.90	31,536.40	37,996.60	32,981.10	5,015.50
1980	143,226.10	107,651.70	35,574.40	34,777.60	28,032.20	6,745.40
1981	164,667.40	124,769.00	39,908.40	40,984.20	32,871.50	8,112.70
1982	193,270.00	148,778.30	44,491.70	41,759.80	33,015.80	8,744.00
1983	240,759.30	190,296.80	50,462.50	33,763.00	24,750.80	9,012.20
1984	269,134.10	210,918.30	58,215.80	26,583.30	17,086.80	9,496.50

Sources: World Bank, *World Debt Tables* (1986); and DRI, External Debt File.
 The countries included are: Argentina, Bolivia, Brazil, Chile, Colombia, Côte d'Ivoire, Ecuador, Mexico, Morocco, Nigerian, Peru, Philippines, Uruguay, Venezuela and Yugoslavia.

Table 8.3 Debt outstanding and yearly disbursements: fifteen developing countries nominal and real rates of growth, 1971–84 (in percentage change and indices, 1970 = 100)[a]

Year	Debt outstanding				Yearly disbursements/nominal growth		
	Nominal growth		Growth deflated by terms of trade		Total	Official creditors	Private creditors
	Index	In per cent	Index	In per cent			
1971	114.92	14.92	117.58	17.58	6.76	−1.35	12.39
1972	140.32	22.10	141.77	20.57	55.65	31.24	70.51
1973	174.36	24.26	152.64	7.67	26.08	14.83	31.35
1974	229.04	31.36	199.09	30.43	43.04	44.13	42.59
1975	276.76	20.84	314.56	58.00	12.89	10.47	13.90
1976	356.97	28.98	378.79	20.42	38.43	−11.81	58.63
1977	456.61	27.91	418.64	10.52	21.39	33.24	18.75
1978	600.39	31.49	621.35	48.42	50.56	2.49	62.61
1979	715.37	19.15	679.13	9.30	13.51	9.82	14.10
1980	822.03	14.91	711.73	4.80	−8.47	34.49	−15.01
1981	945.17	14.98	897.85	26.15	17.85	20.27	17.26
1982	1,109.25	17.36	1,002.89	11.70	1.89	7.78	0.44
1983	1,381.79	24.57	1,127.45	12.42	−19.15	3.07	−25.03
1984	1,544.71	11.79	1,163.98	3.24	−21.26	5.37	−30.96

Note:
[a] Terms of trade are defined as the index of own export unit values divided by the index of US export unit values. Deflated data are weighted averages for fifteen developing countries, with the weights given by the share of each country's debt in total debt.

Source: Same as Table 8.1; and IMF, *International Finance Statistics*, various issues.

The evolution of foreign indebtedness of the sample countries shows a huge rise, from $17.5 billion to $269.1 billion, in the fifteen-year period. While in 1970 55 per cent of the total debt was owed to official institutions, the percentage had fallen to less than 22 per cent by 1984. As indicated in Table 8.3, the average rate of growth of total debt exceeded 20 per cent yearly during the 1970s, and fell below 17 per cent between 1980 and 1984. When deflated by changes in the terms of trade of the countries involved, the rate of growth of debt outstanding fell from an average of 27 per cent a year between 1971 and 1975 to about 12 per cent between 1980 and 1984.[18] Such a reduction in the rate of growth of total indebtedness was caused mainly by a large contraction in disbursements of new debt after 1982. As also shown in Table 8.3, the rate of growth of new disbursements fell from an average increase of 30 per cent a year in the 1970s to an average contraction of about 7.5 per cent a year in the 1980s. Notice, however, that such a reduction on new disbursements was largely accounted for by a contraction in new lending by private creditors (of about 10 per cent a year), while

Table 8.4 Public debt statistics: interest payments and net flows, fifteen developing countries, 1970–84 ($US millions)

Year	Interest payments			Net capital flows		
	Total	Private creditors	Official creditors	Total	Private creditors	Official creditors
1970	856.40	500.30	356.10	1,179.30	549.70	629.60
1971	941.60	552.10	389.50	1,271.60	730.40	541.20
1972	1,058.70	605.80	452.90	3,125.20	2,207.90	917.30
1973	1,530.00	938.30	591.70	3,379.80	2,512.20	867.60
1974	2,151.40	1,461.10	690.30	5,687.10	3,953.30	1,733.80
1975	2,949.30	2,073.20	876.10	5,807.20	4,069.10	1,738.10
1976	3,495.60	2,446.30	1,049.30	9,625.20	8,697.50	927.70
1977	4,389.80	3,136.60	1,253.20	11,225.00	9,678.00	1,547.00
1978	6,473.60	4,907.70	1,565.90	14,416.70	13,209.90	1,206.80
1979	9,807.00	7,913.70	1,893.30	11,297.50	10,757.10	540.40
1980	13,994.30	11,902.60	2,091.70	5,670.20	3,526.10	2,144.10
1981	16,931.30	14,649.60	2,281.70	8,301.50	5,376.50	2,925.00
1982	20,472.00	17,809.10	2,662.90	5,973.60	3,372.80	2,600.80
1983	19,762.30	16,957.40	2,804.90	1,282.80	−885.40	2,168.20
1984	24,274.30	20,943.00	3,331.30	−9,658.50	−12,351.70	2,693.20

Source: See Table 8.2.

official creditors continued to lend, albeit at a lower rate than before. As a whole public external debt increased by more than 1,400 per cent in nominal terms and more 1,000 per cent in real terms. Another important feature is the continuous increase in the amount of interest payments made by these countries. Table 8.4 shows that interest payments rose from less than $1 billion in 1970 to more than $24 billion in 1984, which implies an effective increase in the rate of interest paid from 5 per cent to more than 9.5 per cent[19] (see Table 8.5).

Table 8.6 summarises the impact of the above developments by showing the burden of public debt and interest payments on the economies of the countries involved. Debt outstanding increased from 10 per cent of GNP in 1970 to more than 36 per cent at the end of 1984, an increase mainly accounted for by the sixfold rise in the ratio to GNP of credit from private sources. The increase in the burden of

Table 8.5 Average interest on new commitments and effective interest rate paid, 1971–84[a]

Year	Interest rate on new commitments			Effective interest rate paid		
	Average	Private creditors	Official creditors	Average	Private creditors	Official creditors
1971	6.64	7.48	5.75	5.03	6.32	3.89
1972	6.59	7.41	5.63	4.74	5.53	3.98
1973	7.64	8.93	6.01	5.63	6.48	4.60
1974	8.70	10.15	6.24	6.15	7.35	4.53
1975	8.28	8.89	6.99	6.73	7.96	4.89
1976	7.80	7.96	7.32	6.36	6.98	5.19
1977	7.98	8.18	7.47	6.19	6.53	5.42
1978	9.19	9.91	6.74	7.01	7.47	5.75
1979	10.97	11.93	7.00	8.54	9.36	6.23
1980	11.86	13.17	7.84	10.44	11.82	6.23
1981	14.14	16.03	8.62	11.02	12.63	6.03
1982	12.88	13.95	9.78	11.42	12.97	6.29
1983	11.20	11.81	9.12	9.09	9.94	5.86
1984	10.76	12.04	9.04	9.52	10.43	6.13

Note:
[a] Effective interest rate is defined as interest payment in year (t) divided by the average of debt outstanding between year (t) and $(t-1)$. All data are weighted averages for fifteen developing countries, with weights given by share of each country's debt in total.
Source: See Table 8.2.

Table 8.6 Ratios of debt outstanding and interest payments to GNP: fifteen developing countries, 1970–84[a] (in percentage terms)

Year	Debt outstanding and disbursed/GNP			Interest payments/GNP		
	Total	Private creditors	Official creditors	Total	Private creditors	Official creditors
1970	10.07	4.59	5.47	0.49	0.29	0.21
1971	10.29	4.86	5.43	0.48	0.28	0.20
1972	11.11	5.60	5.51	0.48	0.28	0.21
1973	11.26	6.19	5.08	0.57	0.35	0.22
1974	11.13	6.49	4.65	0.60	0.41	0.19
1975	11.73	7.07	4.66	0.72	0.50	0.21
1976	13.28	8.74	4.54	0.75	0.52	0.22
1977	15.26	10.52	4.74	0.84	0.60	0.24
1978	17.34	12.49	4.85	1.07	0.81	0.26
1979	17.08	12.76	4.32	1.34	1.08	0.26
1980	16.69	12.55	4.15	1.63	1.39	0.24
1981	17.54	13.29	4.25	1.80	1.56	0.24
1982	22.86	17.60	5.26	2.42	2.11	0.32
1983	33.68	26.62	7.06	2.76	2.37	0.39
1984	36.84	28.87	7.97	3.32	2.87	0.46

Note:
[a] Weighted average of individual country ratios. The weights are given by proportion of each country in total GNP.
Source: See Table 8.2.

interest payments in relation to the total product of these countries is also illustrated in Table 8.6: interest payments increased from less than half a per cent of GNP to 3.3 per cent of GNP by 1984.

A more dramatic illustration of the developments related to foreign debt in the fifteen Baker countries is given by the net capital flows columns of Table 8.4. Net capital flows (i.e. disbursements net of debt service) indicate the availability of foreign savings transferred through the capital account. The combination of higher interest payments and lower disbursements resulted in a negative net transfer of about $10 billion in 1984 (compared with a positive net capital flow of $14.4 billion in 1978). Probably, the fall in net capital flows and the outflow of resources from developing countries are the most drastic examples of the consequences of the debt crisis of 1982. It is, however, important to observe that the negative net capital flows result from a combination of large outflows of resources to service the foreign debt owed to private creditors, while official creditors continue to be net lenders at about the same rate as in the early 1980s.[20]

Additional indications of the magnitude of the burden imposed by foreign public debt are given in Table 8.7, where magnitudes of stocks and flows are compared. While new disbursements amounted to more than 30 per cent of the debt outstanding in the late 1970s (almost 40 per cent private creditors), disbursements were less than 10 per cent compared with the stock of debt in 1984. Again, this reduction in disbursements relative to the outstanding stock is explained exclusively by the reduction in new lending by private creditors. Even more important is the potential use of the yearly gross inflows. As shown in this table, more than 90 per cent of new credit was offset by outflows of interest payments in 1984. It is noticeable that this relationship between interest payments and disbursements stood at below 20 per cent in 1978 and at 25 per cent in 1979, even if the average interest rate was not substantially different. The last two columns of this table indicate that in 1984 there was a clear transfer (even excluding repayments) from official to private creditors, since interest payments

Table 8.7 Disbursements and interest payments ratios: fifteen developing countries, 1970–84 (in percentage terms)

	Disbursements/debt outstanding			Interest payments/disbursements		
	Total	Private creditors	Official creditors	Total	Private creditors	Official creditors
1970	22.45	29.05	16.91	21.90	21.67	22.23
1971	20.86	27.42	14.97	22.55	21.28	24.64
1972	26.58	35.91	17.11	16.29	13.69	21.83
1973	26.97	34.83	17.40	18.67	16.15	24.84
1974	29.37	35.64	20.62	18.36	17.63	20.11
1975	27.44	32.46	19.81	22.29	21.97	23.10
1976	29.45	36.57	15.73	19.09	16.34	31.37
1977	27.95	32.42	18.03	19.74	17.64	28.12
1978	32.00	38.36	15.61	19.34	16.98	34.29
1979	30.49	35.42	15.90	25.81	23.99	37.75
1980	24.28	26.04	18.96	40.24	42.46	31.01
1981	24.89	26.35	20.33	41.31	44.57	28.13
1982	21.61	22.19	19.65	49.02	53.94	30.45
1983	14.02	13.01	17.86	58.53	68.51	31.12
1984	9.88	8.10	16.31	91.31	122.57	35.08

Source: See Table 8.2.

to the latter exceeded their disbursements while interest payments to the former were about one-third of their disbursements.

It is evident from the above discussion that debt service is imposing a serious burden on highly indebted countries. Some casual empiricism shows that the level of the debt and the rates of growth of these economies are highly negatively correlated.[21] In a regression between the rate of growth and the level of foreign debt as a proportion of GNP in the fifteen Baker countries involved and over the period 1972–84, the results are:

$\hat{Y} = 5.64 - 0.254$ (debt/GNP) $R^2 = 0.446$
(4.05) (9.77)   SEE = 4.94

$\hat{Y} = 2.51 - 0.178$ (debt/GNP) $+ 3.48\ DM$ $R^2 = 0.483$
(1.56) (5.39)   (3.58)   SEE = 4.78

where $\hat{Y}$ is the rate of growth of real income, and DM is a dummy variable (1:1972–80; 0:1981–4) that distinguishes between the experiences before and after the sharp adjustments induced by the debt crisis. The observations are a time series, cross-section pool and include fourteen country-specific dummies. The figures in parentheses are t-values.

Given the importance of the debt factor, and in order to complete the picture presented in the previous sections of this chapter, in what follows we elaborate on some of the empirical determinants of the overall evolution of foreign debt and of its relative weight in the national economy. For this purpose, a more formal empirical analysis is carried out in the next section.

5.2 The Sources of Growth of Foreign Debt – Regression Results

The purpose of this section is to investigate some of the main factors that determine the changes in the stock of debt, both at the absolute level and as a percentage of GNP, highlighting the importance of the fiscal deficit, relative to other variables affecting the accumulation of debt. Two types of relationships were estimated pooling the data for the fifteen Baker countries over the period 1972–84. The first specification explains the changes in the level of external debt outstanding and disbursed (ΔDt). In additional to the fiscal deficit as a percentage of GDP (Def_t), whose role has been discussed in the previous sections, three variables related to the external sector are

Table 8.8 Changes in debt outstanding and disbursed, fifteen developing countries, 1972–84

$$\Delta D_t = a_1 + a_2 \operatorname{Def}_t + a_3 i_{t-1} + a_4 BoT_t + a_5 \hat{T}T_t$$

	Constant	Def_t	i_{t-1}	BoT_t	$D(BoT)_t$	$\hat{T}T$	$\hat{E}UV$	R^2/SEE
Total								
1.	−390.5 (0.69)	111.4 (3.75)	149.6 (3.58)	164.1 (3.65)		4.934 (1.20)		0.627 1350.3
2.	−348.3 (0.60)	109.8 (3.62)	147.3 (3.45)	175.4 (3.97)			2.132 (0.65)	0.625 1354.2
3.	−633.5 (1.16)	96.3 (3.22)	197.1 (3.57)	233.4 (4.49)	−219.6 (2.55)	6.73 (1.64)		0.641 1329.6
4.	−637.6 (1.09)	96.3 (3.17)	146.6 (3.49)	243.3 (4.73)	−214.6 (2.47)		3.72 (1.13)	0.638 1334.9
Official sources								
5.	76.96 (0.62)	23.42 (4.24)	25.76 (2.23)	16.33 (1.97)		−1.13 (0.15)		0.473 250.5
6.	79.57 (0.62)	23.25 (4.17)	25.53 (2.17)	16.30 (2.00)			−0.95 (.16)	0.473 250.5
7.	74.03 (0.59)	23.20 (4.11)	25.65 (2.21)	17.30 (1.76)	−2.99 (0.11)	−0.88 (0.11)		0.473 251.2
8.	76.07 (0.59)	23.17 (4.06)	25.48 (2.16)	17.24 (1.78)	−2.94 (0.18)		−0.73 (.12)	0.413 251.2

Private sources

9.	−458.1 (0.79)	85.2 (2.85)	106.5 (2.88)	157.2 (3.53)		4.561 (1.11)	0.575 1351.5
10.	−393.3 (0.67)	82.9 (2.72)	102.9 (2.75)	169.3 (3.88)			1.59 (.49)	0.573 1355.4
11.	−779.9 (1.35)	69.9 (2.30)	108.7 (2.99)	227.7 (4.45)	−277.6 (2.65)	6.52 (1.59)		0.592 1329.0
12.	−736.2 (1.24)	68.7 (2.25)	106.5 (2.89)	238.2 (4.70)	−221.3 (2.55)		0.33 (1.02)	0.588 1334.6

Notes:
The regressions are a time series, cross-section pool
ΔD = change in the outstanding stock of foreign public debt
Def = fiscal deficit as percentage of GDP
i = average interest rate on new commitments
BoT = balance of trade surplus
$E\hat{U}V_i$ = rate of change of export unit values of country i
$\hat{T}T$ = rate of change of terms of trade defined as: $EUV_i - EUV_{US}$
$D(\ )$ = indicates a slope dummy variable (1:1972–80; 0:1981–4).
All equations include fourteen country dummies; t-values are in parentheses; SEE is the standard error of the estimate.

included. The cost of foreign credit, represented by the interest rate faced by the country, may affect the stock of debt in two opposite directions. An increase in interest rates may reduce the demand for new loans, but since most of the outstanding stock is subject to adjustable interest rates it may result in an increase in the stock of debt since countries may be forced to borrow more to service previous commitments. In order to capture the two effects, we include in the equation the average interest rate on new commitments in the previous year (i_{t-1}). Since foreign debt could certainly be contracted to close payments gaps, the balance of trade surplus (BoT) is added to the equation together with variations in the international prices faced by the country. This last variable would indicate whether changes in the stock of debt indeed respond to cyclical variations in international markets. It is measured, alternatively, by changes in the terms of trade $(\hat{T}T)$ or by changes in the export unit values $(E\hat{U}V)$. The estimated equation is therefore:

$$\Delta D_t = a_1 + a_2 Def_t + a_3 i_{t-1} + a_4 BoT_t + a_5 \hat{T}T_t$$

This equation was estimated for changes in the total stock of debt and separately for changes in debt originating from official and private sources. The general pattern of results, reported in Table 8.8, clearly confirm the importance of fiscal deficits in the determination of foreign debt. The coefficients of Def are highly significant in all the estimated equations, as are those of the interest rate faced by the country which turn out to have positive signs. Changes in the external prices of imports and exports, on the other hand, do not seem to have affected the changes in the absolute level of debt.

Regarding the balance of trade results, equations (8.1)–(8.2), (8.5)–(8.6), and (8.9)–(8.10) seem to indicate a positive relationship between the changes in the level of debt and the outcome of the balance of trade. This result, however, is not stable for the whole period under study. When a slope dummy variable with a value of 1 during the period 1972–80 and zero during 1981–4 is included multiplicatively with the balance of trade variable, the coefficient is significant and has an opposite sign with a magnitude similar to the balance of trade coefficient. This result suggests that during the 1970s external imbalances did not lead to changes in external debt, but in the 1980s increases in external debt were correlated with balance of trade surpluses, both of which moved positively during that later period. This last result, however, applies mainly to private sources.

Since the units of measurement differ somewhat for the different variables included in Table 8.8, in order to determine the relative influence of the various explanatory variables we calculate the beta coefficients that measure the change in the dependent variable, other things being equal, for a unit change in each of the independent variables. The beta coefficients are independent of units of measurement and can be compared directly within and across equations. The calculated beta coefficients corresponding to the twelve equations in Table 8.8 are presented in Table 8.9. The main results are the following: for changes in total outstanding foreign debt, the fiscal deficit shows up as having the strongest effect relative to the other variables. Such an effect is particularly marked in the equations explaining borrowing from official sources (equations (8.5)–(8.8)). In these equations the interest rate and balance of trade variables have an effect only half as big as the fiscal deficit.

The second specification estimated relates changes in the ratio of debt outstanding to GNP. The estimated equation for this specification is the following:

$$\Delta(D/GNP)_t = b_1 + b_2 \text{Def}_t + b_i i_{t-1} + b_4(BoT/GNP) + b_t \hat{T}T$$

Table 8.9 Values of beta coefficients–equations for the change in the debt outstanding

Equation number	Def	i	BoT	D(BoT)	$\hat{T}T$	$E\hat{U}V$
Total debt						
(1)	0.246	0.189	0.220	—	0.065	—
(2)	0.242	0.185	0.236	—	—	0.035
(3)	0.213	0.186	0.314	−0.192	0.088	—
(4)	0.213	0.185	0.327	−0.188	—	0.061
Official sources						
(5)	0.332	0.149	0.140	—	−0.009	—
(6)	0.331	0.147	0.140	—	—	−0.010
(7)	0.329	0.148	0.149	−0.017	−0.007	—
(8)	0.328	0.147	0.148	−0.017	—	−0.008
Private sources						
(9)	0.201	0.151	0.225	—	0.064	—
(10)	0.195	0.146	0.243	—	—	0.028
(11)	0.163	0.154	0.326	−0.213	0.091	—
(12)	0.162	0.151	0.342	−0.207	—	0.058

Table 8.10 Changes in the ratio of debt outstanding and disbursed to GNP, fifteen developing countries, 1972–84

$$\Delta(D/\text{GNP})_t = b_1 + b_2 \text{Def}_t + b_d{}^3 i_{t-1} + b_4 (BoT/\text{GNP}) + b_5 \hat{T}T$$

	Constant	Def_t	i_{t-1}	BoT/GNP	$D(BoT)/GNP$	$\hat{T}T$	$E\hat{U}V$	R_2/SEE
Total								
13.	−4.14 (1.74)	0.390 (3.03)	0.688 (3.96)	0.189 (1.70)		−0.027 (1.14)		0.208 5.815
14.	−2.97 (1.22)	0.353 (2.74)	0.627 (3.58)	0.233 (2.17)			−0.356 (2.33)	0.223 5.759
15.	−3.95 (1.70)	0.327 (2.57)	0.589 (3.41)	0.433 (3.22)	−0.424 (3.06)	0.021 (1.11)		0.248 5.681
16.	−3.00 (1.26)	0.301 (2.36)	0.546 (3.14)	0.455 (3.48)	−0.399 (2.87)		−0.287 (1.90)	0.258 5.644
Official sources								
17.	−3.89 (2.82)	0.167 (2.69)	0.541 (4.26)	0.048 (0.88)		−0.013 (1.49)		0.282 2.802
18.	−3.44 (2.38)	0.157 (2.50)	0.509 (3.88)	0.054 (1.01)			−0.013 (1.78)	0.286 2.794
19.	−3.77 (2.70)	0.158 (2.53)	0.513 (3.93)	0.084 (1.23)	−0.060 (0.87)	−0.013 (1.39)		0.285 2.804
20.	−3.35 (2.31)	0.150 (2.37)	0.483 (3.63)	0.085 (1.28)	−0.054 (0.78)		−0.012 (1.64)	0.286 2.798

Private sources							
21.	−2.27 (1.21)	0.205 (2.06)	0.337 (2.83)	0.122 (1.44)		−0.014 (0.94)	0.131 4.47
22.	−1.50 (0.78)	0.130 (1.80)	0.306 (2.57)	0.158 (1.91)			−0.022 (1.87)	0.144 4.44
23.	−2.36 (1.30)	0.150 (1.54)	(0.291) (2.50)	0.326 (3.20)	−0.358 (−3.42)	−0.008 (0.57)		0.186 4.34
24.	−1.79 (0.96)	0.135 (1.38)	0.271 (2.32)	0.344 (3.47)	−0.340 (3.23)		−0.015 (1.32)	0.193 4.32

Notes: See Table 8.8.

The results for this specification are reported in Table 8.10. Again, the estimated coefficients for the fiscal deficit (as a percentage of GDP) and for interest rates turn out to be highly significant while the balance of trade variable shows a similar pattern as in the previous table, i.e. no significant effect over the 1970s and co-movements in the last four years. An important difference is the negative sign of the coefficient for changes in the export unit value. This seems to indicate that, *ceteris paribus*, a fall in the export prices faced by a country tends to increase the ratio of debt to GNP, probably through a combination of increased debt and a reduction in economic activity.

Regarding the beta coefficients for equations (8.13)–(8.24) (Table 8.11), they indicate that as far as the ratio of total debt to GNP is concerned, fiscal deficits and interest rates have roughly equivalent effects, but the impact of interest rates seems to be a more important determinant in explaining the changes in the ratio of official credit to GNP.

To summarise, fiscal deficits and interest rates seem to be the most important variables determining changes in the stock of foreign debt. Concerning the changes in the absolute level, the effect of fiscal deficits emerges as the more important factor, particularly in determining borrowing from official sources. The balance of trade did not affect

Table 8.11 Values of beta coefficients–equations for the changes in the ratio of debt to GNP

Equation number	Def	i	BoT/GNP	$D(BoT)/GNP$	$\hat{T}T$	$E\hat{U}V$
Total debt						
(13)	0.292	0.294	0.204	—	−0.122	—
(14)	0.264	0.268	0.251	—	—	−0.199
(15)	0.245	0.252	0.466	−0.375	−0.095	—
(16)	0.225	0.233	0.490	−0.352	—	−0.160
Official sources						
(17)	0.247	0.326	0.101	—	−0.121	—
(18)	0.232	0.305	0.115	—	—	−0.146
(19)	0.235	0.310	0.178	−0.105	−0.114	—
(20)	0.222	0.292	0.182	−0.095	—	−0.137
Private sources						
(21)	0.208	0.207	0.179	—	0.085	—
(22)	0.184	0.189	0.231	—	—	0.166
(23)	0.153	0.179	0.478	−0.431	0.051	—
(24)	0.138	0.167	0.505	−0.409	—	0.116

external exposure during the 1970s and is positively correlated with the changes in debt in the 1980s. The overwhelming importance of fiscal management in the evolution of foreign debt is therefore strongly confirmed by these sets of results.

5.3 The Interest Rate on Public Debt

Given the importance of the rate of interest faced by the borrowing countries in the determination of changes in total indebtedness, it seems important to try to determine some of the main factors affecting this rate. As is well known, the charges paid by the countries on their external debt are usually determined by the LIBOR rate plus a spread, which reflects the countries' specific risk premia. Of course, official and concessional credits do not carry a free market-determined rate but its variations may well be subject to influences similar to forces as those determining free market rates. Without attempting to provide an exhaustive explanation of the determinants of LIBOR spreads for the countries considered, we estimate a number of equations in this section that assess the role played by different variables in affecting the cost of external debt.

Given that the interest rate on official debt usually reflects concessional objectives, it is expected that some of the factors affecting it are substantially different from those influencing the private, or commercial, rate. For this reason, we estimate here separately an equation for the average interest rates charged by private creditors and by official creditors. The variables that are considered to affect the evolution of interest charges are the following: the fiscal deficit as a proportion of GDP; the changes in terms of trade; the rate of growth of the economy; the stock of debt from private (official) sources as a proportion of GNP or, alternatively, the total stock of debt as a proportion of GNP; and the ratio of private (official) sources of debt total debt.

The results of the estimations are reported in Table 8.12. The following pattern of results emerges from these estimations.

Regarding the interest rate charged by private creditors, the stock of debt from private sources, both as a proportion of GNP and as a proportion of total debt, has a significant positive effect on the rate. The ratio of total debt to GNP, however, does not significantly affect it. This result seems to indicate that risk premia increase as the proportion of concessional credit falls or, in other words, that private creditors are more concerned with the stock of debt that has to be

Table 8.12 Determinants of average interest rates on new commitments – fifteen developing countries, 1972–84

Private Creditors

(25) $i_p = 3.74^{**} - 0.024\,\text{Def} + 0.039^{**}(D_p/\text{GNP}) + 0.022^{**}(D_p/D)$
    (7.30)   (0.82)   (2.89)   (2.32)

   $- 0.0076^{**}\hat{T}T + 0.004\hat{Y} + 0.637^{**}\text{LIBOR}$ $R^2 = 0.782$
   (2.02)   (00.20)   (18.55)   SEE = 1.336

(26) $i_p = 3.53^{**} - 0.025\,\text{Def} + 0.012(D/\text{GNP}) + 0.033^{**}(D_p/D) - 0.0069^{*}\hat{T}T$
    (6.74)   (0.83)   (1.31)   (3.63)   (1.81)

   $+ 0.007\hat{Y} + 0.636^{**}\text{LIBOR}$ $R^2 = 0.733$
   (0.35)   (18.14)   SEE = 1.361

Official Creditors

(27) $i_o = 9.23^{**} + 0.066^{**}\,\text{Def} + 0.011(D_o/\text{GNP}) - 0.027^{**}(D_o/D) - 0.003\hat{T}T$
    (9.01)   (2.05)   (0.59)   (2.66)   (0.79)

   $- 0.075^{**}\hat{Y} + 0.112^{**}\text{LIBOR}$ $R^2 = 0.511$
   (3.51)   (3.03)   SEE = 1.423

(28) $i_o = 8.69^{**} + 0.578^{*}\,\text{Def} + 0.025^{**}(D/\text{GNP}) - 0.022^{**}(D_o/D) - 0.004\hat{T}T$
    (8.60)   (1.84)   (2.63)   (2.33)   (1.02)

   $- 0.052^{**}\hat{Y} + 0.106^{**}\text{LIBOR}$ $R^2 = 0.529$
   (2.39)   (2.96)   SEE = 1.397

Notes: See Table 8.8.
Additional notation is as follows:
i_p = average interest rate on new commitments from private creditors
i_o = average interest rate on new commitments from official creditors
D = total debt outstanding
D_p = debt outstanding from private sources
D_o = debt outstanding from official sources
$\hat{Y}$ = rate of growth of real income.

LIBOR: London Interbank Overnight Rate. Dollar denominations, six months.
** Significant at the 5 per cent level.
* Significant at the 10 per cent level.

serviced on commercial terms than with the volume of indebtedness.

2. An improvement in the terms of trade tends to have a negative impact on commercial interest rates. This may be caused by a reduction in the perceived risk, given the improvement in the ability of the countries to service their debts. On the other hand, the rate of growth of the economy does not, nor does the fiscal deficit, exert any influence on interest charges from private sources.

3. Regarding the interest charges on official credit, a somewhat different pattern of results emerges. In the first place, the effect of the fiscal deficit is highly significant while that of the terms of trade is not. It is therefore possible that official creditors do attach a much higher risk premium to fiscal imbalances than to external price developments. Thus, as far as official credit is concerned, the fiscal deficit may have an additional impact on the economy. By increasing the interest charges on new commitments, the fiscal deficit tends to increase further the burden of external debt on the economy.[22]

4. While the stock of official credit relative to GNP does not have a significant effect, the total stock of debt does have a positive effect on interest rates on official credit. The proportion of concessional debt to total debt is also a significant variable: the higher the proportion, the lower the interest charges. Clearly, official institutions appear to attach some degree of risk to the magnitude of commercial debt held by the countries involved. This result, however, carries the undesirable implication that countries with a larger exposure to commercial credit may also end up paying higher charges on their official loans.[23]

5. An interesting result of equations (8.27) and (8.28) in Table 8.12 is the highly significant negative coefficient of the rate of income growth. Although there may be a problem of bi-directional causality, the results point out that a better growth performance is negatively correlated with the interest charges on official credit.

6. Although the coefficients of LIBOR are always highly significant, they are also significantly different from unity in all the equations. This indicates that, everything being equal, an increase in LIBOR tends to reduce the spread. As expected, however, the coefficients for private credit are more than six times higher than for official credit.

6 CONCLUDING REMARKS

This paper has attempted to survey the public debt situation of a group of developing countries referred to as the fifteen Baker countries. It has shown that in recent years there has been, first, a sharp increase in foreign borrowing, accompanied by an equally sharp accumulation of foreign debt, followed by a sharp deceleration in net foreign borrowing as foreign credit became very expensive and much less readily available. The switch has reversed the net flow of resources, forcing the developing countries to run very large trade surpluses. This situation has necessitated drastic changes in economic policy. Some of these changes have inevitably had a significant impact on the performance of these economies. In recent years there has been an ongoing debate over whether the imbalances of the developing countries should be financed or whether these countries would have to adjust. We are now well beyond that debate: the countries have been adjusting, and on a large scale. In fact, some would say on too large a scale. It is hoped that more financing will be once again available to those countries willing to pursue policies consistent with growth.

Notes

The views presented in this chapter are strictly personal and do not necessarily reflect official Fund positions. The authors are grateful to L. Leiderman, A. Mohammed, M. Xafa, and the participants of the Conference for useful comments, and to Z. Farhadian for her valuable assistance.

1. The fifteen Baker countries are: Argentina, Bolivia, Brazil, Chile, Colombia, Côte d'Ivoire, Ecuador, Medico, Morocco, Nigeria, Peru, Philippines, Uruguay, Venezuela and Yugoslavia.
2. In some of these cases, the government has 'borrowed' the reserve requirements that commercial banks are required to keep with the Central Bank. Thus, the government has paid interest to the central bank and the latter has paid interest to the commercial banks (see Tanzi, 1985). The same applies to some type of 'trustee' securities that insurance companies and pension funds are required to hold as a percentage of their total portfolio.
3. This type of risk perception arises particularly when the growth of public financial debt exceeds that of government revenues since this may be seen as an indication that adjustments and reform programmes may be implemented, including capital levies on bond holders or higher income taxes on interest incomes.
4. This impact is reduced by the real rate of growth of the economy (see Friedman, 1971).
5. This implies that countries that bring about a programme of price stabilisation, such as the Plan Austral in Argentina and the stabilisation plan in Israel (both initiated in 1985), and the 1986 Cruzado Plan in Brazil, will experience an automatic increase in the share of tax revenue in GDP. Furthermore, their fiscal deficit as conventionally measured will decline even more because the reduction in the rate of inflation will reduce nominal interest rates and thus interest payments.
6. It will also tend to increase the demand for dollar bills. This phenomenon, generally referred to as dollarisation of the economy, has acquired great importance in Argentina, Brazil, Mexico, and other developing countries. Dollarisation reduces even more the net gains, in terms of revenue, from inflationary finance.
7. Debt service payments as a percentage of exports of goods and services increased from 12.7 per cent in 1973–4 to 23 per cent in 1983–5. For

the fifteen Baker countries, this ratio increased from 18.2 per cent in 1973–74 to 42.6 per cent in 1983–5 (see International Monetary Fund, *World Economic Outlook*, 1986).

8. Since for developing countries the domestic rate of inflation is often much greater than the rest-of-the-world rate, this problem is particularly related to domestic debt. For a country with mostly foreign debt, the two measures of deficit tend to be much closer together.
9. Generally, academicians have favoured the inflation adjusted deficit while most practitioners have favoured the conventional measure.
10. Additional distorting effects which bear on potential growth may arise when a growing debt is perceived as a harbinger of future tax increases.
11. Export subsidies often violate international trade agreements and generate resentment and retaliation. A high rate of growth in industrial countries, of course, helps the growth of exports by developing countries. For this reason the solution to the debt crisis will be facilitated by a good economic performance by the industrial countries. Estimates made by the IMF staff suggest that a 1 per cent change in industrial countries' real GNP is associated, on average, with about a 3.5 per cent change in the same direction for export earnings of developing countries.
12. Imports fell by $54.5 billion between 1981 and 1984. For a discussion of these trends in the Latin American context, see ECLA (1985).
13. Even if it were able, the private sector might not gain access to the foreign exchange required.
14. This effect arises not only from portfolio pressures and competition for loanable funds but also from the effects of expectation regarding future monetisation created by continuous debt-financed deficits which generally add a real risk premium to interest rates. Furthermore, if the individuals are rational they will expect the government to raise taxes in the future as the ratio of debt to GDP rises. Thus, they may not invest in assets that are more exposed to possible taxation.
15. Or unless the domestic debt is denominated in foreign currency, which makes it quite similar to foreign debt.
16. It should also be mentioned that the ordering of projects may also be drastically altered according to the different capital, labour, and imported inputs and intensities of the different projects.
17. The table presents data on long-term, public and publicly guaranteed external debt with an original maturity of over one year. Publicly guaranteed debt is an external obligation guaranteed for repayment by a public entity. The data reported represent only the debt outstanding disbursed, i.e. total outstanding debt drawn by borrowers at year-end. Disbursements are the drawings on outstanding loan commitments during the year. Debt from official creditors comprises loans from international organisation and from governments and their agencies. Private creditors are suppliers, financial markets and other unclassified private creditors.
18. Although nominal debt has been frequently deflated using some measure of international inflation or, alternatively, changes in export unit prices of the debtor countries, deflating the changes in the nominal volume of foreign debt by changes in the terms of trade is, probably, the most

appropriate measure of the changes in the real value of the outstanding liabilities of the country. This is so because external inflation that does not change relative prices between imports and exports does not change the burden of the debt in terms of purchasing power or of the ability of a country to pay. On the other hand, an improvement in the terms of trade reduces the real value of the debt even in the absence of international inflation.

19. The effective interest rate is defined as total interest payments in year t, divided by the average amount of outstanding debt in years t and $t-1$. This increase in the effective interest rate paid should be, however, qualified since it may be partly biased by the nominal appreciation of the dollar over the period. This is so because the stock of debt denominated in other currencies is converted into dollars at the exchange rate prevailing at the contracting dates while interest payments are converted at the rate at the time of payment. In this case, the stock outstanding is understated and the interest ratio overstated.

20. This observation, although applicable to the sample as a whole, does not necessarily hold for individual countries.

21. However, the large borrowing that took place in earlier years had contributed to higher rates of growth in some countries. This is particularly true in those countries where borrowing had gone toward productive channels, increasing the size and efficiency of the economy and facilitating the servicing of the debt.

22. This would also be due to the fact that a high fiscal deficit is likely to lead to debt-servicing problems and rescheduling; given that moratorium interest is usually higher than interest on spontaneous lending, this would raise the sensitivity of the interest rate of fiscal deficits.

23. It should be noted, however, that countries that have better access to private markets also have less justification for concessional funds.

References

Cagan, Phillip (1956) 'The Monetary Dynamics of Hyperinflation', in Friedman, M. (ed.), *Studies in the Quantity Theory of Money* (Chicago: University of Chicago Press), pp. 25–117.
Economic Commission for Latin American (ECLA) 1985 *Preliminary Overview of the Latin American Economy* (Santiago, Chile) December.
Friedman, Milton (1971) 'Government Revenue from Inflation', *Journal of Political Economy*, vol. 79, no. 4, pp. 846–56.
International Monetary Fund (1986) *World Economic Outlook*, April (Washington, DC).
Mendelsohn, Stefan and Group of Thirty (1983) *Commercial Banks and the Restructuring of Cross-Border Debt* (New York: Group of Thirty).
Tanzi, Vito (1977) 'Inflation, Lags in Collection, and the Real Value of Tax Revenue', *Staff Papers*, International Monetary Fund (Washington, DC), vol. 24, no. 1, pp. 154–67.
Tanzi, Vito (1978) 'Inflation, Real Tax Revenue, and the Case for Inflationary Finance: Theory with an Application to Argentina', *Staff Papers*, International Monetary Fund (Washington, DC), vol. 25, no. 3, pp. 417–51.

Tanzi, Vito (1985) 'Fiscal Management and External Debt Problems', in Mehran, H. (ed.), *External Debt Management* (Washington, DC: International Monetary Fund), pp. 65–87.

Tanzi, Vito and Mario, I. Blejer (1982) 'Inflation, Interest Rate Policy, and Currency Substitution in Developing Economies: A Discussion of Some Major Issues', *World Development*, vol. 10, no. 9, pp. 781–9.

9 Benefits and Burdens of Indexed Debt: Some Lessons from Israel's Experience

Ephraim Kleiman*
THE HEBREW UNIVERSITY OF JERUSALEM AND THE
MAURICE FALK INSTITUTE FOR ECONOMIC RESEARCH
IN ISRAEL

1 INTRODUCTION

Despite the considerable growth of professional interest in indexation in the last decade, and the rich theoretical literature on the subject, we still seem to lack an applicable model, which would allow us to estimate the effects of indexation as actually practiced. In particular, we would wish to compare the results with those of a counterfactual world where, under the same circumstances, indexation has not been introduced. In the absence of such a model (and given the limitations of the present author), what follows here is a rather impressionistic, stylised facts description of public debt indexation as it has been practiced in Israel.

The introduction of debt indexation is analysed in Sections 2 through 5 in terms of the distinction between the expected, *ex ante*, real rate of interest and the *ex post* realised one. This emphasises the uncertainty reducing aspects of indexation, the effects of which on the Israeli economy are surveyed in Sections 6 through 8. Finally, Section 9 takes a summarising look on the effects of indexation on public finance in the traditional, narrow, sense of the term.

A word of caution: many of the developments discussed here result from specific attributes to Israeli society, and of its economic and political structure, no less than they result from indexation.

2 EXPECTED VERSUS REALISED REAL RATES OF INTEREST

In a world of nominal credit contracts, inflation, or more precisely inflationary uncertainty, introduces a wedge between the real interest expected *ex ante*, $\bar{r}$, and that realised *ex post*, r^*. In the absence of money illusion, nominal rates quoted by either lenders or borrowers may be expected to represent some underlying real interest rate, and the corresponding agent's expectations regarding the future rate of inflation. For the present purpose it may be convenient to think in terms of the future purchasing power of money, expressed as an index to its present base, $q = 1/(1+x)$, where x is the future rate of price inflation. The nominal interest rate, i, which, given some $\bar{q} = E(q)$, satisfies the expected real one, $\bar{r}$, can then be expressed as:

$$i(\bar{r}, \bar{q}) = [(1+\bar{r})/\bar{q}] - 1 \tag{9.1}$$

while the realised, *ex post* real rate of interest is, of course

$$r^*(i, q) = (1+i)q^* - 1 \tag{9.2}$$

where q^* is the actually realised purchasing power of money. With the rate of change in the price level known with certainty, $q^* = \bar{q}$, and for any value of i at which a credit contract was negotiated, $r^* = \bar{r}$.

Generally speaking, future changes in the purchasing power of money are not known with certainty. Probably the only exceptions are those changes which result from the lopping off of redundant decimal points on the currency, for example with the introduction of the Franc Nouveau in France or, quite recently, of the New Sheqel in Israel. On other occasions, however, economic agents envisage not point estimates, but some probability distributions of the future inflation or deflation rate, x. In the present context, these distributions provide the probabilities for the realised, *ex post*, purchasing power of money, $q^* = 1/(1+x^*)$, differing from its *ex ante* expected value, represented by the appropriately weighted mean of the corresponding distribution, $\bar{q} = E(q)$.[1] The uncertainty represented by these probabilities carries over also to the real interest rate. Under our assumption of no money illusion, any nominal rate quoted by an economic agent will always be adjusted for the expected changes in the value of money so that, other things being equal, the corresponding *ex ante* expected real rate of interest, $\bar{r}$, will be independent of the value of $\bar{q}$. But each such *ex ante* rate will now have associated with it a probability distribution of the actually realised one, r^*, differing from its expected value $\bar{r}$ as a result of q^* differing from $\bar{q}$. For any given nominal interest rate contracted, this difference between the expected and the realised rates amounts

$$\bar{r} - r^* = (1 + \bar{r})\left(1 - \frac{q^*}{\bar{q}}\right) \qquad (9.3)$$

which is distributed with the same probability as that of $q^*/\bar{q}$ deviating from unity.

The effects of interest rate uncertainty on the behaviour of economic agents differ with their position in the credit market, besides depending, of course, on their attitude towards risk. For lenders, interest payments constitute an addition to their wealth. The smaller $q^*/\bar{q}$, and the larger, therefore, $\bar{r} - r^*$, the smaller their realised wealth, as compared to that expected at the time the loan was contracted. If lenders are risk averse, the possibility of the realised rate of interest earned by them exceeding the expected one by a certain amount will not compensate them for an equal probability of its falling short of the expected value by the same amount. From the lender's point of view, therefore, for all symmetric and left-skewed distributions of $q^*/\bar{q}$, the certainty equivalent of the probability distribution of r^* will fall short of its expected value, $\bar{r}$.

The opposite is true of borrowers, for whom interest payments constitute a depletion of their wealth. In their case, the smaller $q^*/\bar{q}$, and the larger, therefore, $\bar{r} - r^*$, the larger (i.e less depleted) their realised wealth, as compared to that expected at the time the loan was contracted. But if borrowers are risk averse, such a possibility will not compensate them for an equal probability of r^* exceeding $\bar{r}$ by the same amount. Because of this reversal, relative to the case of lenders, in the role of interest, the certainty equivalent to the borrowers of the same probability distribution of r^* will exceed its expected value $\bar{r}$. To put it in different words, the risk to the lender is that the value of money may fall by more than he or she expected, so that the realised real rate will fall short of the real rate expected at the time the loan was negotiated; the risk to the borrower, on the other hand, is that the value of money may fall by less than expected, so that the realised real rate will exceed that expected *ex ante*. For their behaviour in the capital markets to remain unaffected will not be by uncertainty regarding r^*, the *ex ante* expected real interest rates demanded by lenders have to rise, and those offered by borrowers have to fall, relative to those demanded and offered under conditions of full certainty.

3 UNCERTAINTY'S EFFECT ON CAPITAL MARKETS

The effect, which uncertainty with respect to the realised rate of interest may have on capital markets, is illustrated in Figure 9.1. There, the volume of credit traded on the market, in real, constant price values, c, is measured along the horizontal axis, while the real rate of interest, at which this credit is contracted, is measured along the vertical one. In a world of nominal contracts, credit can be contracted only at the *ex ante* expected real rate, $\bar{r}$. However, if lenders and borrowers are not risk neutral. the supply and demand for credit can be assumed to be functions not of $\bar{r}$, but of the certainty equivalent of the corresponding probability distribution. It is only in the special case, when the rate

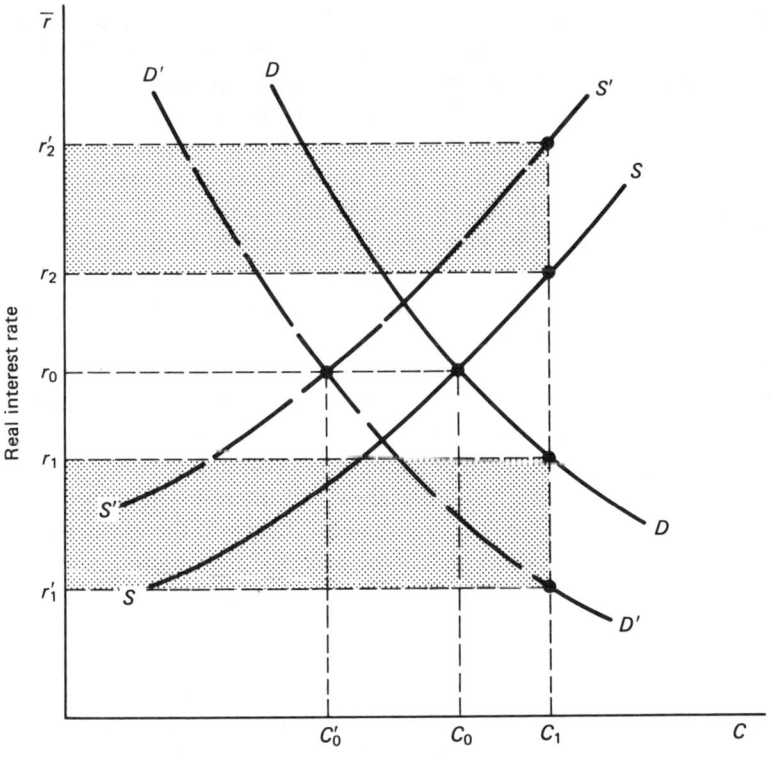

Real volume of credit

Figure 9.1

which will actually be realised, r^*, is known with certainty, that these two rates, the expected one and its certainty equivalent, coincide. In Figure 9.1, the supply and demand curves, SS and DD respectively, are arbitrarily postulated to correspond to this case. In the absence of money illusion, they are presumed to be invariant to future inflation, if its rate is known with certainty.[2]

Suppose, however, that the future purchasing power of money is not known with certainty, and $\bar{q}$, and consequently $\bar{r}$, are only the expected values of probability distributions. As has been pointed out in the previous section, this means that, from the point of view of the lenders, the certainty equivalent corresponding to any given value of $\bar{r}$ will now fall short of the latter. Consequently, the quantities of credit offered at different values of $\bar{r}$ will be reduced correspondingly, and the whole supply curve will shift leftwards, from SS to $S'S'$. To put it in other words, the risk to the lender is that the value of money may fall by more than was expected, so that the realised real interest rate will fall short of that which was expected when the loan was negotiated. Lenders will lend the same sums as before, only if they are compensated for the extra risk involved. The vertical measures of the shift from SS to $S'S'$ represents the risk premium demanded by them, i.e. that increase in the expected real rates of interest which raises the corresponding certainty equivalents to their previously held levels.

Similar considerations also apply to borrowers. In their case, the same uncertainty with respect to r raises its certainty equivalent, to exceed its expected value $\bar{r}$. At the same values of the latter they will now wish to borrow less than under full certainty, and the whole demand curve will also shift leftward, from DD to $D'D'$. In similarity to the case of the supply curve, the vertical, in this case downward, shift of the demand curve represents the wish of the borrower to be compensated for the risk that, with the purchasing power of money falling by less than was expected, the realised real rate of interest will exceed that expected when the loan was negotiated. They will, therefore, fail to borrow as much as before, unless the expected real interest rates are rebated enough to lower the corresponding certainty equivalent to their previously held levels.

We need not, for the present purpose, go into the question whether, as implied by the way these shifts are depicted in Figure 9.1, the risk premia demanded are independent of the level of the expected rate, or are of the same absolute size for lenders and borrowers. The answers to these questions obviously depend on the form risk aversion is postulated to assume, and on its relative strength in these two groups.

But they do not affect the direction of the shifts. (Though whether the equilibrium rate of interest will rise or fall, as a result of uncertainty, can be seen to depend on whether or not lenders are more risk averse than borrowers.) It may also be queried whether, in fact, both the supply and demand for credit are, as is assumed here, functions only of the real interest rate's certainty equivalent. In particular, as has been pointed many years ago by Mundell (1963), the risk of changes in the purchasing power of money may result in shifts in the public's financial portfolio from cash balances, towards interest bearing assets. The question, whether such a shift will offset the accompanying shift from financial towards real assets, like the associated one of uncertainty's effect on saving, cannot be answered unambiguously on *a priori* grounds. For our purpose it will be sufficient to assume that the expansion of credit supply, resulting from an attempt to hedge against (expected) inflation, is smaller than the contraction due to inflationary risk aversion.

With both demand for, and supply of credit reduced by uncertainty, the volume of credit cleared in the market may be expected to shrink, from c_0 to c_0'. This does not necessarily imply that the volume of investment in the economy is reduced correspondingly. To avoid the risk of nominal contracts, firms which would have otherwise lent surplus funds on the market may prefer to invest internally, in their own expansion; for the same reason, households may prefer to invest their savings internally by purchasing consumer durables. However, the marginal efficiency of capital then can be expected to be lower than when such funds are channelled through the market. In the extreme case, the shifts of $S'S'$ and $D'D'$ may be so large, that they fail to intersect any longer in the positive quadrant. In a development familiar to those who experienced rapid inflations, this depicts the case where the market for purely nominal contracts for medium- and long-term credit collapses and ceases to function altogether.

4 COSTS OF INTERVENTION AND INDEXATION

Suppose now that, in order to ensure its growth target for the economy, the government wishes to raise the volume of credit traded on the market to some $c_1 < c_0$. It can do so by means of a subsidy, which would bridge the difference between the real interest rate demanded by lenders, and that offered by borrowers, at this volume of credit. Under conditions of full certainty, where in the absence of government intervention the market could have been equilibrated at c_0, the expansion of the volume traded to c_1 would require a subsidy of $(r_2 - r_1)$, represented in Figure 9.1 by the vertical distance, at c_1, between DD and SS.

As we have just seen, inflationary uncertainty raises the *ex ante* real rate demanded by lenders, and lowers that offered by borrowers, by the respective uncertainty premia demanded by them. Consequently, with the shift to $S'S'$ and $D'D'$, the subsidy required to maintain the volume of credit traded at the level desired by the government, c_1, has now to be increased by the sum of these two premia $r'_2 - r_2$ and $r'_1 - r_1$, respectively, from $r_2 - r_1$ to $r'_2 - r'_1$. As these are real interest rates, uncertainty increases the real capital subsidy expenditures necessary to maintain c_1, by a sum represented by the two shaded rectangles of Figure 9.1. As the inflationary conditions, which generate such increases, are more often than not due to government deficit spending, the additional subsidy will only increase the deficit, adding fuel to the inflationary process.

Given government insistence on maintaining c_1, capital subsidy payments can be kept at their previous level only if a way is found to prevent realised interest rates from diverging from the expected ones, thereby restoring the supply and demand curves to their full certainty positions of SS and DD respectively. In principle, this could be done in two ways. The first is that of aligning the realised rate with the expected one, by ensuring that the realised future value of money does not diverge from the expected one, $\bar{q}$. The degree of the required pump priming, and the need for this not only to happen, but for the public to believe *ex ante* that it will indeed occur, rules out this possibility altogether. The alternative way is to align the expected rate with the ultimately realised one or, to put it, perhaps, more precisely, to have credit transactions conducted in terms of the realised, rather than of the expected rate of interest. This may seem impossible in the absence of price omniscience. But, in fact, it is what the indexation of financial assets, and of public debt instruments in particular, is about.

Somewhat surprisingly, the terms value linking, indexation and monetary correction, have been often used in a rather imprecise manner. For one purpose we may wish to distinguish between what in another context has been termed *ex ante* and *ex post* indexation (Kleiman, 1977). *Ex ante* indexation may be best described as the addition, to the initial nominal interest rate, of some further element intended to compensate for the expected inflation and presumably also for the uncertainty surrounding it. Under the name of monetary correction it was widely applied to public debt instruments in, for example, Brazil, where the 'correction' used to reflect the Finance Ministry's prognosis of price increases in the relevant period in the future. Unless the government can be expected to be able to ensure always that its forecasts are, in fact, fulfilled, such *ex ante* indexation cannot equalise the expected and realised interest rates. The latter objectives can, however, be achieved through *ex post* indexation. This consists of a contractual agreement for the *ex post* revision of nominal interest payments, to compensate for those changes in the purchasing power of money which actually took place. Credit is contracted then not at some expected, *ex ante* real interest rate, but at what is going to be the *ex post* realised one. To put it somewhat differently, the contract specifies the real rate of interest which is to be realised, and its realisation is affected through the *ex post* payment of the appropriate indexation differentials, reflecting the changes in the value of money which actually took place.

By ensuring that, irrespective of the value of $q/\bar{q}$, the expected rate of interest, $\bar{r}$, will always be realised, *ex post* indexation removes the inflation uncertainty element from the credit market. In terms of Figure 9.1, it means that the supply and demand curves remain fixed at SS and DD, whatever the dispersion in the probability distribution of q. To put it in different words, indexation makes it possible for both lenders and borrowers to waive their demand for uncertainty premia. In terms of the particular government financing problem considered here, financial indexation is seen to isolate the size of the credit subsidy, necessary to maintain c_1, from the level and variability of inflation. Given indexation, and assuming other things to remain constant, the total subsidy payments will vary only with the volume of credit which the government wishes to see traded on the market. In the presence of inflationary expectations, a government intent on some level of capital market activity has, therefore, a strong incentive to introduce indexation in this market, in order to reduce the subsidy payments, and presumably the resultant budget deficit, required to achieve it.

5 THE CREATION OF INDEX DEBT

The maintaining of capital market activity at a level exceeding the equilibrium one does not necessitate public debt creation. In principle, at least, a subsidisation of medium or long-term credit may be obtained through direct credit or investment subsidies, financed out of tax revenues. But, for both political and administrative expediency reasons, it may take the form of government iself intermediating in the capital market, borrowing from lenders at a higher rate of interest than that at which it lends the proceeds to investing entrepreneurs. This is so, because the contracting of debt for investment purposes is, probably, more easily defensible than its contraction to finance current deficits, especially as such a debt may be expected, on the face of it, to be self-liquidating. In this case, the introduction of indexation in order to prevent the rise in the government's capital subsidy outlays, translates into the creation of an indexed, or otherwise value linked, public debt.[3] This, in fact, is what happened in Israel.

It should be pointed out that the public sector's borrowing requirements, by themselves, do not necessarily provide an incentive for the introduction of indexation to cope with inflationary uncertainty. This may be illustrated with the help of Figure 9.2, where the left-hand panel describes the market for private, and the right-hand one that for public, debt. As before, real volume of credit is measured on the horizontal axes and the (expected) real rate of interest on the vertical ones, and SS and DD represent the private supply and demand of credit under conditions of full certainty. The supply of credit facing the government, represented by S_G in the right-hand panel of Figure 9.2, is the excess of the quantities along SS over those along DD. In the absence of the public sector's demand for credit, the market would have cleared C_0 of private credit at an interest rate r_0. With the volume demanded by the government fixed, for convenience, say at C_g, the market will

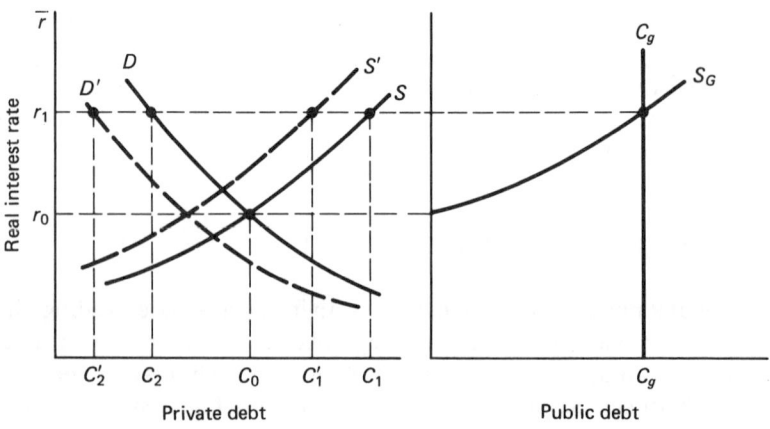

Figure 9.2

clear at the rate r_1, and total volume C_1, of which the private sector will borrow C_2, and the public sector $C_g = C_1 - C_2$.[4]

As has been shown before, uncertainty with respect to the purchasing power of money, translating into uncertainty with respect to the *ex post* realised real interest rate, may be expected to shift both *SS* and *DD* leftward, to $S'S'$ and $S'D'$ respectively. These shifts may, but need not necessarily, affect the credit supply curve facing the public sector. As drawn here, the effects of uncertainty on the quantities of credit supplied and demanded are assumed to be the same. Consequently, the real interest rate which would obtain in the absence of government borrowing, r_0, the excess supply curve facing the latter, S_G, and the ultimate equilibrium rate r_1, remain unaffected. In this case, $C_1' - C_2' = C_1 - C_2$, and the government is able to borrow as much as before at the same cost, the whole effect of uncertainty expressing itself in the shrinking volume of credit contracted in the private market. More generally, however, the rate of interest may either rise or fall, depending on the relative sizes of the uncertainty premia demanded by lenders and borrowers, and of the elasticities of the private supply and demand schedules for credit. Indeed, if the decline in the volume of credit offered falls short of that demanded privately, the supply facing the government will increase, so that the real interest rate at which it borrows will decline as a result of uncertainty. Even in this case, of course, the introduction of indexation on its own debt will be worthwhile, in that it will reduce the real interest rate the government itself has to pay. But assuming governments to be satisfisers, rather than maximisers, and to be more sensitive to rises in costs rather than to their levels, the incentive to introduce indexation may be expected to be weaker in the last two cases than when borrowing becomes more costly in the present of uncertainty. On the other hand, if the government's objective is to maintain the total volume of credit cleared by the market at above its equilibrium level, uncertainty will always (provided economic agents are, on the net, risk averse) raise the cost of doing so. It is possible that the variance observed in governments' attitudes towards indexation may be due to such differences in either their objectives with regard to the volume of private credit, or in the net effect of uncertainty on their credit markets.

6 EFFECT ON ECONOMIC PERFORMANCE

The creation of indexed public debt instruments may be expected to facilitate the spread of financial value linkage throughout the economy.

If has been often asserted that, because of the risk of relative price variability, private firms would shy away from issuing indexed bonds of their own (e.g. Liviatan and Levhari, 1977). Besides being based on some rather strong assumptions regarding the relationship between price dispersion and inflation (compare Marquez and Vining, 1984), this argument cannot explain the failure of highly diversified multiproduct firms to issue indexed bonds. It also ignores the fact that, because of the tax treatment of linkage differentials, and of foreign exchange controls often imposed in the wake of inflation, private indexation may be unprofitable, if not even outright illegal, unless sanctioned by the government. Nevertheless, it seems that both in Israel in the early 1950s, as well as in the post First World War hyper-inflations of central and eastern Europe, the linkage of private short and medium-run credits, though not of bonds, to either the price of gold or to foreign exchange, was not a rare occurrence (although, because of its semi- or outright illegality, it was rather poorly documented).[5] In Israel, for example, linkage to black-market exchange rates was illegal and before the government itself entered the indexed market, courts regarded all financial indexation as 'inimical to the public weal' (see sources cited in Kleiman, 1977). The legal provisions of such an entry will usually service private contracts as well, especially in the treatment of linkage differentials for tax purposes, or as in the Israeli case, in their exemption from a anti-usury law which severely restricted the nominal interest rate. At the same time, the availability of government issues, or guaranteed, indexed bonds provides an asset against which private indexed obligations, such as, say, life insurance policies, can now be issued.

The most obvious result of widespread financial indexation is a drastic reduction in the wealth redistribution which would occur in its absence mainly within the private sector, and of which the redistribution between the private and the public sector, in the form of an inflation tax, is only the proverbial iceberg's tip. The decline in the risk of such a redistribution may be expected to have a positive effect on savings: admittedly, the effect of inflationary uncertainty on savings cannot be ascertained on *a priori* grounds. But it can be argued that, for high enough inflation rates, their substitution effect on savings must outweigh their income effects, if only because the saving then of even the whole present income will not suffice significantly to affect future consumption. Further, even if the volume of savings remained unaffected by inflation then, as shown in Section 3 above, the share of them placed through the market may be expected to decline, and with it also the efficiency of the investment financed by them. Coupled with the overall diversion of entrepreneurial activity towards the search for anti-inflationary hedging, inflation may thus be expected to result in a decline in economic performance in general.

Table 9.1 presents some indicators of the performance of the Israel economy in the last fifteen years. As can be seen from the first row of the table, inflation accelerated dramatically in this period. Nevertheless,

Table 9.1 Inflation and economic performance: selected indicators, Israel 1970–85[a] (per cent)

	1970–3	1974–8	1979–82	1983	1984	1985
1. Price increase during the year	15.6	41.7	119.3	190.7	445.0	185.0
2. Private saving ratio	34.4	32.1	30.9	25.0	35.3	28.4
3. GNP growth	8.9	3.3	3.1	2.7	1.7	3.8
4. Unemployment rate	3.2	3.4	4.5	4.5	5.9	6.7
5. Total factor productivity	3.7	0.0[b]	1.0[c]	1.2	−2.9	1.4

Notes:
[a] Figures for year-groups are arithmetic averages; periodisation by rate of inflation.
[b] 1975–7.
[c] 1978–82.

Sources and definitions:
Line 1: Consumer Price Index, December over December of previous year. CBS, Statistical Abstract of Israel, various years
Line 2: Saving of private sector as per cent of private disposable income from all sources, corrected for credit subsidy. Bank of Israel, Annual Reports, various issues
Line 3: Annual rate of growth of real GNP. 1970–8, CBS, Statistical Abstract of Israel, 1983; 1979–85, Bank of Israel, Annual Report, 1985, Table II–A1
Line 4: Unemployed as per cent of civilian labour force. 1970–83, CBS, Statistical Abstract of Israel, 1983; 1984–5, Bank of Israel, Annual Report, 1985
Line 5: 1970–3: Total factor productivity in the economy. Bank of Israel Annual Report, 1975. Thereafter, total factor productivity in the business sector, calculated for output growth derived from individual industry figures. Bank of Israel Annual Report, 1983–5.

despite the obviously tremendous uncertainty regarding future rates of inflation, the private saving ratio was both high and fairly stable. It may be argued that this reflects the high proportion of contractual savings, and that the discretionary component of the saving ratio was, most probably, much more volatile. But the public's readiness to contract heavily for institutionalised, long-term saving could itself hardly have been expected in the absence of indexation. Of the other indicators, the great decline of GNP growth, compared to the pre-1974 years, reflects factors other than inflation, though the further slowdown before the beginning of stabilisation in 1985 may probably be ascribed to it, as well as some of the rise in unemployment. On the other hand, total factor productivity in the private sector, though reduced far below its annual rate of growth of over 3 per cent in the preceding decade, shows no systematic association with inflation. Altogether, while some deterioration in economic performance is visible in the data of Table 9.1, the emerging picture is by no means that of an economy reduced to barter and riven by industrial disputes, as may have been expected, perhaps, when prices rise on the average by as much as 10, or even 15, per cent a month. That no such disintegration occurred is due, most probably, to a large extent to the comprehensiveness of the indexation system, through which Israel society tried to protect itself from the worst ravages of inflation, and of which the financial part was made possible by the existence of indexed public debt instruments. Indexed government bonds, introduced initially to ease the financing problem of the public sector, became ultimately the means of insuring the operation of all medium and long-run financial markets.

7 INDEXED MONEY AND PRICE INDETERMINACY

As a matter of record, it may be worth pointing out that protecting savers was not the government's prime objective in introducing indexation. The immediate requirements which prompted it were the erosion of the credits which the government extended to investors, and the difficulties it encountered in borrowing domestically. Indeed, savings accounts were the last to be indexed, and that only after considerable public pressure. But both firms and households were quick to avail themselves of this opportunity of safeguarding themselves against inflation. For all practical purposes, the supply of indexed debt instruments was virtually unlimited, as the government was ready to satisfy all demand at real interest rates which did not change with market conditions. Consequently, the public could adjust its holdings of them at will, in accord with its inflationary expectations. This is illustrated by the data in line 2a of Table 9.2, which shows the proportion of purely nominal unlinked assets in the public's short and medium-run monetary portfolio to have decreased dramatically as inflation accelerated. Supporting the view that this development reflected changes in inflationary expectations is the fact that this trend reversed itself sharply in the last year covered in the table, when a stabilisation policy considerably slowed down the inflation rate, at least for the time being.

To provide some idea of the absolute magnitude of the change in the public's monetary portfolio, made possible by the availability of indexed government obligations and of the indexed assets packed by them, we present in line 3 of Table 9.2 the amounts of means of payments held per capita, expressed in terms of constant, December 1970 purchasing power. In the years preceding the resurgence of inflation in the wake of the Yom Kippur war, the real value of the money balances held by the public had been increasing more rapidly than population growth. In particular, their per capita value increased by nearly one quarter within the brief span of the earliest period considered here. From 1974 onwards, however, real money balances have been shrinking rapidly as the cost of holding them, in terms of purchasing power lost, increased with inflation. By the end of 1984, the average money balance held could purchase no more than one-seventh of what could have been purchased with that held eleven years earlier.

A comparison between the relative changes in lines 2a and 3 of Table 9.2 suggests that the decline in money balances held was accompanied by a transition towards the holding not of physical real assets, but of some other, value linked monetary ones. The fact that money balances fell by only one-sixth, when the inflation rate more than doubled between 1983 and 1984, indicates the very high value which economic agents attach, at the margin, to the liquidity services provided by traditional means of payments. It is obvious that in some situations there is not substitute for ready money. But the very low level to which money balances fell – amounting to no more than $125 per capita in 1984 – provides at the same time an indication of the relatively high liquidity of at least some of the assets substituted for them.

Traditionally, sales of government bonds to the public are expected to reduce demand, both directly and indirectly, through their effect on interest rates. Both these effects required such bonds to be regarded by the public as significantly less liquid than the money balances with

Table 9.2 Inflation and financial behaviour: some selected ratios, Israel 1970–85[a] (per cent)

	1970–3	1974–8	1979–82	1983	1984	1985
1. Price increase during the year	15.6	41.7	113.3	130.7	445.0	185.0
2. Share in public's monetary portfolio of:						
a. unlinked assets	40.6	20.0	8.5	7.7	6.8	14.5
b. exchange-rate linked assets	22.9	22.0[b]	36.2[c]	44.3	44.5	34.1
3. Means of payments per capita, in 1970 IS	127	91	41	24	20	24
4. 'Velocity' of monetary portfolio with respect to domestic resources	2.3	2.2	2.3[d]	—	—	—
5. 'Velocity' of liquid assets with respect to GDP	—	—	2.6	2.7	2.6	2.2

Notes:
[a] See Table 9.1.
[b] 1974–7; see explanation to line 2b.
[c] 1982.
[d] 1979–80.

Sources and definitions:
Line 1: As in Table 9.1

Line 2a: Means of payments, time deposits and CD's (certificates of deposit) held by the public, expressed as per cent of the public's total portfolio of short and medium term financial assets (M_5), consisting, in addition to the above, also of saving and other linked deposits, tradable indexed bonds, and foreign exchange linked deposits. End-of-year figures: 1970–4, Falk Institute, indexation research project files; 1975–85, Bank of Israel, *Annual Report*, various issues

Line 2b: Exchange-rate linked deposits (PATAM) and restitution's deposits (PATAP), as per cent of M_5. Exclusive of exchange-rate linked bonds and of bank shares, which were virtually turned into bonds in October 1983. PATAM deposits not in existence before November 1977. 1970–8, from Fischer (1982) Table 3; 1982–5, Bank of Israel, *Annual Reports*

Line 3: Means of payments divided by total population, end-of-year figures. Deflated by consumer price index, to the basis of December 1970. (The Sheqel was introduced only in 1980. '1970 IS' is only a convenient which they were purchased. However, to increase the attraction of government bonds, the Bank of Israel used, until quite recently, to support their prices by intervening in the secondary market. By providing a floor to the market, such intervention affected the public's perception of the liquidity of all government obligations (besides monetising, of course, that part of the public debt thus purchased from time to time by the Bank). It thus resulted in what amounted in practive to the monetisation of the bonds held by the public. For some purposes they could substitute perfectly for cash, or even beat it on its own grounds: short-term bearer bonds, popular in the 1960s, were known to have been used in large underground economy transactions, being available in much higher denominations than currency notes. Though over the years the government made it progressively more costly to shift in and out of linked assets, the costs of doing so remained trifling compared with those of holding unlinked balances. As a result, while the government accumulated debt in the belief that it was 'absorbing' the public's liquidity, the public continued to regard itself, for most practical purposes, as maintaining its liquidity levels constant.

The last conclusion is supported by the stability of the ratio between the corresponding monetary aggregates and income, represented alternatively by domestic use of resources (net of direct defence imports) or by GDP. Because of changes in definitions, as well as in the legal and other characteristics of some monetary assets, as well as in the legal and other characteristics of some monetary assets, this stability is illustrated in Table 9.2 with the help of two different ratios, corresponding to different periods, but overlapping in the early 1980s, to make a continuous comparison possible.[6] The stability of these ratios is especially remarkable in that the corresponding financial assets are net of long-run, difficult to break contractual assets such as pension

---

        compression of 'IS', at constant 1970 prices.) Underlying data from CBS, *Statistical Abstract of Israel*, various years

Line 4: Total domestic use of resources, net of direct defense imports, divided by average annual balance of the public's short and medium-term financial assets (M_5). 1970–8, from Fischer (1982, Table 2); 1979–80, from Kondor (1981)

Line 5: Gross Domestic Product divided by the average annual balance of the public's liquid assets (equal to M_5 minus saving accounts, and indexed time deposits). Calculated from Bank of Israel, *Annual Report*, 1983 and 1985

fund balances. For comparison, the similarly calculated circulation velocity of the means of payment rose from 8.4 in 1970 to 55.7 in 1984! The stability in the relative size of the monetary portfolio in the face of accelerating inflation can be viewed from two different angles: on the one hand, value linking made it possible for firms and households to hold substantive monetary assets without having the real value of these assets eroded by inflation. On the other hand, however, with more than nine-tenths of these assets value linked in one way or another, the nominal value of the monetary portfolio adjusts itself automatically with inflation. Such automatic monetary accommodation means that the economy no longer possesses a nominal anchor, so that the price level becomes indeterminant. Under these circumstances, relatively minor shocks can result in relatively major upward shifts in the inflationary trajectory, as they seem to have done, in fact, in Israel in the past few years (see, e.g. Bruno and Fischer, 1986). Thus, financial indexation, made possible by the creation of indexed debt, had two diametrically opposed results: it neutralised the effects of inflation with respect to asset holding, thereby preventing not only its redistributive effects, but also the flight towards real assets, which, up to a point, would have fuelled inflation even further. But indexation achieved this at the cost of a price indeterminancy which raised inflation to levels at which traditional indexation mechanisms could no longer fulfil their original function, and had to be substituted, or supplemented, by ones which were considerably more costly in real terms.

8 CHOICE OF LINKAGE STANDARDS AND UNCERTAINTY

As has been shown in earlier sections, the indexation of financial assets eliminates the uncertainty with respect to the *ex post*, realised real rate of interest. It has been argued, however, that the total amount of uncertainty in the economy is not reduced by indexation, but is only shifted – in this case from the real to the nominal rate of interest (see, e.g. Samuelson, 1986). This raises two questions: to what extent is the former type of uncertainty eliminated in practice by indexation, and are the real costs of uncertainty reduced by such a shift. In the Israeli context, the answers to both questions are closely interrelated with that of the value base to which public debt instruments were linked.

Different economic agents may use different standards to deflate nominal into real values, depending on the uses to which they intend to put their wealth or their income. The most widely accepted measure of the consumption value of money in Israel in the consumer price index (CPI) which measures changes in the cost of the average consumption bundle or urban wage and salary earners. For many years, the CPI used to be the linkage standard for most indexed bonds, besides being used also as the basis for wage indexation. With forward currency markets precluded by exchange controls, linkage to the CPI could not, however, answer the hedging needs of those groups whose revenues or outlays were foreign exchange oriented, such as exporters, or purchasers of imported investment goods. For these, as well as for other reasons, linked government bonds were initially linked either to the CPI or to the dollar exchange rate (and so were also the government's credits). But under the fixed exchange rate regime of the 1950s and 1960s, and a government known to be averse to formal devaluations, the exchange rate varied discretely in a step-function manner, while the general price level grew more or less continuously, even if not at a constant rate. A quick profit could, thus, be made by shifting in and out of exchange linked bonds at the opportune moment. To put it in the terms used in the earlier sections of this paper, this situation generated uncertainties regarding both the real interest rate, defined in terms of the CPI, which would be realised through the purchase of exchange linked bonds, and that defined in dollars, which could be realised through the purchase of CPI linked ones. But as long as devaluations were infrequent enough, occurring only once every five years or so, the real costs of these uncertainties could not have been very large. The effects of another uncertainty, that regarding the realised nominal rate on indexed bonds, were considerably restricted with the introduction of option bonds, which allowed their holders to choose, *ex post*, between an indexed redemption and a nominal one with a higher rate of interest. Uncertainty with respect to relative prices, on the other hand, need not have been affected by indexation.[7]

The CPI is calculated on a monthly basis, and is published with a fortnight's lag. For the sake of administrative simplicity, indexed bonds are linked to the 'last known index'. Assuming the index for any given month to correspond, more or less, to the price level in the middle of the month, this causes the linkage standard to be outdated by thirty to sixty days at the time indexation differentials are calculated. This may be of little consequence when the inflation rate is constant, as roughly the same lag occurs at both ends of a bond's life. But as inflation accelerated, these lags, as well as the discrete nature of the whole CPI linkage, became much more significant. With the purchasing power of money, at which the redemption value of an indexed bond was calculated, reduced, on occasion, by as much as 20 per cent by the time of its actual redemption, the uncertainty with respect to realised real rates of interest was no longer negligible, even in the presence of indexation. But since late 1977 unrestricted linkage to the exchange rate, which has been discontinued in the 1960s, again became available, following a temporary liberalisation of the exchange regime, in the form of dollar denominated time and demand deposits.[8]

Known by their acronym, PATAM, these deposits provided their holders with a highly liquid asset with practically continuous value linkage, being redeemable at the, by that time daily changing, rate of exchange with only a day's lag. Unlike in the case of the exchange denominated deposits in existence until then, which were restricted, in the main, to the recipients of private restitution payments from West Germany, the creation of PATAM required no foreign exchange. They constituted, in effect, daily indexed money. The loss of nominal anchor, referred to earlier, and the resultant, and otherwise difficult to account for, successive accelerations of inflation, can, most probably, be traced to the introduction of PATAM accounts.

As can be seen from the figures in the third line of Table 9.2, the share of exchange linked assets in the public's monetary portfolio rose rapidly following the introduction of PATAM and the acceleration of inflation, until they accounted, at one stage, for nearly half of the total. In fact, these data underestimate the role of PATAM, as deposits originating in restitution monies could not, by their very nature, keep pace with the rest of the portfolio. Nevertheless, the effects of changing expectations are illustrated there by the change in the share of exchange linked assets over time, and especially by the jump in it in 1983, which resulted in a stock exchange crash, as the public, expecting a devaluation, was trying to shift over to PATAM. In fact, present data underestimate the shift towards exchange linked assets, in that they do not include the, by all indications, substantiated illegal holdings of foreign currency, either in currency notes or in bank deposits abroad, which the Israeli public accumulated in the last few years in an attempt to protect itself against both inflation and the possibility of such anti-inflationary measures as a capital levy on financial assets.

From the present point of view, these shifts reflect the uncertainty regarding the relative returns on two differently linked types of assets, further aggravated by the introduction, in the 1980s, of high interest, short-run nominal debt instruments, in the form of negotiable CD's and seven days' time deposits. It is widely accepted in Israel, that hedging against inflation has become the major preoccupation of management there; and that the resultant deflection of entrepreneurial efforts, from production to financial dealings, may be the cause of the poor growth record of recent years. In an attempt to calculate some of the shoe leather costs of inflation, the inflation caused expansion of the banking system, and the corresponding time cost to firms and households, were estimated to amount to as much as 3 to 4 per cent of GNP (Kleiman, 1984). These observations do not imply, however, that the costs of inflationary uncertainty were not reduced by indexation.

In particular, indexation of debt instruments reduced the risk of ruin, which many firms and households would have faced in its absence. Introspection suggests that risk averters could be expected to make much greater efforts, i.e. incur greater costs, to avert total ruin than they will make to obtain a gain. Therefore, though indexation did not eliminate all uncertainty with respect to real interest rates, and transformed the rest of it into uncertainty with respect to nominal rates, it probably did significantly reduce the economic effects of inflationary uncertainty.[9]

9 THE EFFECT ON GOVERNMENT FINANCE

An evaluation of indexation's effect on public finances is complicated by the role which the Israeli government performs in the country's capital markets, which made it introduce debt indexing in the first instance. For most practical purposes, the government became the ultimate financial intermediary in the country, channelling funds from, savers to investors. As I have recounted elsewhere (e.g. Kleiman, 1986), this resulted in the politisation of the debt. In other words, it exposed the government to pressures from enterprises as well as from households for preferential treatment, especially in their role as borrowers. This most often took the form of the government foregoing the indexation clause on credits granted by it directly, or out of funds borrowed under its guarantee. From the politician's point of view, this had the advantage of not being reflected in current expenditure and, unlike budgetary decisions, requiring the approval only of a parliamentary sub-committee.

As a result of such pressures, and of the government's belief, at one stage, that inflation had been subdued for good (!), its capital position became highly asymmetric by the early 1970s, with nearly all of its internal debt value linked, but nearly all of its credits to the public unlinked. Had the value linkage of government credits not been abandoned, its revenues, from interest and repayments of the credits it extended, would have equalled, except for some constant capital subsidy element, its expenditures on debt servicing. As can be seen from the second line in Table 9.3, such revenues, plus returns from direct government investments, financed nearly three-quarters of its domestic debt servicing in the period 1970–3. But as inflation accelerated, the indexation asymmetry caused this proportion to fall rapidly, until it amounted to less than one-tenth by 1984. This greatly reduced the government's ability to lessen its debt burden by withdrawing gradually from the capital market, just at the time when growing public fears, of the government reneging on its indexed obligations, made the recycling of its debt more difficult than before.

Though indexation prevents the erosion of the public debt by inflation, it need not, by itself, increase the burden of the debt, relative to GNP or to the government's own budget. Other things being equal,

Table 9.3 Inflation and the public finance aspects of indexed debt, Israel 1970–85[a] (per cent)

	1970–3	1974–8	1979–82	1983	1984	1985
1. Price increase during the year	15.6	41.7	119.3	190.7	445.0	185.0
2. Revenue from capital/ domestic debt servicing	74.6	29.4	25.4	13.0	8.0[b]	—
3. Net total domestic debt/GNP	55	96	112	114	123	143
4. Domestic debt servicing/ government civilian expenditures	12.9	18.1[c]	24.5	25.0	33.0[b]	—
5. Inflation tax/GNP	1.5	2.9	2.4	1.9	2.9	0.9
6. Inflationary credit subsidy/GNP	5.3	9.5	7.7	4.5	3.5	2.1

Notes:
[a] See Table 9.1.
[b] Temporary estimates, based on budgeted rather than on actual revenues and expenditures.
[c] 1975–8.

Source: Kleiman, 1986, Table 1 (updated where possible for 1984 and 1985).

the debt burden under indexation may be expected to be roughly the same as in the absence of both inflation and indexation. But under the circumstances which evolved in Israel, this is no longer true of the net debt burden, i.e. that exclusive of the government's claim on the public. As can be seen from the third line of Table 9.3, with the acceleration of inflation, the net burden became, on the average, nearly twice as high in 1974–8 than it was in 1970–3. As the gross debt burden rose by only a quarter, between the same two periods, the heavy increase in net indebtedness can be ascribed to the erosion of government's outstanding credits, without a similar development occurring on the debt side of its domestic capital account.

From the view of public finance, inflation imposes a tax on the holders of nominal government obligations. In fact, such a tax has often been considered to underly government's inflationary policies. As it results from the erosion of the real value of the money base and of the domestic debt, this tax may have been expected to rise with inflation. As can be seen from line 4 of Table 9.3, this did, indeed, happen between 1970–3 and 1974–8, when, expressed as a per cent of GNP, the inflation tax nearly doubled. But in the following years, despite the acceleration in inflation, the tax actually declined, regaining its 1974–8 level only in 1984, when the inflation rate was ten times higher! The cause of this seeming paradox is, of course, the same which explains the altogether low level of the inflation tax rate: with the whole public debt indexed, the inflation tax's base is greatly reduced – in the present case, as can be seen from line 3 in the table, from a magnitude exceeding that of annual GNP, to only a small fraction of the latter. And the availability of indexed debt instruments allows the public to try to avoid some of the inflation tax by shifting into them at the expense of nominal money holdings as inflation rises, thereby further eroding the inflation tax base. In Israel, this process was made even more extreme by the extension of unlinked credits by the government to the private sector. It may be questioned what part of the inflation caused by decline in this sector's real indebtedness to the government should be regarded as pure rent, in excess of the capital subsidy which, as discussed earlier, the government intended to grant also in the absence of inflation. But even if we allow for some margin of definitional error, the order of magnitude of the inflation credit subsidy, shown in the last line of Table 9.3, can be seen to have considerably exceeded the corresponding inflation tax.

By eroding the inflation tax rate, indexation caused inflation to be no longer 'functional', in so far as the financing of the public sector was concerned. The granting by the government of unlinked credits to

286   Aspects of Public Debt Theory and Practice

the private sector, on the other hand, provided inflation with the rather unusual function of transferring purchasing power from government to public. As the former was unwilling to curtail its expenditures, and unable to increase tax revenues, this redistributive effect of inflation forced it to borrow more, in excess of what it required for the recycling of its existing net debt. Thus, the indexation asymmetry in the government's capital position not only prevented an easing of the debt burden, but resulted in a further increase in it, as inflation accelerated.

Notes

* The author wishes to thank the University of Illinois at Urbana-Champaign, where most of this paper was written for its hospitality.

1. We do not pursue here the question of whether economic agents tend in fact to think in terms of x or of $q = 1/(1 + x)$. The latter seems, however, to be the variable to consider in analysing uncertainty. We note, in passing, that the relationship between x and a being that between an arithmetic and a harmonic mean, $\bar{q} \neq 1/(1 + x)$ (Jansen's inequality).
2. This means that, had it been the nominal, rather than the real rate of inflation, which was measured on the vertical axis of Figure 9.1, the expectation with certitude, that the price level will rise at the rate of $\bar{x}$ would have shifted both supply and demand curves upwards by this same rate. Or, in other words, that the nominal rates at which different volumes of credit are demanded or offered, adjust themselves to a certain decline in the value of money according to the expression of equation (9.1).
3. It may be also argued that the introduction of indexation, in order to reduce capital subsidy outlays, cannot be easily effected except through the creation of an indexed public debt.
4. And where $C_0 - C_2$ represents the displacement of private by public debt.
5. For some information on the east European linkage practices in the early 1920s, see, e.g. Szturm de Sztrem (1924).
6. In particular, there was the change, to be discussed later, in both the formal and actual status of bank shares in 1983, which turned them into exchange linked bonds, practically speaking. The view, that it is the most broadly defined monetary aggregate, which should be considered for policy purposes, has been long pressed in a series of internal memoranda, by Yaakov Kondor, formerly of the Israel Economic Planning Authority (e.g. Kondor, 1981; see also Fischer, 1982).
7. It has been sometimes argued that firms refrained from borrowing or indexed because of the uncertainty regarding the divergence of their own prices from the general price level. But such an uncertainty exists also in a purely nominal system, if the *ex ante* nominal rate of interest there is based on the expected change in some general price level. The preference for nominal borrowing was due first and foremost to the nominal rate of interest falling, for a long period, to adjust itself fully to the rate of inflation.
8. Unlike government bonds, such deposits do not have to be redeemed out

of the government budget. But for most macroeconomic purposes, obligations of the monetary authority may be regarded as part of the public debt. In fact, in the Israeli state budget a certain portion of the reserves against exchange linked deposits is regarded as being lent to the Treasury, rather than deposited with the Bank of Israel.

9. It is an act of faith with economists that increased choice increases welfare. But one cannot help wondering whether the public would not have been better of with a narrower range of inflation hedging financial assets to choose from. The expansion of this range increases the uncertainty with respect to the relative rates of return earned. If choice is not costless, and costs of regret are also taken into account, the game may, perhaps, not be worth the candle.

References

Bruno, M. and Fischer, S. (1986), 'The Inflationary Process: Shocks and Accommodation', in Ben-Porath, Y. (ed.), *The Israeli Economy: Maturing through Crises*, (Cambridge: Harvard University Press), pp. 347-74.

Fischer, S. (1982) 'Monetary Policy in Israel', *Bank of Israel Economic Review*, no. 53, May, pp. 5-30.

Kleiman, E. (1977) 'Monetary Correction and Indexation: The Brazilian and Israeli Experience', *Explorations in Economic Research*, vol. 4 no. 1, pp. 141-76.

Kleiman, E. (1984) 'The Cost of Inflation', *Economic Quarterly*, vol. 30, no. 119, pp. 859-64 (in Hebrew).

Kleiman, E. (1984) 'The Indexation of Public Debt in Israel', in Herber, B. (ed.), *Public Finance and Public Debt* (Wayne State University Press), pp. 193-204.

Kondor, Y. (1981) 'The Velocity of Money Circulation: The Evidence of the 1980 Data', Memorandum No. 11, Economic Planning Authority, Jerusalem, July (in Hebrew).

Liviatan, N. and Levhari, D. (1977) 'Risk and the Theory of Indexed Bonds', *American Economic Review*, vol. 67, June, pp. 366-75.

Marquez, J. and Vining, D. (1984) 'Inflation and Relative Price Behaviour: A Survey of the Literature', in Ballabon, M. B. (ed.), *Economic Perspectives: An Annual Survey of Economics*, vol. 3 (New York, Hardwood Academic Publishers), pp. 1-56.

Mundell, R. (1963) 'Inflation and Real Interest', *Journal of Political Economy*, vol. 71, no. 3, pp. 280-3.

Samuelson, L. (1986) 'Inflation, Indexing, and Economic Development'. Paper presented at a Seminar on the Resurgence of Inflation in Latin American, Center for Latin American and Caribbean Studies, University of Illinois, 4-5 April.

Szturm de Sztrem, T. (1924) *The Inflation Tax* (Warsaw, IGS) (in Polish).

DISCUSSION

Professor Jean-Paul Fitoussi was the principal discussant of Ephraim

Kleiman's chapter. Fitoussi prefaced his remarks by noting that there was no strong welfare argument for or against indexation. He cited three traditional arguments favouring indexation. The first was due to Tobin, that indexation allows monetary policy to be more effective. The second was due to Richard Musgrave, that indexed bonds encourage saving, and so lowers the rate of interest that must be paid on debt. The third was that indexed bonds are said to discourage inflation. Fitoussi noted that Kleiman uses all three arguments.

Fitoussi suggested that governments issue indexed debt only when they have to, i.e. in situations where inflation is apt to be high, and indexed debt is the only debt that people will want to hold. Thus, indexed debt will be desired when there is risk aversion and price level uncertainty.

Fitoussi then outlined Kleiman's basic framework. Kleiman analyses the benefits and burdens of indexed debt, but only in a partial equilibrium framework. Fitoussi noted that in Kleiman's Figure 9.1, the supply and demand for debt may not intersect when there is hyperinflation. Such a situation would be marked by dynamic inconsistency, in which the realised real rate of return will differ from the expected rate. *Ex post* indexation would remove the inflation uncertainty, and so everyone would be better off.

Fitoussi noted that the argument was similar to the Musgrave argument. Indexation encourages people to move from physical inflation hedges to financial assets. And this is precisely what happened in Israel. Indexation led to: (1) a reduction in the wealth redistribution due to inflation; (2) a reduction in the real impacts of inflation; (3) a large reduction in real money balances since index bonds provided a substitute for cash.

This last feature had the potential for undermining the benefits of indexation, since it removed the nominal anchor of the economy. So indexation had two effects. While it helped to neutralise the impact of inflation on the economy, it had the effect of making the price level indeterminate.

Fitoussi then turned to his criticisms of the paper. First, he remarked that it was rather strange that there was no treatment of the real interest rate. This left unanswered the question of the impact of indexation on the real interest rate, and what it was that determined whether firms hold financial rather than real assets. Also, the paper did not incorporate any economic costs to the introduction of bonds. In particular, it failed to discuss the future taxes that must be raised to finance the interest payments.

Fitoussi concluded by pointing out the limitations of the partial equilibrium approach. He noted that the partial equilibrium approach left the conclusions less robust than they might have been. In particular, this framework does not allow Kleiman to say anything about the impact of indexed bonds on the consumption/investment choice. All that is discussed is the impact of indexation on the form of investment. Fitoussi speculated that the rise in the variance of inflation might reduce consumption, when there is indexation.

Professor Kleiman began his response with a critique of his own Chapter 9. He noted that it was an impressionistic paper, that the arguments were sequential, but not rigorous.

Having completed the paper, Kleiman realised that an interesting comparison would be between high inflation countries with and without indexation. He noted that in countries without indexation, people had come up with other devices for minimising the effects of inflation, such as daily pay. He thus realised that he may be claiming too much for indexation.

Turning to Fitoussi's specific comments, Kleiman said that he had not considered the real rate of interest because until recently, there had been no market determined interest rate in Israel. Credit rationing was widespread, and credit was tightly controlled. He also noted that even in the current, freer markets, it was difficult to measure the *ex ante* real rate, since it was difficult to know the expected rate of inflation.

On the questions of the impact of inflation and indexation on the consumption/investment choice, Kleiman referred to his Table 9.1. He noted that until inflation reached 200 per cent per annum, inflation had had essentially no impact on saving, so that ignoring this effect seemed fairly safe.

Kleiman then discussed the historical evolution of indexation in Israel. He said that indexation originated out of a desire by the government to intervene in the capital market, to engage in lending policy. But the loans that the government made to the private sector were unindexed, while the government raised the money with indexed bonds. This was illustrated in Table 9.3. Kleiman noted that indexation meant giving up the collection of the inflation tax on bonds. At the same time, when inflation increased, the inflation tax base shrank, because, for example, people reduced their real money holdings. These factors combined to lead to an inflation subsidy that exceeded the inflation tax, as illustrated on lines 5 and 6 of Table 9.3.

Kleiman concluded his remarks by asking whether or not indexation simply shifted inflation uncertainty. He wondered how one would measure the 'total amount of uncertainty in the economy'.

The general discussion began with a question from *Professor Paul Pieper* as to why the consumer price index (CPI) was used for the indexation of government debt. *Professor Kleiman* responded that the reasons were partly historical, since the CPI had been used since the 1940s for wage indexation, and partly practical, since the CPI was calculated monthly, but the GNP deflator, only quarterly.

Professor Guido Tabellini asked Kleiman how reserve requirements were affected by the use of indexed bonds. *Kleiman* answered that indexed deposits were backed with bonds as reserves. Kleiman noted the problems created by exchange-linked deposits which did not have to actually be backed by foreign exchange.

Professor Michael Boskin mentioned the feeling many US legislators have, that introducing indexation contributes to inflation by reducing the constituency opposed to inflation. *Kleiman* felt that this was a valid point. He said that in the 1970s, the government delayed for a long time before reintroducing indexation on its credits, arguing that such a step would be taken to be a signal that it was planning to inflate in the future. He suggested that indexation works, to a point, at a very low cost. But recalculation of prices at half-daily intervals becomes costly. As the economy approaches hyperinflation, shoe-leather costs become significant, as, for example, people spend more and more time in bank queues.

In response to a question from *Dr Christophe Chamley*, *Professor Kleiman* suggested that indexation does not eliminate the need for governments to inflate. Although indexation should eliminate the inflation tax base, governments often inflate anyway. In Israel, the motivation seems to have been a desire to improve the balance of payments by depreciating the currency.

Dr Vito Tanzi pointed out that eventually a government must issue indexed bonds, or else they will not be able to sell the bonds at all.

Tanzi also wanted to reiterate the idea that it is the conventional measure of the deficit, and not the 'real' or 'inflation-adjusted' deficit, that is the relevant measure of fiscal prudence. Emphasis on the inflation adjusted deficit is little more than a cosmetic improvement. Tanzi noted that, in Argentina, perhaps five billion dollars in US currency was being held as a hedge against accelerating prices on that country. This alone led to a $500 million a year drain in export earnings as a result of lost interest income. Treating the inflation tax as a normal source of government revenue gives a false impression of the fiscal strength of a country.

As regards indexation, Tanzi felt that it led to a loss of inflation tax revenue, and thus to a loss in the war on inflation. On the positive side, though, Tanzi saw a benefit in that stabilisation will be more successful when there has been indexation, because relative prices will be undistorted.

Professor Kleiman agreed with Tanzi, that it would be best not to have inflation in the first place. But the question becomes, once there is inflation, how best to deal with it. Kleiman agreed that indexation was beneficial in reducing the distortionary effects of inflation, but he also agreed that shoe-leather costs would eventually become important with or without indexation. What indexation allowed was for the damage to be minimised as long as the rates of inflation were not too high.

Professor Eisner wondered whether, given the high level of uncertainty that accompanied high inflation, the presence or absence of a real return of three or four per cent was important. *Professor Kleiman* agreed, saying that the principal benefit of indexation was to avert the risk of ruin that was always a possibility in a high-inflation environment.

10 Debt, Wealth and the Rate of Growth: An Exercise in Equilibrium Dynamics

Stefano Gorini
UNIVERSITY OF SASSARI

1 INTRODUCTION

The purpose of this chapter is to work out certain stylised relationships between budget balance, wealth and growth. The theoretical basis will be provided by the standard Domar references on the subject of growth (Domar, 1946, 1947). Our analysis may appear old-fashioned, because it is carried out under the conventional assumption that public debt acts in the economy as a component of private wealth (a negative component, when public debt is negative), just like private physical capital, thereby disregarding the modern revival of Ricardo's equivalence hypothesis. Also, it is framed exclusively in terms of *real* output growth, with no explicit account of the problems of monetary growth and inflation. Although these are strong limitations, in our view the exercise, which requires no more than elementary algebra, does retain some meaningful economics.

The issue dealt with in Section 2 is the steady state relationship between deficit (positive or negative), wealth and the equilibrium, or 'warranted', growth rate. We derive such relationship by extending a Domar growth model to include, in the conventional way, (1) a deficit, and (2) a role for private net wealth in determining the average propensity to save out of disposable income. By definition, the equilibrium growth rate remains the standard Domar one, namely the ratio of private saving less the deficit to income times the output capital ratio, but allowing for a conventional wealth effect introduces an interesting variation into the standard picture. With a balanced budget, and no steady state debt, there is again a unique equilibrium growth rate, obviously lower than that which would be generated in the absence of a wealth effect. But with a positive deficit there would in general be two distinct equilibrium growth rates, both lower, of course, than the balanced budget one. Indeed, with perfectly feasible values of the parameters an equilibrium growth rate may simply not exist. With a surplus there would again be a unique equilibrium growth rate, obviously higher than the balanced budget one.

As will be readily shown, the qualitative result of two distinct equilibrium growth rates, or of none, follows directly from the fact that with a given deficit income ratio and a conventional wealth effect of debt, the steady state ratio of saving less the deficit to income depends on the growth rate itself (it rises with the rise of the growth rate), because this affects the steady state state debt income ratio (which declines as the growth rate rises). The dependence of the two equilibrium growth rates on the values of the parameters, notably the deficit income ratio, the wealth coefficient and the output capital ratio, will be readily shown through simple formulae and the figures.

In Section 3 the reasoning is reversed. The economy is assumed to exhibit some actual trend growth rate, and we see how the model determines the equilibrium, or 'required', deficit income ratio corresponding to that trend growth rate, i.e. the deficit income ratio required to ensure steady state full capacity output market equilibrium for an exogenously given growth rate. If, for a given growth rate and given values of the parameters, there is excess supply (excess saving), then the existence of a conventional wealth effect of the debt affects the level of the deficit income ratio required to close the gap, because the closing of the gap is brought about both by the increased deficit income ratio *and* the increased debt income ratio. Moreover, if the economy starts off with a debt income ratio lower than the steady state one, then the deficit income ratio required to ensure continuous full capacity output market equilibrium along the adjustment path declines as the debt income ratio increases approaching its steady state value. The original motivation for the exercise in Section 3 has been to redefine and revisit, in a simple general growth setting and in purely theoretical terms, the economics of the classical argument (Lerner, 1943, resumed and qualified later by Dernburg, 1962) that through the demand augmenting wealth effect of debt the requirement of a deficit finance to ensure full employment output market equilibrium would tend to be self-eliminating, and therefore temporary.

In Section 4 the steady state relationships are worked out between average tax burden on gross disposable income, average real interest on government debt, the budget deficit and growth, and integrate them logically into the preceding discussion. In the resulting framework Domar's 'burden of the debt' concept (Domar, 1944), adjusted for inflation and for a variable composition of the debt itself, will coincide by definition with the average tax burden when the deficit income ratio is equal to the expenditure income ratio, i.e. when total tax revenues cover exactly the real debt interest bill.

Though the notation used is explained throughout, for easy reference purpose it is listed in the Appendix.

2 BUDGET BALANCE, WEALTH AND EQUILIBRIUM GROWTH

As indicated above, in this section the working of a Domar growth model is described and is extended to include, in the conventional way, (1) a deficit (positive or negative), and (2) a positive wealth effect of debt on private demand. The model is in real (and inflation adjusted) terms. Let y be real output (income), $\theta = g/y$ the income ratio of government expenditure on goods and services, $\delta = d/y$ the income ratio of government debt, and $\eta = \dot{d}/y$ the income ratio of the real, inflation adjusted, deficit.[1] $g - \dot{d} = (\theta - \eta)y$ are thus real government revenues (real net transfers to the government less real interest on public debt), and $y_d = (1 - \theta + \eta)y$ is real private net disposable income. Real private saving is assumed to be a linear function of real net disposable income and of total private wealth, K (real physical capital) plus d. according to a simple expression like

$$S = -\alpha k + [\sigma(1 - \theta + \eta) - \alpha\delta]y.[2] \qquad (10.1)$$

with the given definition of $\dot{d}$, rearranging terms the expression for real private saving less the deficit becomes

$$s - \dot{d} = -\alpha k + (\sigma(1 - \theta) - [(1 - \sigma)\eta + \alpha\delta])y. \qquad (10.2)$$

Let v be Domar's 'capital coefficient', so that

$$y_{fc} = vk \qquad (10.3)$$

is full capacity output (supply), and let $i = \dot{k}$ be investment, so that

$$\frac{i}{k} = \hat{k} = \gamma \tag{10.4}$$

is the (real) growth rate of capital and of full capacity supply.[3] Full capacity saving and saving less the deficit, both expressed as ratios to k, are given, respectively, by

$$\left(\frac{s}{k}\right)_{fc} = -\alpha + \sigma(1 - \theta + \eta - \alpha\delta)v \tag{10.1'}$$

and

$$\left(\frac{s-\dot{d}}{k}\right)_{fc} = -\alpha + (\sigma(1-\theta) - [(1-\sigma)\eta + \alpha\delta])v. \tag{10.2'}$$

As is well known the steady state debt income ratio is given by

$$\delta_\infty = \frac{\eta}{\gamma} \tag{10.5}$$

so that in steady state (2') becomes

$$\left(\frac{s-\dot{d}}{k}\right)_{fc,\infty} = -\alpha + [\sigma(1-\theta) - \left(1 - \sigma + \frac{\alpha}{\gamma}\right)\eta]v \tag{10.2''}$$

Excess demand is the difference between investment and saving less the deficit. Our basic expression is the ratio of steady state full capacity excess demand to capital as a non-linear function of the growth rate:

$$ed_\infty(\gamma) = \frac{i}{k} - \left(\frac{s-\dot{d}}{k}\right)_{fc,\infty}$$

$$= \gamma - [\sigma(1-\theta)v - \alpha] + \left(1 - \sigma + \frac{\alpha}{\gamma}\right)v\eta. \tag{10.6}$$

To slightly simplify notation we put

$$a_1 = \sigma(1-\theta)$$
$$a_2 = 1 - \sigma \tag{10.7}$$

and, rearranging, rewrite (10.6) as

$$ed_\infty(\gamma) = \gamma - (a_1 v - \alpha) + \left(a_2 + \frac{\alpha}{\gamma}\right) v\eta. \tag{10.6}$$

The graph of this function is represented in Figure 10.1.

If we take α (the wealth effect coefficient), v (Domar's capital coefficient) and η (the deficit income ratio) as our basic parameters, it is a plain exercise to see how they affect the shape and position of the

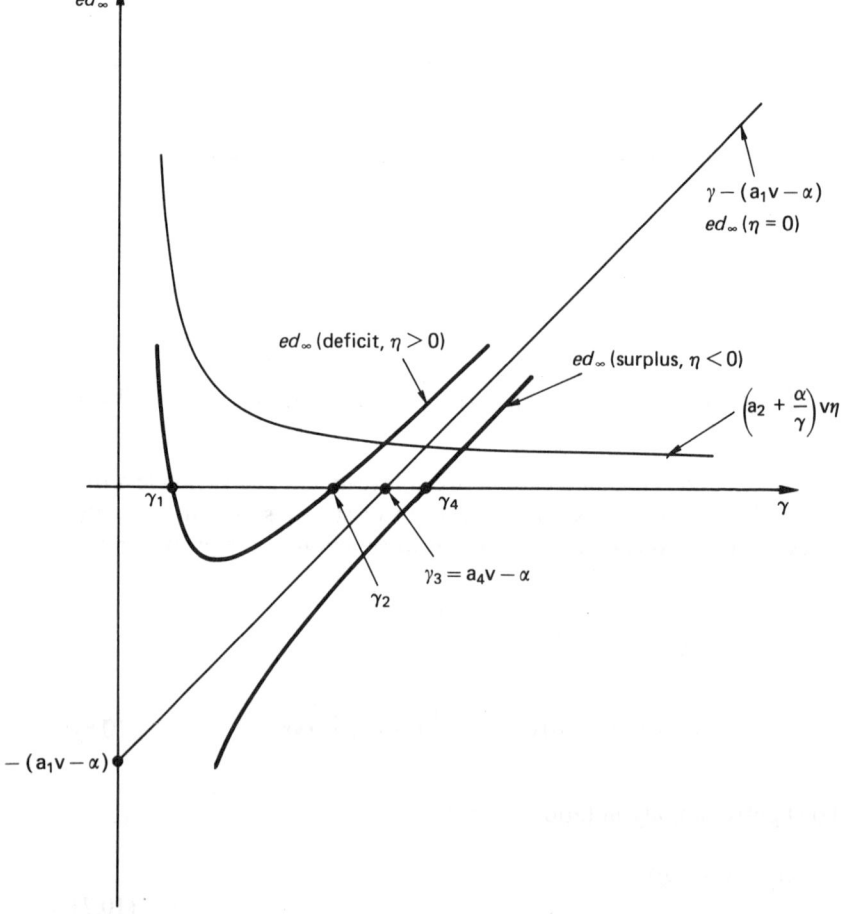

Figure 10.1   Growth and steady state full capacity excess demand

$ed_\infty(\gamma)$ curve. For a given α and v, with a balanced budget ($\eta = 0$) $ed_\infty(\gamma)$ coincides with the straight line $\gamma - (a_1 v - \alpha)$, and the equilibrium growth rate is $a_1 v - \alpha = \gamma_3$. As η becomes positive (a deficit), $ed_\infty(\gamma)$ takes up a shape like the thick curve to the left of the $\gamma - (a_1 v - \alpha)$ line. There would be two equilibrium growth rates like γ_1 and γ_2, both lower than γ_3. As η rises further these two growth rates move towards each other, until they meet at some intermediate point where the curve $ed_\infty(\gamma)$ just touches the horizontal axis. A further rise in η lifts $ed_\infty(\gamma)$ fully above the horizontal axis, and an equilibrium growth rate would no longer exist. Due to the wealth effect of public debt such a deficit would, in the long run, be 'unsustainable' with *any* growth rate, in the sense that no growth rate, however high, would be capable of absorbing the excess demand caused by such deficit through the wealth effect. On the other hand, as η becomes negative (a surplus), $ed_\infty(\gamma)$ takes up a shape like the thick curve to the right of the $\gamma - (a_1 v - \alpha)$ line, this time again with a single equilibrium growth like γ_4, higher than γ_3.

Predictably, the effects of a rise in α for given η (positive) and v are qualitatively similar to those of a rise in η. The $ed_\infty(\gamma)$ curve would move upwards, with a rise in the lowest equilibrium growth rate and a decline in the highest one.

The effects of a rise in v for given η and α are especially meaningful, because such a rise may be interpreted as an improvement in the general productivity of the economy. But we shall postpone its discussion because the present formulation, as represented by Figure 10.1 is not suited to it.[4]

As a purely computational problem, the conditions for the existence of equilibrium growth rates may be derived from the quadratic formula of elementary algebra. (10.6') may be rewritten as

$$ed_\infty(\gamma) = \frac{\gamma^2 - [(a_1 - a_2 \eta)v - \alpha]\gamma + \alpha \eta v}{\gamma}, \quad \gamma \neq 0 \qquad (10.6'')$$

and the zeros of the numerator are given by

$$\gamma_e = \frac{[(a_4 - a_2 \eta)v - \alpha] \pm ([(a_4 - a_2 \eta)v - \alpha]^2 - 4\alpha \eta v)^{\frac{1}{2}}}{2}. \qquad (10.8)$$

Provided $[(a_4 - a_2 \eta)v - \alpha]$ and $4\alpha \eta n$ are both positive, there will be two distinct real and positive values of γ_e, or only one, or none, according to the relationship

$$[(a_1 - a_2\eta)v - \alpha]^2 \gtreqless 4\alpha\eta v. \tag{10.9}$$

In order to provide a more intuitive reference for the foregoing arguments it is useful to illustrate them in terms of a different diagram, such as Figure 10.2. We represent on the vertical axis (1) the ratio of investment to capital, which is equal to the growth rate of full capacity supply (equation (10.4) above), and (2) the steady state full capacity ratio of saving less the deficit to capital (equation (10.2″) above).

For given values of η and γ (10.2″) is shown in the diagram as a straight line originating in $0'$, with $\alpha = \overline{00'}$ and with slope $[a_1 - (a_2 + \alpha/\gamma)\eta]$. For a given v, say v_0, the distance between γ and the intersection of such line with the vertical in v_0 represents the steady

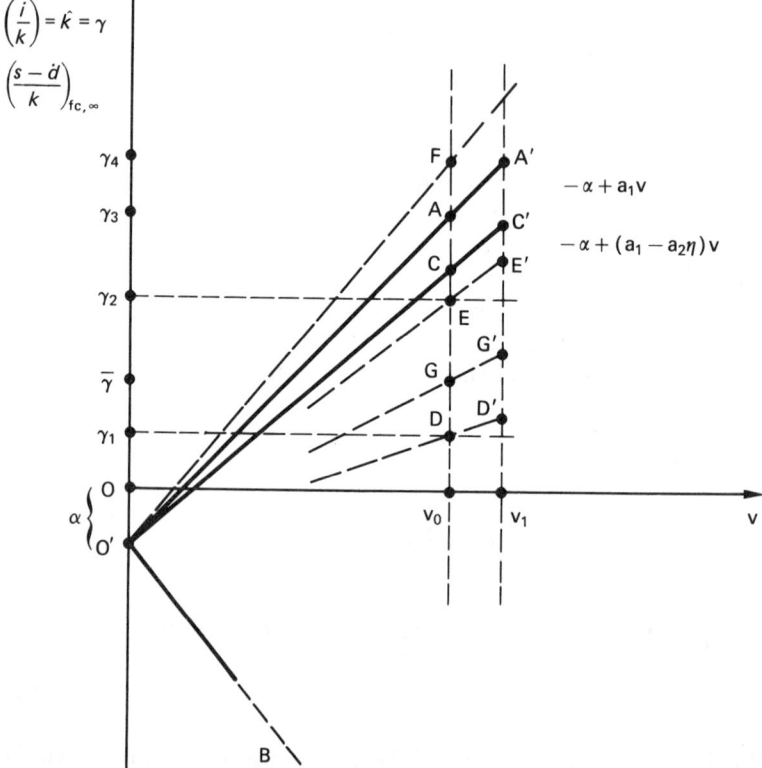

Figure 10.2 Full capacity output, budget balance, and equilibrium growth

state full capacity excess demand (10.6′). With a balanced budget ($\eta = 0$) the line would be $\overline{O'A}$, with slope a_1 and equilibrium growth γ_3. With a deficit ($\eta > 0$) the slope of the line depends on γ. With a very low γ, close to zero, the line is negatively sloped and very steep, such as $\overline{O'B}$ (excess demand). As γ rises the line rotates upwards, and for very high values of γ it tends to approach $\overline{O'C}$, with slope $(a_1 - a_2\eta)$. In the process the intersection of the line with the vertical in v_o will first catch up with γ, say at $D = \gamma_1$, then, over a limited range, lie above it (excess supply), until the two coincide again, say at $E = \gamma_2$, while thereafter the excess of γ over the intersection will continue to grow. With a surplus ($\eta < 0$) the intersection of the line with the vertical in v_o will lie above A for any γ, while the identification of the latter's equilibrium value (say, $F = \gamma_4$) is obtained by the same type of reasoning as in the deficit case. At an equilibrium growth rate like γ_4 a budget surplus finances part of private investment, and indeex in steady state total private net wealth is less than the stock of physical capital.

The present formulation, as represented by Figure 10.2, lends itself to a direct identification of the effects of an increase in v on the equilibrium growth rates. Suppose v increased from v_o to v_1. It can be seen that, at v_1, γ_1 is no longer an equilibrium growth rate. D' lies above it, which means that there is excess supply. As γ decreases, the line $\overline{O'DD'}$ rotates downwards, until its intersection with the vertical line through v_1 comes to coincide with some new γ, positive but lower than γ_1. Similarly, at v_1 there is excess supply also at the growth rate γ_2, because E' lies above it. But here output market equilibrium is reached through an *increase* in γ. This rotates $O'EE'$ upwards. Its intersection with the vertical in v_1 also rises, but at a decreasing speed, until γ catches up with it. Thus inspection of Figure 10.2 shows unambiguously that an increase in v raises the highest of the two equilibrium growth rates, while it depresses the lowest one. In terms of Figure 10.1 this means that the curve $ed_\infty(\gamma)$ moves downwards, thereby raising also the level of the highest deficit sustainable by some equilibrium growth.

An increase in v may be interpreted as an increase in the productivity of productive capacity, in the sense that a given productive capacity is capable of producing more output. This interpretation of v provides the simplest way of here dealing with the supply side role of public expenditure, which many regard as a more important one, in the long run, than its demand side role.

One standard approach to the macroeconomics of the supply side role of public expenditure (on goods and services) is to decompose it into a consumption and an investment component. The first, treated as part of aggregate consumption, has no supply side effects, while the latter, treated as part of aggregate capital accumulation (public capital), acts on supply precisely as such, as an increase of productive capacity. Now, while any precise distinction between consumption and investment expenditure is to some extent arbitrary, whether in the public *or* in the private sector, it is bound to be much more so in the former than in the latter, due to the peculiar, non market nature of most public expenditure items.

For this reason, a useful alternative approach would be to consider all public expenditure as having potentially some positive supply side effects. In various ways and to various degrees (depending on the nature, quality and technical efficiency of the services provided) all its components are required for, or may contribute to, the satisfactory functioning of the private, market sector of the economy, and thereby favour its overall productivity. As exceptions, at one end of the spectrum, there may be items which are strict substitutes of true private consumption. These would have no appreciable supply side effects, while they may or may not affect the private propensity to save. The simplest way to incorporate this view into the present model would be to let v be an increasing function of θ, with the understanding that v may also be affected, positively or negatively, by changing quality and composition of a given level of θ.

3 ACTUAL GROWTH, WEALTH AND THE REQUIRED BUDGET BALANCE

In this section, the reasoning of the preceding one is reversed. In Figure 10.2 let $G = \bar{\gamma}$ be an exogenously given growth rate. With a balanced budget the line $\overline{O'A}$ would show a full capacity excess supply measured by the excess of A over G. As the deficit rises the line rotates downwards, until it becomes $\overline{O'G}$. Such 'required' deficit absorbs full capacity excess supply and makes $\bar{\gamma}$ into an equilibrium growth rate. If exogenous growth were at something like γ_4 the required budget balance would be a surplus, which would absorb full capacity excess demand through a partial financing of private investment. Formally the 'required' steady state full capacity budget balance for an exogenous growth rate is obtained from (10.6'), by setting $ed_\infty(\gamma) = 0$ and then expressing η_∞ as a nonlinear function of γ:

$$\eta_\infty(\alpha) = \frac{[(a_1 v - \alpha) - \alpha]\gamma}{a_2 v \gamma + \alpha v} \qquad (10.10)$$

which is the inverse of the previous paragraph's relationship associating two distinct values of the growth rate to each value of the deficit. Equation (10.10) is represented in Figure 10.3.

The required budget balance of equation (10.10) is a steady state one. It is of some interest to widen the picture by considering what would be the required budget balance for an economy which starts off from a non-steady state position. In any period, the budget balance required for full capacity output market equilibrium is given by

$$\frac{\dot{d}}{k} = \left(\frac{s-i}{k}\right)_{fc} = \left(\frac{s}{k}\right)_{fc} - \gamma \qquad (10.11)$$

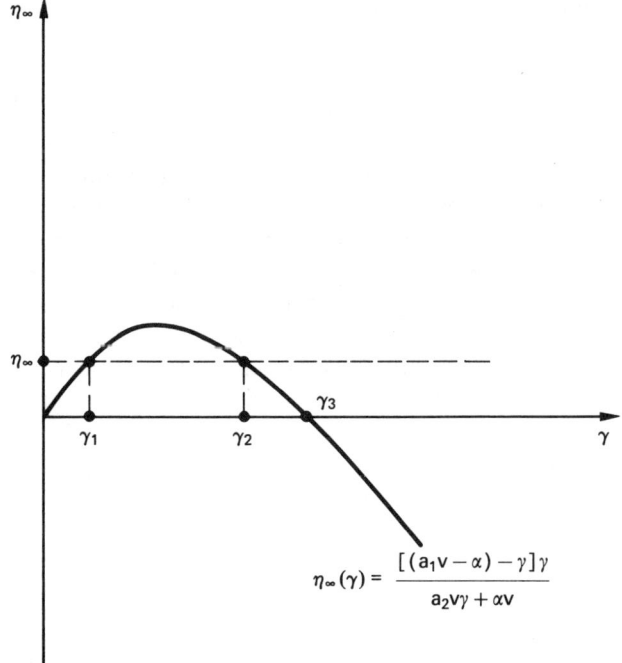

Figure 10.3 Exogenous growth and required budget balance

By simple manipulation[5] (10.11) translates into the following elementary differential equation in δ:

$$\dot{\delta} + \frac{a_2\gamma + \alpha}{a_2}\delta = \frac{(a_1v - \alpha) - \gamma}{a_2v} \tag{10.12}$$

To simplify notation we put

$$b_1 = \frac{a_2\gamma + \alpha}{a_2} = \gamma + \frac{\alpha}{a_2}$$

$$b_2 = \frac{(a_1v - \alpha) - \gamma}{a_2v} \tag{10.13}$$

and rewrite (10.12) as

$$\dot{\delta} + b_1\delta = b_2. \tag{10.12'}$$

Its solution

$$\delta(x) = Ae^{-b_1x} + \frac{b_2}{b_1} \tag{10.14}$$

(where x is time) gives the time path of the debt income ratio $\delta(x)$, under an exogenous growth rate and a budget balance which is being continuously adjusted to ensure persistent full capacity output market equilibrium (assuming the average real interest on debt and the income ratio of government expenditure to remain unchanged, the budget adjustment will have to come through taxation). By the definition of b_1 in (10.13), if there is a positive wealth coefficient $\alpha > 0$, then $b_1 > \gamma \geqslant 0$ (only non-negative growth rates are considered). Thus, starting from any initial level δ_o, δ converges to its steady-state value $\delta_\infty = b_2/b_1$, with $A = \delta_o - \delta_\infty$.

On the other hand, substitution of (10.14) into $\eta = \dot{\delta} + \delta\gamma$[6] gives the time path of the required deficit income ratio (10.15)

$$\eta(x) = \dot{\delta}(x) + \delta(x)\gamma = (\gamma - b_1)Ae^{-b_1x} + \frac{b_2}{b_1}\gamma. \tag{10.15}$$

Since $(\gamma - b_1) < 0$ we see that, if $\delta_o < \delta_\infty$ ($A < 0$), then $\eta(x)$ rises as $\delta(x)$ declines, while $\delta_o > \delta_\infty$ ($A > 0$) implies the opposite.

This behaviour over time of the debt and deficit income ratios can be readily visualised in Figure 10.2. It has been previously seen that with an exogenous actual growth like $\bar{y}$ the steady state line making it into an equilibrium one would be $\overline{0'G}$, which is equation (10.2″) with $\gamma = \bar{y}$ and η equal to the steady state required deficit. If the economy starts off with a debt income ratio *lower* than the steady state one, then the relevant equation for full capacity saving less the deficit becomes (10.2′). Let's put $\delta_o < \delta_\infty$ in (10.2′). If we want the line represented by (10.2′) to coincide with that represented by (10.2″), namely $\overline{0'G}$, then the required *initial* value of η in (10.2′) must be *higher* than its required steady state value in (10.2″). But over time such higher deficit pushes the debt income ratio upwards, and as this rises towards its steady state value δ_∞ the required full capacity deficit declines, because of the wealth effect of the rising δ. Due to a low initial debt income ratio, the deficit income ratio required to absorb full capacity excess supply is sufficiently high as to cause the debt income ratio to grow. On the other hand, starting with a debt income ratio *higher* than the steady state one, persistent full capacity output market equilibrium would require a similar but opposite process.

The first of the above cases is just a generalisation to a growth setting of the conventional idea that if full capacity equilibrium requires a certain deficit, and if demand is wealth dependent, then the initially required deficit may be self-reducing because the induced debt growth tends to close the excess supply gap. As is intuitive, in a growth setting the initially required deficit: income ratio might instead be *self-increasing*, if the induced debt growth were slower than the trend growth of capital and output.

The foregoing discussion, although containing statements on the economics of fiscal policy, is based on a highly stylised model. This does not detract from the meaningfulness of such statements, but the stages of reasoning and empirical assessments required to move from them to practical propositions about actual situations are very many indeed, and we do not propose to embark on them here. However, we mention briefly two of the issues which would be met at the very beginning.

The first concerns the relationship between the real, inflation adjusted deficit considered so far, which we have denoted by $\eta = \dot{d}/y$, and the nominal deficit, which we may denote by $\tilde{\eta} = \dot{D}/Y$, where D is nominal debt and Y nominal income. The relationship is the following

$$\eta = \tilde{\eta} \frac{\hat{y}}{\hat{Y}} \qquad (10.16)$$

and is obtained immediately from the definitions.[7] Given some nominal deficit, if there is inflation the corresponding real adjusted deficit will be lower, and the higher the inflation and the lower the growth rate the lower it will be. Through budget policy and authorities have direct control over the nominal deficit. If they are capable, and willing, to separately control inflation, then in principle they can achieve any real deficit they like. But if when they increase the nominal deficit they cannot prevent also inflation from rising, then their possibility of pursuing a 'real' budget policy is weakened, or vanishes altogether.

The second issue concerns the role of employment constraints in the present model. With respect to this our discussion has been based upon two rather strong assumptions, namely that the long-run real growth rate of output is determined by, and coincides with, the rate of capital accumulation ($i/k = \hat{k}$) and changes as this changes, and that there is a long-run tendency for full employment and full capacity labour intensities to coincide. Whether, and to what extent, these assumptions are acceptable will, of course, always be debatable. Whichever position one may take in the controversy, it is useful to appreciate the precise implications of the assumptions within the model itself. The standard way to do so is to view the technology of the model in terms of a fixed coefficients production function, in capital and *effective* labour units as inputs, and then to apply the usual reasoning and interpretations of neoclassical growth theory.

Leaving out the details of the exercise,[8] we shall confine ourselves here to its basic conclusions. In the presence of a dynamic employment constraint, the assumption that the rate of capital accumulation determines, and coincides *tout court* with, the real growth rate of output implies that in the long run the growth rate of *effective* labour supply tends to coincide with that of capital. With a given growth rate (n) of the *natural* labour supply, this would in turn require the rate of technical progress (λ) to rise or fall in line with that of capital accumulation, so as to ensure always $n + \lambda = \hat{k} = \gamma$. This is a strong requirement, but it not altogether implausible. The other assumption is the long-run tendency of full employment and full capacity (effective) labour intensities to coincide. This implies that if, at some time, the former were *lower* than the latter (excess capacity = excess demand for labour), then either the (effective) real wage would tend to rise, bringing forth more labour supply, or the rate of capital accumulation would temporarily slow down, until complete absorbtion of excess capacity is achieved. If the former were *higher* than the latter (insufficient capacity = excess supply of labour), then there would be an opposite process.

4 TAX BURDEN, DEFICIT AND GROWTH

Our discussion has been centered so far on deficit government expenditure and growth. Two further important variables have not been brought out explicitly, namely the average real interest on government debt and the average tax burden, or macro-tax rate. A useful way of doing so is by generalising Domar's 'burden of the debt' formula.

Let R be the nominal interest rate on nominal interest bearing government debt B, M be the nominal non-interest bearing government debt (say, monetary base), and h be the steady state share of the former in total debt $D = B + M$, $\left(\dfrac{B}{D}\right)_\infty = h$. The steady state average nominal interest will be $R_a = hR$, and the average real interest will of course be

$$r_a = hR - \pi \tag{10.17}$$

(π is the inflation rate). The average tax burden is then defined as the ratio of total tax revenues t to private gross disposable income $y + r_a d$

$$t = \tau(y + r_a d).^9 \tag{10.18}$$

By simple manipulation of the definitions we obtain[10]

$$\tau = \frac{r_a \eta + (\theta - \eta)\gamma}{r_a \eta + \gamma}. \tag{10.19}$$

This macro-tax rate is represented, as a function of γ and for given values of r_a, η, θ, in Figure 4. Simple reasoning on the diagram shows that with a balanced budget ($\eta = 0$) the average tax burden coincides, trivially, with the share of government expenditure (the horizontal dotted line at θ). As the deficit rises, with fixed θ, the average tax burden assumes a shape like the dotted curve τ. When η coincides with θ it becomes the thick curve τ_d. As η rises further above θ it approaches the straight dotted line joining 1 on the vertical axis to r_a on the horizontal one. The curve τ_d represents Domar's burden of the debt as a function of the growth rate, because the condition $\eta = \theta$ is equivalent to the condition $\tau(y + r_a d) = r_a d$, i.e. that τ be the ratio of the average real interest bill on government debt to gross private disposable income, such ratio being Domar's measure of the debt burden, adjusted for inflation. It may be noticed that as $\eta = \theta$ rise together, the curve τ_d moves upwards assuming a shape like τ'_d.

It is of some interest to observe that as the average tax burden curve

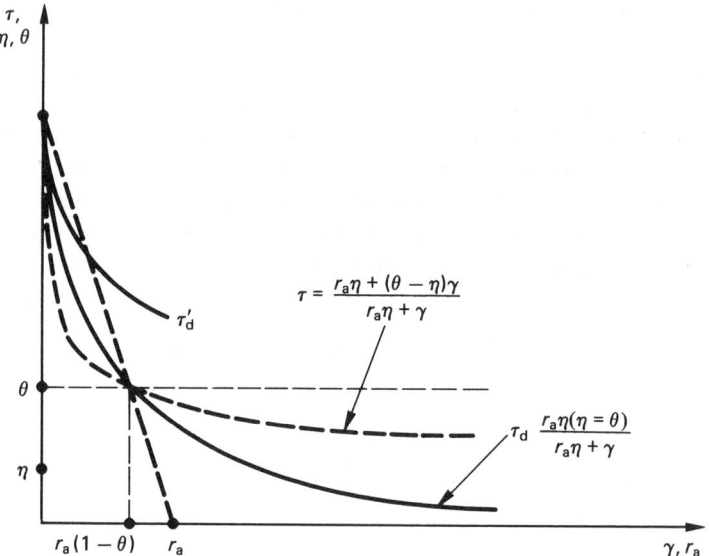

Figure 10.4 Growth, deficit and average tax burden

τ becomes steeper and steeper, due to a rise in η with constant θ, it always keeps passing through the fixed point whose coordinates are $r_a(1-\theta)$ and θ.[11] In steady state, if the real growth rate is greater than $r_a(1-\theta)$ then a rise in the deficit with constant θ *decreases* the average tax burden, or alternatively, a decrease in the average tax burden *increases* the deficit. If the growth rate is less than $r_a(1-\theta)$, then a rise in the deficit *increases* the average tax burden. $r_a(1-\theta)$ is the critical level of real growth. Below that an increase in the deficit generates in the long run such an increase in the interest bill that the average tax burden must itself rise with the deficit. It may also be observed in the diagram how a change in the steady state composition of the debt (a change in h), by changing r_a, would alter the shape of the debt and average tax burden functions.

The logical integration of the relationships of Figure 10.4 into the discussion of the preceding paragraphs is simply obtained by super-imposing Figure 10.3 on to Figure 10.4. Starting from an exogenous growth rate, with given values of θ and r_a the two diagrams together determine the required deficit, and the debt and average tax burdens associated with it. Alternatively, starting with some feasible deficit, the two diagrams determine the two equilibrium growth rates, and the debt and average tax burdens associated with each of these.

APPENDIX: NOTATION

B	interest bearing nominal government debt
d, D	real and nominal total government debt
ed_∞	ratio of steady state full capacity excess demand to physical capital
g	real government expenditure on goods and services
h	share of interest bearing debt into total debt
$i = \dot{k}$	real investment
k	real (private) physical capital
M	non-interest bearing government debt
n	growth rate of natural labour supply
P	price level
R	nominal interest rate
$r_a = hR - \pi$	real average interest rate
$R_a = hR$	nominal average interest rate
s	real private saving
t	real total tax revenues
v	Domar's capital coefficient
y, Y	real and nominal output (income)
y_d	real net disposable income
$y_{fc} = vk$	full capacity output
α	coefficient for wealth induced demand
γ	growth rate of real output
$\delta = \dfrac{d}{y}$	income ratio of government debt
$\eta = \dfrac{\dot{d}}{y}$	income ratio of real (inflation adjusted) deficit
$\tilde{\eta} = \dfrac{\dot{D}}{Y}$	income ratio of nominal deficit
$\theta = \dfrac{g}{y}$	income ratio of government expenditure
λ	rate of (labour augmenting) technical progress
π	inflation rate
σ	marginal propensity to save out of net disposable income
τ	average tax burden (macro tax rate) on gross disposable income
τ_d	Domar's 'burden of the debt'
x	time
$(\dot{\ })$	time derivative
$(\hat{\ })$	time rate of change

Notes

I wish to express special thanks to Ragnar Bentzel, who, as the discussant of this paper, subjected it to a number of critical remarks and suggestions for improvement, all of which I found very precisely valid and relevant. In the revision I benefited from them as well as from the other comments and discussion in and out of the conference room. I alone of course bear responsibility for the final text.

1. See note 7 for the definitional relationship between real, inflation adjusted deficit and nominal deficit.
2. From $s = -\alpha(k+d) + \sigma(1-\theta+\eta)y$, substituting δy for d, and rearranging. α is the coefficient measuring wealth induced consumption demand (a rise in $(k+d)$ decreases saving, i.e. increases consumption, for given disposable income) and σ is the marginal propensity to save out of disposable income. A further specification of the saving function would be to split α into two distinct coefficients, one for real physical wealth and one, presumably lower, for public debt, while an important extension of it in another direction would be to allow saving to depend also on the growth rate itself, as is suggested by many empirical studies.
3. It would be simple, but qualitatively immaterial for our present purposes, to include depreciation in the picture.
4. As can be seen in the diagram, a rise in v would both move the $(a_2 + \alpha/\gamma)v\eta$ curve upwards and shift the line $\gamma - (a_1 v - \alpha)$ downwards, so that the net result on the two equilibrium growth rates is not immediately obvious.
5. (1) substitute ηv for $\dot{d}/K (\dot{d}/K = \dot{d}/y \; y/k = \eta v)$, (2) substitute equation and (4) rearrange terms.
6. See note 5(3).
7. Differentiate $d = D/P$ with respect to time (P is the price level), and divide by y. $\hat{y}$ is the growth rate of real income and $\hat{Y} = \hat{y} + \pi$ is that of nominal income (π is inflation).
8. For an exposition of the analytics and diagrammatic technique, see Wan, 1971, pp. 40ff.
9. $y + r_a d$ is real gross disposable income, adjusted for inflation. In order to concentrate on the debt related magnitudes we define real gross disposable income as real output plus real debt interest payments, while all other transfers from the government to the private economy are deduced from gross tax revenues.
10. (1) $\dot{d} = g - t + r_a d$, (2) by substituting (10.18) into (1), dividing by y, substituting the steady state value η/γ for d/y, and rearranging, we obtain (10.19).
11. This can easily be proved by differentiating τ with respect to η, or, ex post, by substituting $\gamma = r_a(1-\theta)$ into (10.19).

References

Dernburg, T. F. (1962) 'A Note on Productivity, Wealth and Fiscal Policy', *National Tax Journal*, vol. 15, no. 3, September, pp. 327–9.

Domar, E. D. (1944) 'The "Burden of the Debt" and the National Income', *American Economic Review*, vol. 34, December, pp. 798–827.

Domar, E. D. (1946) 'Capital Expansion, Rate of Growth and Employment', *Econometrica*, vol. 14, April, pp. 137–47.

Domar, E. D. (1947) 'Expansion and Employment', *American Economic Review*, vol. 37, March, pp. 34–55.
Lerner, A. P. (1943) 'Functional Finance and the Federal Debt', *Social Research*, vol. 10, no. 1, February, pp. 38–51.
Wan, H. Y. Jr (1971) *Economic Growth* (: Harcourt Brace).

DISCUSSION

The purpose of this paper is to extend the Domar model of growth to incorporate budget deficits. The underlying assumption is that public debt contributes positively to private wealth. In addition, the consumption function is specified as a linear function of income and private wealth.

The first part of the paper deals with the relationship between the deficit, wealth and equilibrium growth rates. With a budget surplus or budget balance, there is a unique equilibrium growth rate. However, with a budget deficit, there is the possibility of two, one, or zero equilibrium growth rates. No equilibrium exists when the deficit is sufficiently large.

The second part of the chapter takes the reverse approach: it asks what deficit is necessary to ensure a given growth rate. A specific formula is presented relating the needed deficit positively to the growth rate.

Professor Bentzel the principal discussant complimented the overall model, but saw some useful modifications. He thought that allowing the government to hold capital would be a realistic and not too difficult extension. He would have liked to see an explicit treatment of inflation.[1] He also believed that the evidence warranted treating saving as a function of the rate of growth as well as disposable income and wealth. Finally, he noted that the lack of treatment of labour issues[2] allowed the odd conclusion that the government could generate any growth rate it wanted, by manipulating the deficit. Some constraint on growth should be included.

Professor Gorini agreed that there was no treatment of inflation; the analysis focused solely on real ratios. He also agreed that including employment would be reasonable and useful. On the lack of government capital, he noted that ideally all public expenditures should contribute to the better working of the private economy, which is the important issue here. He did venture to say that public expenditure that is a close substitute for private consumption should increase the private saving ratio. However, he agreed with *Dr Vito Tanzi*, who said that the overall savings rate would not necessarily be affected.

Professor Michael Boskin noted that in this model a fiscal stimulus at below full employment would increase consumption through the wealth effect and thereby provide a reinforcing expansionary effect. He also wondered if the author had attempted to use any actual parameter values to examine some of the model's implications.

Professor Eisner asked about the possibility of a self-eliminating deficit; i.e. a fiscal stimulus that would raise consumption and aggregate demand sufficiently to remove the need for any further fiscal stimulus. *Professor Gorini* replied that since the debt to capital stock ratio must be constant in a steady state growth equilibrium, debt must continually grow; that is, deficits must be positive. Nevertheless, from an initial point with a low debt:capital ratio, optimal policy would be to have large deficits now followed by small deficits later. This is analogous to the self-eliminating deficits described above.

Professor Eisner then suggested that if the economy is chronically below full employment, then a permanent deficit would be warranted. A number of commentators questioned Eisner's underlying assumptions and the time frame involved.

Notes

1. Some comment on these matters is now included in the revised text.
2. See note 1.

Index

Abe, H. 190
Abreu, D. 68
Adams, G. 111
altruism, intergenerational 71, 86–8, 135, 137–42, 227
amortisation 134–9, 145, 195, 238
see also depreciation
Ando, A. 39, 86
Argentina
  foreigh debt 243, 260, 290
  stabilisation 260
Arrow, K. J. vii, viii, ix, x, xiii–xvii, 40, 118, 197, 223, 224–7
Arrow–Debreu model of general equilibrium 44, 62–3, 70, 73
Aschauer, D. A. 152
assets, government *see* wealth, government
Atkinson, A. B. 43, 54, 68, 70, 174, 189
Atoda, N. 190
Auerbach, A. J. 83, 84, 174, 175, 189, 197
Austro-Hungarian school 117

Bacha, E. L. viii
Bailey, M 86
Baker, Secretary J. 230–1
Baker plan countries 230–63
balance of payments
  and fiscal policy 40, 237–42
  and foreign debt 232–3, 236–49, 252–3
  and government deficit xiv, 20–8, 39, 77, 80, 82, 85, 105–7, 154, 187–8, 236–42
Ballabon, M. B. 287
bankruptcy 48
Barham, B. 79, 94, 95, 107

Barro, R. J. 37, 68, 71, 78, 86, 87, 89, 100, 107, 108, 114, 150–1, 152, 158, 159, 192, 193, 195, 196, 202, 203
Barth, J. R. 87
Bellman equation 123–4
Ben-Porath, Y. 287
Bentzel, R. viii, x, 197, 307, 309
Bernheim, D. x, 75, 76, 86
Beveridge, S. 156, 157
Blanchard, O. J. 152, 192
Blejer, M. I. x, xvi, 230–63
Blinder, A. 68
Bogomolov, O. T. viii
Bolivia, foreign debt 243, 260
bonds, government
  contingent 219–20, 227
  demand 159, 217
  indexation xiv, xvi, 71, 261, 271–83, 286–7
  price 45, 61–8, 71, 205, 232, 234
  and rate of interest 68
  see also debt, public
Borner, S. viii, x
Boskin, M. J. vii, x, xiii–xvii, 40, 77–115, 147, 148, 152, 188, 189, 194–5, 196, 228, 290, 310
Bradford, D. 68
Brahmananda, P. R. viii
Brazil
  foreign debt 230, 236, 243, 260
  stabilisation 260
Brumberg, R. 86
Brunner, K. 108
Bruno, M. 280
Buchanan, J. 145
Buiter, W. H. 108
Burbridge, J. B. 150

311

Cagan, P. 94, 235
Calvo, G. A. 189
Canada
  government deficits 167–8
  growth 3
  capital stock 207–23
Carter, President J. 79
Cass, D. 68
chain-letter mechanism 158–73
Chamley, C. x, 197, 223, 228, 290
Chicago school 117
Chile, foreign debt 243, 260
Colombia, foreign debt 243, 260
Cone, K. 79, 94, 95
consumer durables 99, 107
consumption function
  and expenditure 5–28, 32–7, 89–107, 185–7, 294–306, 308
  and inflation 269, 289
  life-cycle theory 5, 43–5, 49–54, 85–8, 118–28, 147, 155, 160–2, 174–6, 193, 195–6, 228
  permanent income theory 5, 86–8, 114, 192
  and rate of interest 115
  and taxation 49–68, 133–48, 201–23, 224–9
Côte d'Ivoire, foreign debt 243, 260
Cox, W. M. 33, 34
credit restraint 76
Csikós-Nagy, B. viii, x
Currie, D. A. 202

Darby, M. 86
David, M. 86
Deane, P. ix, x
Debreu, G. 44, 62–3, 70, 73
debt, public
  and development 43, 68, 230–60
  foreign 235–6, 242–60
  and inflation 3, 59–61, 71, 94, 234–9, 264–86
  intertemporal transfer 83–7, 133–48, 149–87, 191–7, 202–23
  maturity 44, 48, 61–4, 78, 205, 261
  in national accounting 32–7, 79–88

and private sector 50, 232–3
Say's Law 42–9, 75–6, 87
and wealth 292–306, 309–310
see also deficits, government; investment, crowding in/out
deficits, government
  and balance of payments xiv, 20–8, 39, 77, 80, 82, 85, 105–7, 154, 187–8, 236–42
  and consumption/saving 78–93, 96–107, 133–9, 152, 160–2, 298–300
  and employment 68, 77–86, 93–6, 99–107, 133, 304
  and exchange rate 20, 234
  and growth xvi, 133, 142–4, 147, 230–60, 292–306
  and inflation xiii, xiv, 3, 40, 59–61, 77–8, 80–3, 158, 234–9, 290, 303–4
  and investment 43, 77–88, 90–107, 150, 171–2, 298–304
  and public expenditure 26, 84, 150, 176, 202–23, 231, 233–5, 238, 283–6
  and rate of interest xiii, 3, 40, 82, 85, 153–4, 197, 205–23
  sustainability xiii, 159–68, 297–304, 310
  see also taxation
demand management 143, 154
Denmark, foreign debt 230
depreciation 79, 84, 308
Dernberg, T. F. 293
Diamond, P. A. 68, 86, 149–50, 151, 158, 159, 160, 162, 174, 176, 193, 196
Dicks-Mireaux, L. 86
Djajic, S. 120, 129
Domar, E. D. 292–6, 305, 307, 309
Dornbusch, R. 68, 74

Ecuador, foreign debt 243, 260
Edwards, J. 74
Eisner, R. x, xiv, 3–40, 79, 84, 88, 90, 94, 108, 148, 195, 196, 197, 291, 310
Ellis, H. S. ix

employment
  and government deficits 68,
    77–86, 93–6, 99–107, 133, 304
  and money supply 4–20, 28, 41,
    116–18
  and public debt xiv, 4–20, 43, 48
equivalence, Ricardian xiv, 37, 78,
    89–90, 103, 113, 133–9, 203,
    221, 226, 292
Evans, O. J. 174, 189
exchange control 281, 282
exchange rate
  black-market 274
  and government deficit 20
  risk 83
expectations
  exchange rate 83, 241–2
  government debt 40, 52–4, 56
  government expenditure 89
  inflation 55–8, 242, 265–71
  interest rates 266–73
  money supply 41
  risk 56–8, 266–71
  tax liability 42, 65, 73, 90, 93,
    223, 228

Farhadian, Z. 260
Feldstein, M. S. 79, 83, 87, 88, 89,
    100, 107, 112, 152, 174, 192,
    193, 195
Fellner, W. 112
Ferguson, J. E. 145, 146
fiscal policy see taxation
Fischer, S. 68, 278, 279, 280, 286
Fisher, I. 126
Fitoussi, J.-P. vii, viii, x, 287–9
Flanders, K. J. 74
Flemming, J. S. x, xv–xvi, 115, 118,
    147, 196, 201–29
France
  government deficits 167–8
  growth 3
Franks, J. 74
Friedman, M. 39, 260
Fuchs, V. x
Furstenberg, G. M. von 110

Gale, D. 94, 150, 160, 164
Gale, W. x

Germany, Federal Republic
  government deficits 167–8
  growth 3
Goldsmith, R. W. 114, 115
Gordon, R. H. 109
Gorini, S. x, xvi–xvii, 223, 292–310
Grandmont, J. M. 68
Greenwald, B. 66

Haberler, G. ix, 37
Hahn, F. H. 68, 203
Hammond, P. J. 221
Hansen, A. H. 116
Harris, S. 145
Hausman, J. 86
Heal, G. M. 191
Helpman, E. 108
Herben, B. 287
Hickman, G. B. x, 40
Hillebrandt, P. M. ix
Holloway, T. M. 35, 78, 94
Homma, M. 152, 157
Hotelling, H. 116
Howrey, E. P. 111
Huber, A. 79, 84, 90, 91, 92, 93, 98,
    108
Hughes, G. A. 191
Hulten, C. 90
Hurd, M. 86
Hymans, S. H. 111

Ihori, T. x, xv, 149–91
indexation of government
  bonds xiv, xvi, 71, 261,
    271–83, 286–7
inflation
  and employment 3, 119–22, 129
  and exchange rate 260, 261
  and government deficits xiii, 3,
    40, 59–61, 77–8, 80–3, 158,
    234–9, 261, 290, 309
  and interest rates 40, 51, 269–74,
    288–91
  indexation xiv, xvi, 68, 235,
    261–2, 264–86, 288–91
  neutrality 42, 196
  postwar 274, 277, 286
insurance
  guarantees 112–13, 115

and risk 44, 75, 94, 95, 201, 203–5, 220–1
investment
  crowding in/out xiv–xv, 4, 20, 28, 39–40, 41, 43, 77, 85–7, 145, 147, 149, 172–3, 234, 239
  incentives 84, 148, 205, 242
  residential 85
  and wealth 43, 45–9, 62, 84, 210, 292–306
Ireland, foreign debt 230
Israel
  employment 275–6
  inflation 275–86, 289
  public debt 264–86
  stabilisation 260
Italy
  government deficits 167–8
  growth 3

Japan
  government deficits 167–8, 188, 194
  growth 3
  rate of saving 78, 80–1, 152
Johnson, H. 69

Kanaya, S. 159
Kandori, M. 190
Kaser, M. ix
Kay, J. 111
Keynes, J. M. 116, 129, 140, 145, 196
Keynesian demand management 3, 41, 88, 116–28, 133–5, 142
Keynes–Ramsey rule *see* Ramsey rule
Khachaturov, T. S. ix
King, M. A. 76, 86, 174
Kleiman, E. x, xvi, 40, 114, 147–8, 264–91
Kochin, L. 100, 108, 152
Kohn, M. 74
Kondor, Y. 279, 286
Koret Foundation vii
Kormendi, R. C. 87, 152, 155
Kotlikoff, L. J. 78, 83, 84, 86, 87, 108, 113, 152, 174, 175, 189, 197
Kumar, P. 79, 90, 108

Kurihara, K. E. 111
Kurz, M. x, 76, 113, 115, 118, 191–4, 195, 197, 223, 224
Kyle, P. 68

Lancaster, K. 129
Lange, O. 20
Leeuw, F. de 35, 78, 94
Leiderman, L. 260
Leimer, D. 111
Lerner, A. P. 116, 129, 197, 293
Lesnoy, S. 111
Levhari, D. 274
Levine, P. 202
Lindahl, E. R. ix, 140
Lipsey, R. 110
liquidity 236, 277–80
Liviatan, N 274
Lucas, R. E. 3, 202
Lundberg, E. ix
Luo, Y. ix

McCallum, B. T. 159, 168
Machlup, F. ix
McManus, D. A. 221
Malinvaud, E. ix
Mariano, R. S. 156
Marquez, J. 274
Maurer, S. B. 175
Mayer, C. 74
Meade, J. E. 116, 123, 124, 126, 127, 197
Medicare 95–6
Mehran, H. 263
Meier, G. x
Meiselman, D. 39
Menchik, P. 86
Mexico, foreign debt 230, 236, 243, 260
Meyer, L. H. 108
Miller, M. 79, 94
Millikan, M. 130
Mirer, T. W. 86
Mirrlees, J. A. 118, 203
modelling
  consumption function 44–64, 85–107, 158, 207–21
  employment and money 4–38
  fiscal policy 118–29

government expenditure 44–64,
  98–107
 intertemporal income
  distribution 41–73
 structural 39, 40, 105
Modigliani, F. 39, 86, 149
Moggridge, D. 146
Mohammed, A. 260
money supply
 definition 39–40
 and employment 4–20, 28, 41,
  116–18
 and expectations 41
 and inflation 41, 277
 and public debt xiv, 4–20, 43, 48
 and rate of interest 116
Morocco, foreign debt 243, 260
Motley, B. x
multiplier, foreign trade 26
Mundell, R. 269
Mundell–Fleming demand
 curve 119–20
Musgrave, P. B. 172
Musgrave, R. A. x, xv, 115,
 133–45, 172, 197, 228, 288
Mutch, T. 190

national accounting
 government assets 90–3
 government debt 79–81
 government expenditure 112, 114
Neary, J. P. 65
Nelson, C. R. 156
Newbery, D. 72
Nigeria, foreign debt 243, 260

Okuno, M. 150
Onitiri, H. M. A. x
O'Reilly, T. 79, 90, 108
Organisation of Petroleum
 Exporting Countries
 (OPEC) 236
Ozler, S. 79, 94, 95

Papi, G. U. ix
Pasinetti, L. ix
Pareto efficiency 147, 150
Patinkin, D. ix, 37, 195
Pechman, J. A. 111
Pellechio, A. 87

Penner, R. 111
Persson, T. 202
Peru, foreign debt 243, 260
Peterson, G. 90
Phelps, E. S. x, xv, 116–30
Philippines, foreign debt 243, 260
Phillips curve 119–22, 128, 129
Pieper, P. J. x, xiv, 3–40, 79, 84,
 88, 90, 94, 108, 112–13, 290
Pigou, A. C. 37, 116, 117, 120, 127,
 133–4, 140, 145, 226
Pigou effect 117, 120, 123, 127,
 133–4, 226
population growth 72
portfolio composition 80–4, 269,
 276–80, 282–3
 and public debt 5, 42, 44–9,
  68–76, 83
production function 167, 205, 224,
 304
property rights 79, 92–3, 108,
 112–14, 204
Puffert, D. 109

Radner, R. 221
Ramsey, F. P. 116–30, 224
Ramsey rule xv, 116–29
Ramsey–Meade savings
 rate 123–7
Razin, A. 74
Reagan, President R. 82, 228
real balance effect see Pigou effect
redistribution, intertemporal xiv,
 xv, 41–73, 114, 118, 133–48,
 149–87, 191–7
relevance theorems 42–64, 75–6
Ricardo, D. 133, 146, 159, 226
 see also equivalence, Ricardian
risk
 exchange rate 83, 235
 expectations 43, 48, 53–4, 56–8,
  87, 90, 192, 266–71, 288–90
 government guarantee 241
 insurance 44, 75, 94, 95, 201,
  203–5, 220–1
 intertemporal sharing xiv,
  58–68, 73, 75
 political xvi
 trade in 75

Index

Roberts, J. M.   x, 79, 81, 90, 107, 194, 197
Robinson, E. A. G.   ix, x, 147, 196, 229
Robinson, M.   x, 40, 79, 84, 90, 91, 92, 93, 98, 108, 115, 147, 197
Rockefeller Foundation   vii
Rojo, L. A.   viii, x
Russek, F. S.   87

Sahasakul, C.   109
Samuelson, L.   280
Samuelson, P. A.   ix, xv, 116–17, 129, 149–50, 158, 159, 165
Sandmo, A.   174
Sargent, T. J.   3, 108, 159, 195
Schaefer, S.   74
Scholes, M.   x
Seater, J. J.   156, 187
Seidman, L. S.   175
Sen, A.   viii
Serra-Puche, J.   x
Shell, K.   68, 73
Shiraishi, T.   ix, x
Shoup, C.   145
Shoven, J.   x
Sidrauski, M.   68, 69
Simonsen, M.   74
Skinner, J.   174, 175, 189
social security
   funding   83–7, 95–6, 182–3
   as wealth   103–5, 112, 195, 196
Solow, R. M.   109
Sraffa, P.   146
Stackelberg, H. von   224
Stanford University   vii
Stiglitz, J. E.   x, xiv, 40, 41–76, 114–15, 189, 195, 196, 227, 228
Stokey, N. L.   202
Summers, L. A.   83, 84, 85, 86, 174, 189
supply-side economics   118, 299–300
Svensson, L. E. O.   202
Szturn de Sztrem, T.   286

Tabellini, G.   x, 290
Tanner, J. E.   108, 152
Tanzi, V.   x, xvi, 40, 108, 147, 228, 230–63, 290–1, 309
taxation
   and aggregate production/employment   xiii, xv, xvi, 3, 144–5, 146, 150, 233–5, 305–6, 310
   and consumption   204–23
   incidence   49–68, 150–2, 204–5, 226–8, 233, 293–4
   indexation   271–2
   and intergenerational transfer   60–7, 83–7, 174–82
   intertemporal smoothing   133–48, 168–87, 197, 201–23, 224–9, 231
   lump-sum   44–54, 58–67, 175–6, 183–4, 227
   and portfolio composition   42, 44–9, 68–76, 83
   property   76
   see also transfers
Taylor, J. B.   x, 39–40, 65, 68, 228–9
Thirty, Group of   262
Throop, A.   x
Tice, H. S.   110
Tobin, J.   42, 68, 69, 86
transfers
   intertemporal   108, 133–48
   lump-sum   50, 55–8, 87
Tsiang, S. C.   74
Tsuru, S.   ix

uncertainty   see risk
United Kingdom
   government deficits   167–8
   government expenditure   226
   growth   3
United Nations Educational, Scientific and Cultural Organisation (UNESCO)   vii, ix
United States
   defence expenditure   79, 83
   government assets   90–3
   government deficits   4–32, 77–107, 167–8
   saving   80–107
Urquidi, V. L.   ix

Uruguay, foreign debt   243, 260
utility   122–9, 169, 192–3
   see also consumption function;
   redistribution, intertemporal

Velupillai, K.   x, xv, 116–30
Venezuela, foreign debt   236, 243, 260
Vining, D.   274

Wachter, S.   109, 112
Wallace, N.   68, 70, 108, 159, 195
Wan, jr., H. Y.   309
war finance   140, 145, 212–21, 226, 228, 229, 231–2
wealth
   government   90–3, 97–9, 105–7, 114–15, 134, 172, 196
   and investment   43, 45–9, 62, 84, 210, 292–306
   national   119
   and public debt   292–306
   and taxation   151, 154, 203, 217, 225
Weiss, A.   66
West Germany   *see* Germany, Federal Republic
Wise, D. E.   109

Xafa, M.   260

Yaari, I. E.   68
Yugoslavia, foreign debt   243, 260